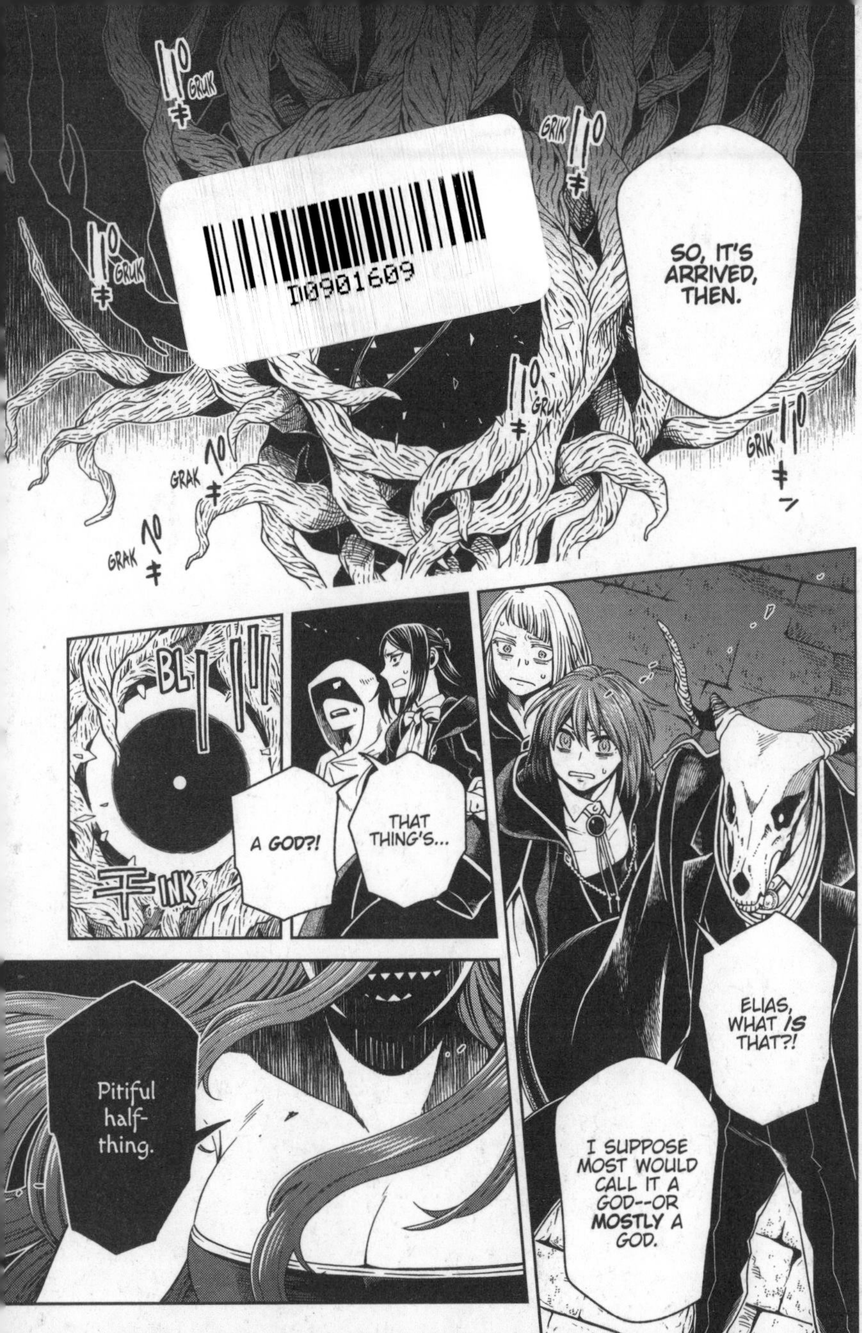

GRIK
SO, IT'S ARRIVED, THEN.
GRUK
GRIK
GRUK
GRUK
GRAK
GRAK
THAT THING'S...
A GOD?!
BL
INK
ELIAS, WHAT *IS* THAT?!
I SUPPOSE MOST WOULD CALL IT A GOD--OR MOSTLY A GOD.
Pitiful half-thing.

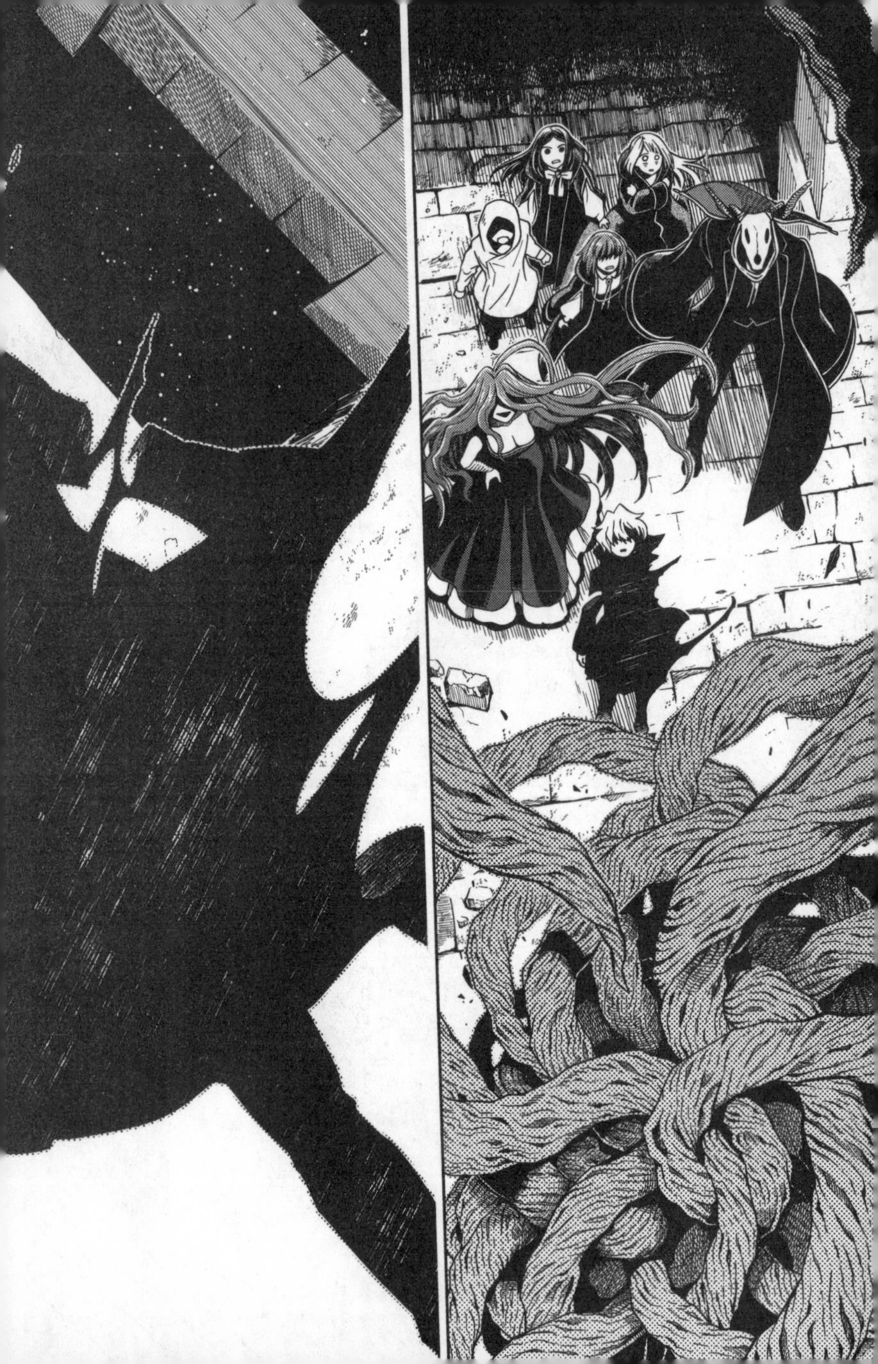

Chapter 91: Of two evils, choose the lesser. II

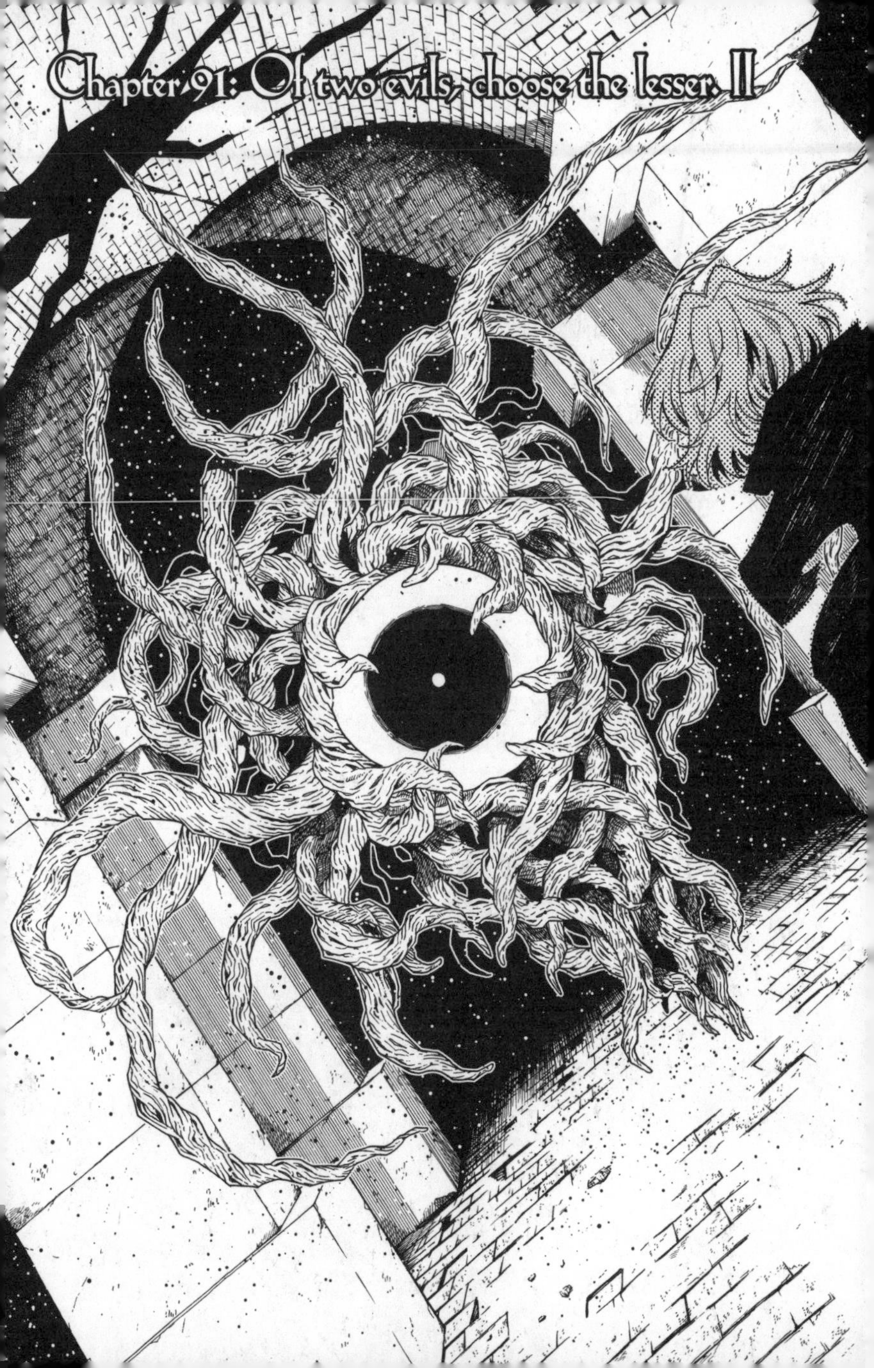

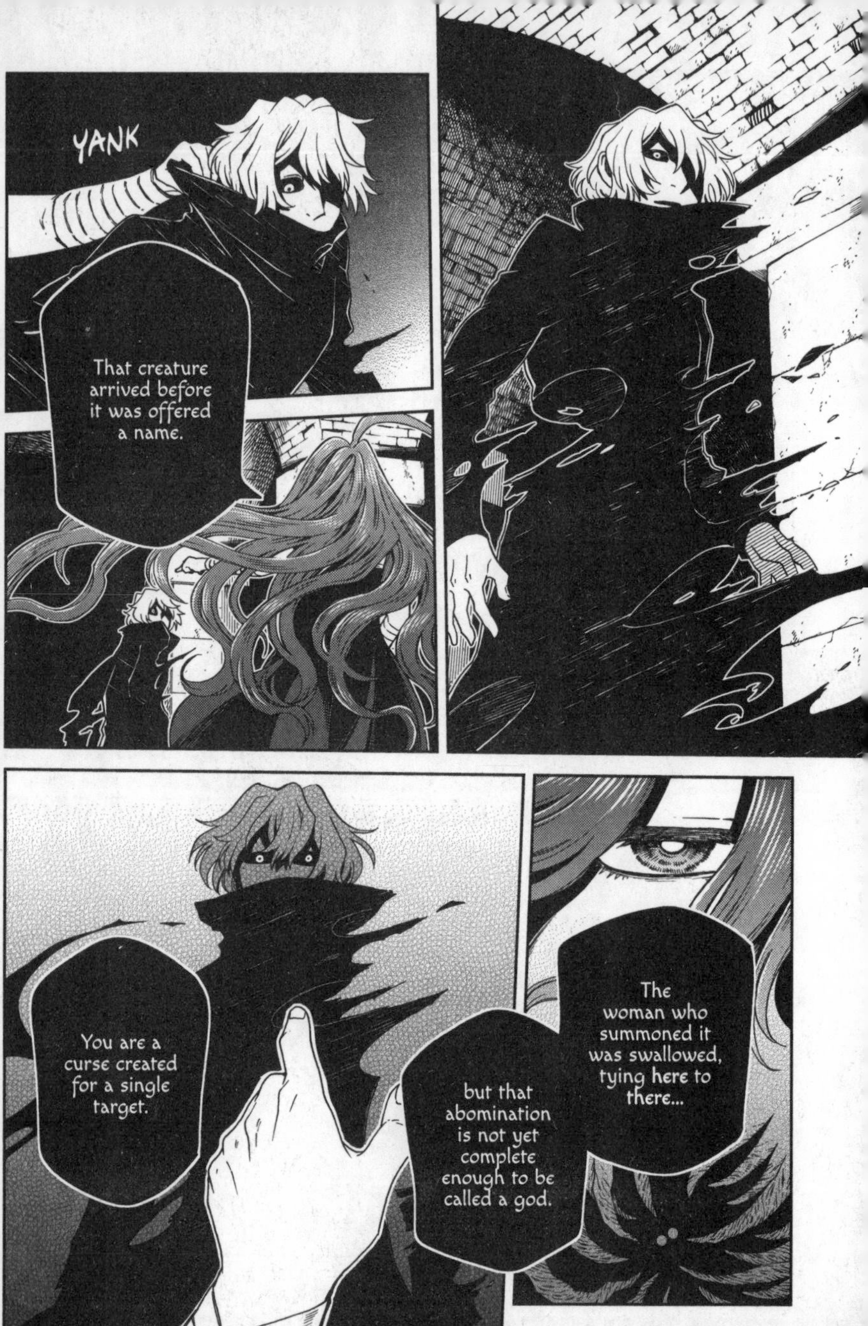

YANK
That creature arrived before it was offered a name.
You are a curse created for a single target.
The woman who summoned it was swallowed, tying here to there...
but that abomination is not yet complete enough to be called a god.

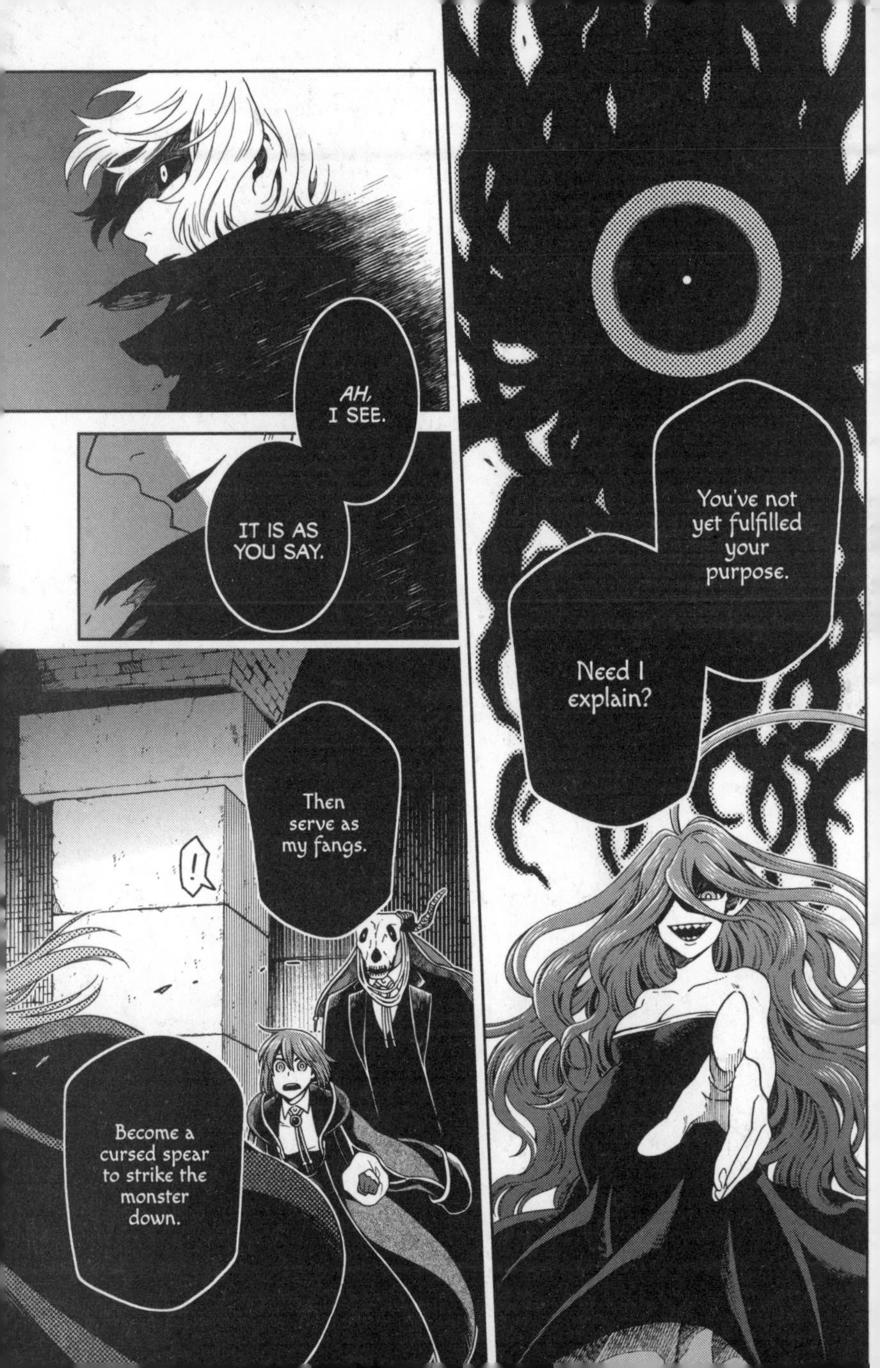
You've not yet fulfilled your purpose.
Need I explain?
AH, I SEE.
IT IS AS YOU SAY.
Then serve as my fangs.
!
Become a cursed spear to strike the monster down.

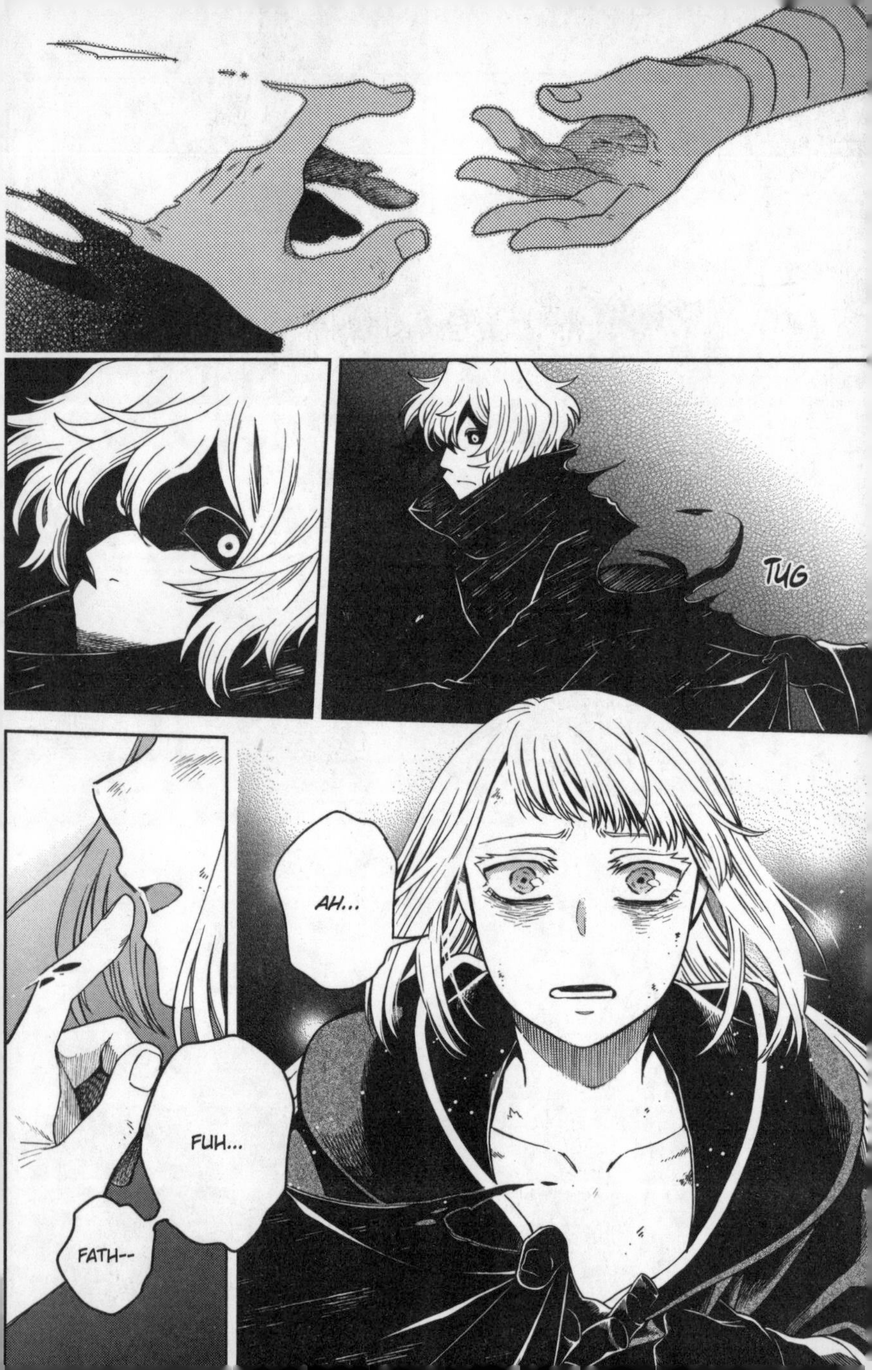
TUG
AH...
FUH...
FATH--

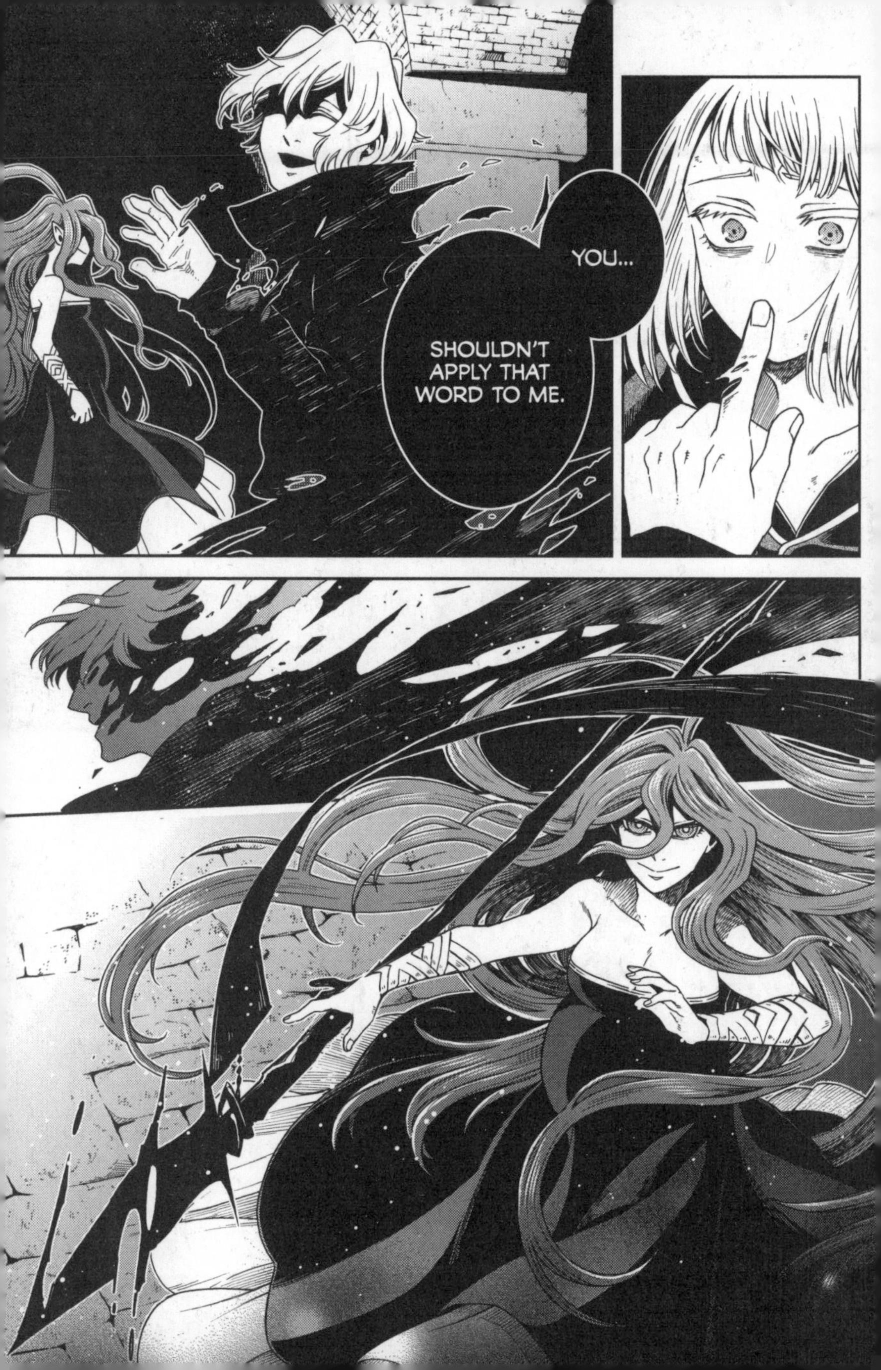
YOU...
SHOULDN'T APPLY THAT WORD TO ME.

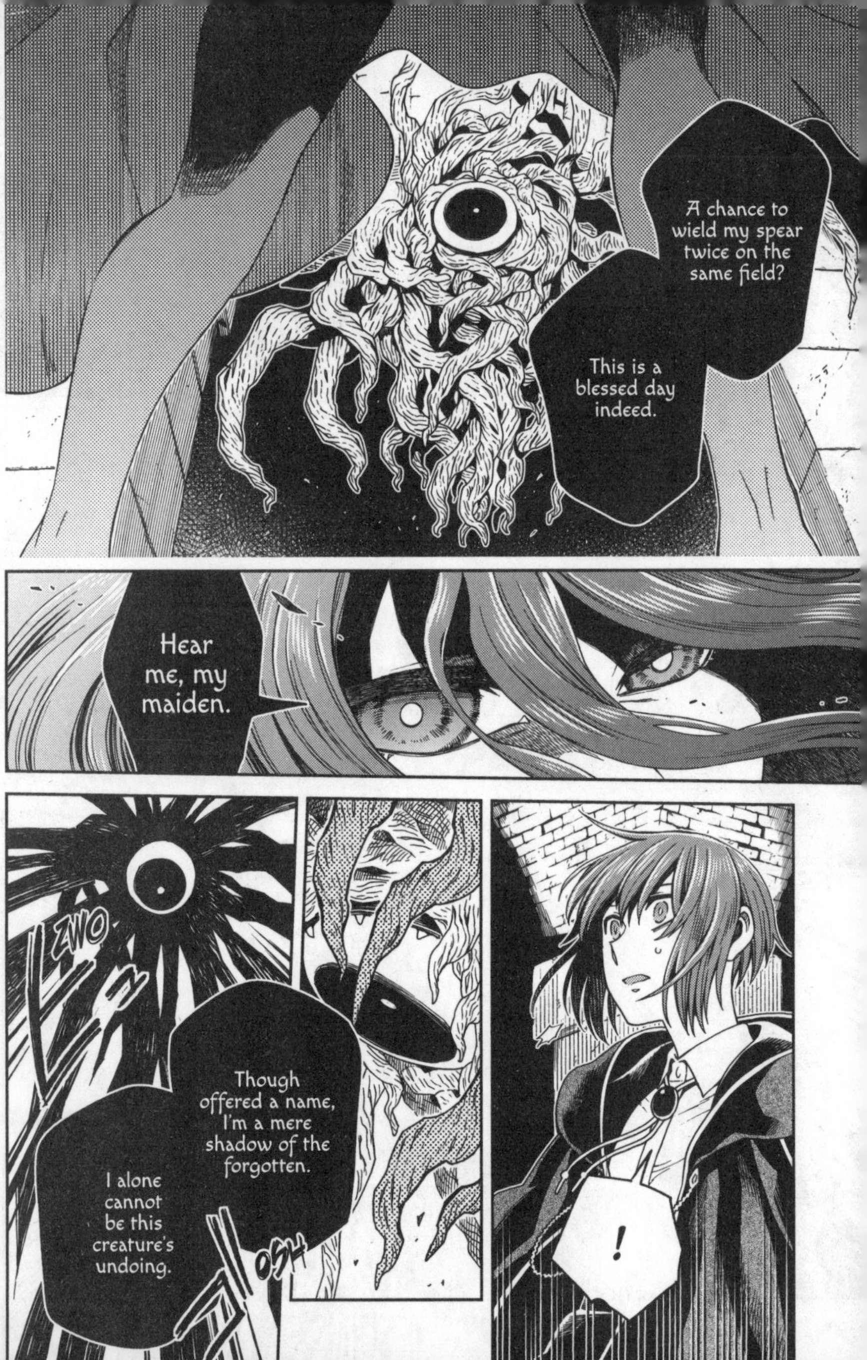
A chance to wield my spear twice on the same field?
This is a blessed day indeed.
Hear me, my maiden.
!
Though offered a name, I'm a mere shadow of the forgotten.
I alone cannot be this creature's undoing.
ZWO
OSH

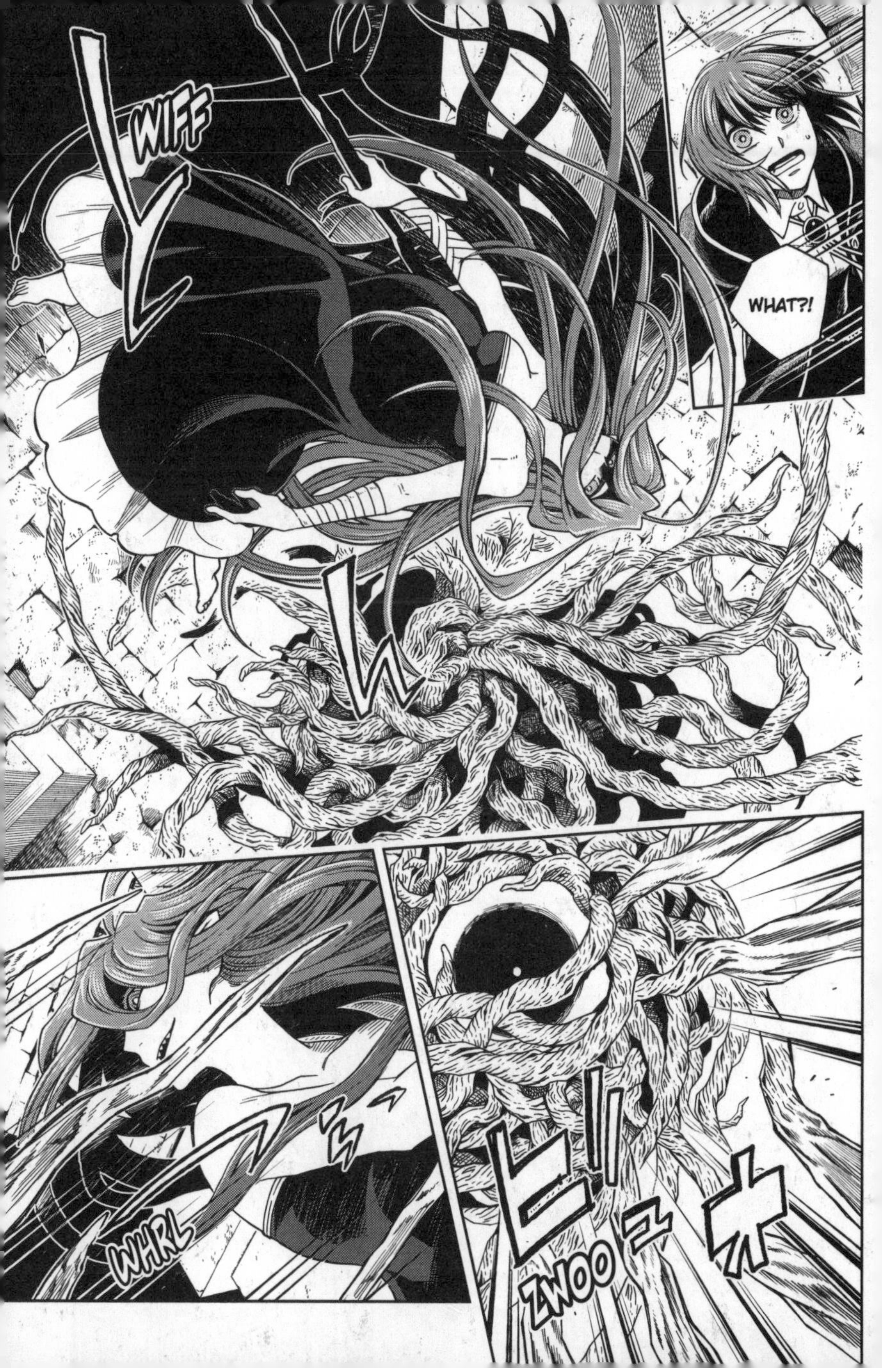
WHAT?!
WIFF
ZWOO
WHRL

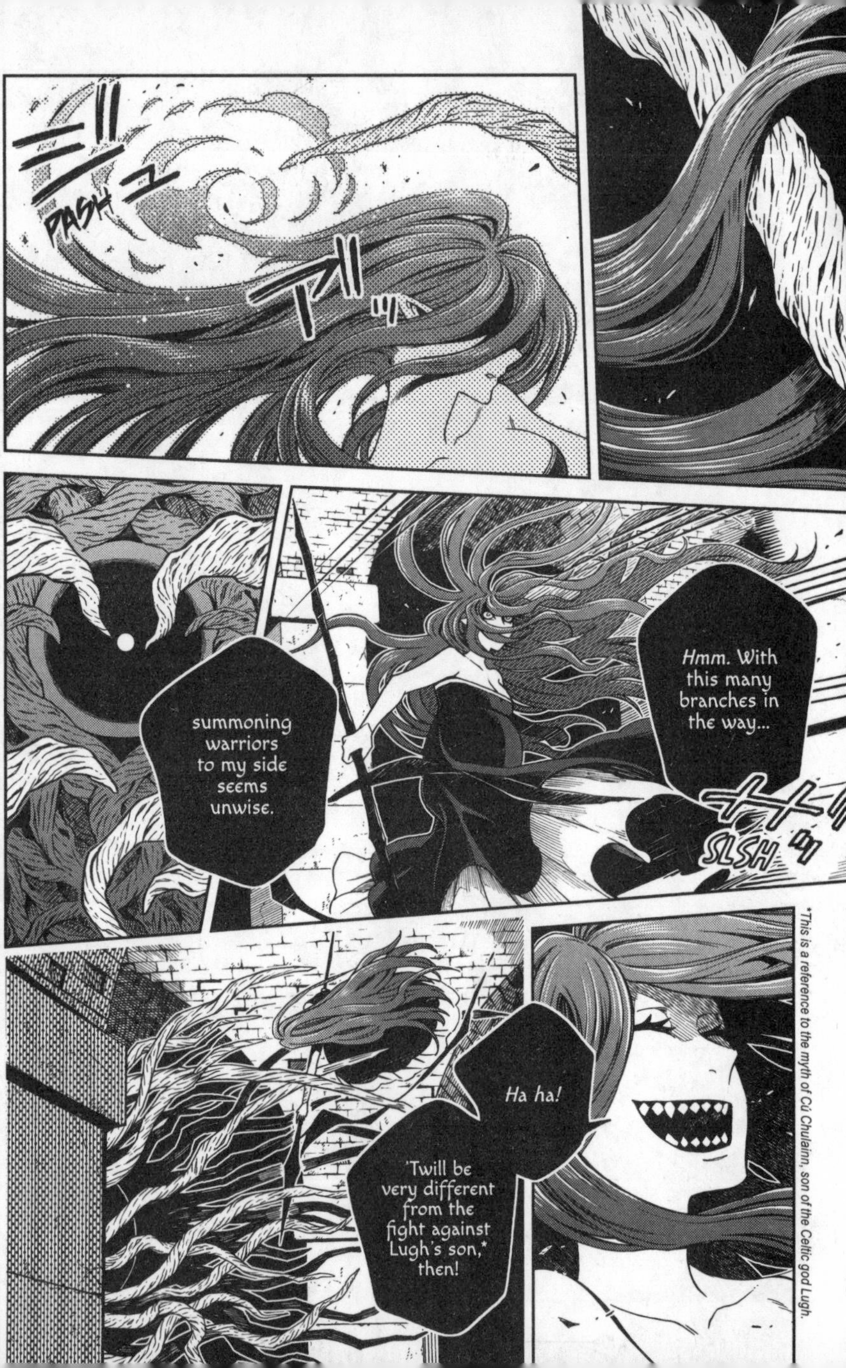
PASH
Hmm. With this many branches in the way...
summoning warriors to my side seems unwise.
SLSH
Ha ha!
'Twill be very different from the fight against Lugh's son,* then!

*This is a reference to the myth of Cú Chulainn, son of the Celtic god Lugh.

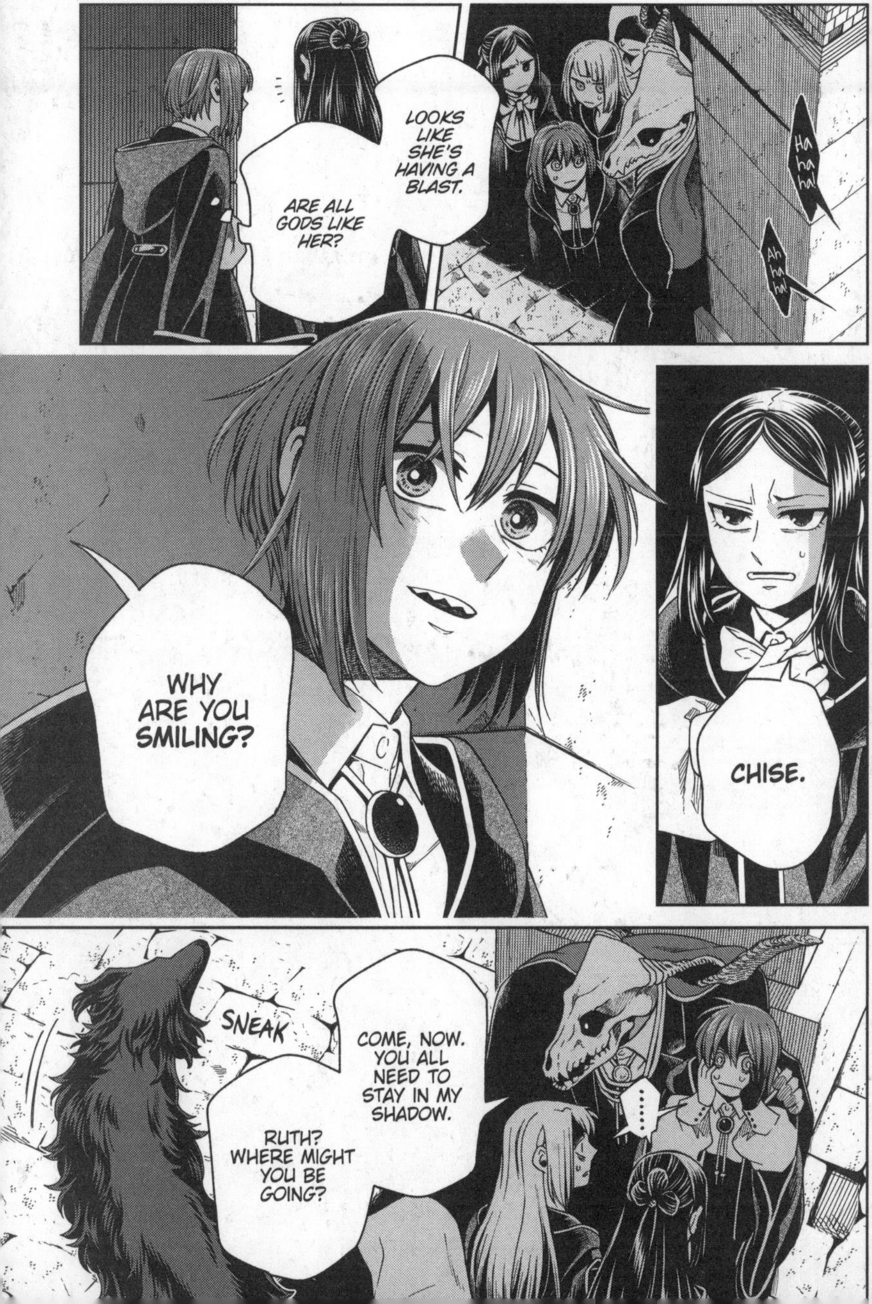
Ha ha ha!
Ah ha ha!
LOOKS LIKE SHE'S HAVING A BLAST.
ARE ALL GODS LIKE HER?
CHISE.
WHY ARE YOU SMILING?
COME, NOW. YOU ALL NEED TO STAY IN MY SHADOW.
RUTH? WHERE MIGHT YOU BE GOING?
SNEAK

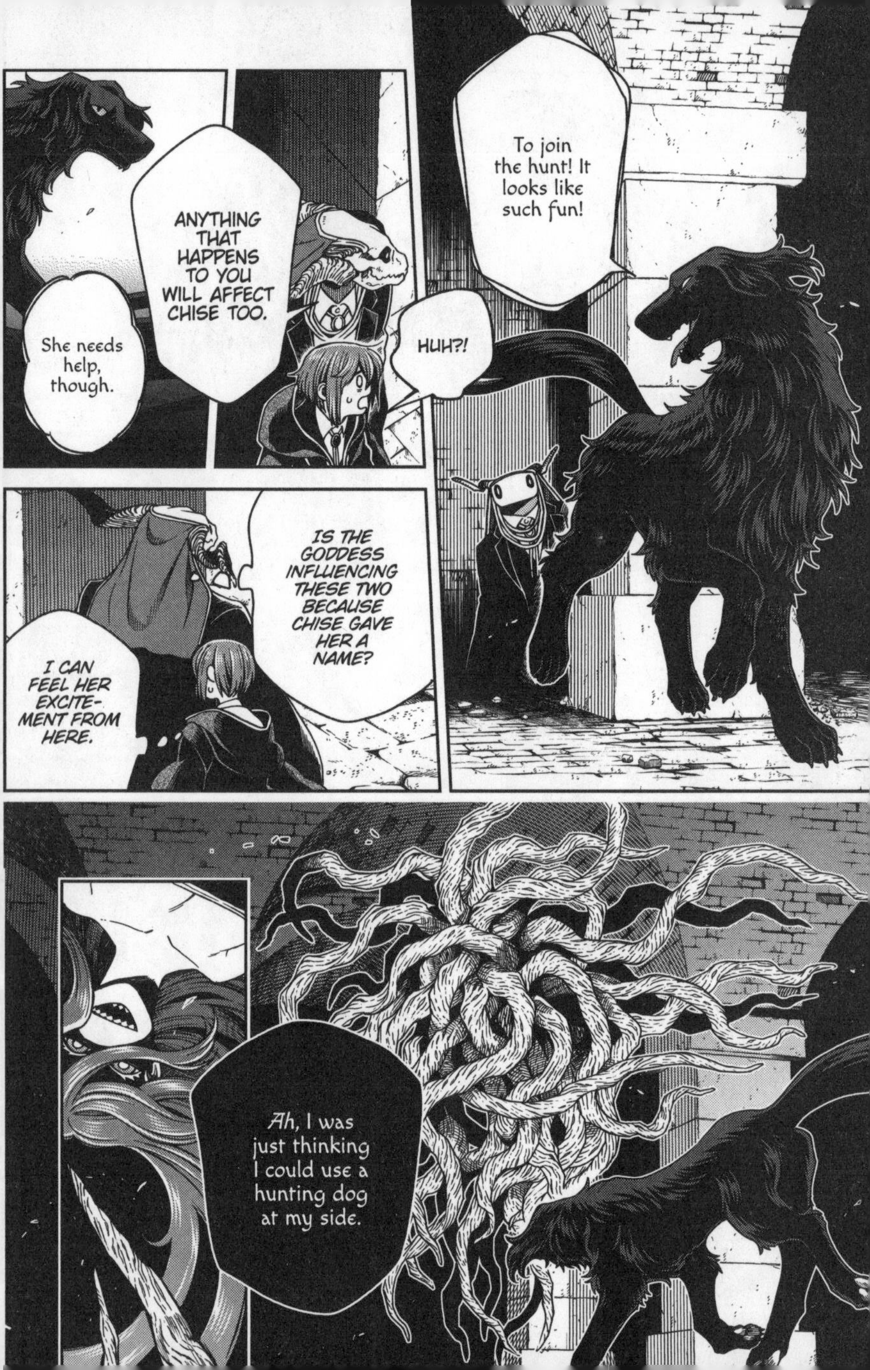
To join the hunt! It looks like such fun!
HUH?!
ANYTHING THAT HAPPENS TO YOU WILL AFFECT CHISE TOO.
She needs help, though.
IS THE GODDESS INFLUENCING THESE TWO BECAUSE CHISE GAVE HER A NAME?
I CAN FEEL HER EXCITE-MENT FROM HERE.
Ah, I was just thinking I could use a hunting dog at my side.

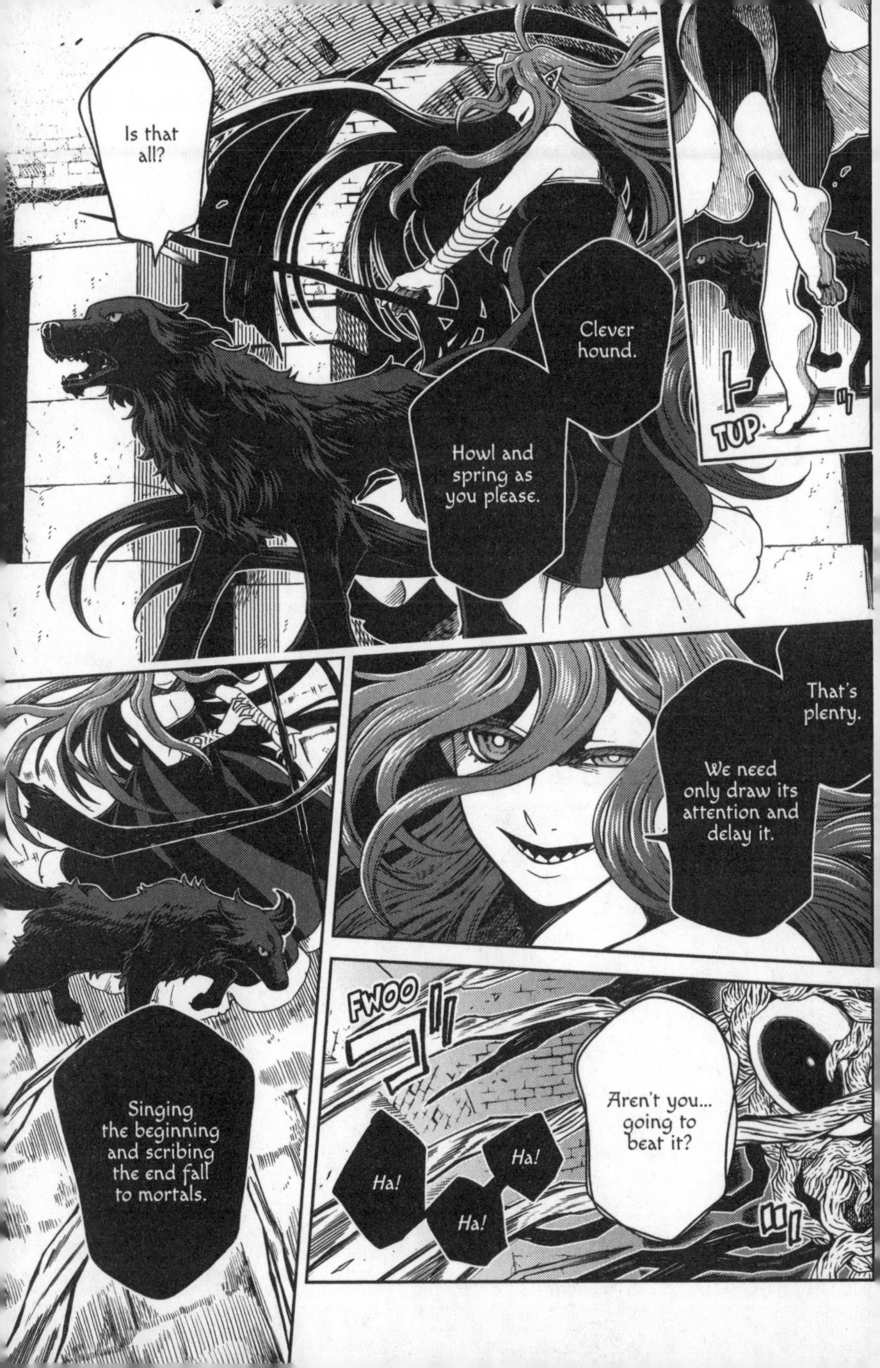
TUP
Is that all?
Clever hound.
Howl and spring as you please.
That's plenty.
We need only draw its attention and delay it.
Singing the beginning and scribing the end fall to mortals.
FWOO
Aren't you... going to beat it?
Ha!
Ha!
Ha!

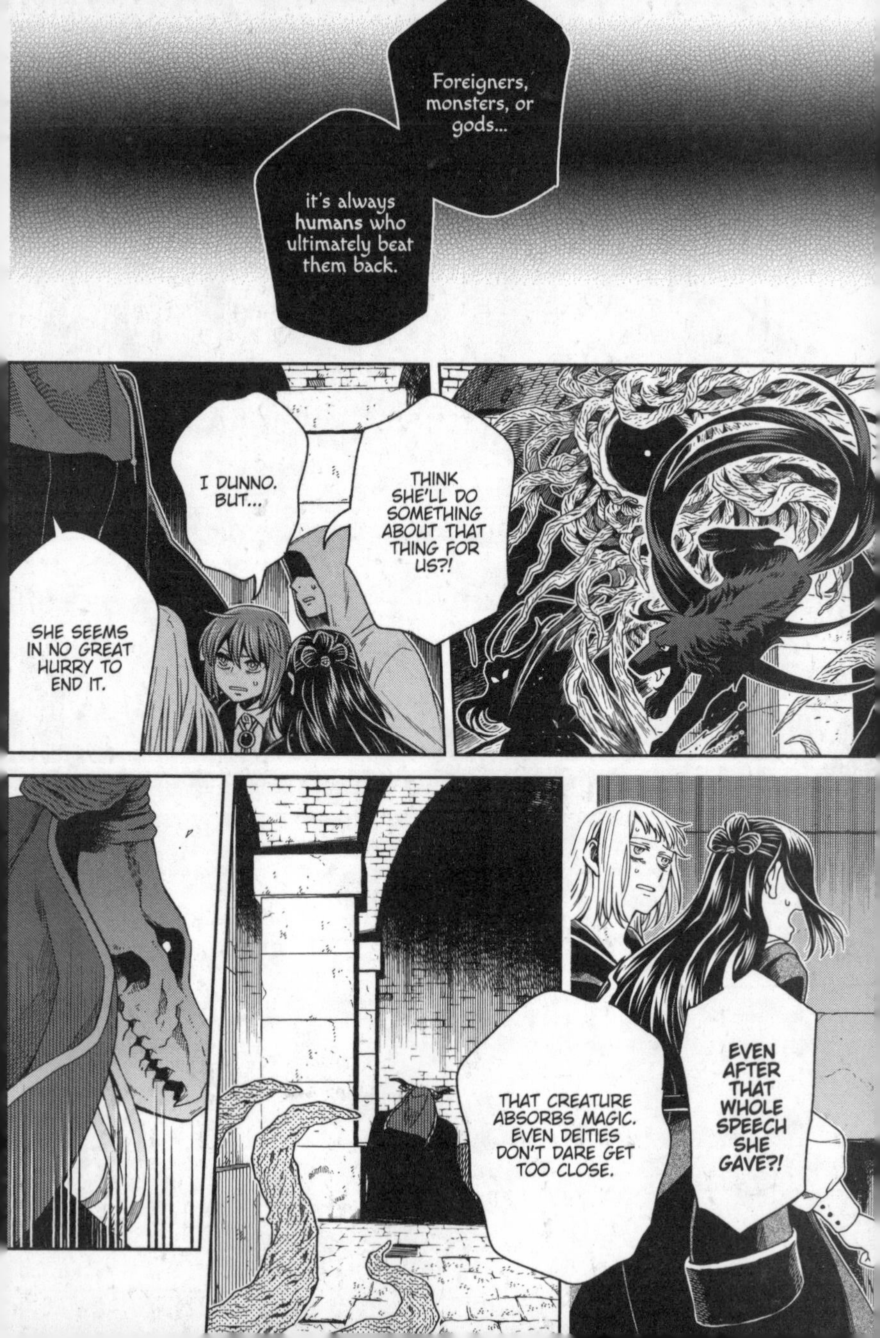
Foreigners, monsters, or gods...
it's always humans who ultimately beat them back.
THINK SHE'LL DO SOMETHING ABOUT THAT THING FOR US?!
I DUNNO. BUT...
SHE SEEMS IN NO GREAT HURRY TO END IT.
EVEN AFTER THAT WHOLE SPEECH SHE GAVE?!
THAT CREATURE ABSORBS MAGIC. EVEN DEITIES DON'T DARE GET TOO CLOSE.

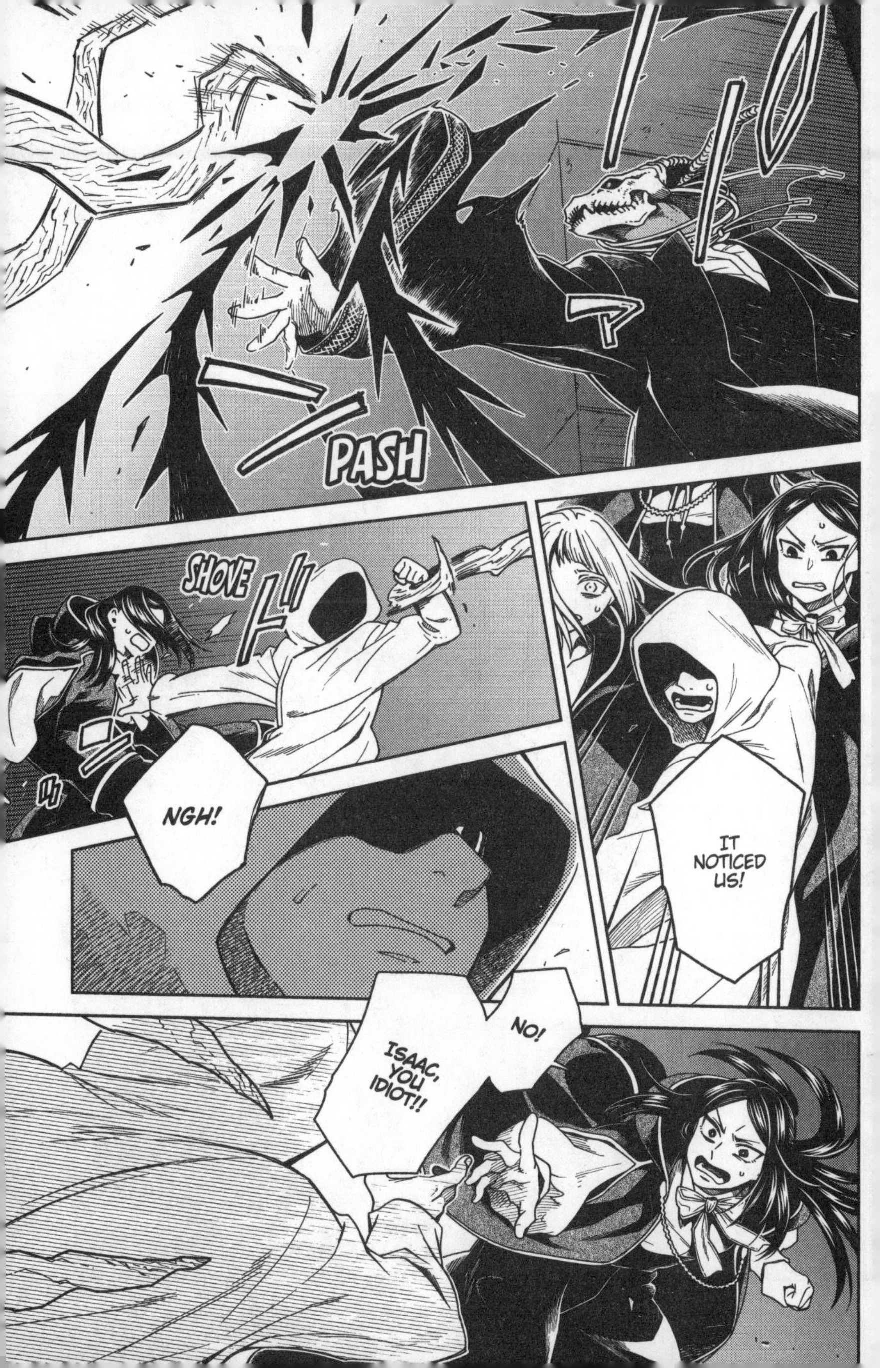
PASH
SHOVE
IT NOTICED US!
NGH!
NO!
ISAAC, YOU IDIOT!!

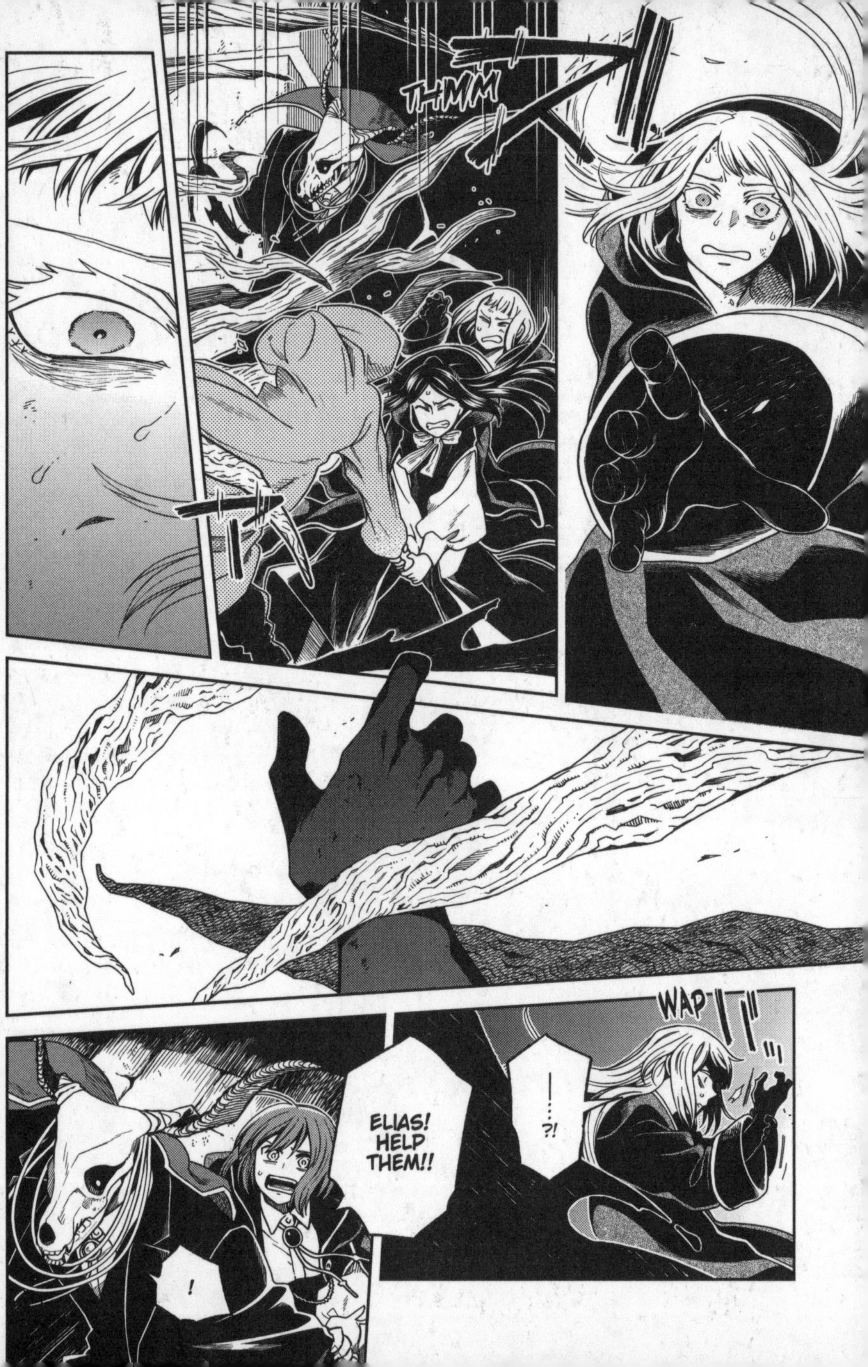
THMM
WAP
…?!
ELIAS! HELP THEM!!
!

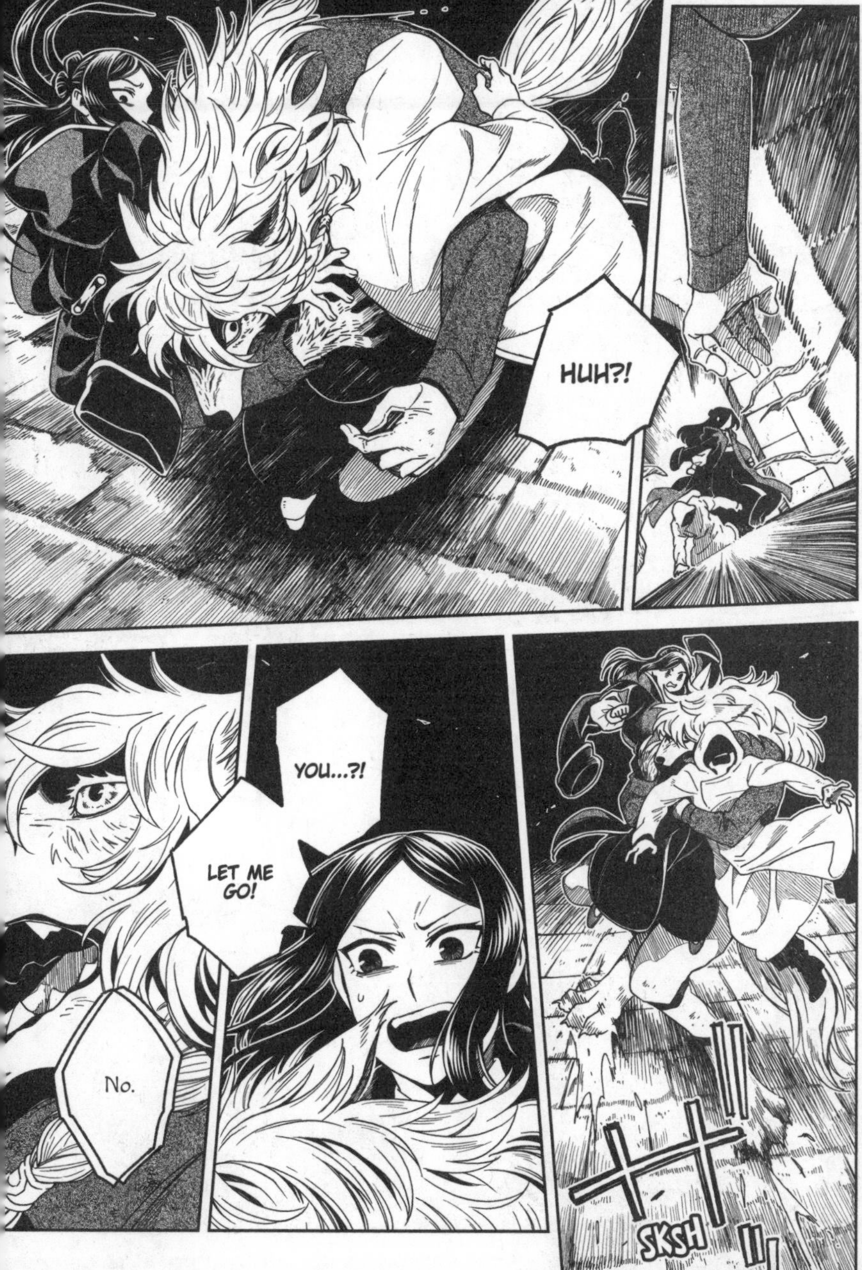
HUH?!
SKSH
YOU...?!
LET ME GO!
No.

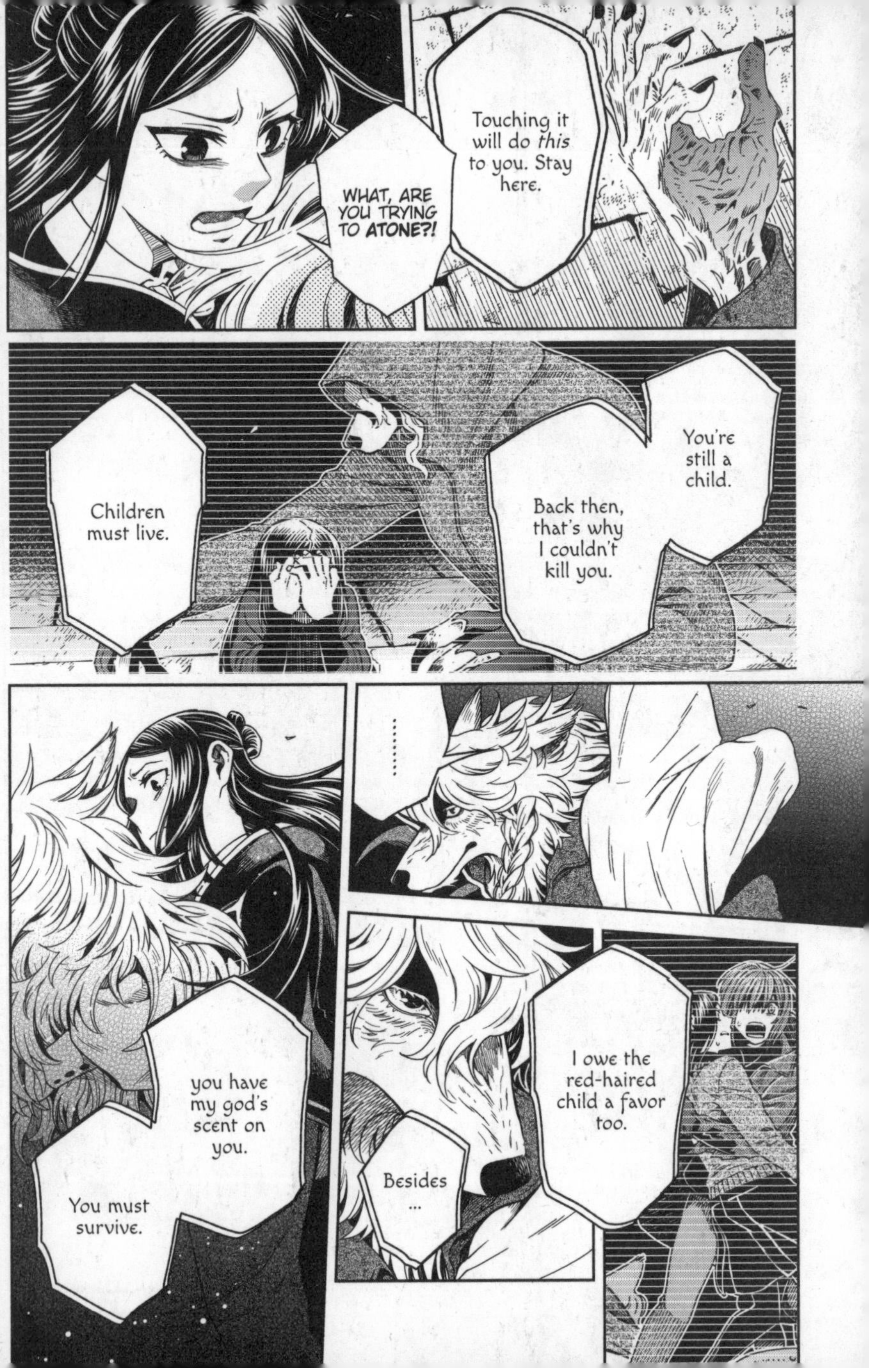
Touching it will do *this* to you. Stay here.
WHAT, ARE YOU TRYING TO ATONE?!
You're still a child.
Back then, that's why I couldn't kill you.
Children must live.
......
I owe the red-haired child a favor too.
Besides ...
you have my god's scent on you.
You must survive.

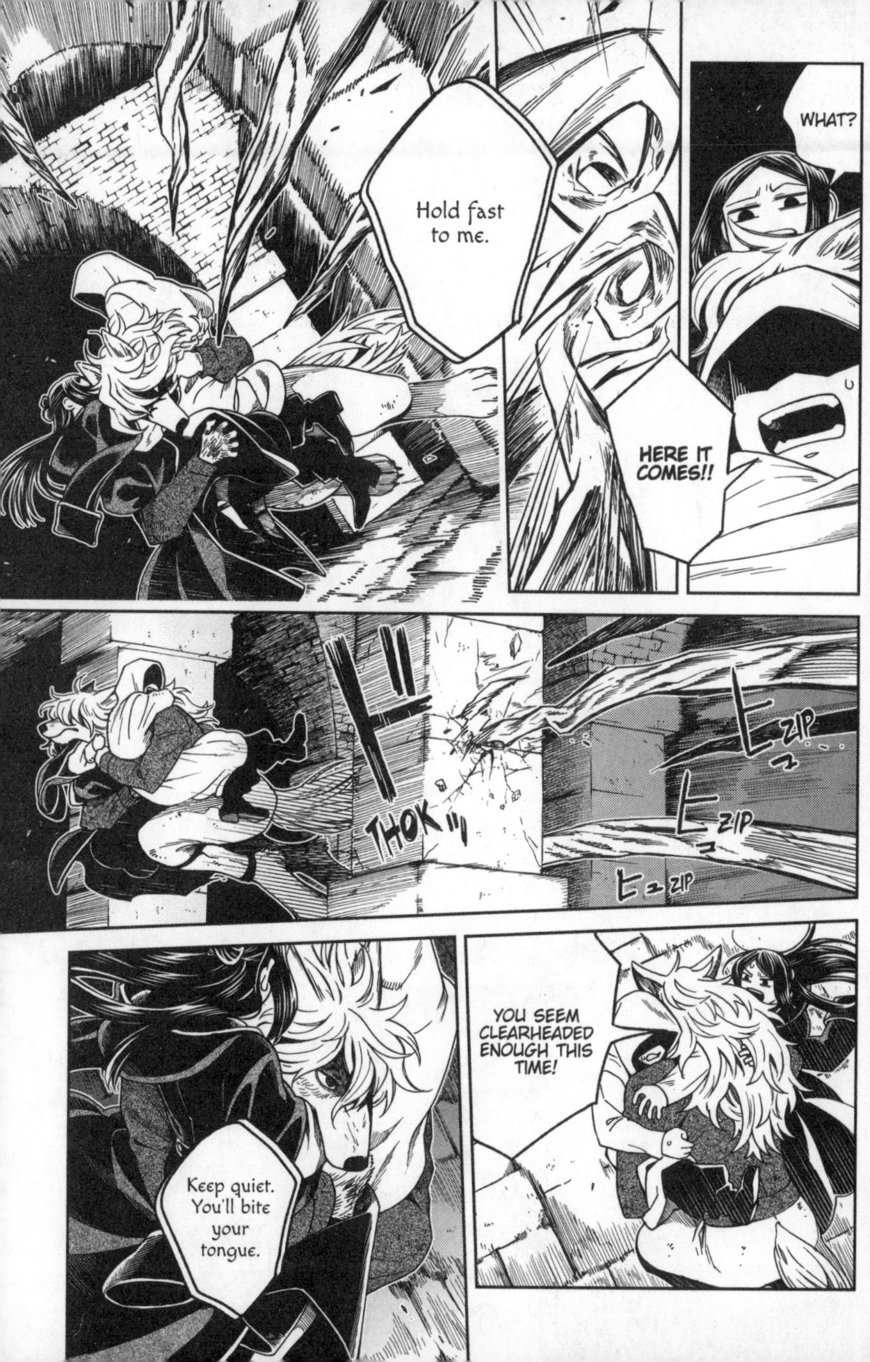
WHAT?
HERE IT COMES!!
Hold fast to me.
ZIP
ZIP
ZIP
THOK
YOU SEEM CLEARHEADED ENOUGH THIS TIME!
Keep quiet. You'll bite your tongue.

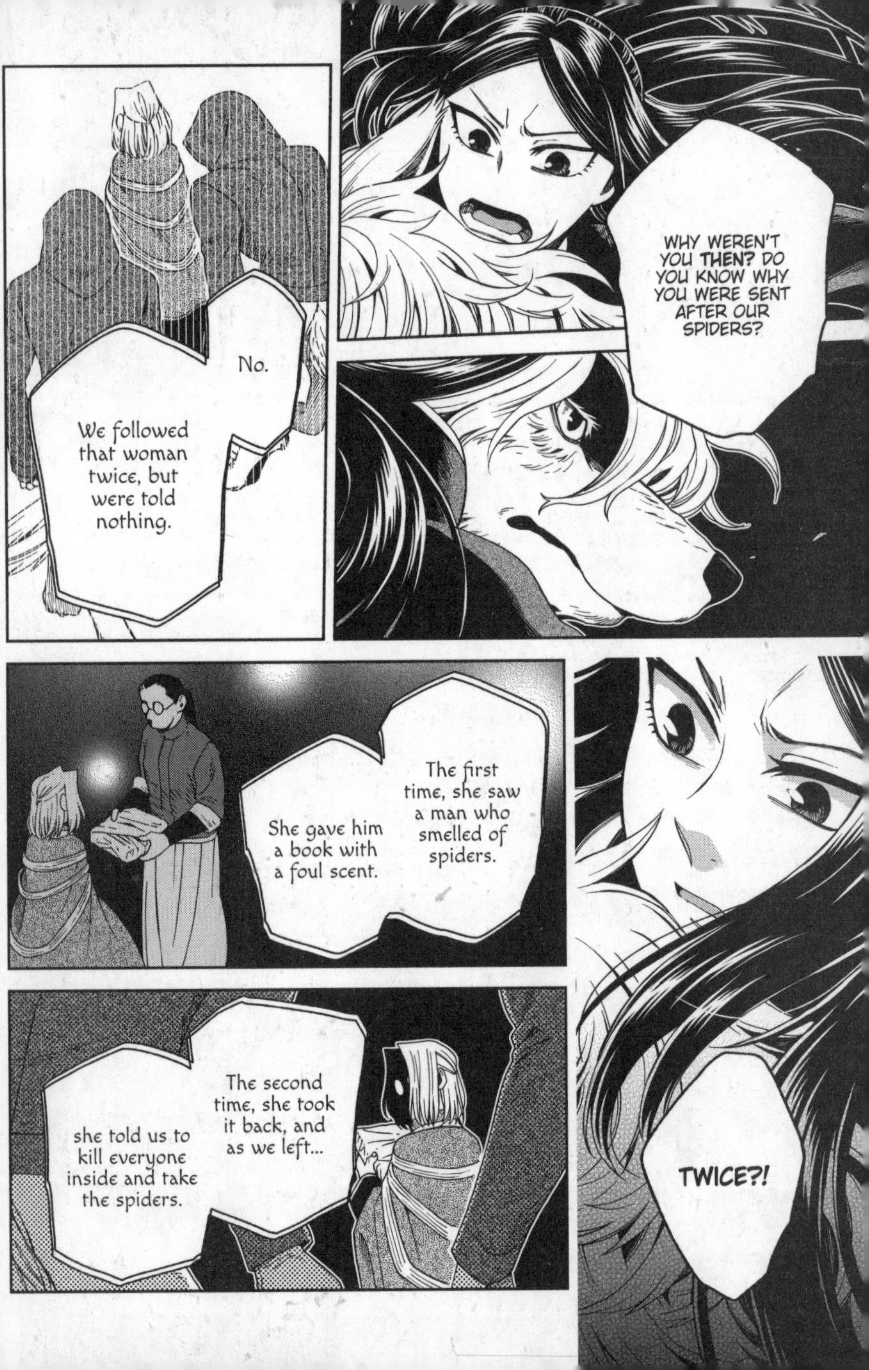
WHY WEREN'T YOU THEN? DO YOU KNOW WHY YOU WERE SENT AFTER OUR SPIDERS?
No.
We followed that woman twice, but were told nothing.
TWICE?!
The first time, she saw a man who smelled of spiders.
She gave him a book with a foul scent.
The second time, she took it back, and as we left...
she told us to kill everyone inside and take the spiders.

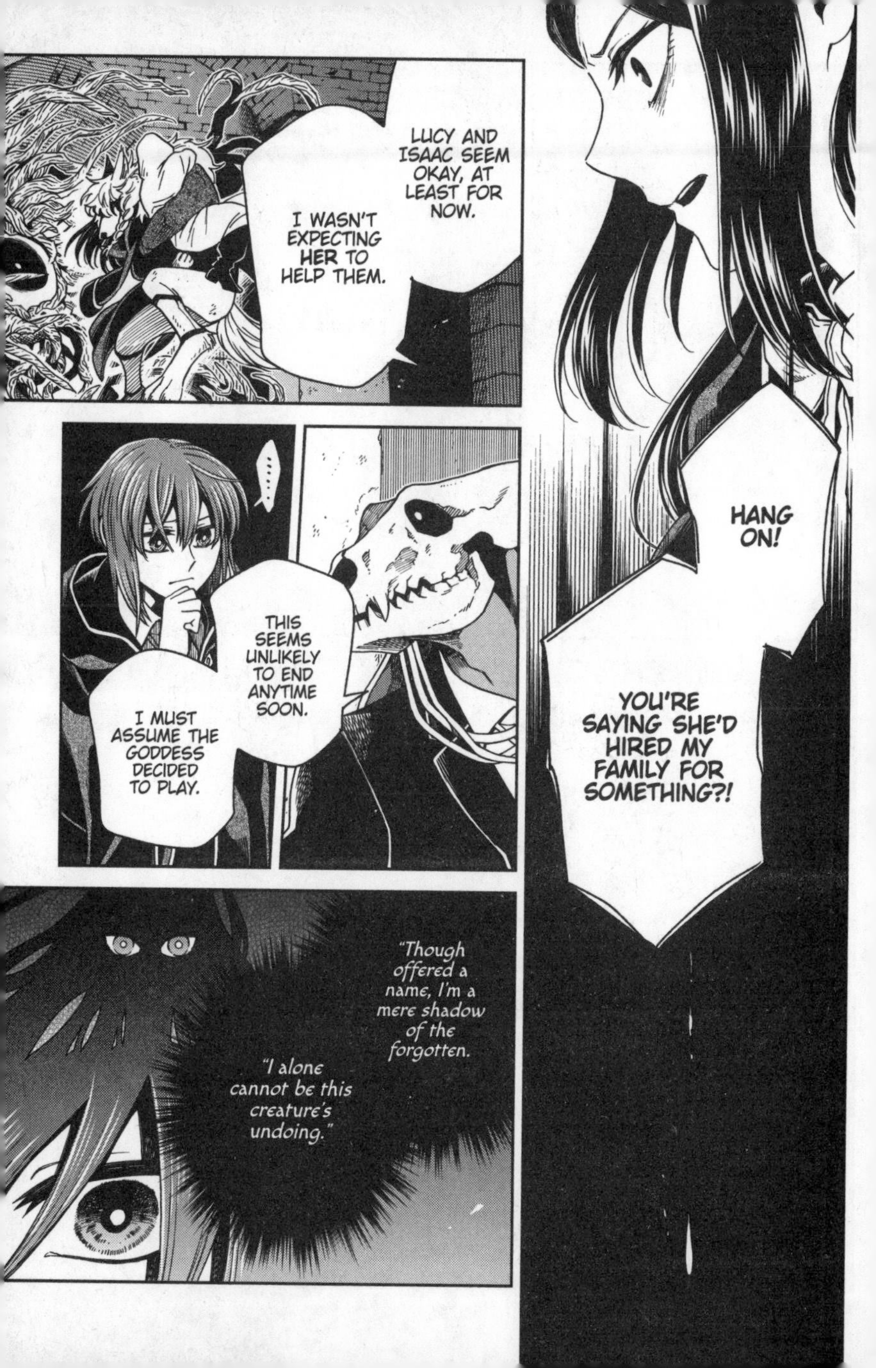

HANG ON!
YOU'RE SAYING SHE'D HIRED MY FAMILY FOR SOMETHING?!
LUCY AND ISAAC SEEM OKAY, AT LEAST FOR NOW.
I WASN'T EXPECTING HER TO HELP THEM.
...
THIS SEEMS UNLIKELY TO END ANYTIME SOON.
I MUST ASSUME THE GODDESS DECIDED TO PLAY.
"Though offered a name, I'm a mere shadow of the forgotten.
"I alone cannot be this creature's undoing."

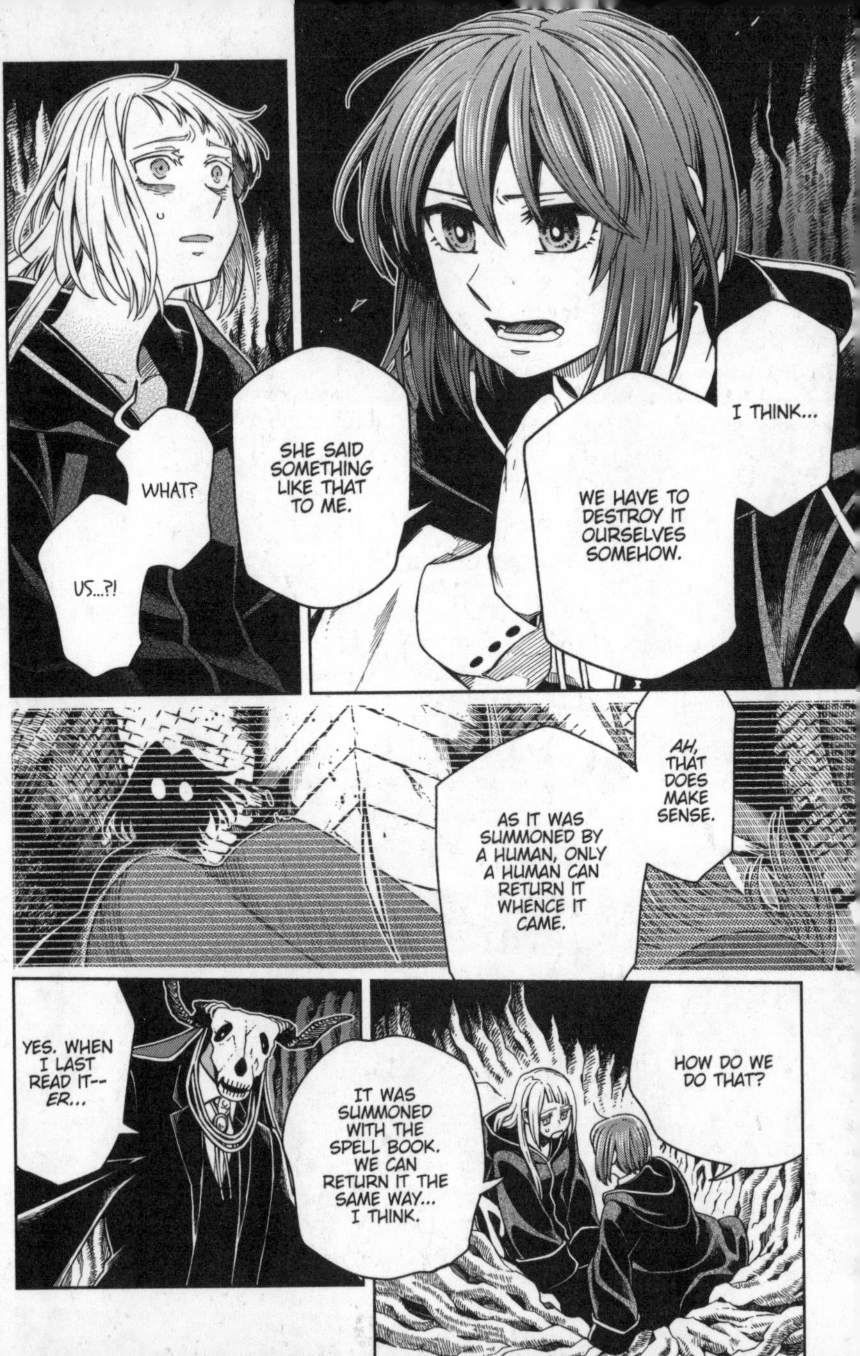
I THINK...
WE HAVE TO DESTROY IT OURSELVES SOMEHOW.
SHE SAID SOMETHING LIKE THAT TO ME.
WHAT?
US...?!
AH, THAT DOES MAKE SENSE.
AS IT WAS SUMMONED BY A HUMAN, ONLY A HUMAN CAN RETURN IT WHENCE IT CAME.
HOW DO WE DO THAT?
YES. WHEN I LAST READ IT-- ER...
IT WAS SUMMONED WITH THE SPELL BOOK. WE CAN RETURN IT THE SAME WAY... I THINK.

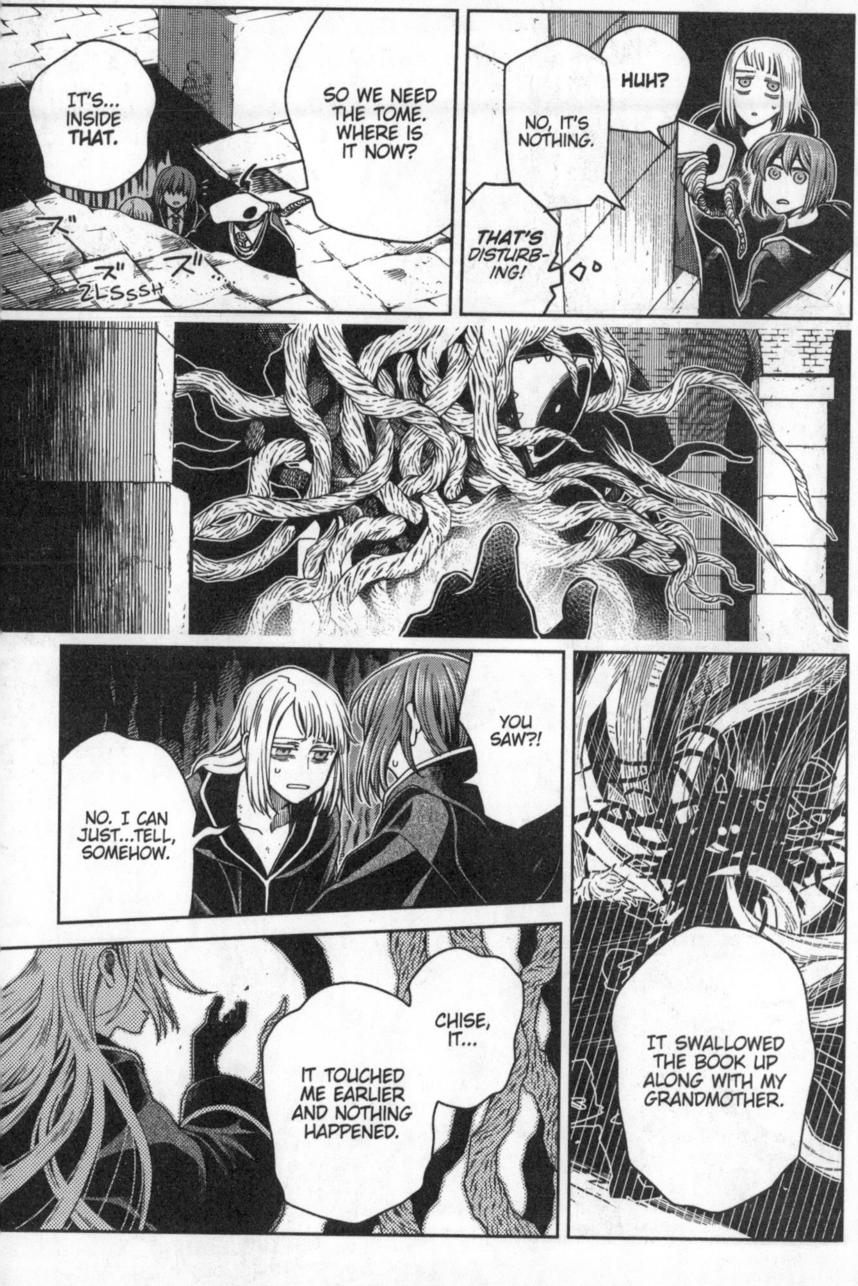
HUH?
NO, IT'S NOTHING.
THAT'S DISTURB-ING!
SO WE NEED THE TOME. WHERE IS IT NOW?
IT'S... INSIDE THAT.
ZLSssH
IT SWALLOWED THE BOOK UP ALONG WITH MY GRANDMOTHER.
YOU SAW?!
NO. I CAN JUST...TELL, SOMEHOW.
CHISE, IT...
IT TOUCHED ME EARLIER AND NOTHING HAPPENED.

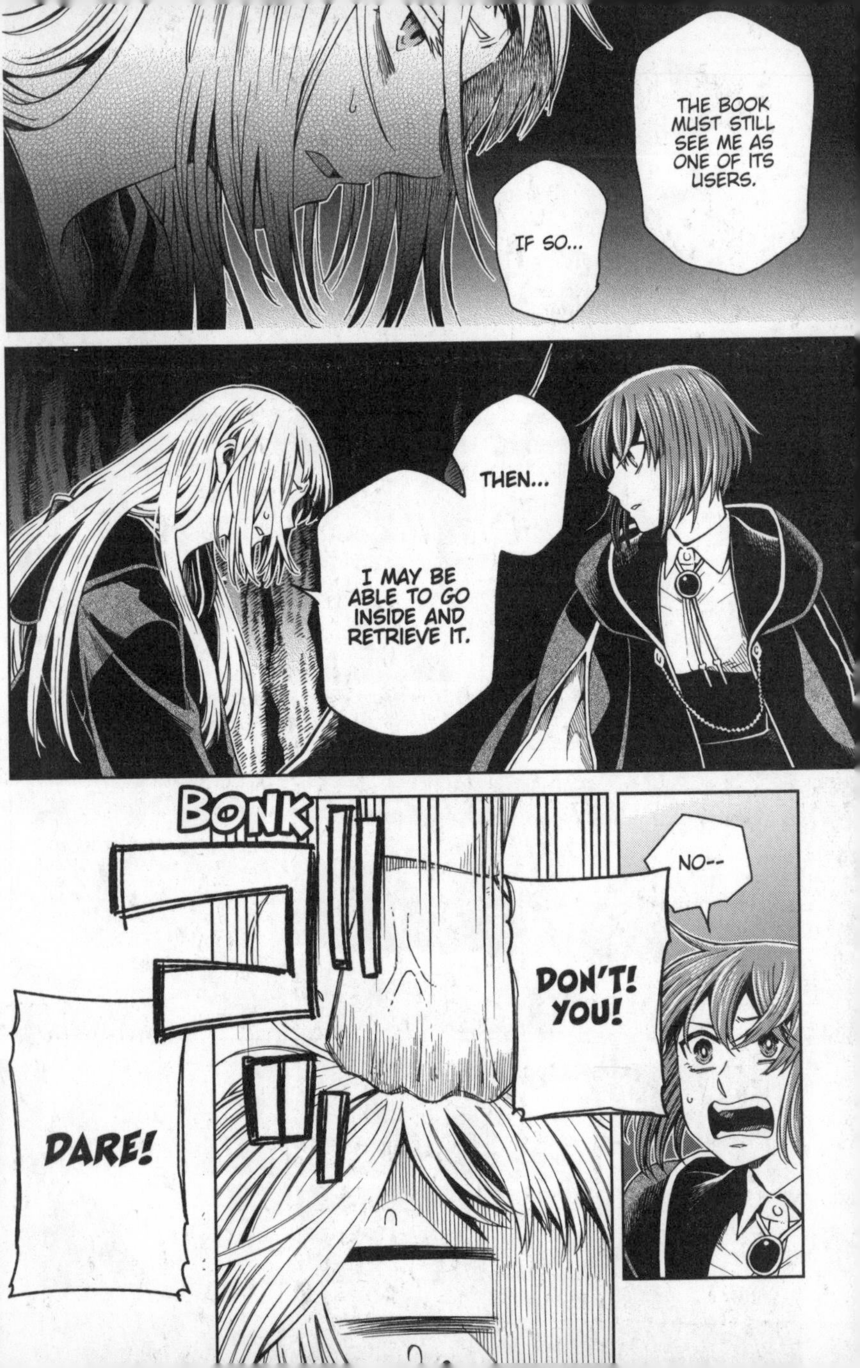
THE BOOK MUST STILL SEE ME AS ONE OF ITS USERS.
IF SO...
THEN...
I MAY BE ABLE TO GO INSIDE AND RETRIEVE IT.
NO--
DON'T! YOU!
BONK
DARE!

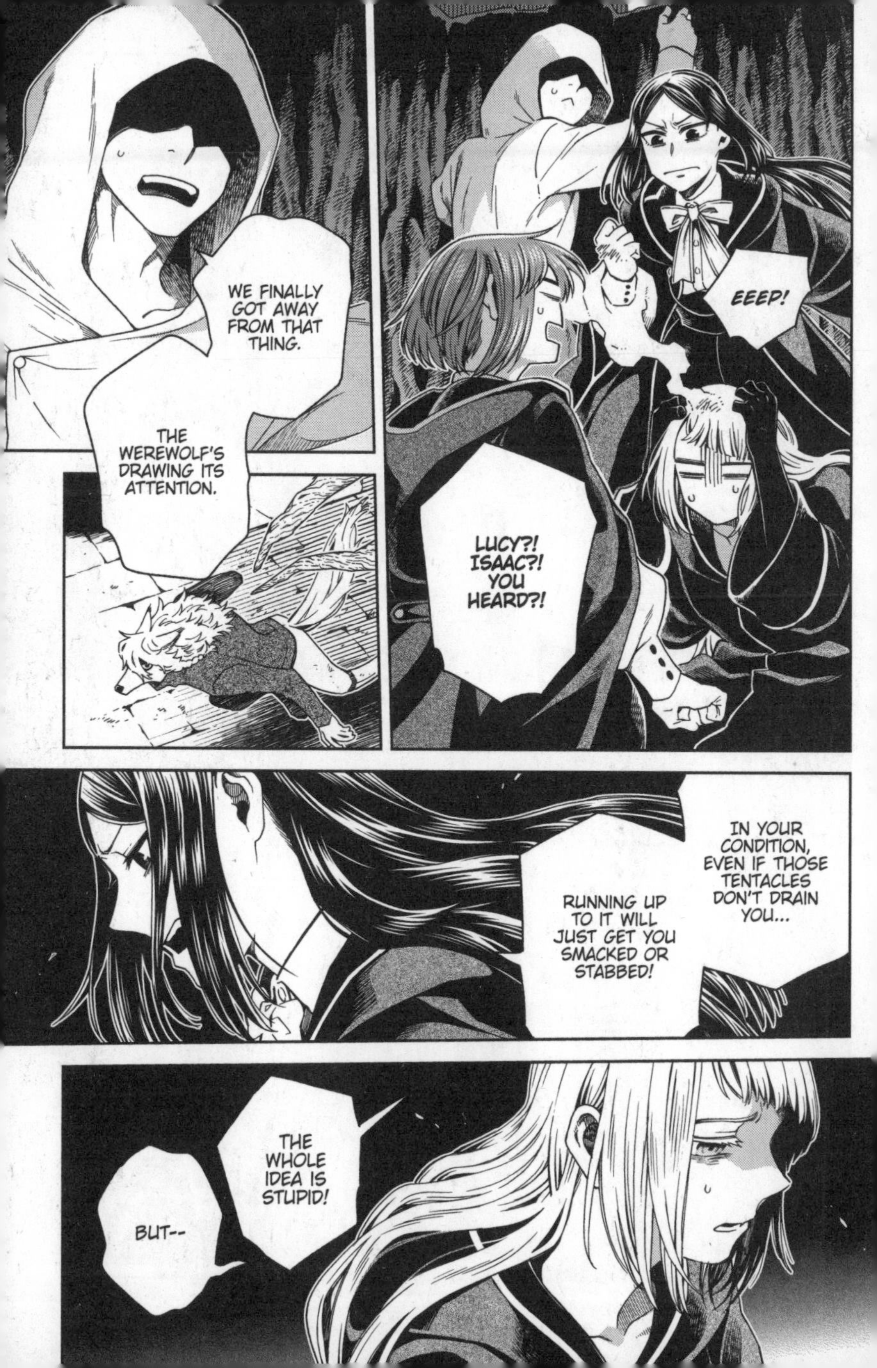
EEEP!
WE FINALLY GOT AWAY FROM THAT THING.
THE WEREWOLF'S DRAWING ITS ATTENTION.
LUCY?! ISAAC?! YOU HEARD?!
IN YOUR CONDITION, EVEN IF THOSE TENTACLES DON'T DRAIN YOU...
RUNNING UP TO IT WILL JUST GET YOU SMACKED OR STABBED!
THE WHOLE IDEA IS STUPID!
BUT--

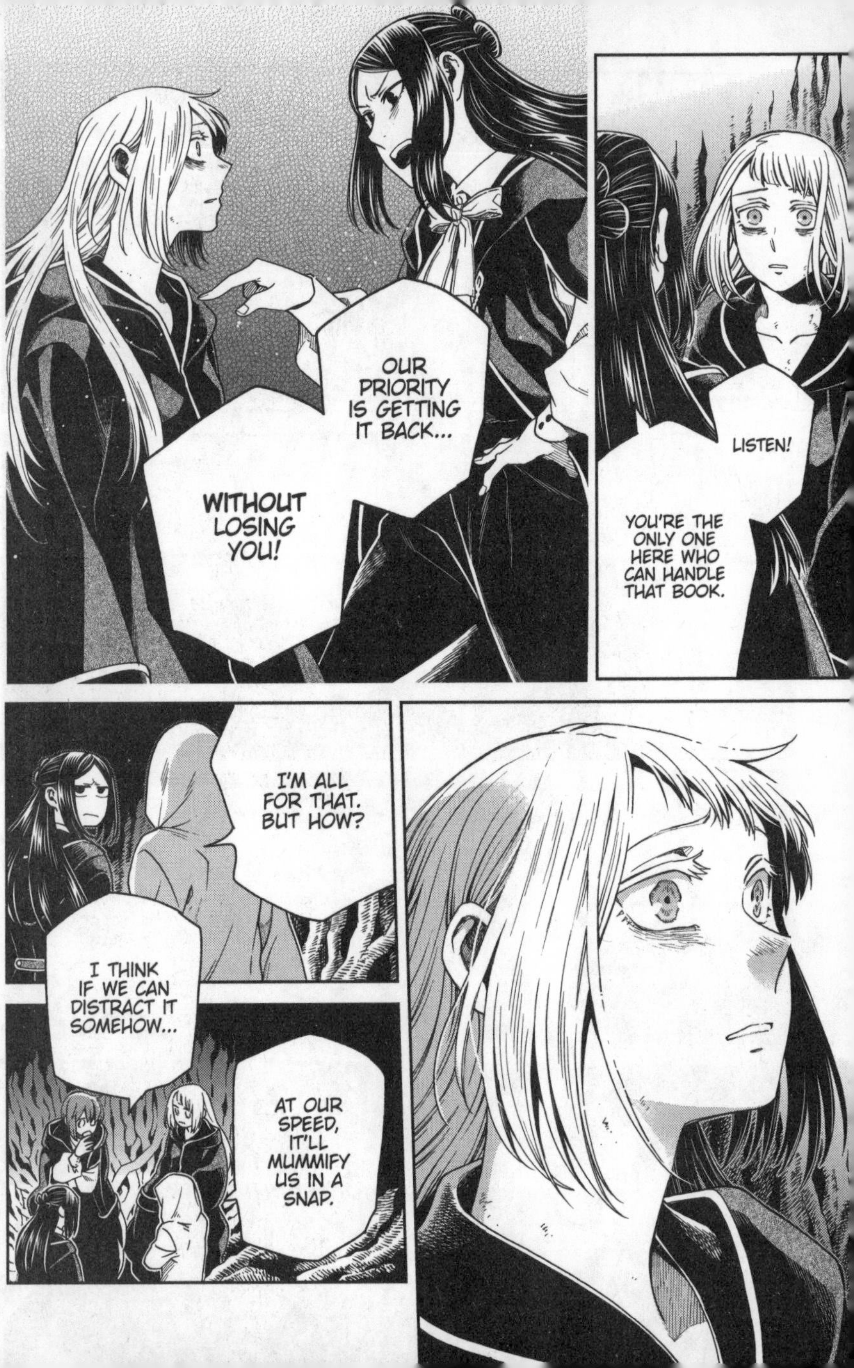
LISTEN!
YOU'RE THE ONLY ONE HERE WHO CAN HANDLE THAT BOOK.
OUR PRIORITY IS GETTING IT BACK...
WITHOUT LOSING YOU!
I'M ALL FOR THAT. BUT HOW?
I THINK IF WE CAN DISTRACT IT SOMEHOW...
AT OUR SPEED, IT'LL MUMMIFY US IN A SNAP.

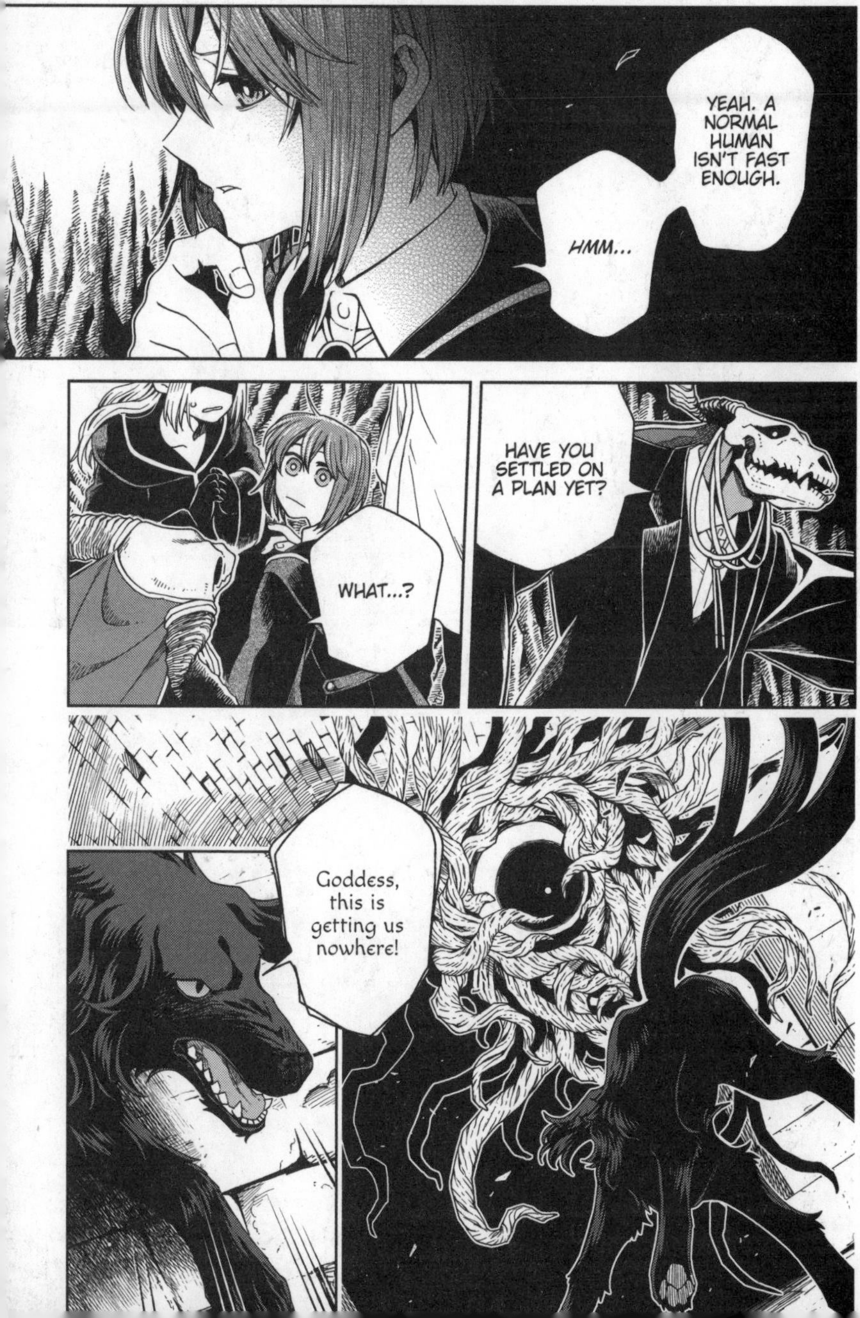
YEAH. A NORMAL HUMAN ISN'T FAST ENOUGH.
HMM...
HAVE YOU SETTLED ON A PLAN YET?
WHAT...?
Goddess, this is getting us nowhere!

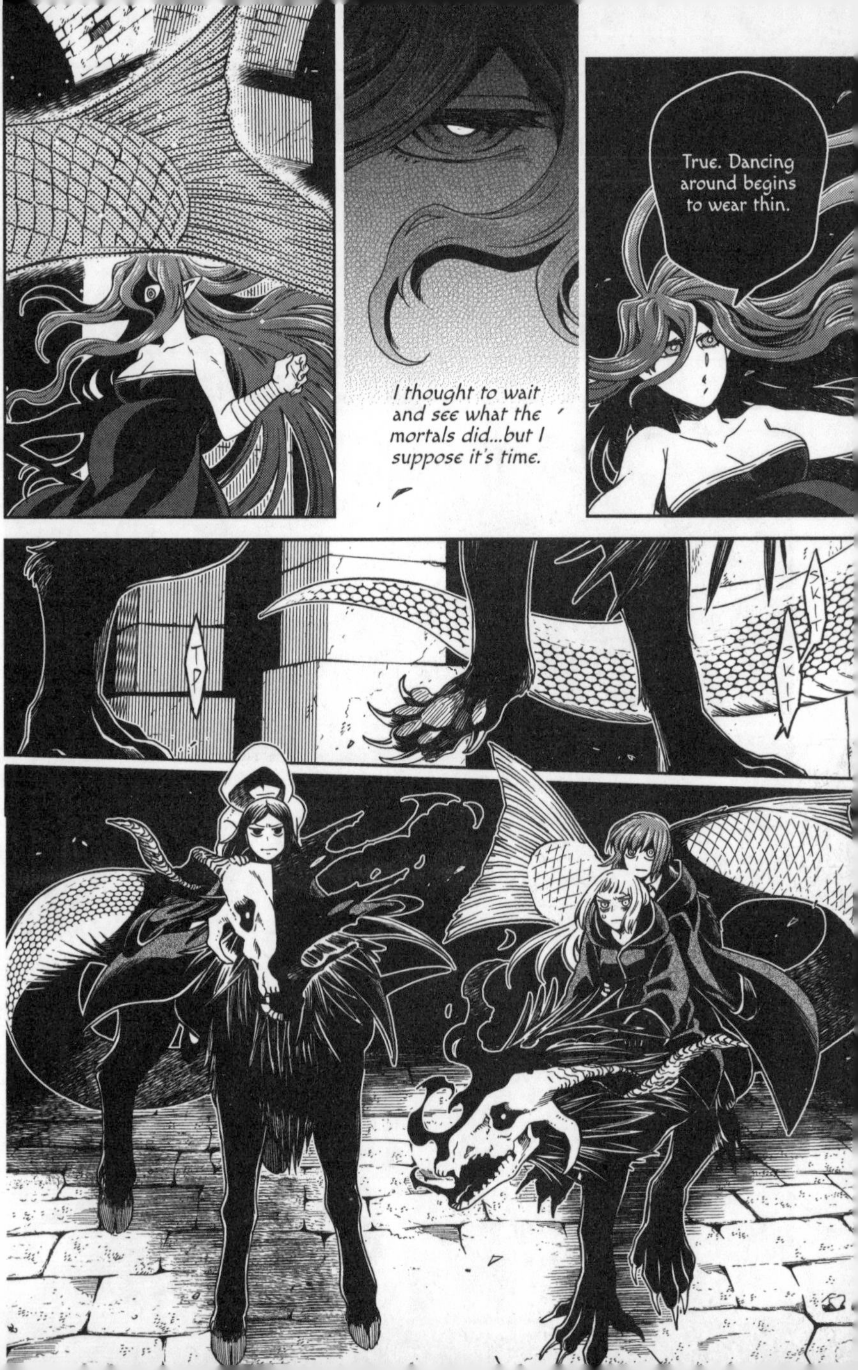
True. Dancing around begins to wear thin.
I thought to wait and see what the mortals did...but I suppose it's time.
TP
SKIT
SKIT

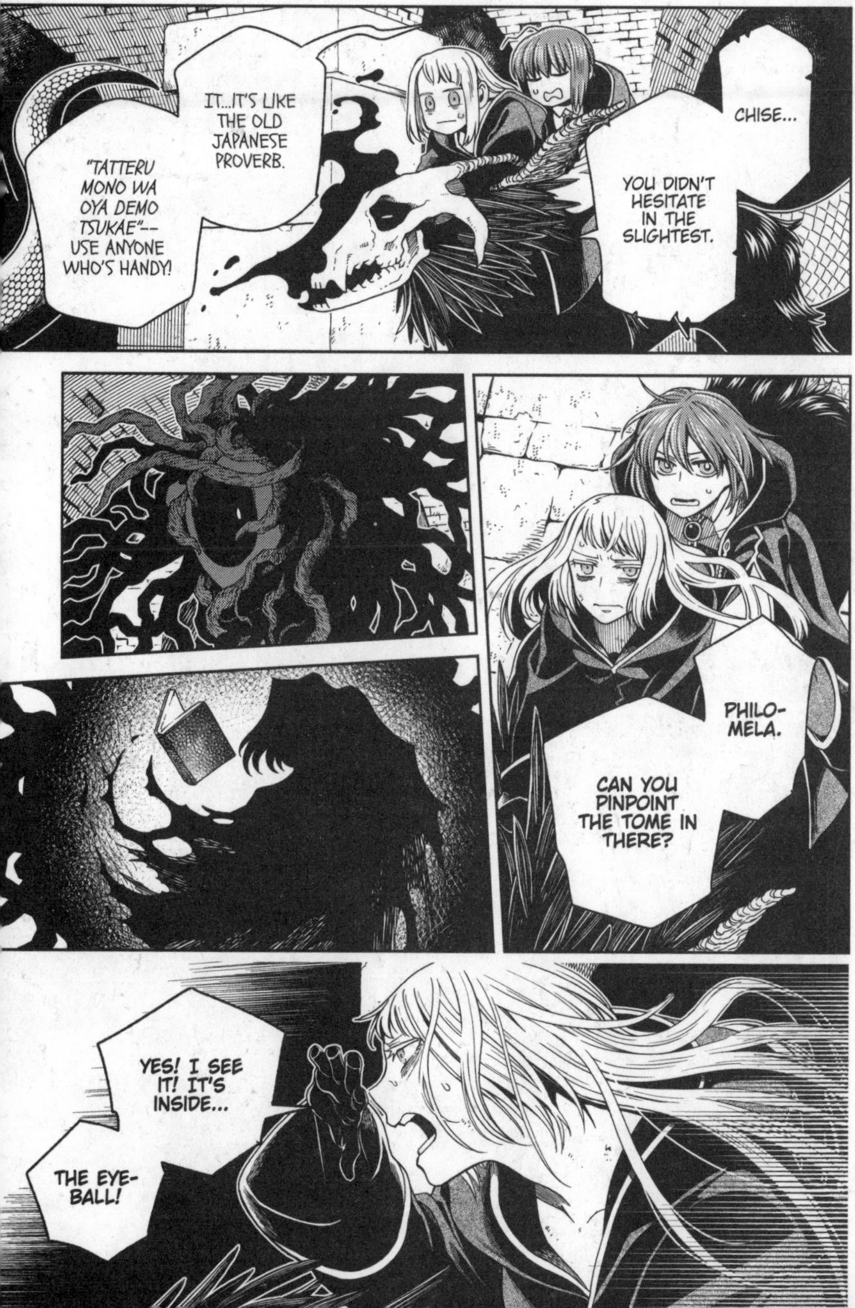
CHISE...
YOU DIDN'T HESITATE IN THE SLIGHTEST.
IT...IT'S LIKE THE OLD JAPANESE PROVERB.
"TATTERU MONO WA OYA DEMO TSUKAE"-- USE ANYONE WHO'S HANDY!
PHILO-MELA.
CAN YOU PINPOINT THE TOME IN THERE?
YES! I SEE IT! IT'S INSIDE...
THE EYE-BALL!

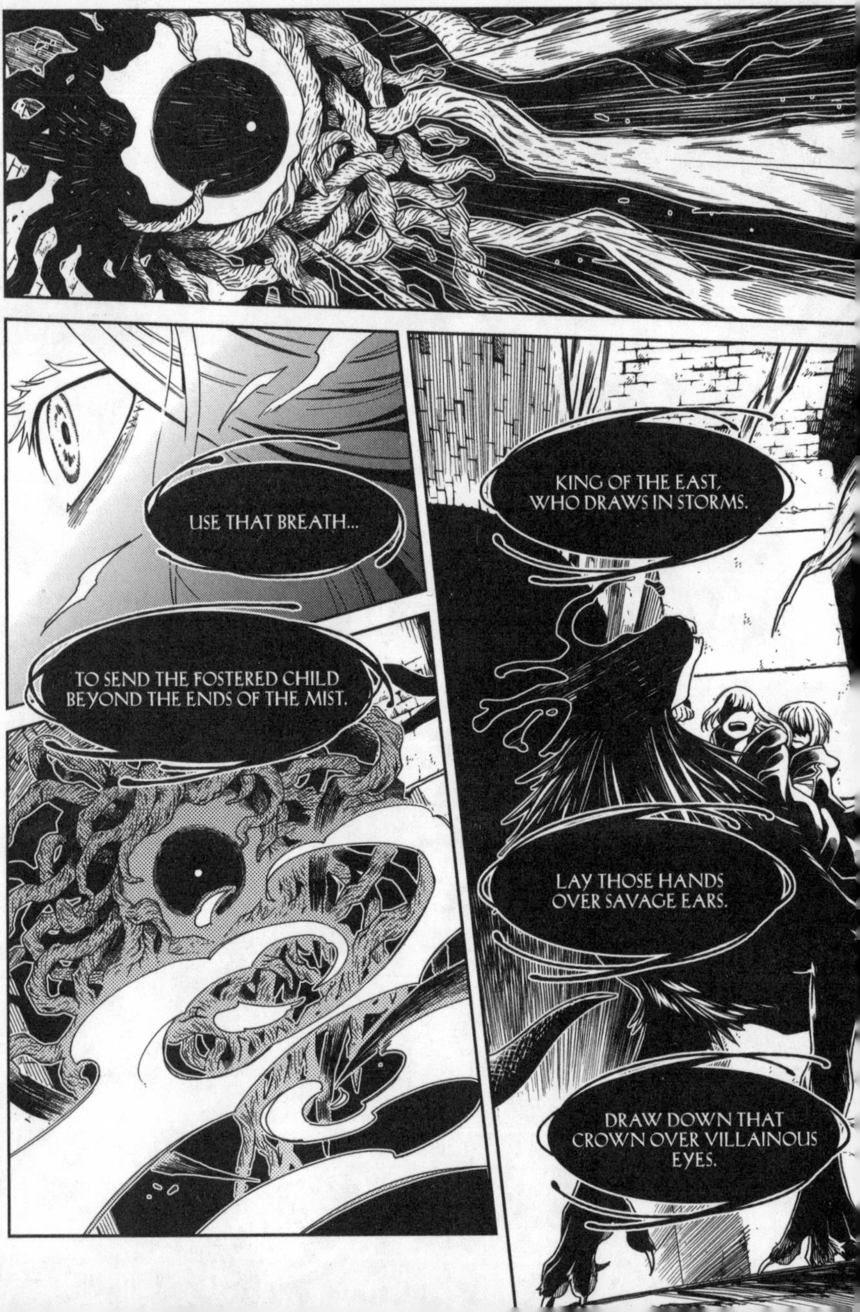
USE THAT BREATH...
TO SEND THE FOSTERED CHILD BEYOND THE ENDS OF THE MIST.
KING OF THE EAST, WHO DRAWS IN STORMS.
LAY THOSE HANDS OVER SAVAGE EARS.
DRAW DOWN THAT CROWN OVER VILLAINOUS EYES.

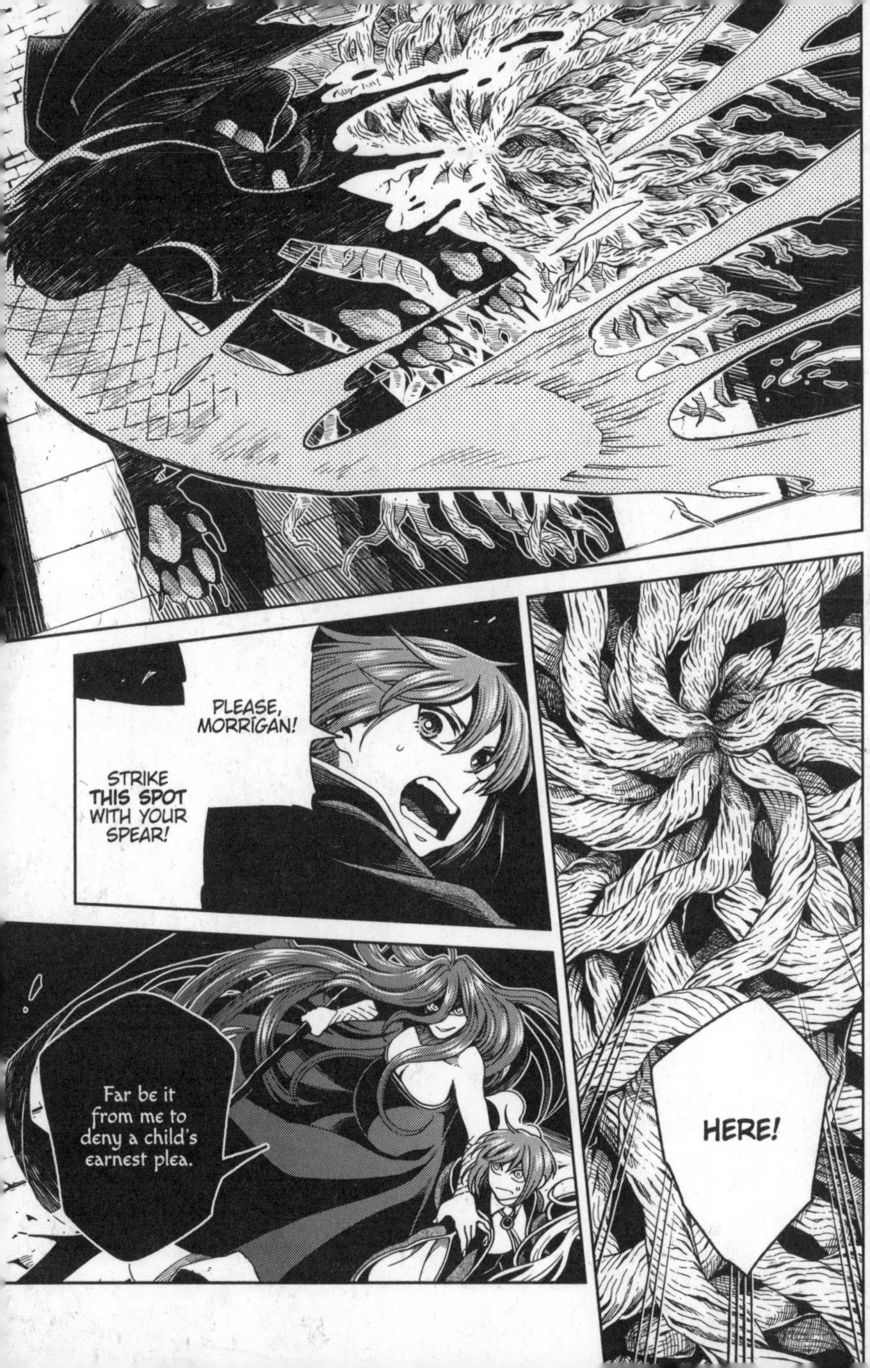
HERE!
PLEASE, MORRIGAN!
STRIKE THIS SPOT WITH YOUR SPEAR!
Far be it from me to deny a child's earnest plea.

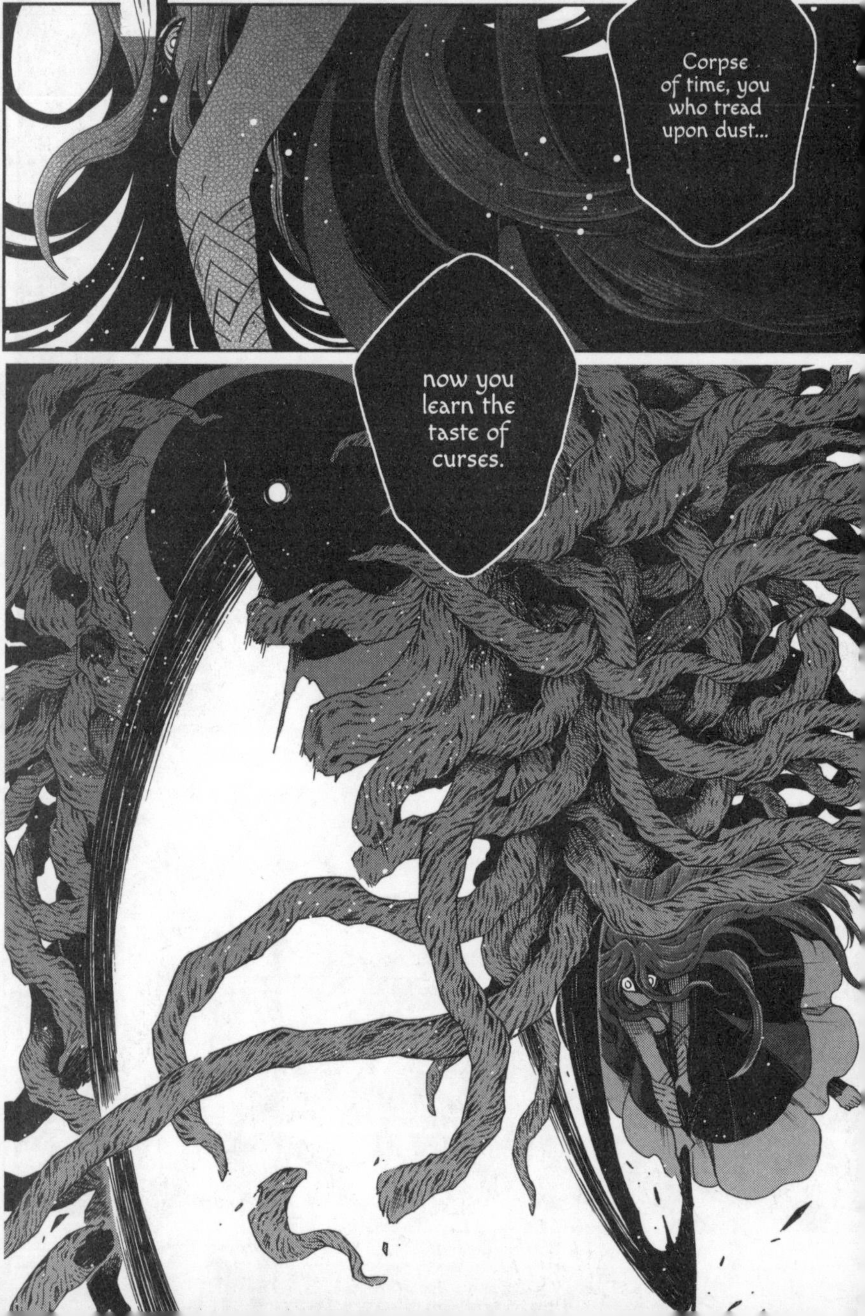
Corpse of time, you who tread upon dust...
now you learn the taste of curses.

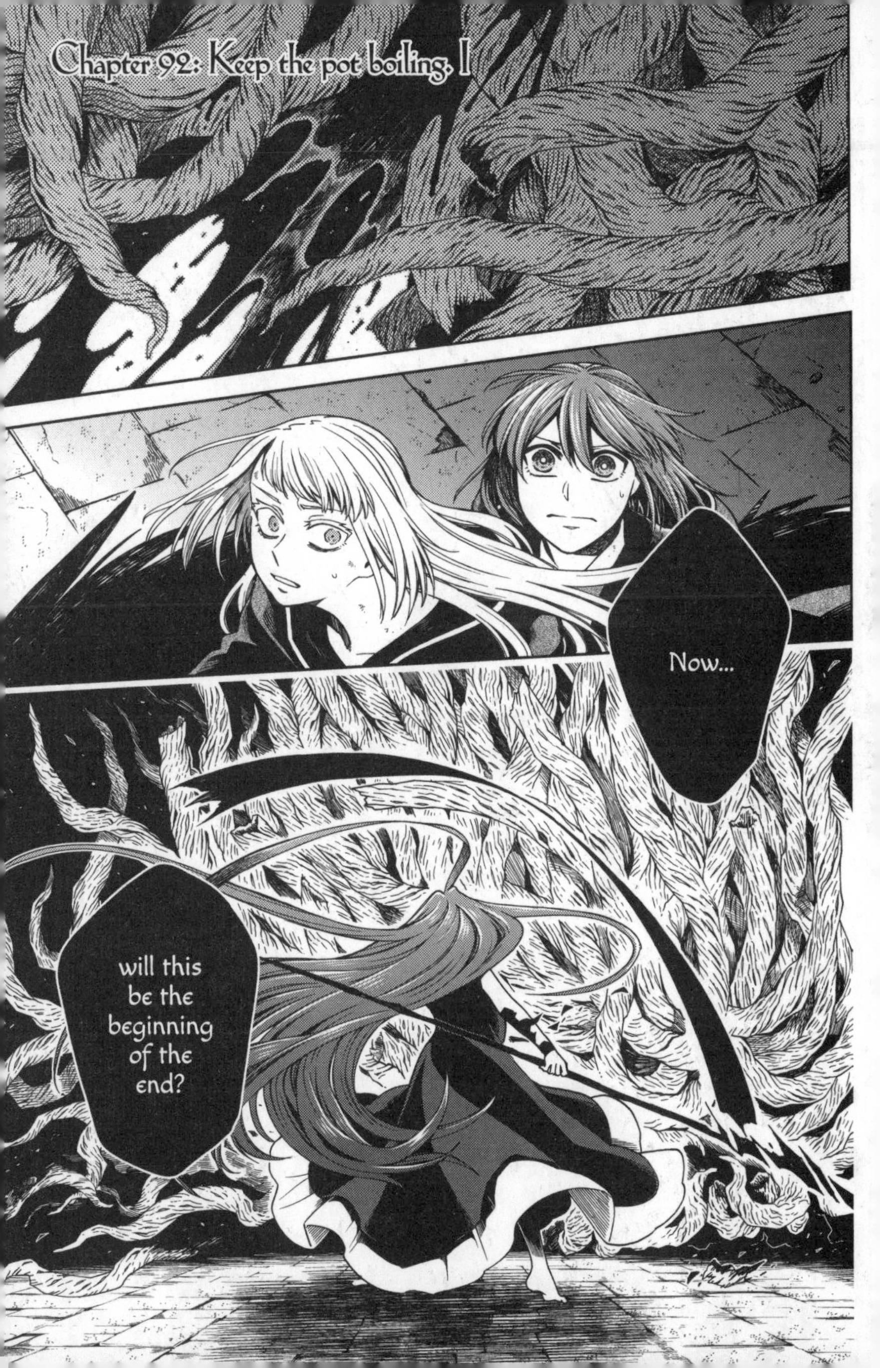
Chapter 92: Keep the pot boiling. I
Now...
will this be the beginning of the end?

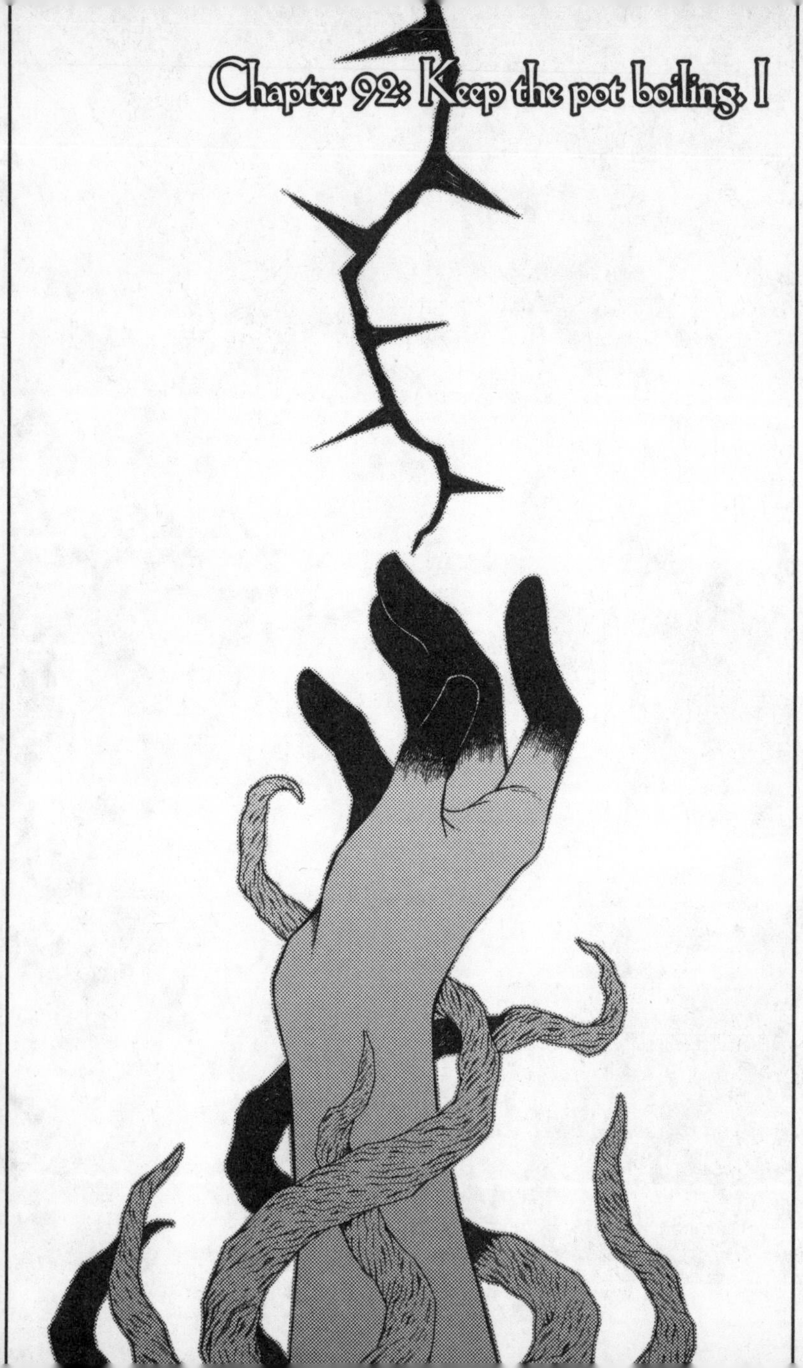
Chapter 92: Keep the pot boiling. I

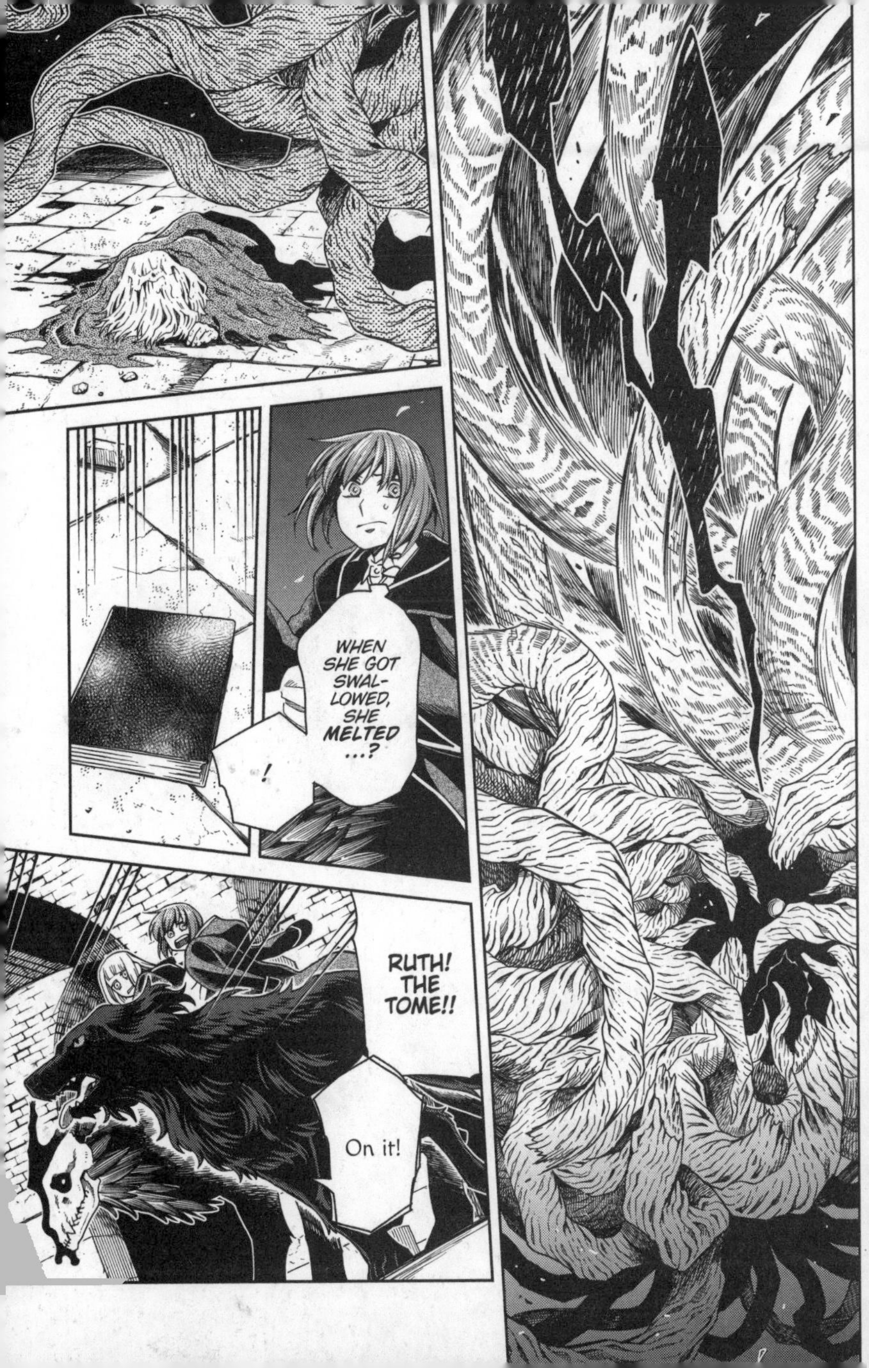
WHEN SHE GOT SWAL-LOWED, SHE MELTED ...?
!
RUTH! THE TOME!!
On it!

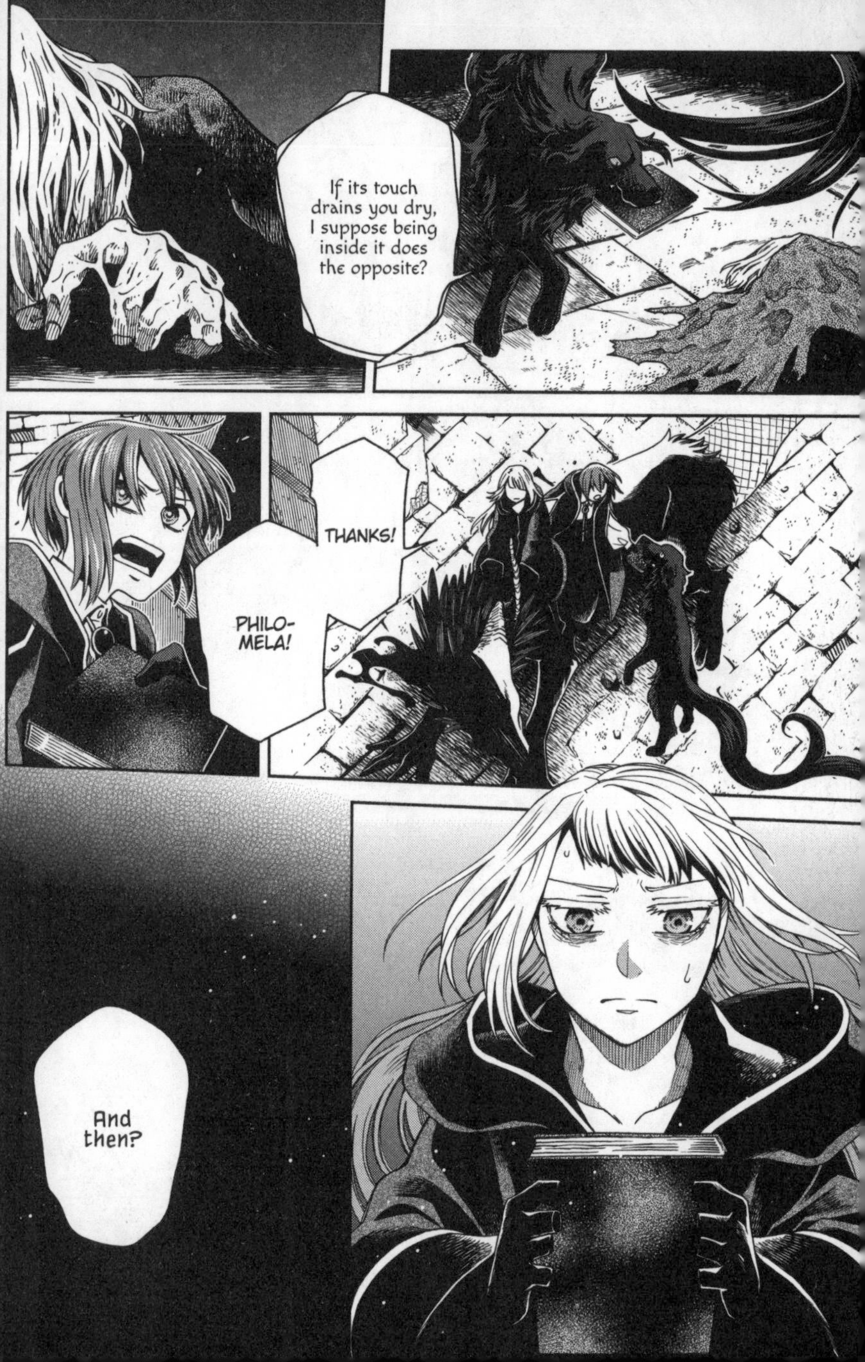
If its touch drains you dry, I suppose being inside it does the opposite?
THANKS!
PHILO-MELA!
And then?

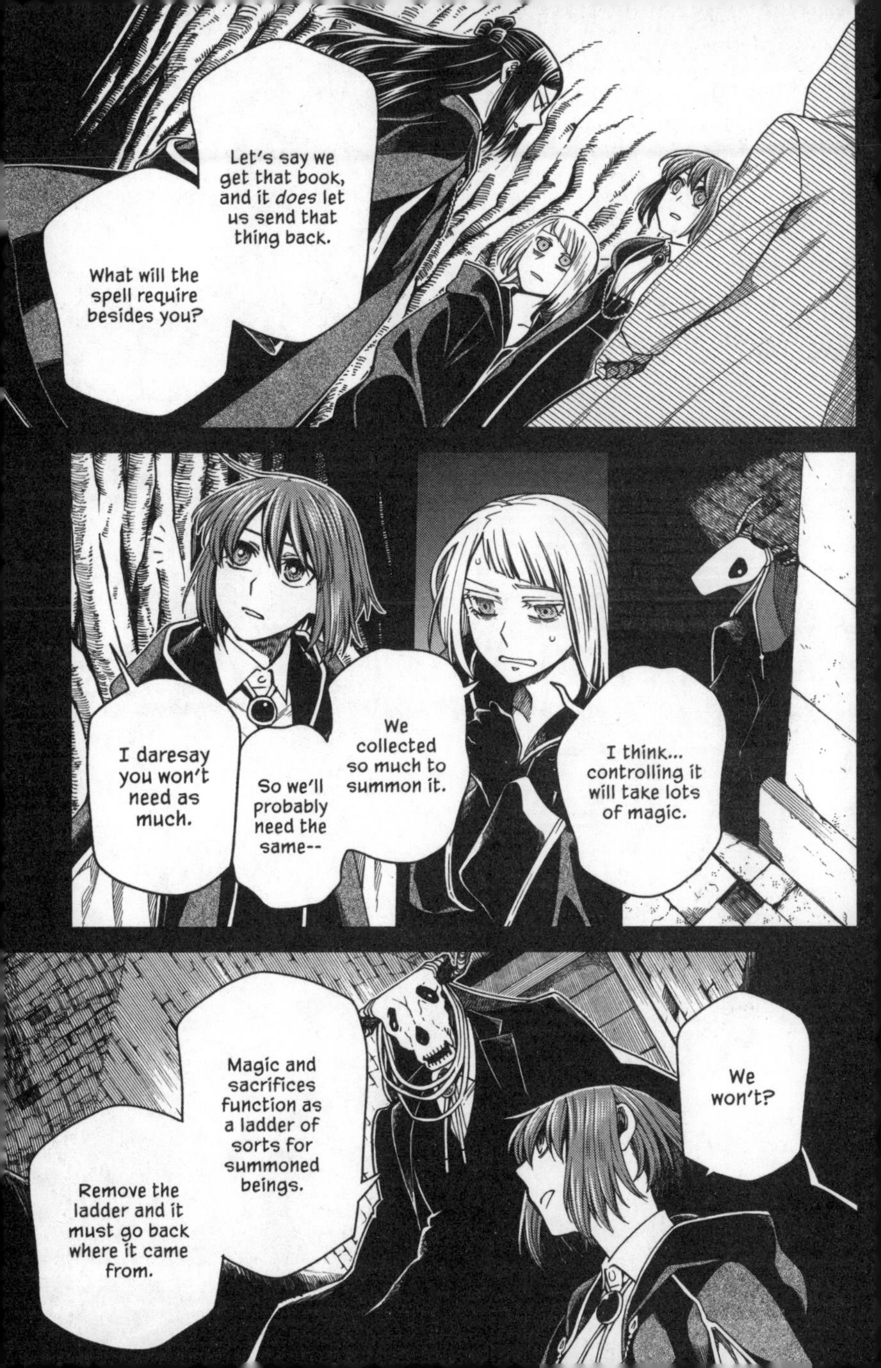
Let's say we get that book, and it *does* let us send that thing back.
What will the spell require besides you?
I think... controlling it will take lots of magic.
We collected so much to summon it.
So we'll probably need the same--
I daresay you won't need as much.
We won't?
Magic and sacrifices function as a ladder of sorts for summoned beings.
Remove the ladder and it must go back where it came from.

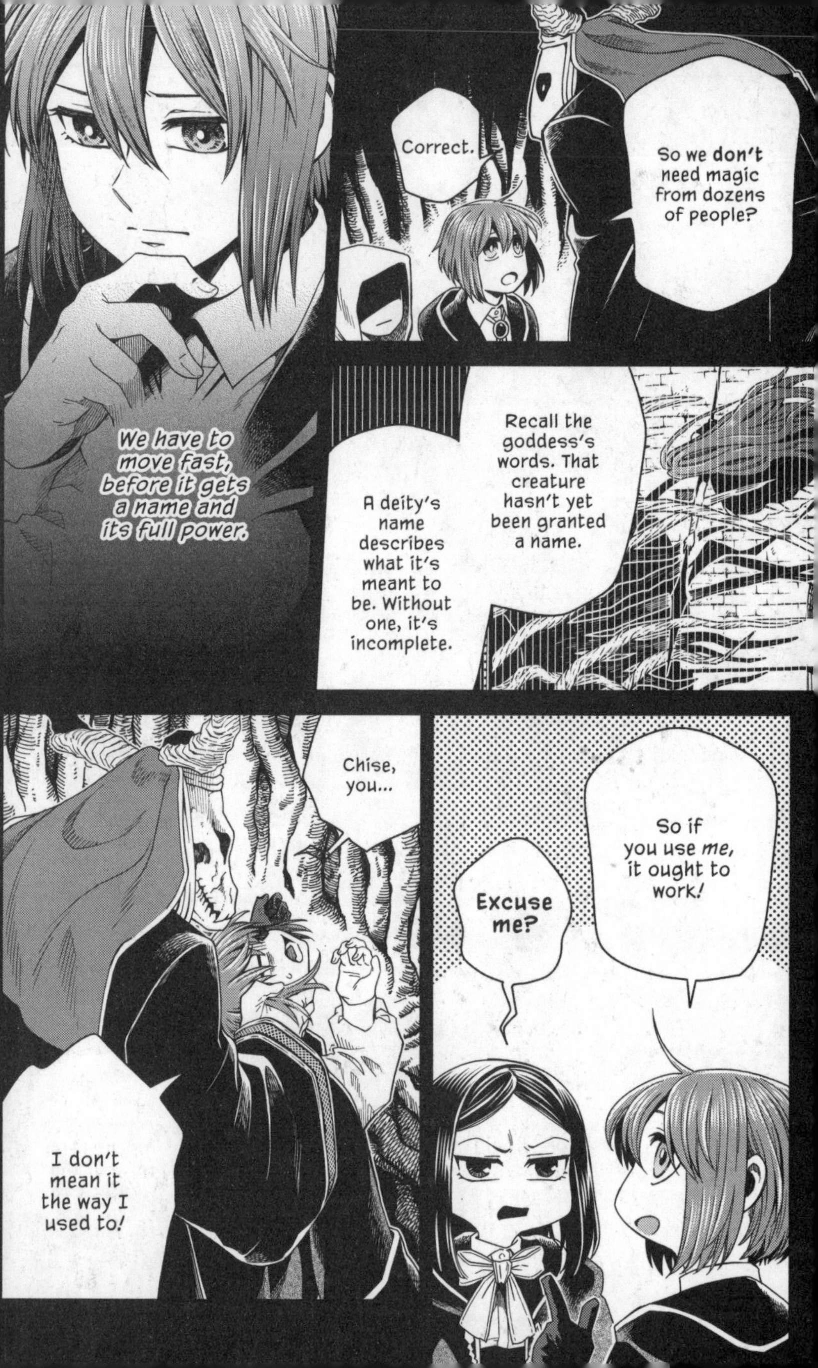
So we **don't** need magic from dozens of people?
Correct.
Recall the goddess's words. That creature hasn't yet been granted a name.
A deity's name describes what it's meant to be. Without one, it's incomplete.
We have to move fast, before it gets a name and its full power.
So if you use *me*, it ought to work!
Excuse me?
Chise, you...
I don't mean it the way I used to!

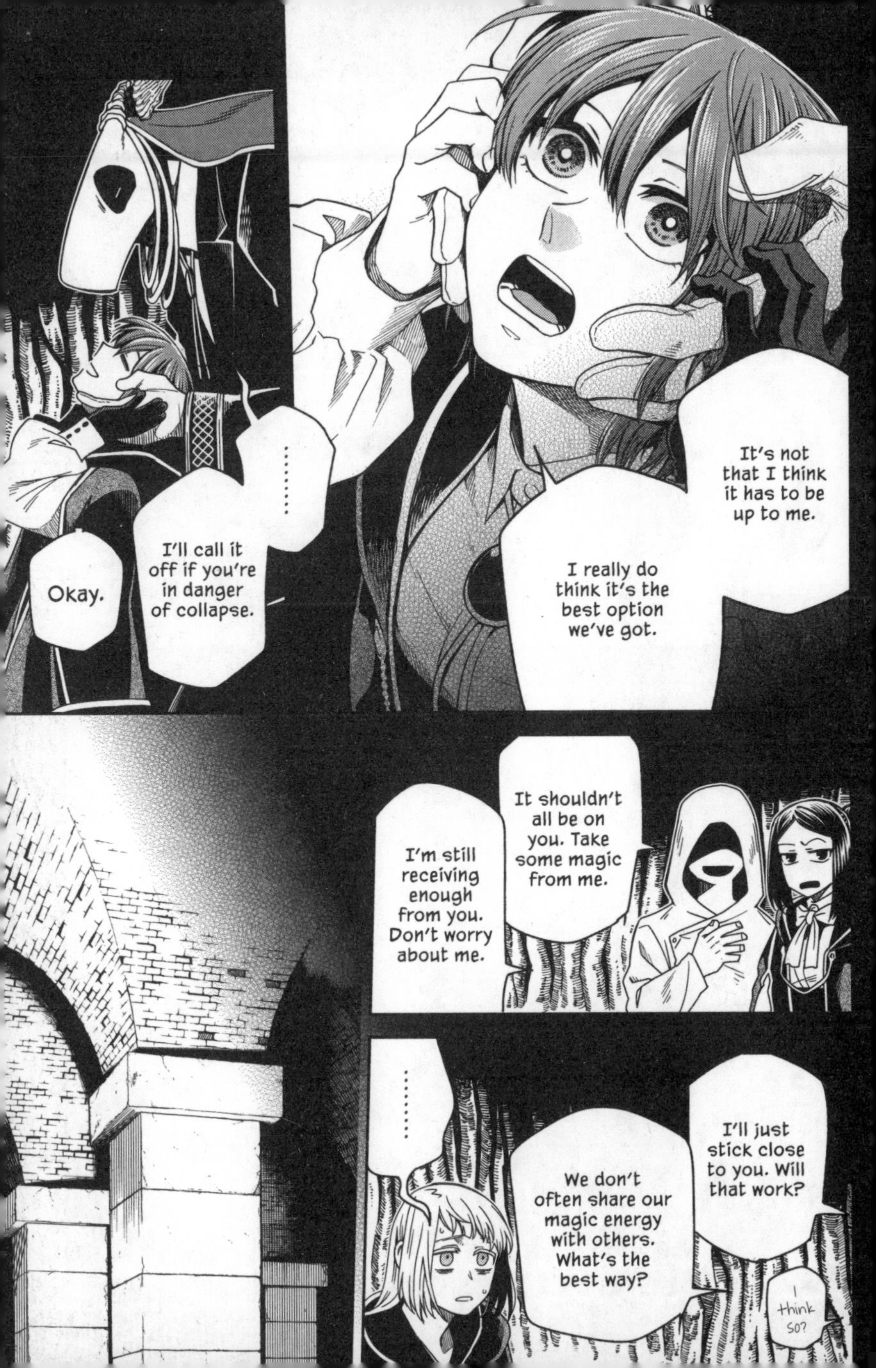
It's not that I think it has to be up to me.
I really do think it's the best option we've got.
......
I'll call it off if you're in danger of collapse.
Okay.
It shouldn't all be on you. Take some magic from me.
I'm still receiving enough from you. Don't worry about me.
I'll just stick close to you. Will that work?
I think so?
We don't often share our magic energy with others. What's the best way?
......

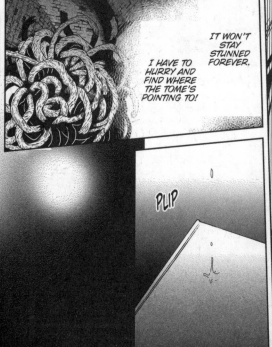

IT WON'T STAY STUNNED FOREVER.

I HAVE TO HURRY AND FIND WHERE THE TOME'S POINTING TO!

PLIP

I MUST DO THIS.

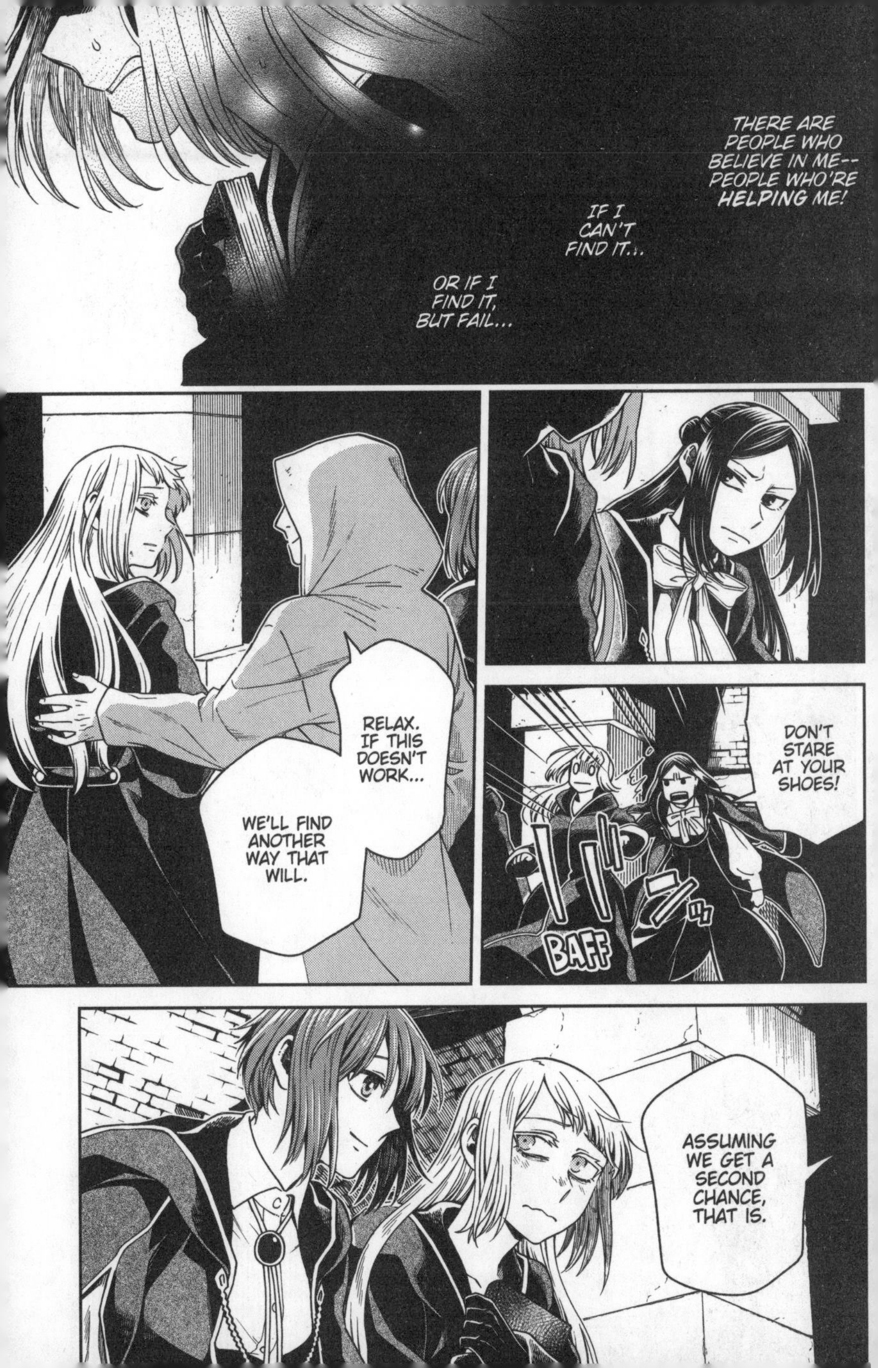
THERE ARE PEOPLE WHO BELIEVE IN ME-- PEOPLE WHO'RE HELPING ME!
IF I CAN'T FIND IT...
OR IF I FIND IT, BUT FAIL...
DON'T STARE AT YOUR SHOES!
BAFF
RELAX. IF THIS DOESN'T WORK...
WE'LL FIND ANOTHER WAY THAT WILL.
ASSUMING WE GET A SECOND CHANCE, THAT IS.

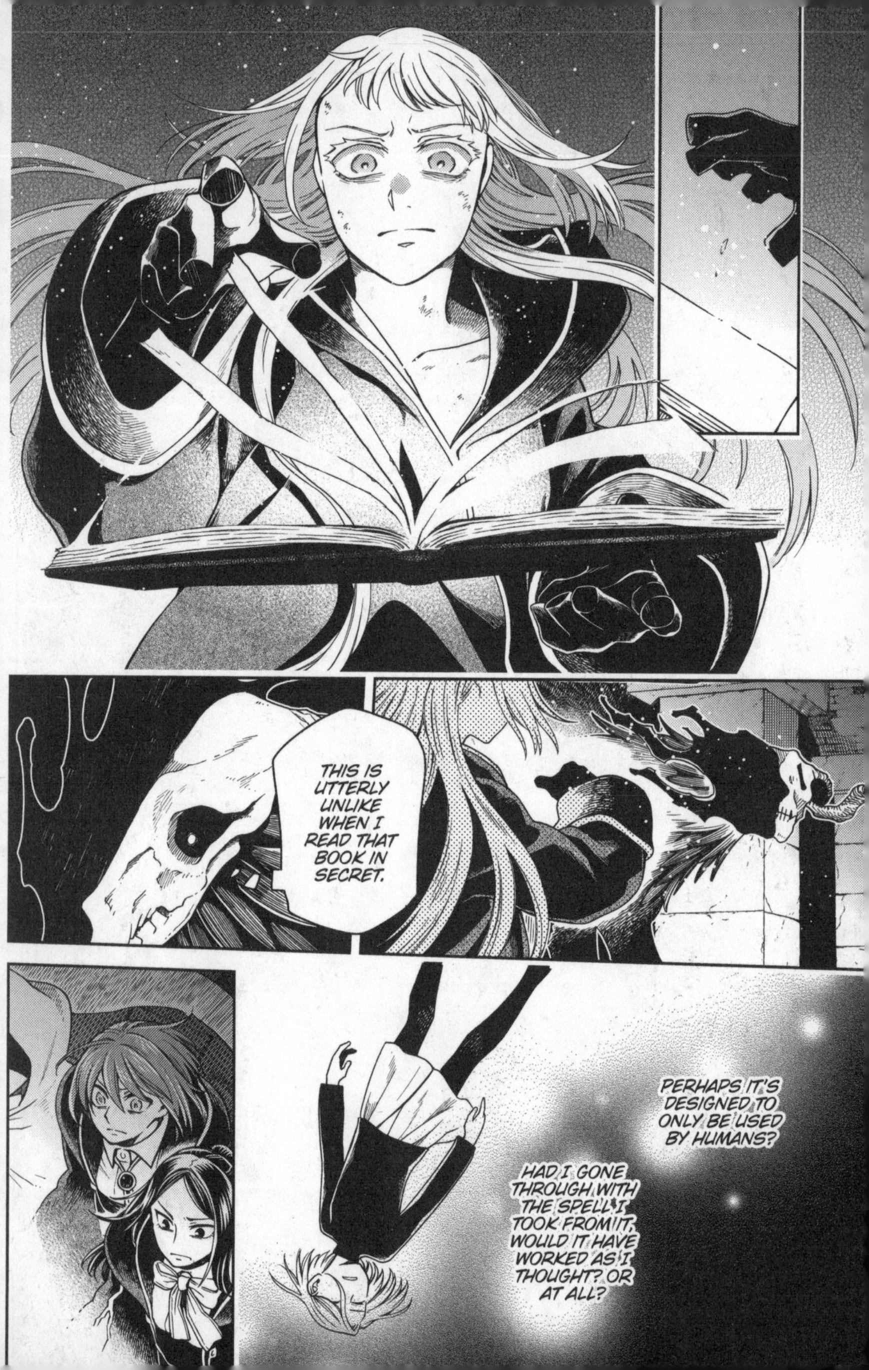
THIS IS UTTERLY UNLIKE WHEN I READ THAT BOOK IN SECRET.
PERHAPS IT'S DESIGNED TO ONLY BE USED BY HUMANS?
HAD I GONE THROUGH WITH THE SPELL I TOOK FROM IT, WOULD IT HAVE WORKED AS I THOUGHT? OR AT ALL?

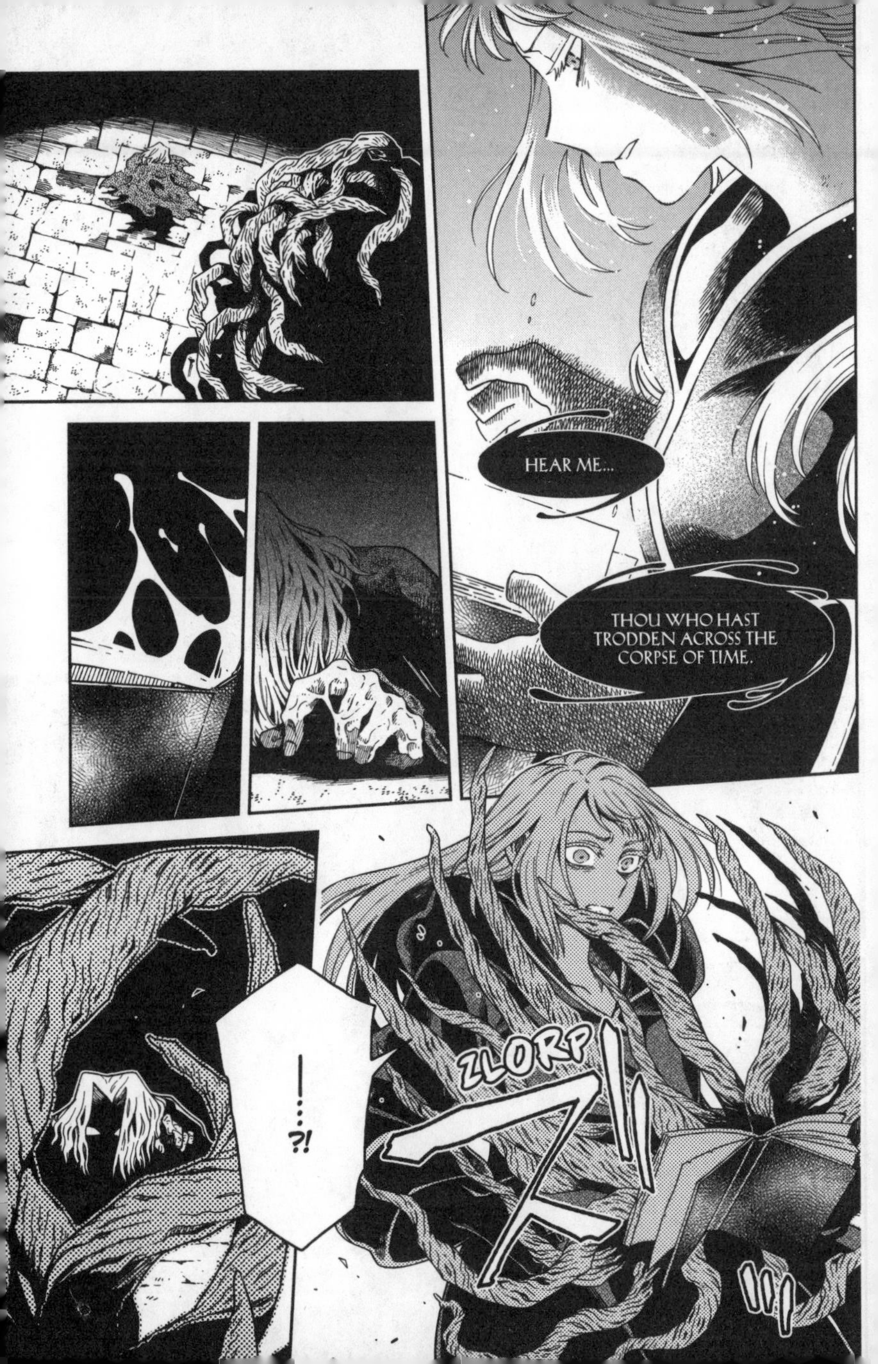
HEAR ME...
THOU WHO HAST TRODDEN ACROSS THE CORPSE OF TIME.
...?!
ZLORP

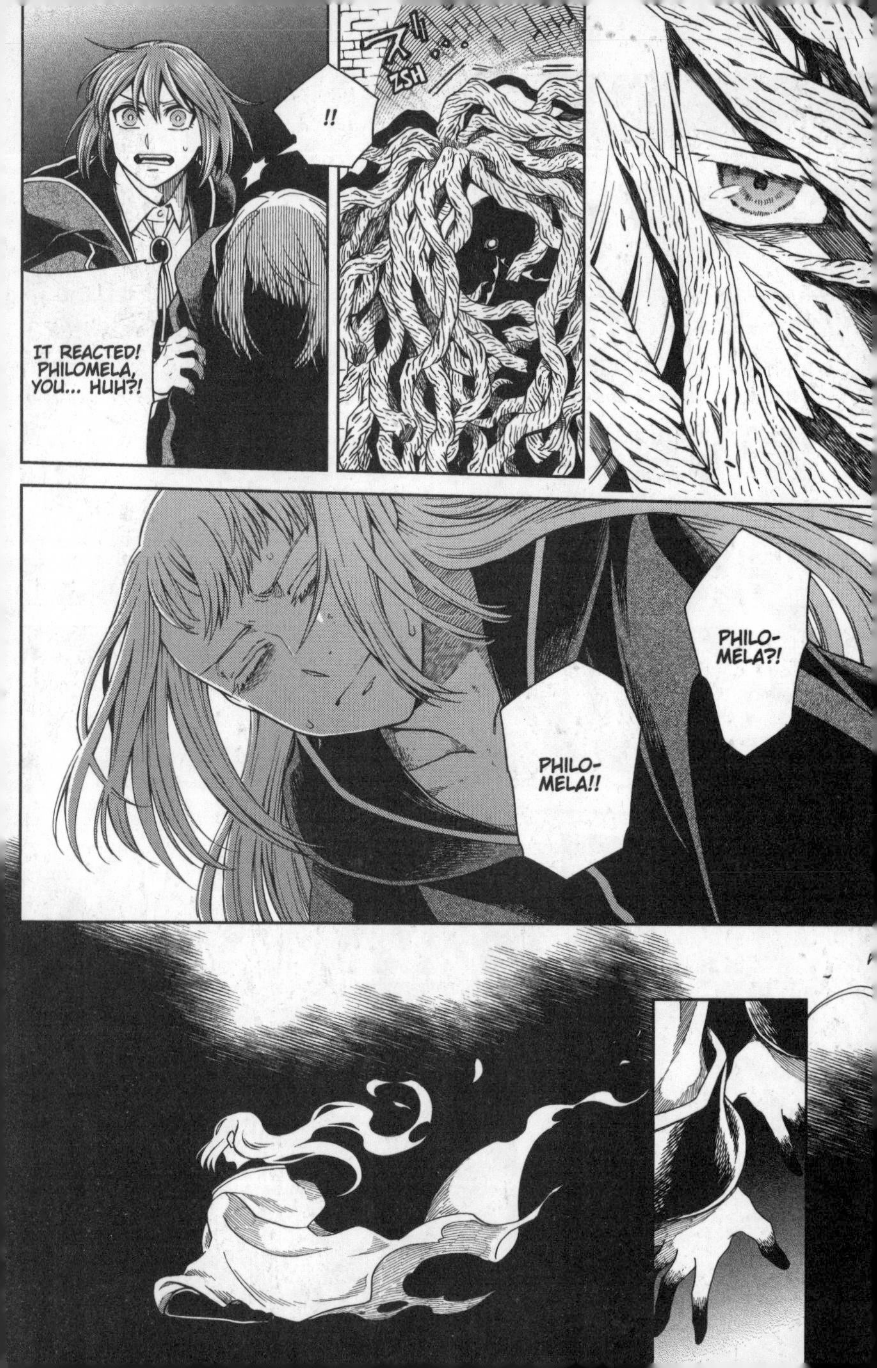
ZSH
!!
IT REACTED! PHILOMELA, YOU... HUH?!
PHILO-MELA?!
PHILO-MELA!!

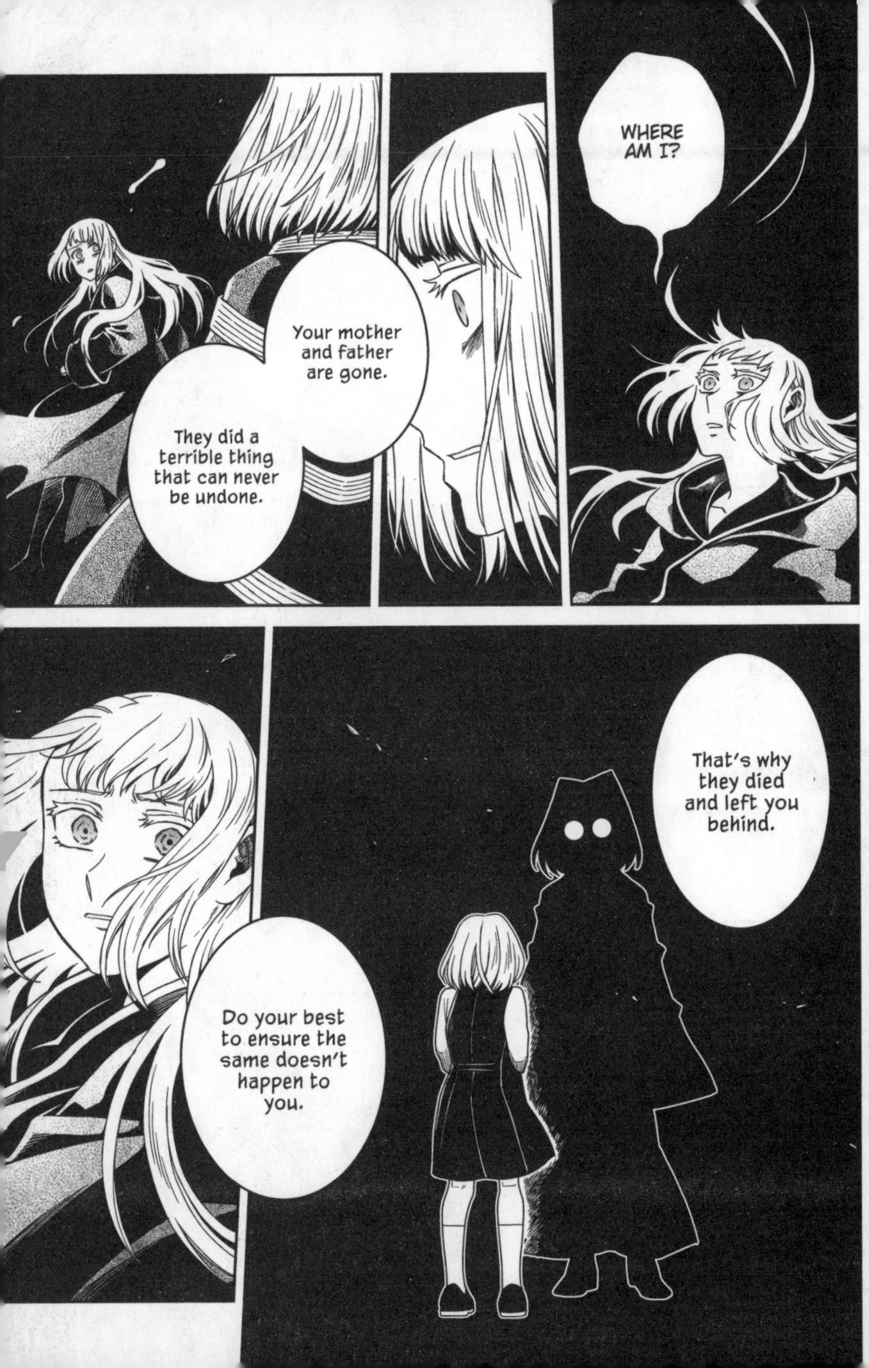
WHERE AM I?
Your mother and father are gone.
They did a terrible thing that can never be undone.
That's why they died and left you behind.
Do your best to ensure the same doesn't happen to you.

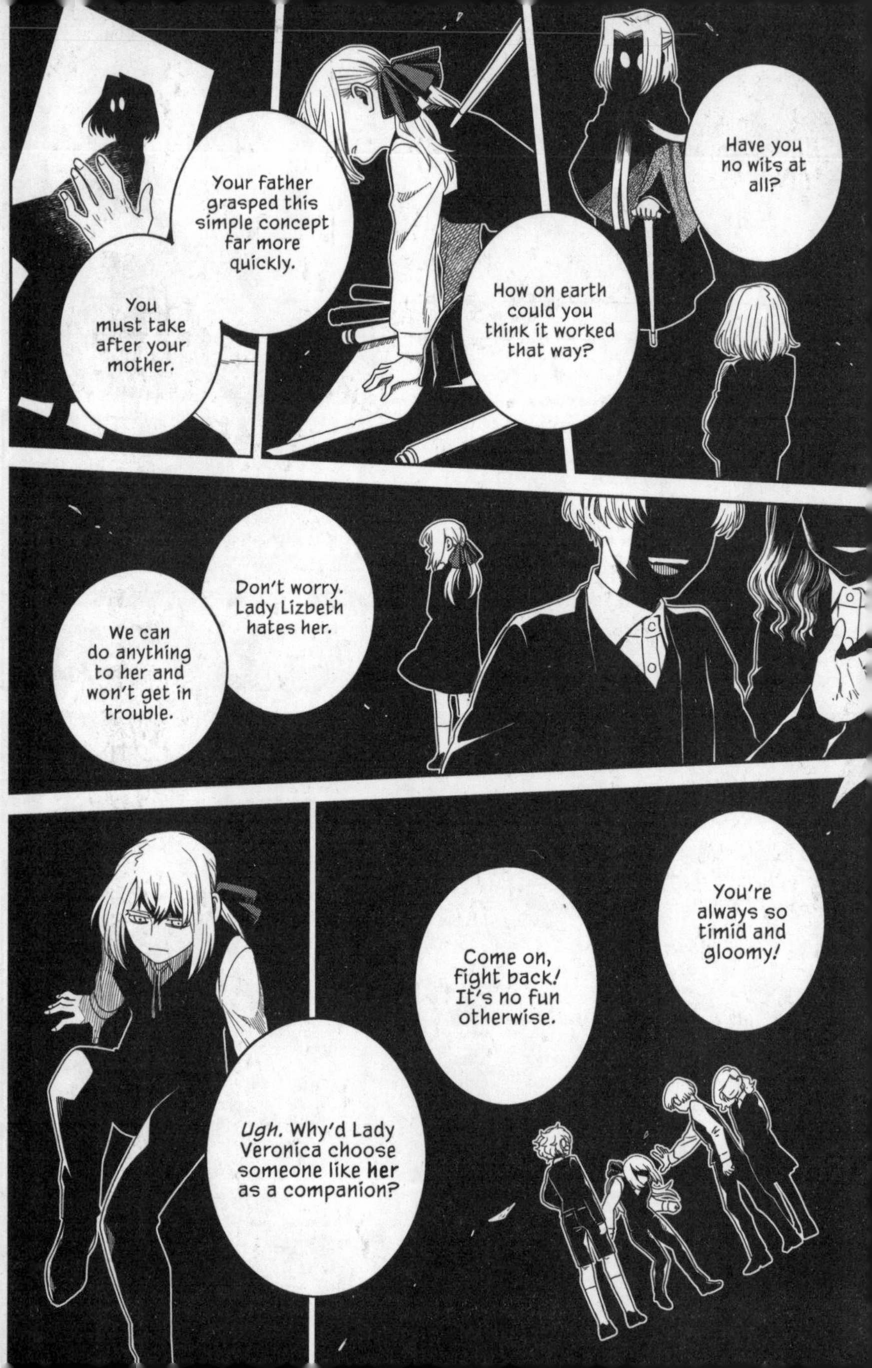
Your father grasped this simple concept far more quickly.
You must take after your mother.
Have you no wits at all?
How on earth could you think it worked that way?
Don't worry. Lady Lizbeth hates her.
We can do anything to her and won't get in trouble.
You're always so timid and gloomy!
Come on, fight back! It's no fun otherwise.
Ugh. Why'd Lady Veronica choose someone like **her** as a companion?

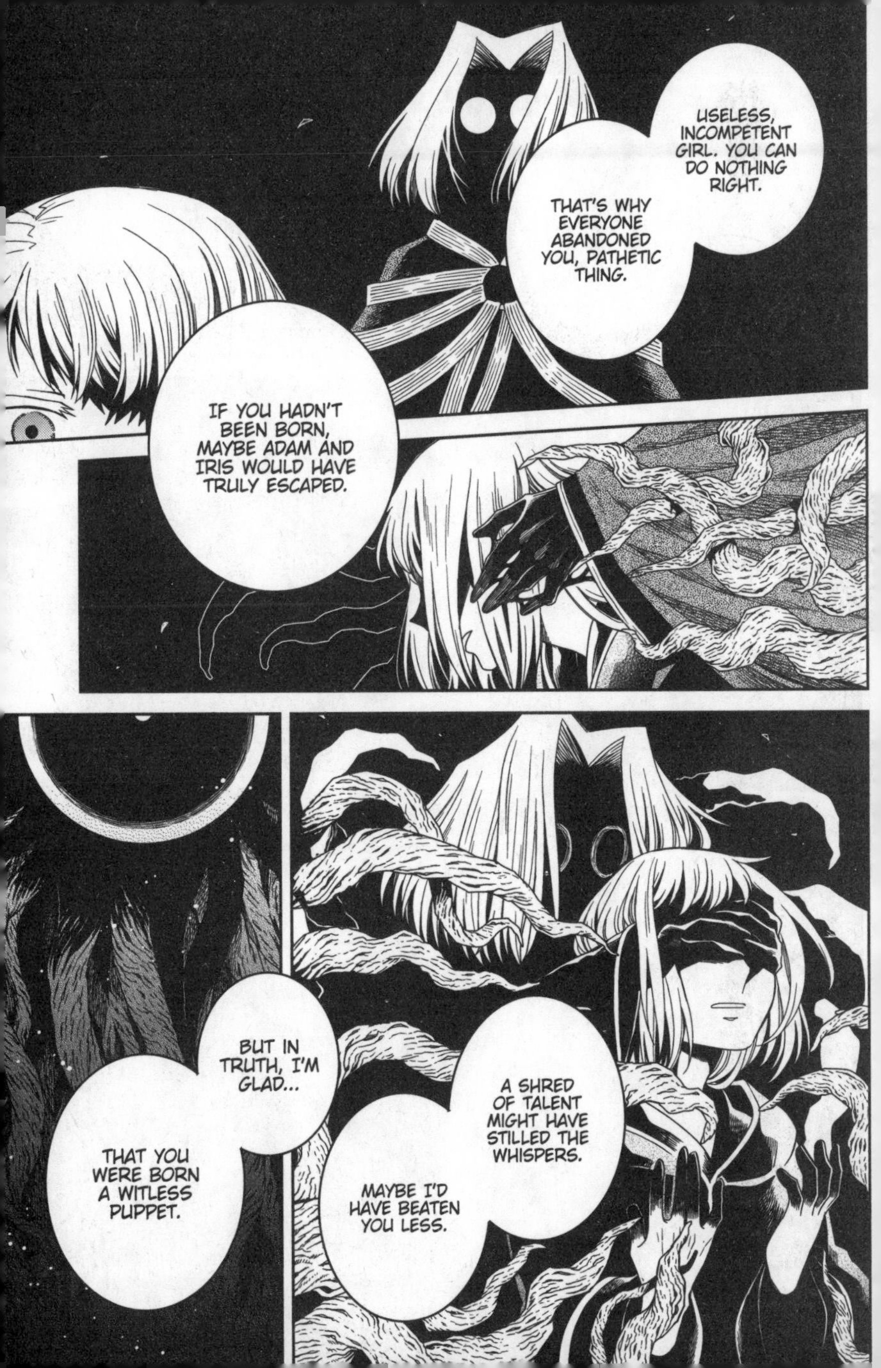
USELESS, INCOMPETENT GIRL. YOU CAN DO NOTHING RIGHT.
THAT'S WHY EVERYONE ABANDONED YOU, PATHETIC THING.
IF YOU HADN'T BEEN BORN, MAYBE ADAM AND IRIS WOULD HAVE TRULY ESCAPED.
A SHRED OF TALENT MIGHT HAVE STILLED THE WHISPERS.
MAYBE I'D HAVE BEATEN YOU LESS.
BUT IN TRUTH, I'M GLAD...
THAT YOU WERE BORN A WITLESS PUPPET.

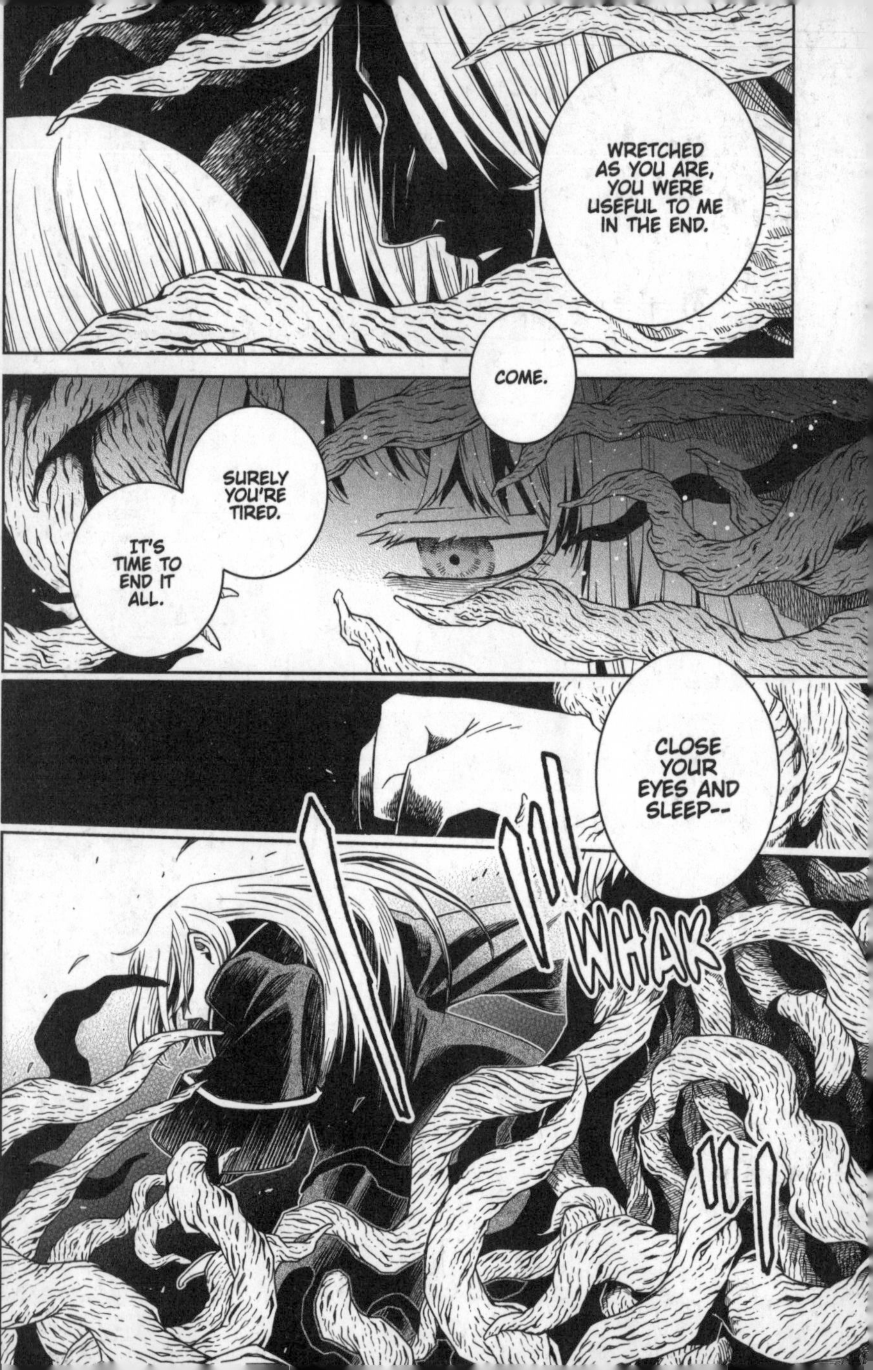
WRETCHED AS YOU ARE, YOU WERE USEFUL TO ME IN THE END.
COME.
SURELY YOU'RE TIRED.
IT'S TIME TO END IT ALL.
CLOSE YOUR EYES AND SLEEP--
WHAK

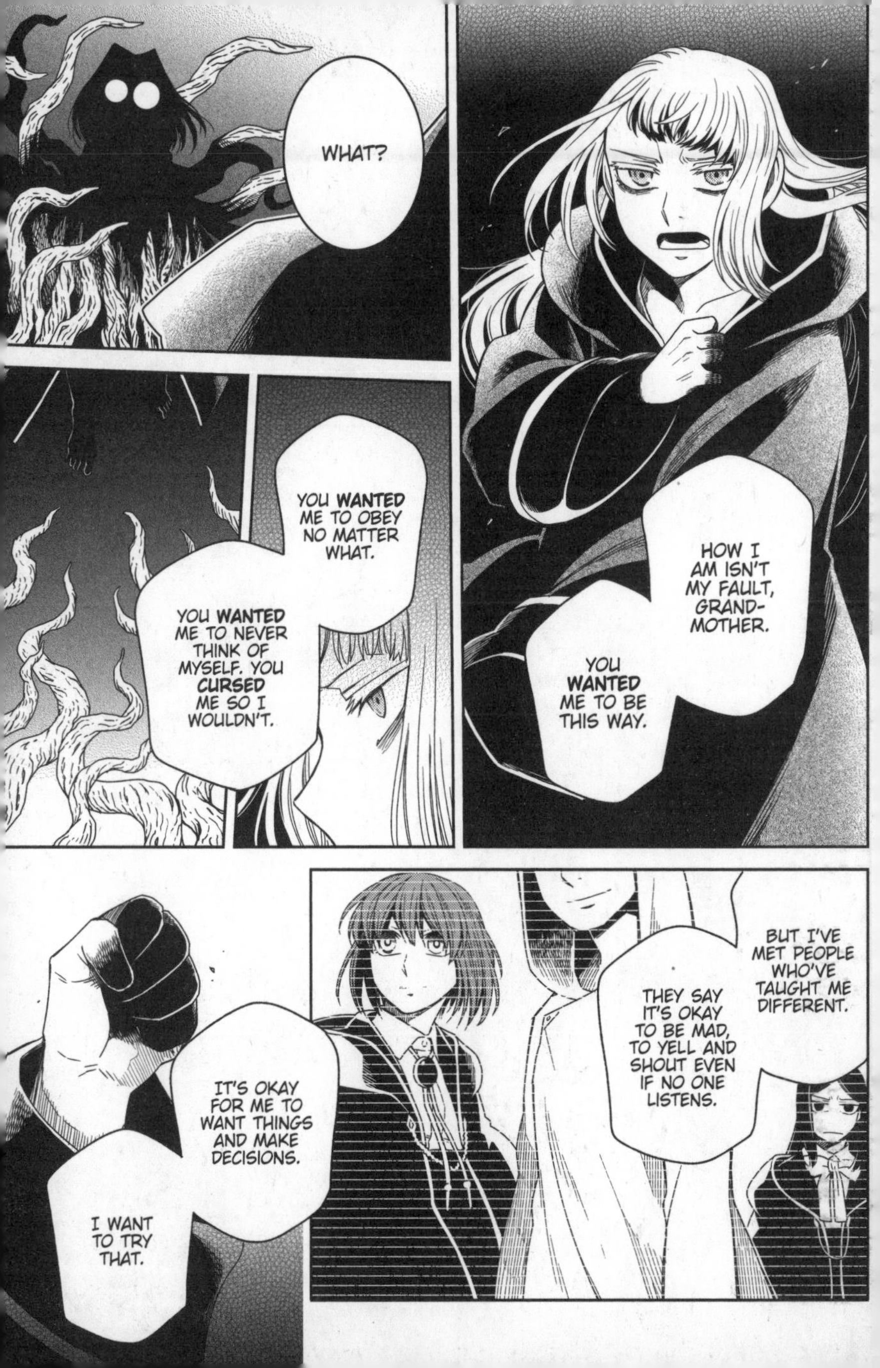
HOW I AM ISN'T MY FAULT, GRAND-MOTHER.
YOU WANTED ME TO BE THIS WAY.
WHAT?
YOU WANTED ME TO OBEY NO MATTER WHAT.
YOU WANTED ME TO NEVER THINK OF MYSELF. YOU CURSED ME SO I WOULDN'T.
BUT I'VE MET PEOPLE WHO'VE TAUGHT ME DIFFERENT.
THEY SAY IT'S OKAY TO BE MAD, TO YELL AND SHOUT EVEN IF NO ONE LISTENS.
IT'S OKAY FOR ME TO WANT THINGS AND MAKE DECISIONS.
I WANT TO TRY THAT.

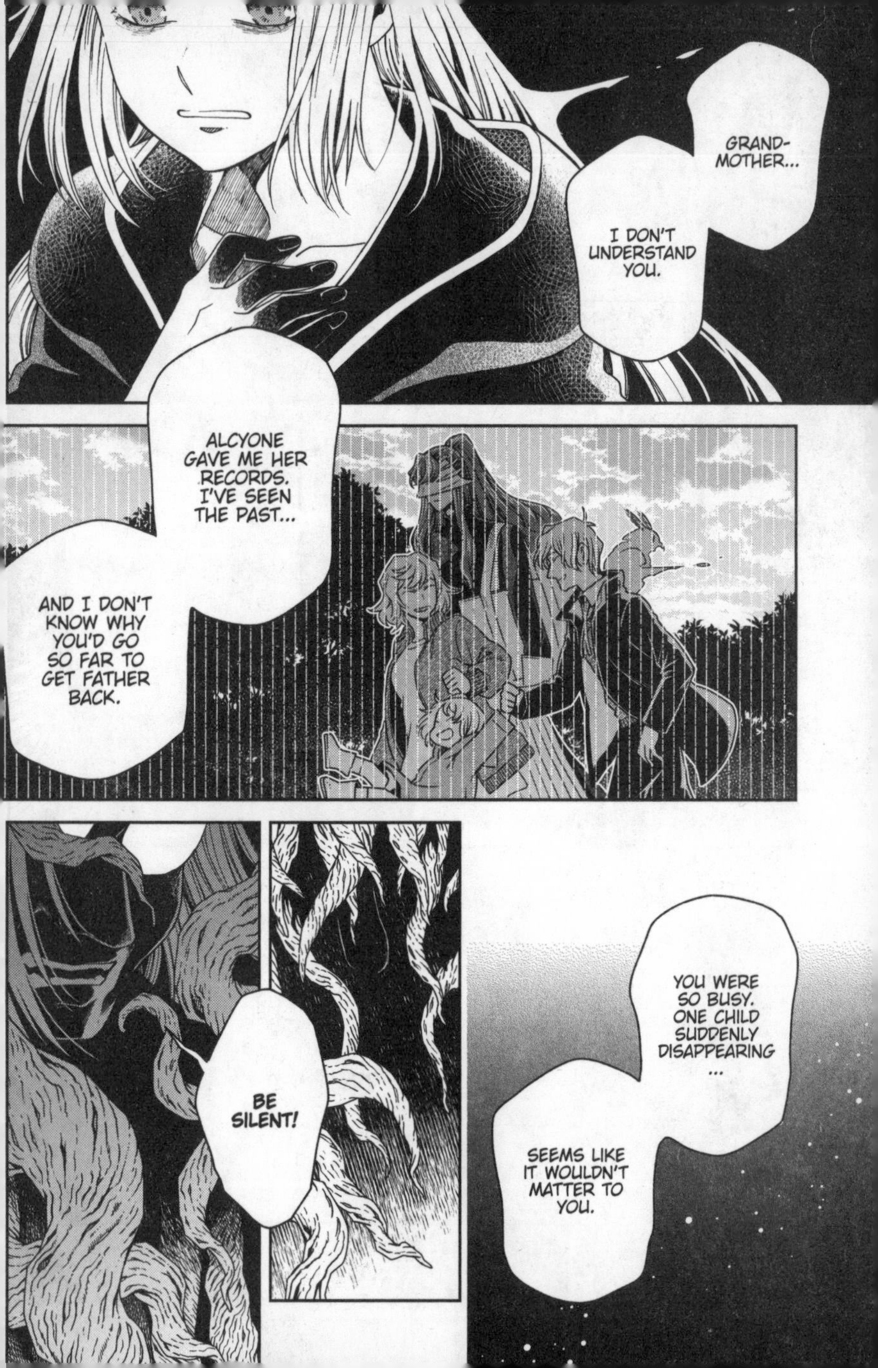
GRAND-MOTHER...
I DON'T UNDERSTAND YOU.
ALCYONE GAVE ME HER RECORDS. I'VE SEEN THE PAST...
AND I DON'T KNOW WHY YOU'D GO SO FAR TO GET FATHER BACK.
YOU WERE SO BUSY. ONE CHILD SUDDENLY DISAPPEARING ...
SEEMS LIKE IT WOULDN'T MATTER TO YOU.
BE SILENT!

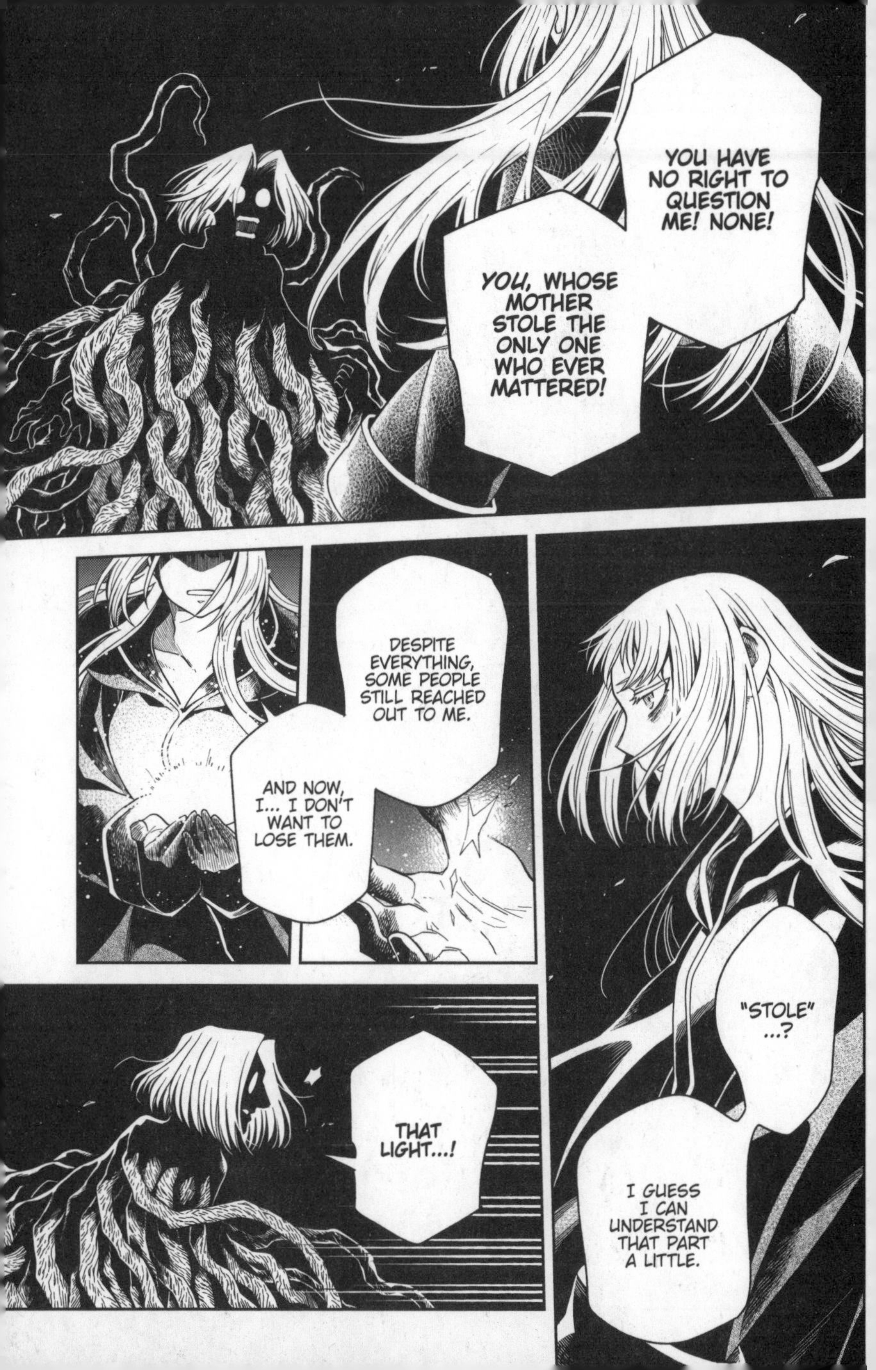
YOU HAVE NO RIGHT TO QUESTION ME! NONE!
YOU, WHOSE MOTHER STOLE THE ONLY ONE WHO EVER MATTERED!
"STOLE" ...?
I GUESS I CAN UNDERSTAND THAT PART A LITTLE.
DESPITE EVERYTHING, SOME PEOPLE STILL REACHED OUT TO ME.
AND NOW, I... I DON'T WANT TO LOSE THEM.
THAT LIGHT...!

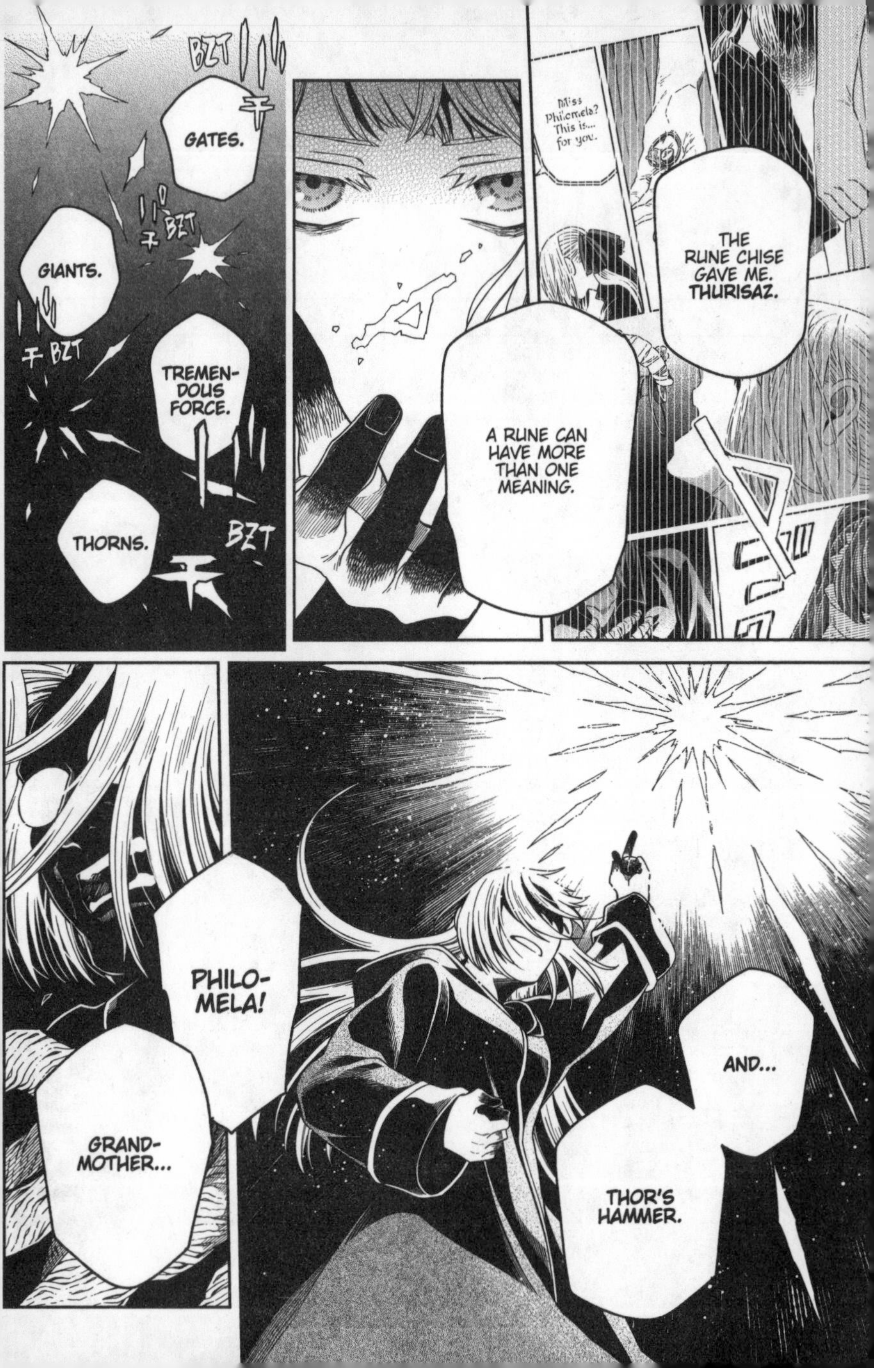
Miss Philomela? This is... for you.
THE RUNE CHISE GAVE ME. THURISAZ.
A RUNE CAN HAVE MORE THAN ONE MEANING.
BZT
GATES.
BZT
GIANTS.
BZT
TREMEN-DOUS FORCE.
BZT
THORNS.
AND...
THOR'S HAMMER.
PHILO-MELA!
GRAND-MOTHER...

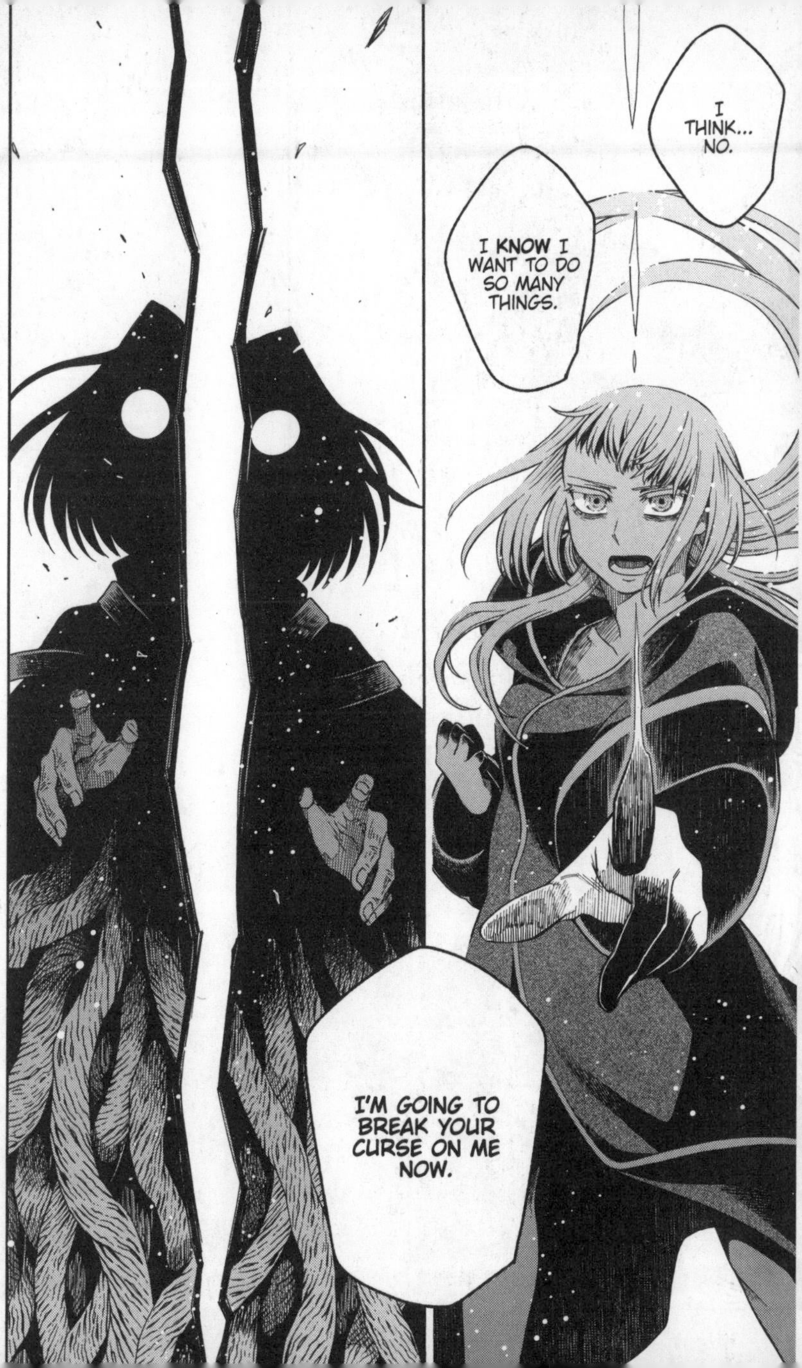
I THINK... NO.
I KNOW I WANT TO DO SO MANY THINGS.
I'M GOING TO BREAK YOUR CURSE ON ME NOW.

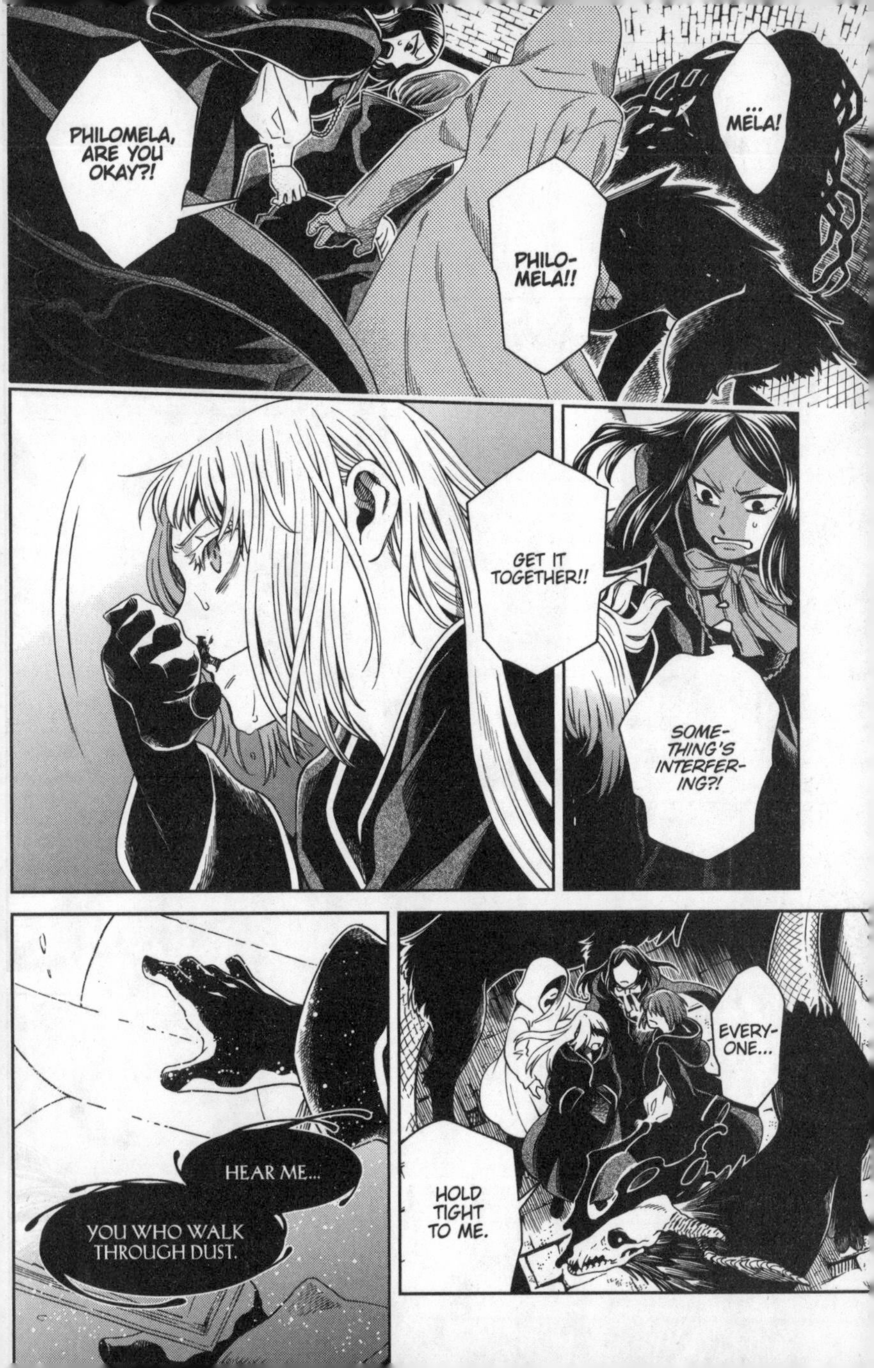
...MELA!
PHILO-MELA!!
PHILOMELA, ARE YOU OKAY?!
SOME-THING'S INTERFER-ING?!
GET IT TOGETHER!!
EVERY-ONE...
HOLD TIGHT TO ME.
HEAR ME...
YOU WHO WALK THROUGH DUST.

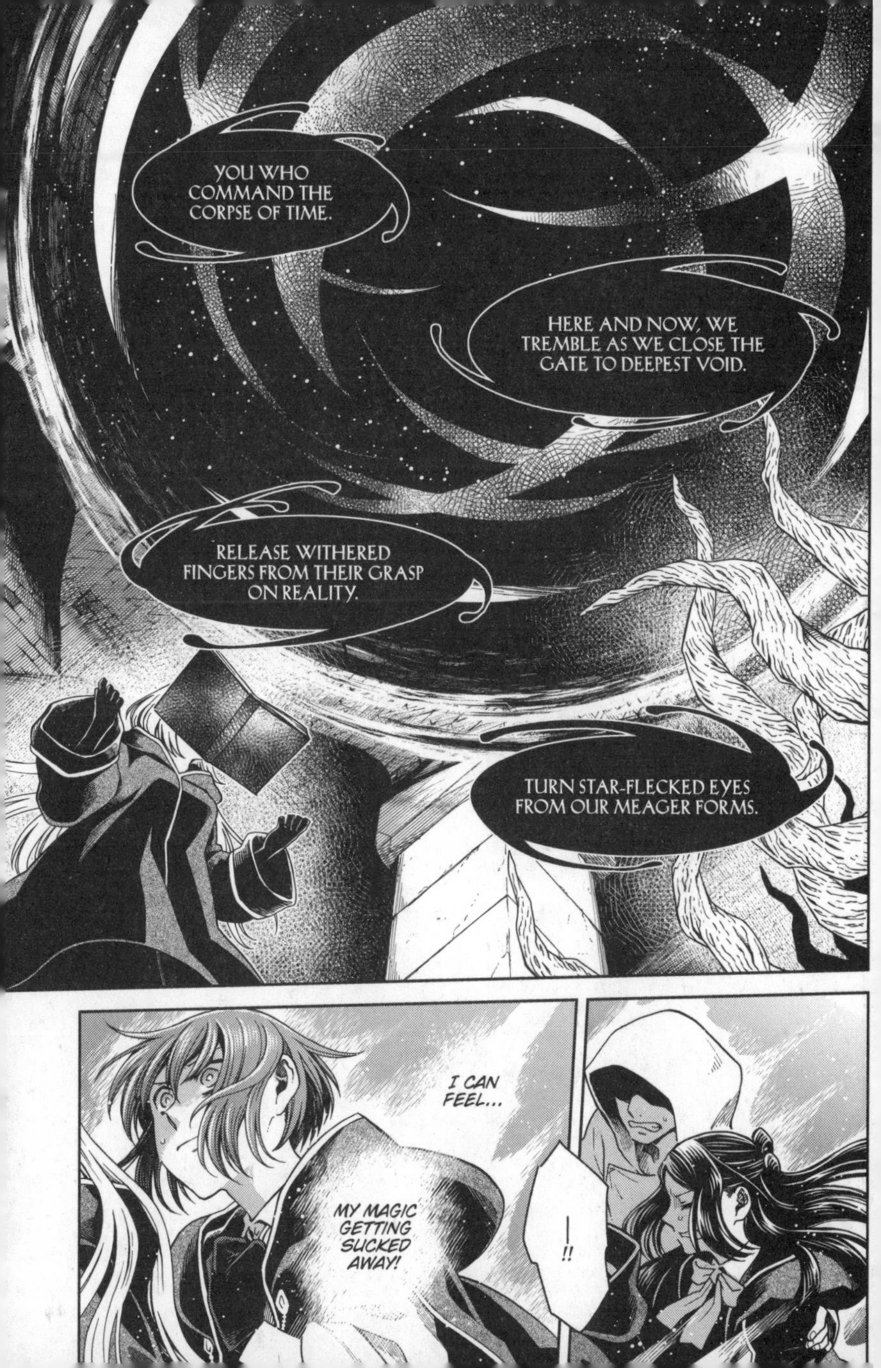
YOU WHO COMMAND THE CORPSE OF TIME.
HERE AND NOW, WE TREMBLE AS WE CLOSE THE GATE TO DEEPEST VOID.
RELEASE WITHERED FINGERS FROM THEIR GRASP ON REALITY.
TURN STAR-FLECKED EYES FROM OUR MEAGER FORMS.
—!!
I CAN FEEL...
MY MAGIC GETTING SUCKED AWAY!

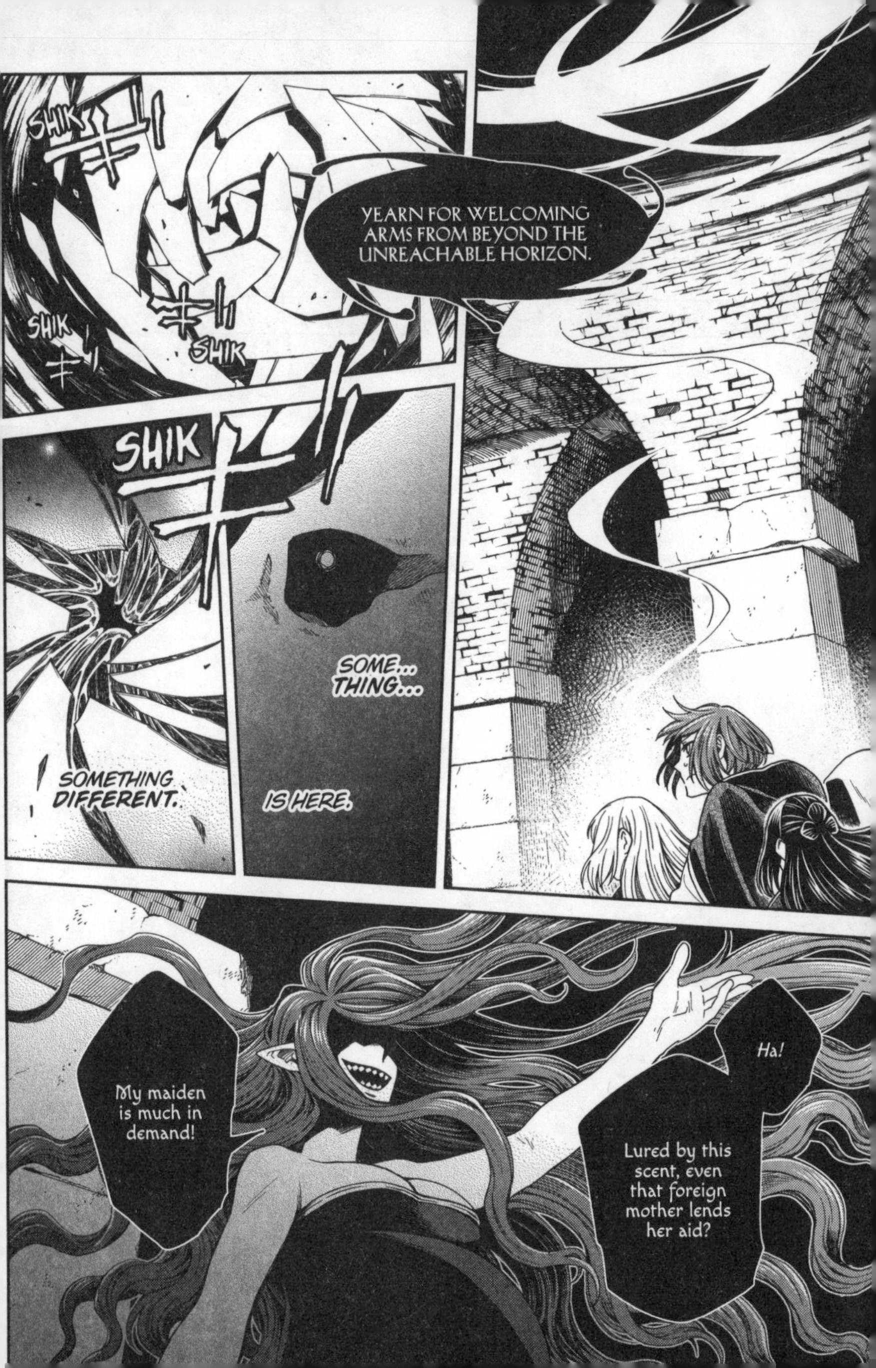
YEARN FOR WELCOMING ARMS FROM BEYOND THE UNREACHABLE HORIZON.
SHIK
SHIK
SHIK
SHIK
SOME... THING...
IS HERE.
SOMETHING DIFFERENT.
Ha!
Lured by this scent, even that foreign mother lends her aid?
My maiden is much in demand!

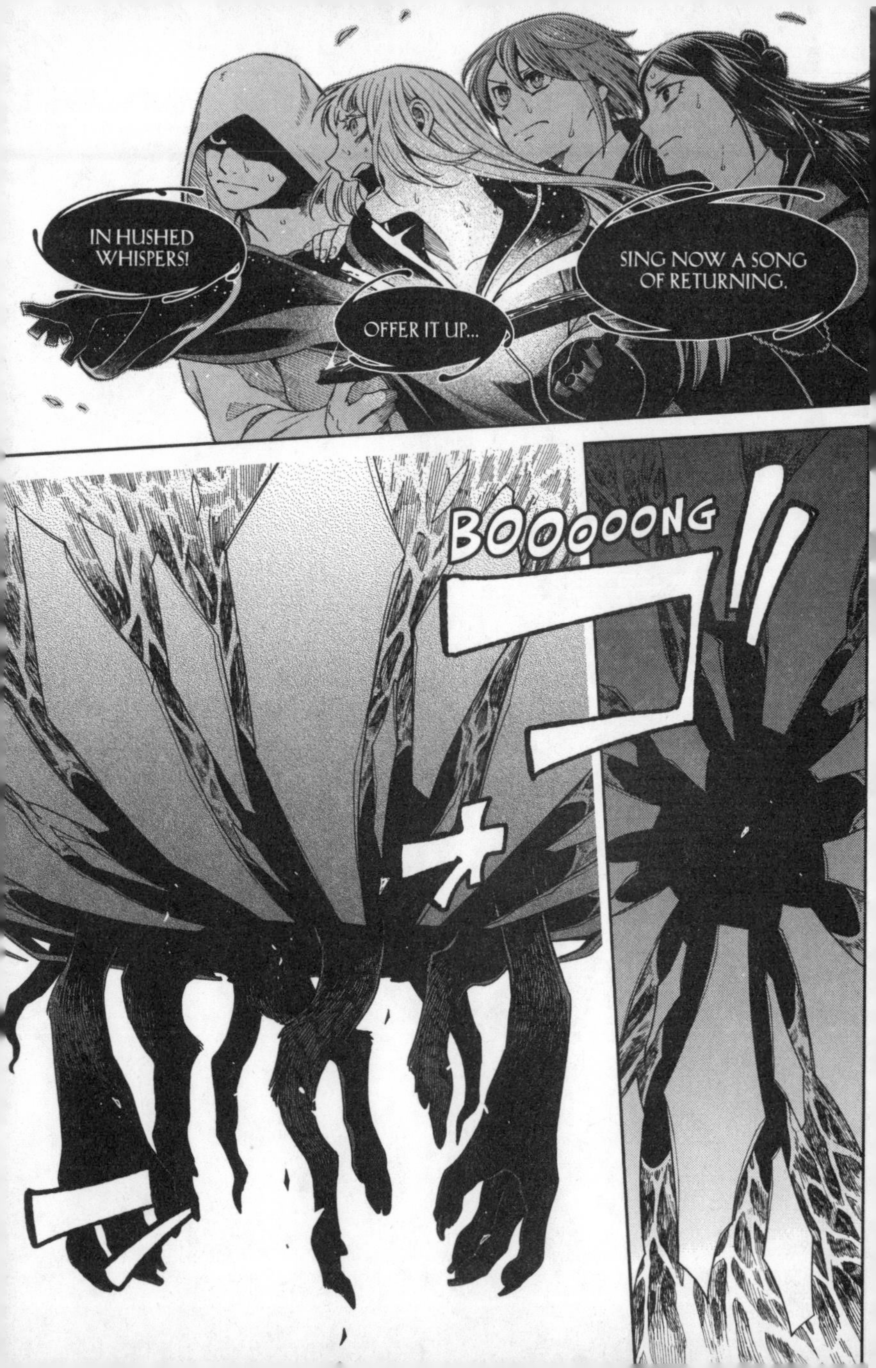
SING NOW A SONG OF RETURNING.
OFFER IT UP...
IN HUSHED WHISPERS!
BOOOOOONG

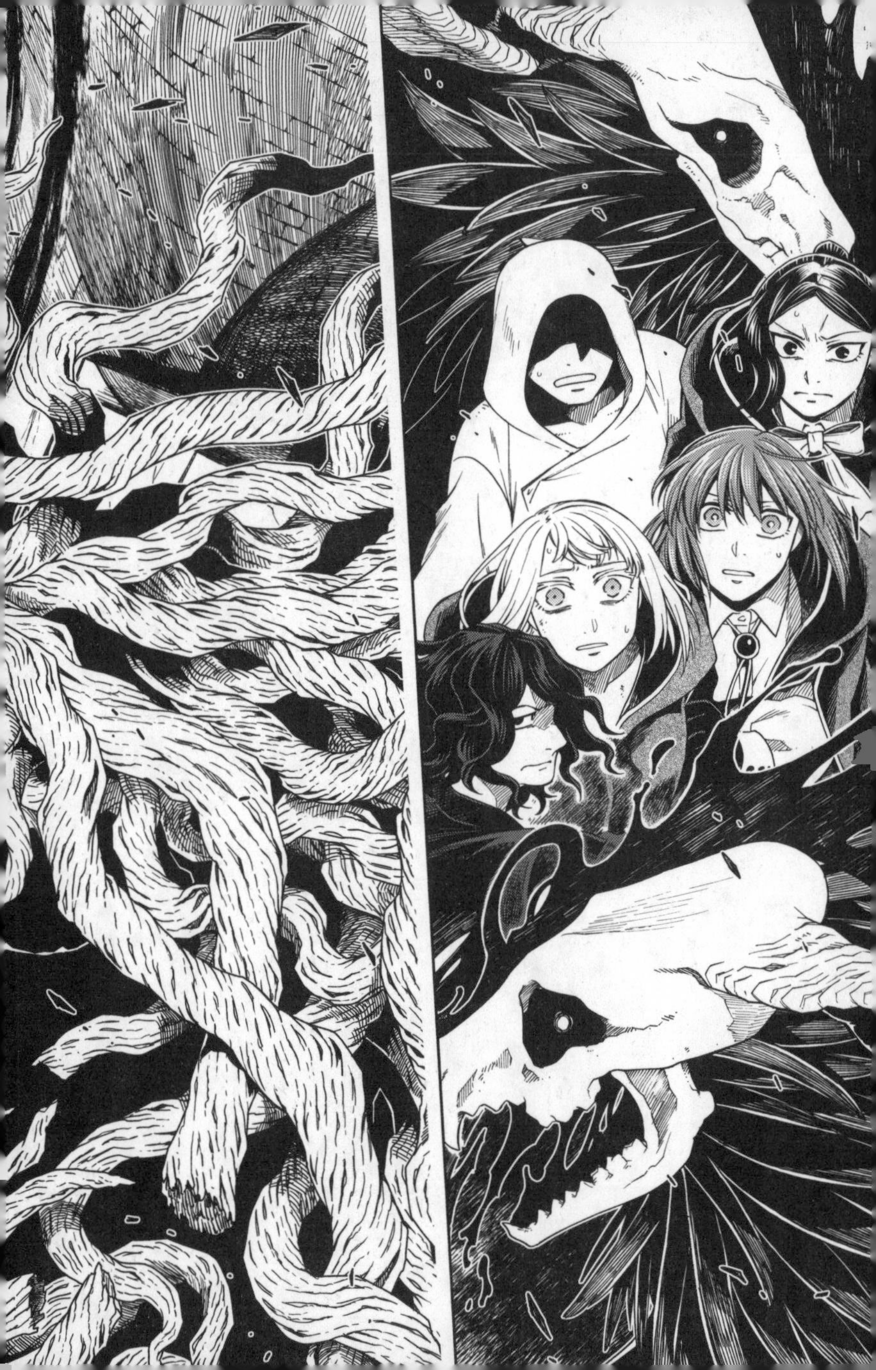

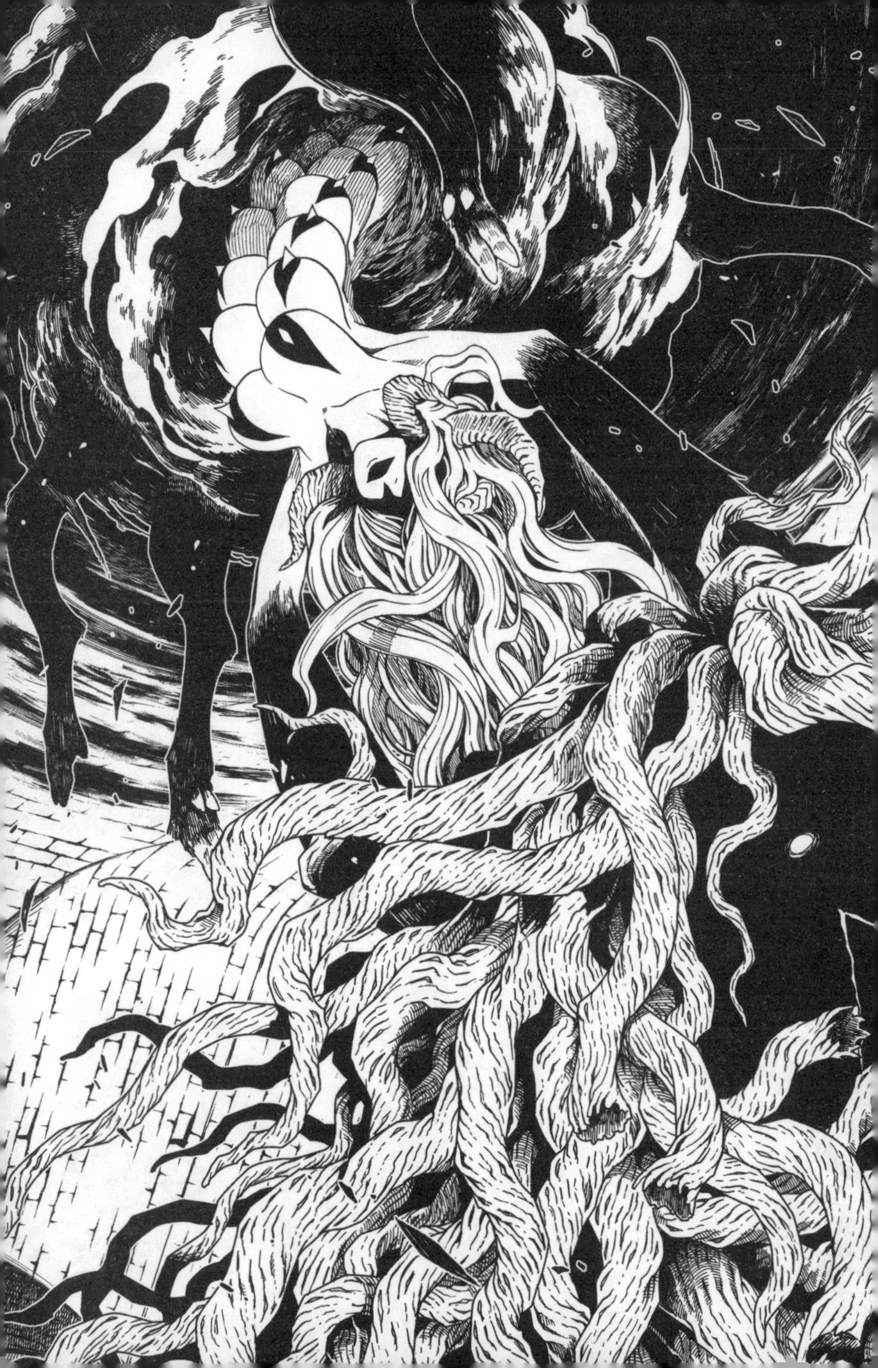

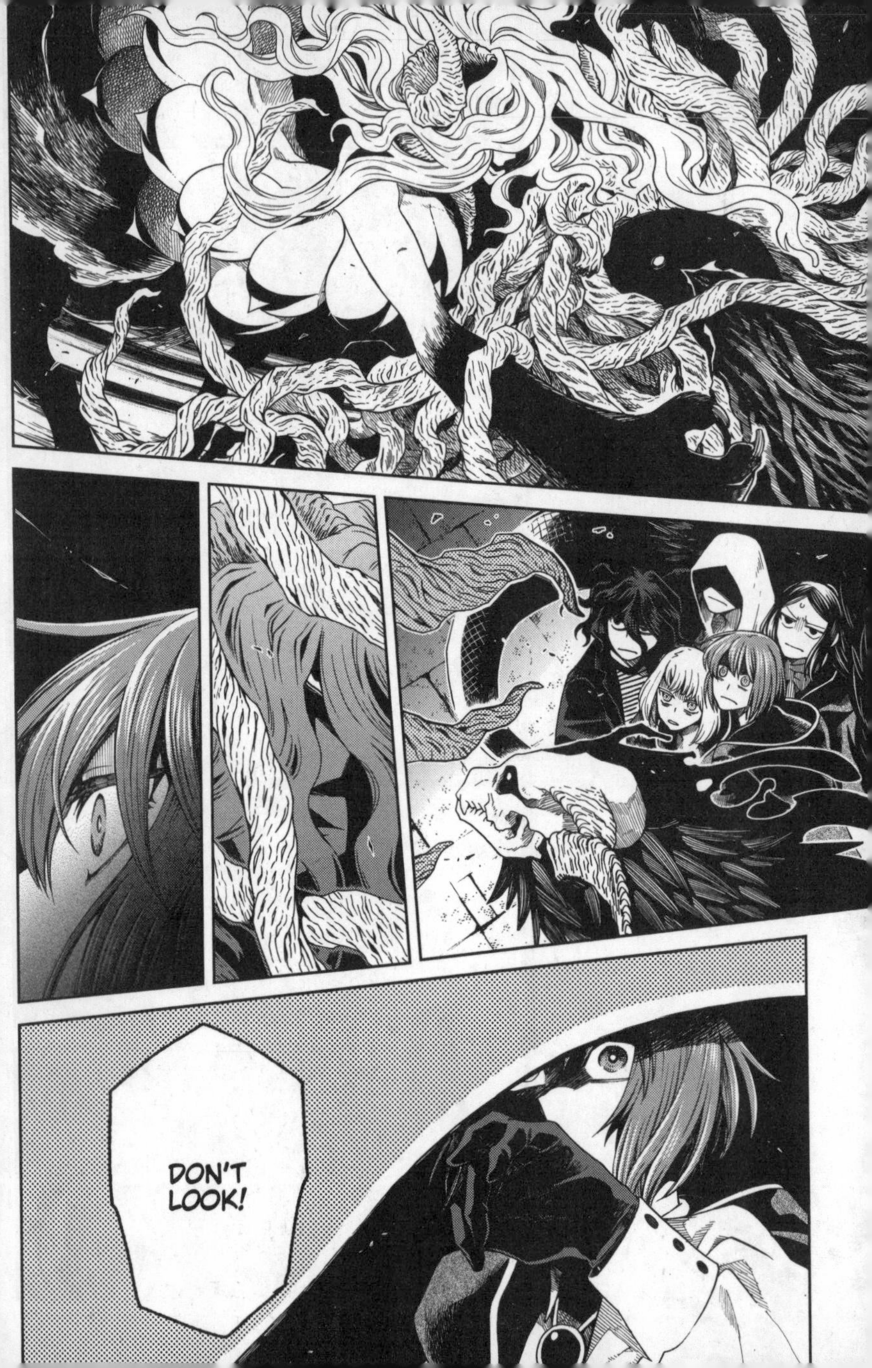
DON'T
LOOK!

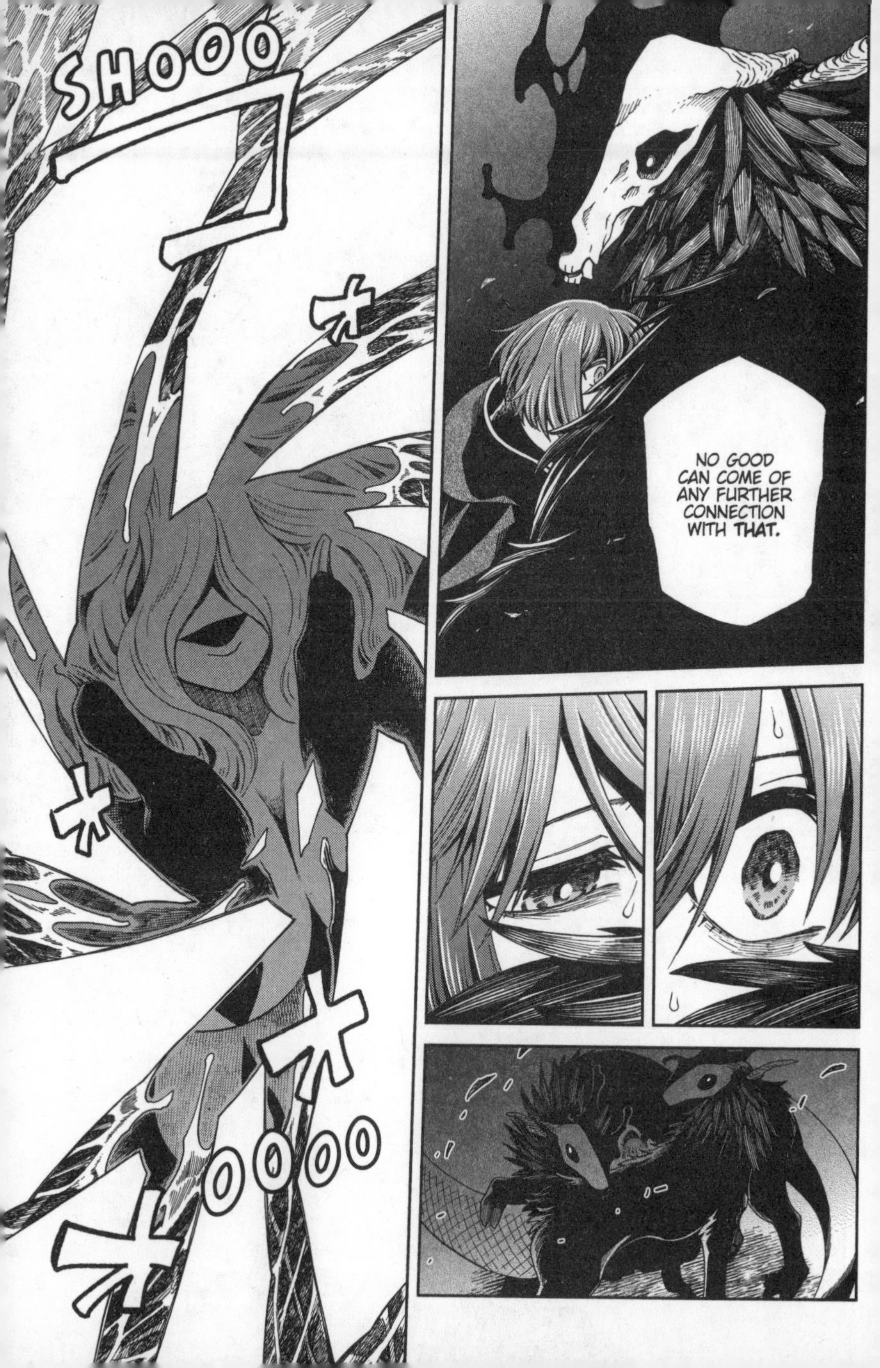
NO GOOD CAN COME OF ANY FURTHER CONNECTION WITH THAT.
SHOOOOOOO

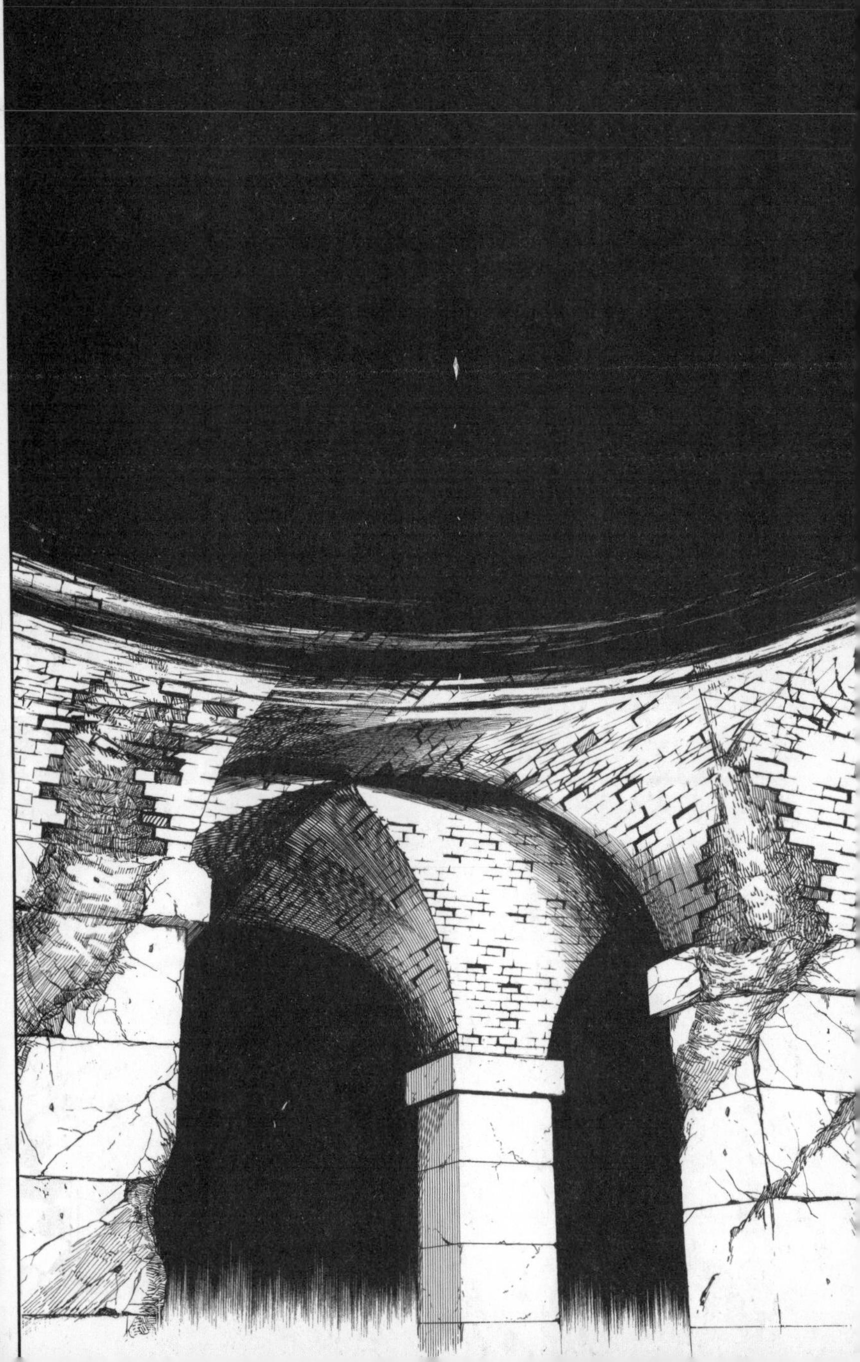

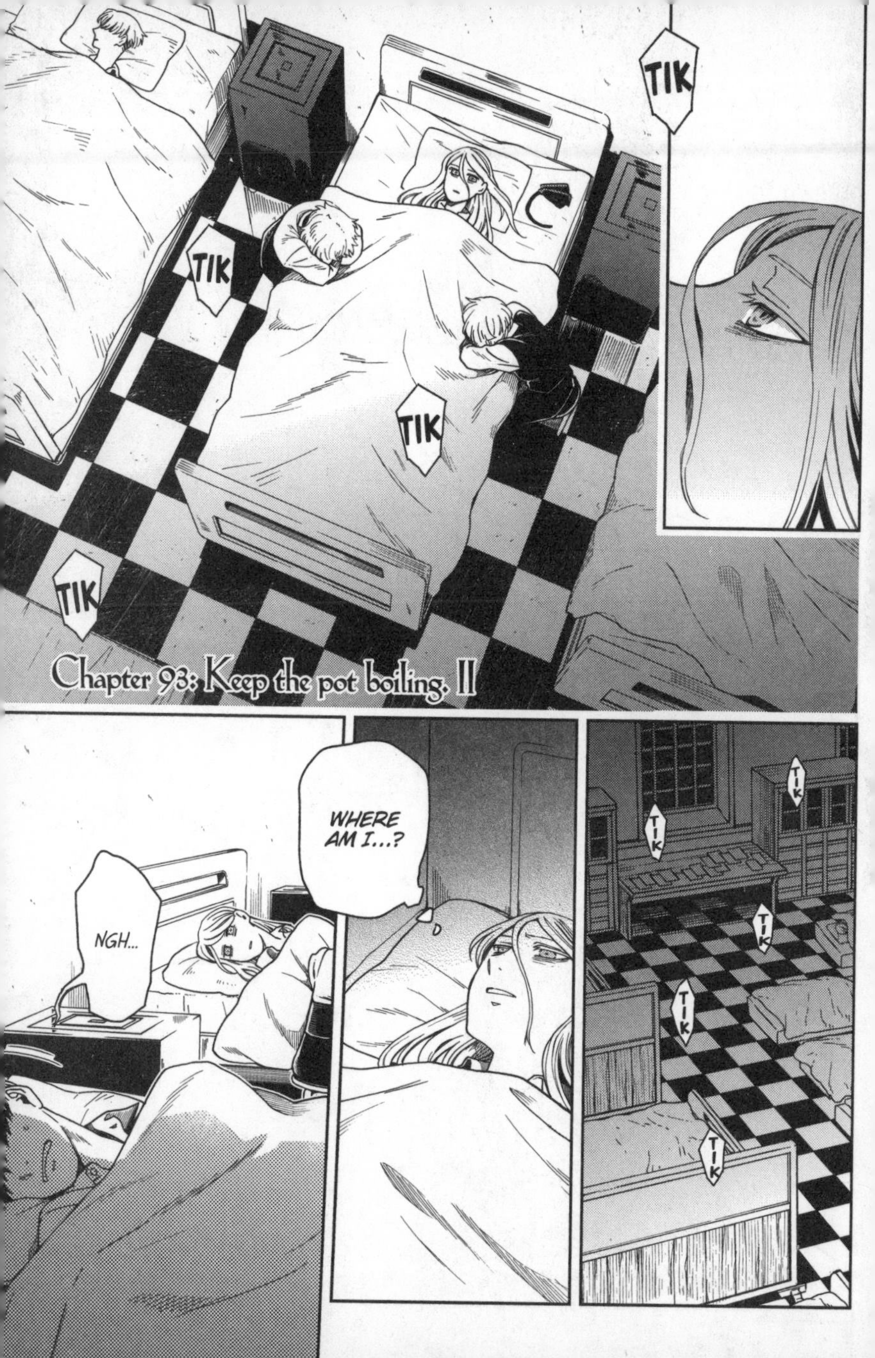
TIK
TIK
TIK
TIK
Chapter 93: Keep the pot boiling. II
TIK
TIK
TIK
TIK
TIK
WHERE AM I...?
NGH...

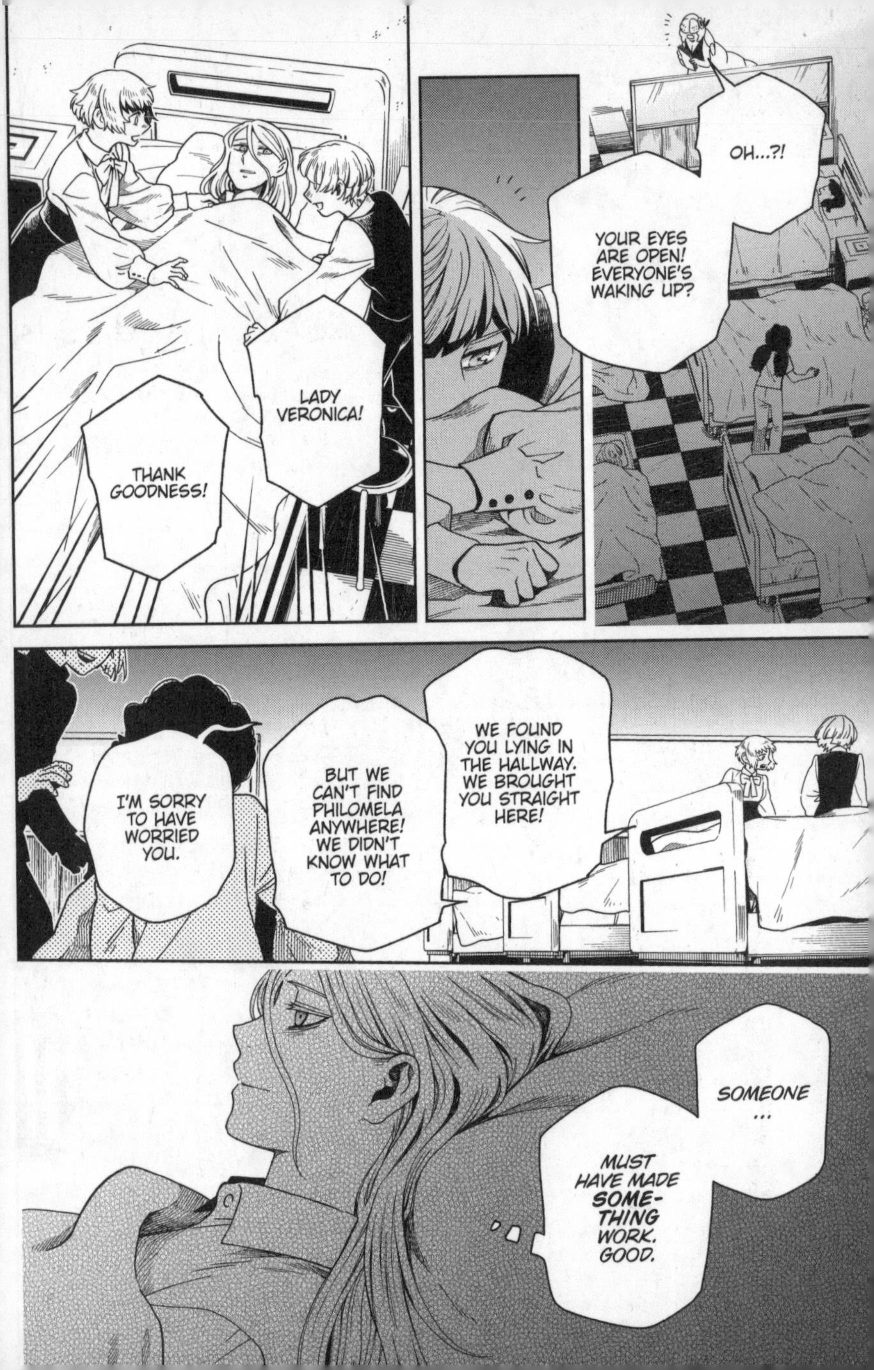
OH...?!
YOUR EYES ARE OPEN! EVERYONE'S WAKING UP?
LADY VERONICA!
THANK GOODNESS!
WE FOUND YOU LYING IN THE HALLWAY. WE BROUGHT YOU STRAIGHT HERE!
BUT WE CAN'T FIND PHILOMELA ANYWHERE! WE DIDN'T KNOW WHAT TO DO!
I'M SORRY TO HAVE WORRIED YOU.
SOMEONE ...
MUST HAVE MADE SOMETHING WORK. GOOD.

Chapter 93: Keep the pot boiling. II

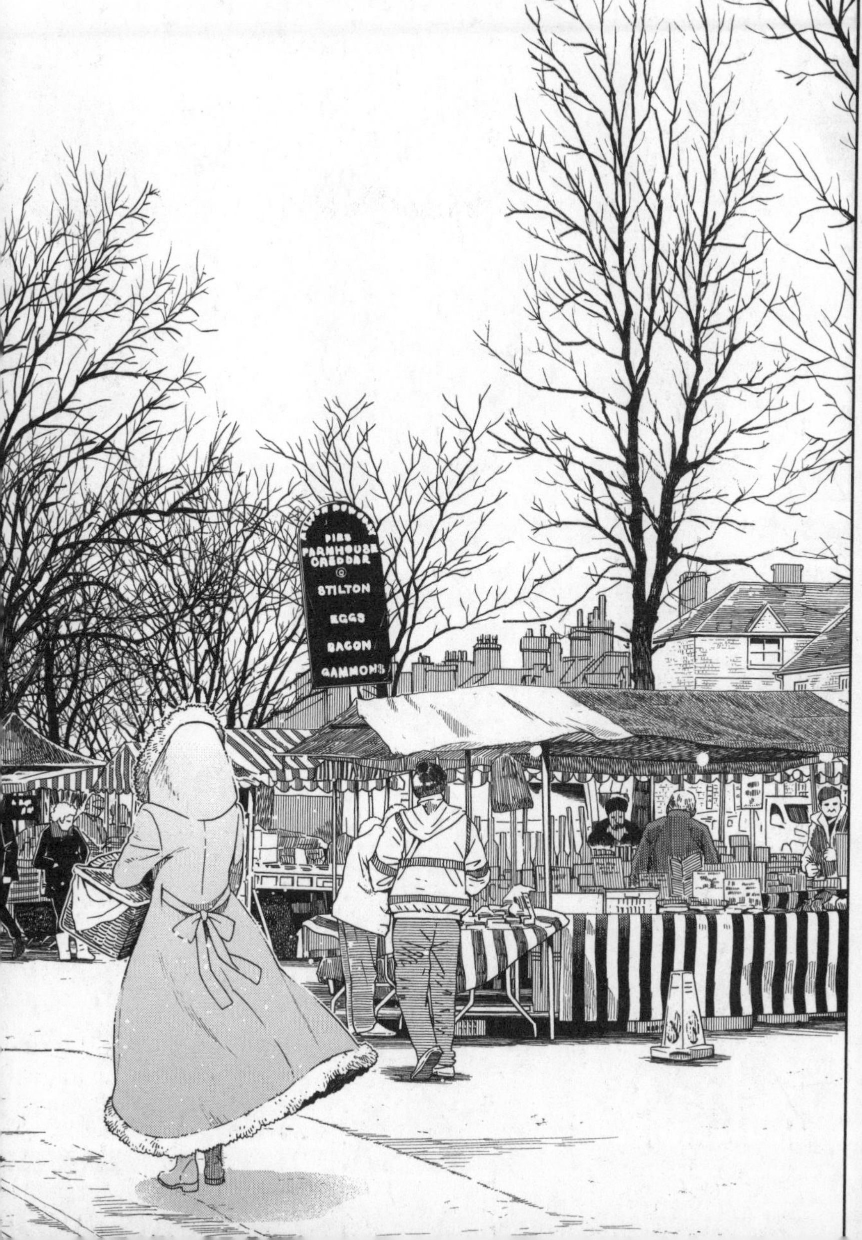
PIES
FARMHOUSE
CHEDDAR
@
STILTON
EGGS
BACON
GAMMONS

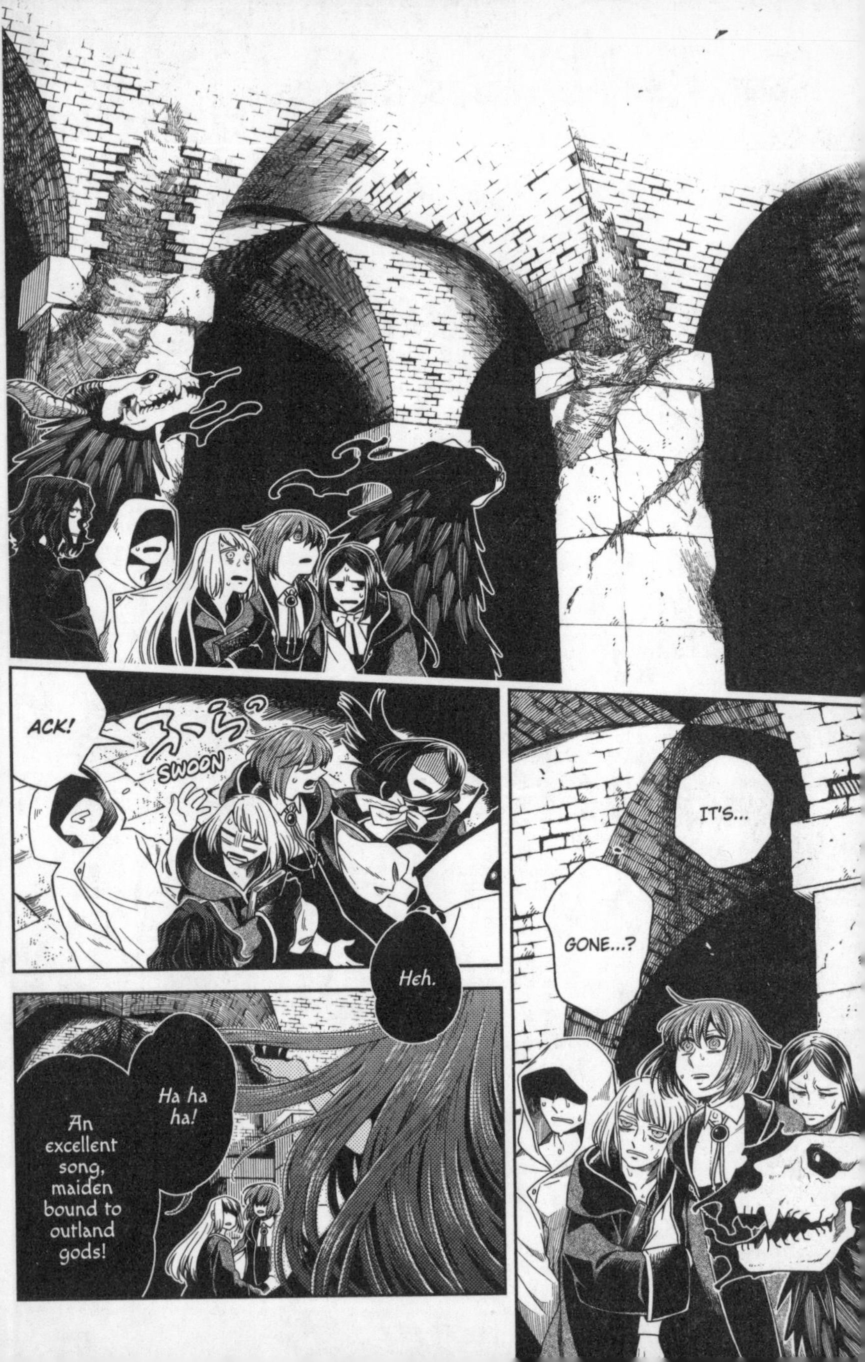

ふら
SWOON
ACK!
IT'S...
GONE...?
Heh.
Ha ha ha!
An excellent song, maiden bound to outland gods!

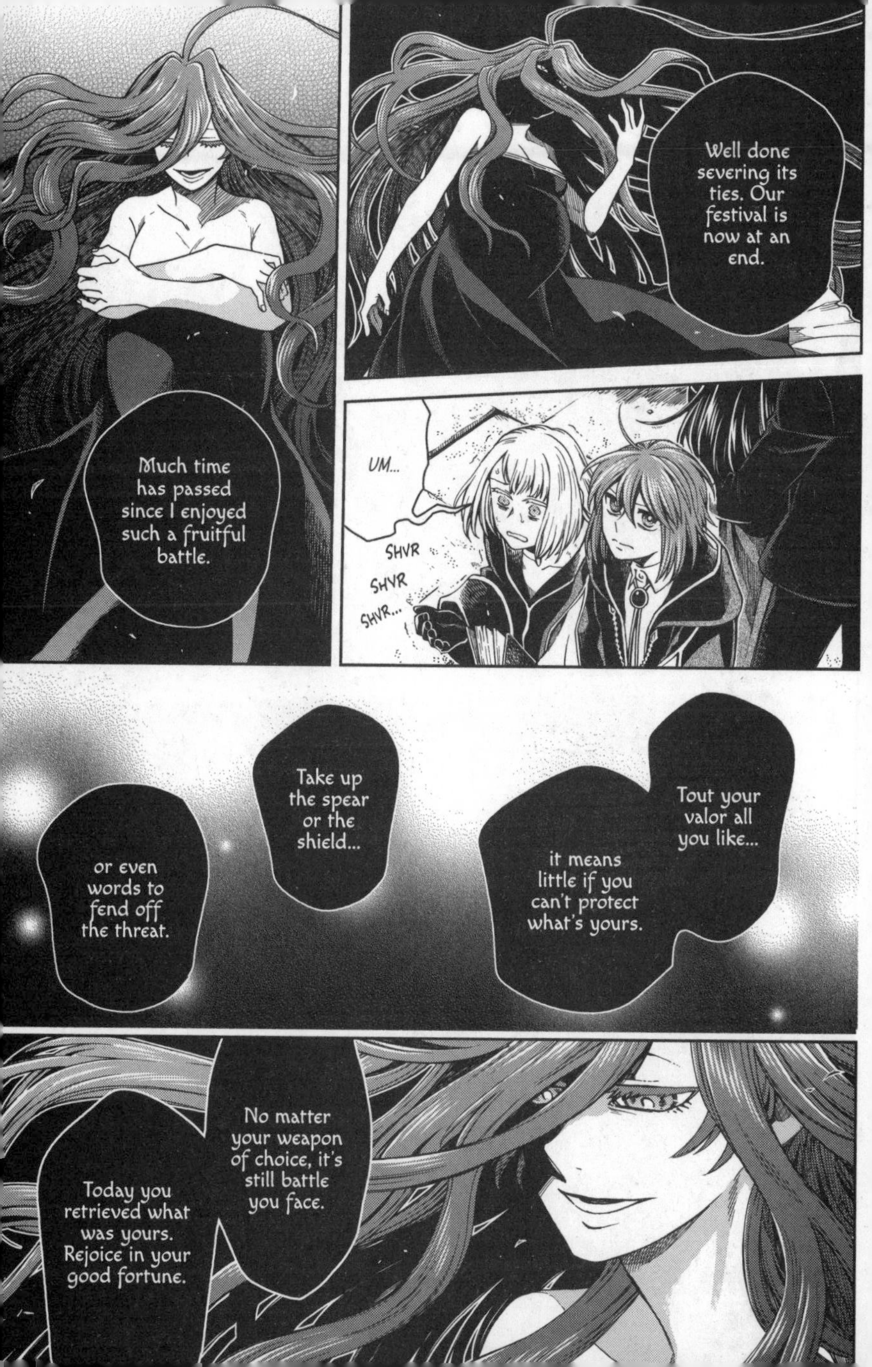
Well done severing its ties. Our festival is now at an end.
Much time has passed since I enjoyed such a fruitful battle.
UM...
SHVR
SHVR
SHVR...
Tout your valor all you like...
it means little if you can't protect what's yours.
Take up the spear or the shield...
or even words to fend off the threat.
No matter your weapon of choice, it's still battle you face.
Today you retrieved what was yours. Rejoice in your good fortune.

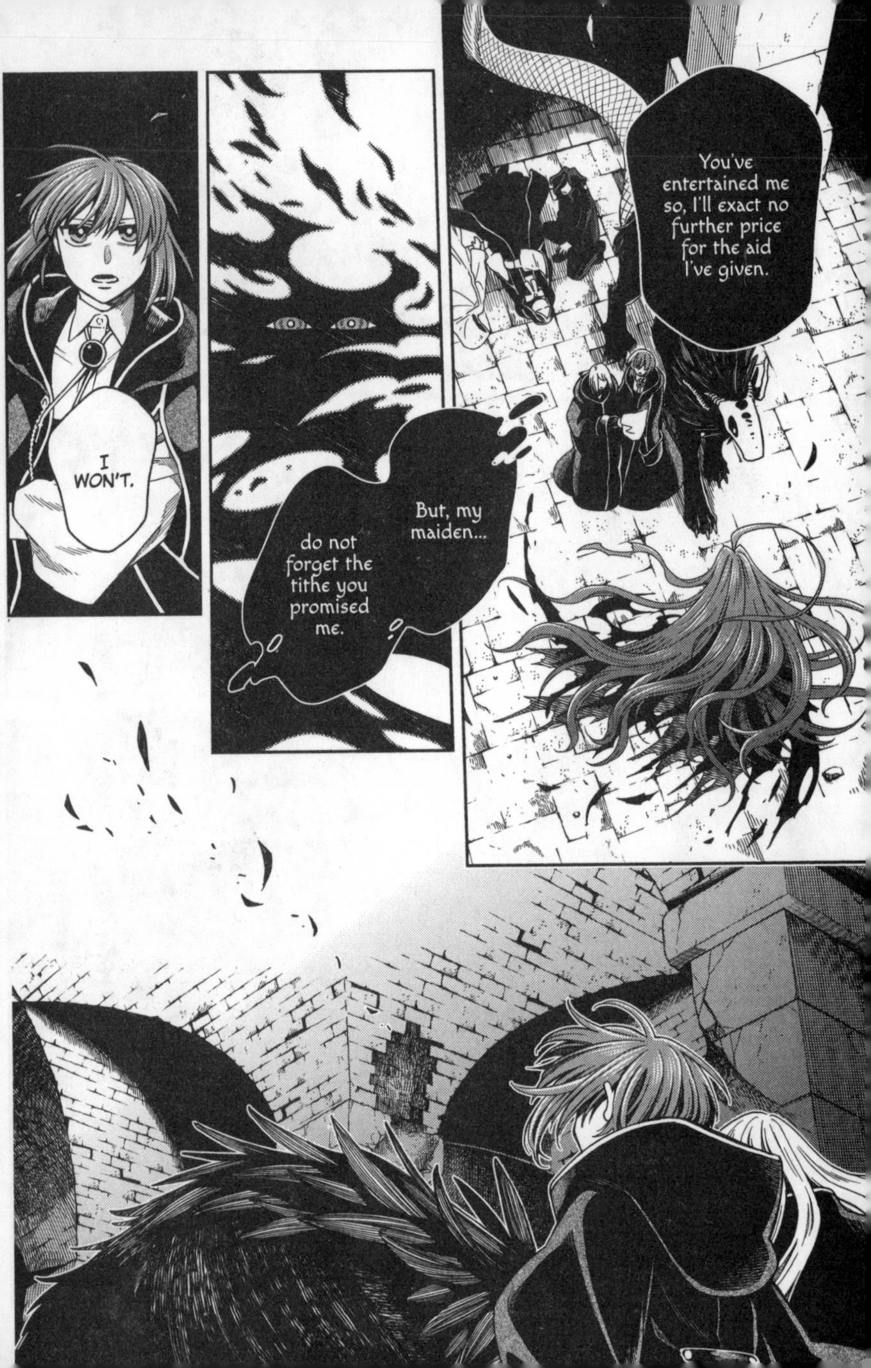
You've entertained me so, I'll exact no further price for the aid I've given.
But, my maiden...
do not forget the tithe you promised me.
I WON'T.

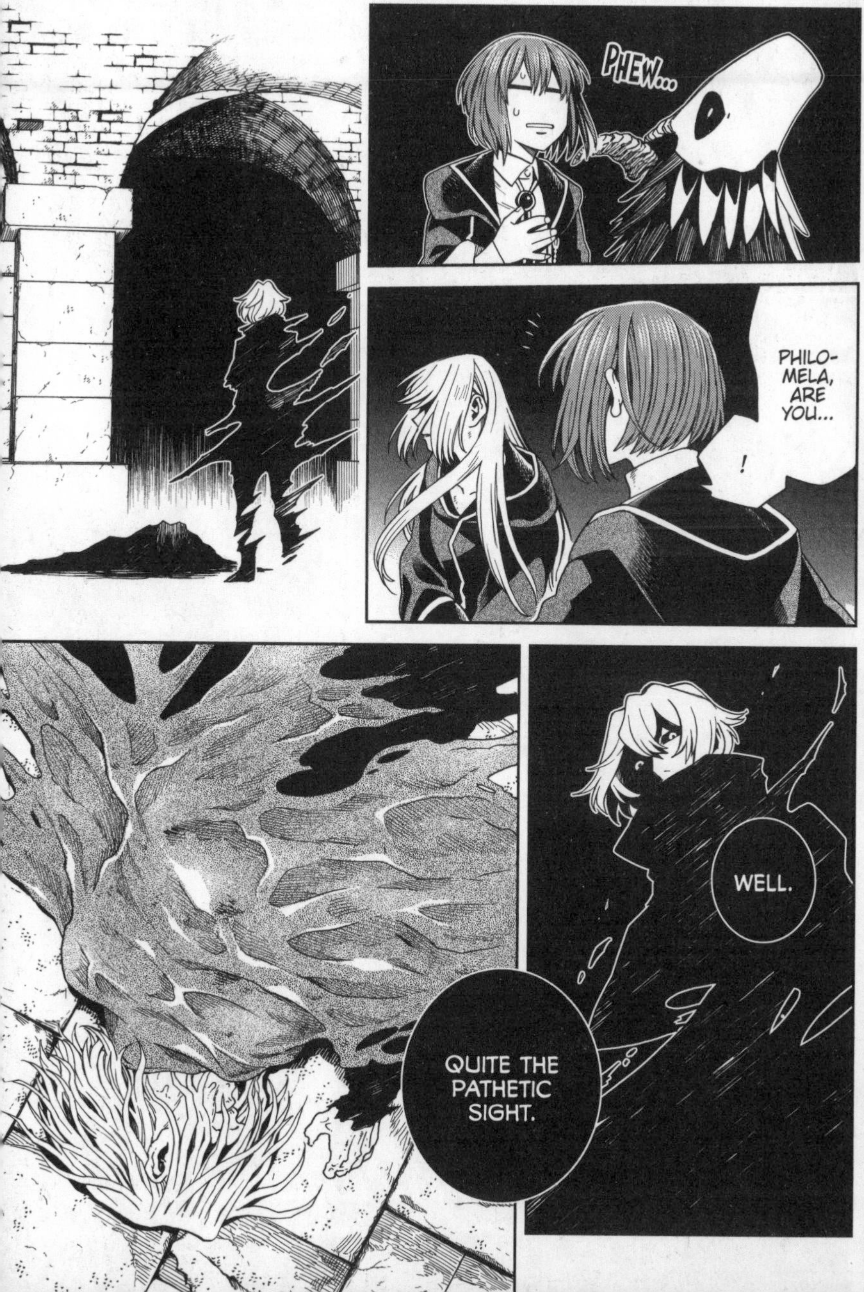
PHEW...
PHILO-MELA, ARE YOU...
!
WELL.
QUITE THE PATHETIC SIGHT.

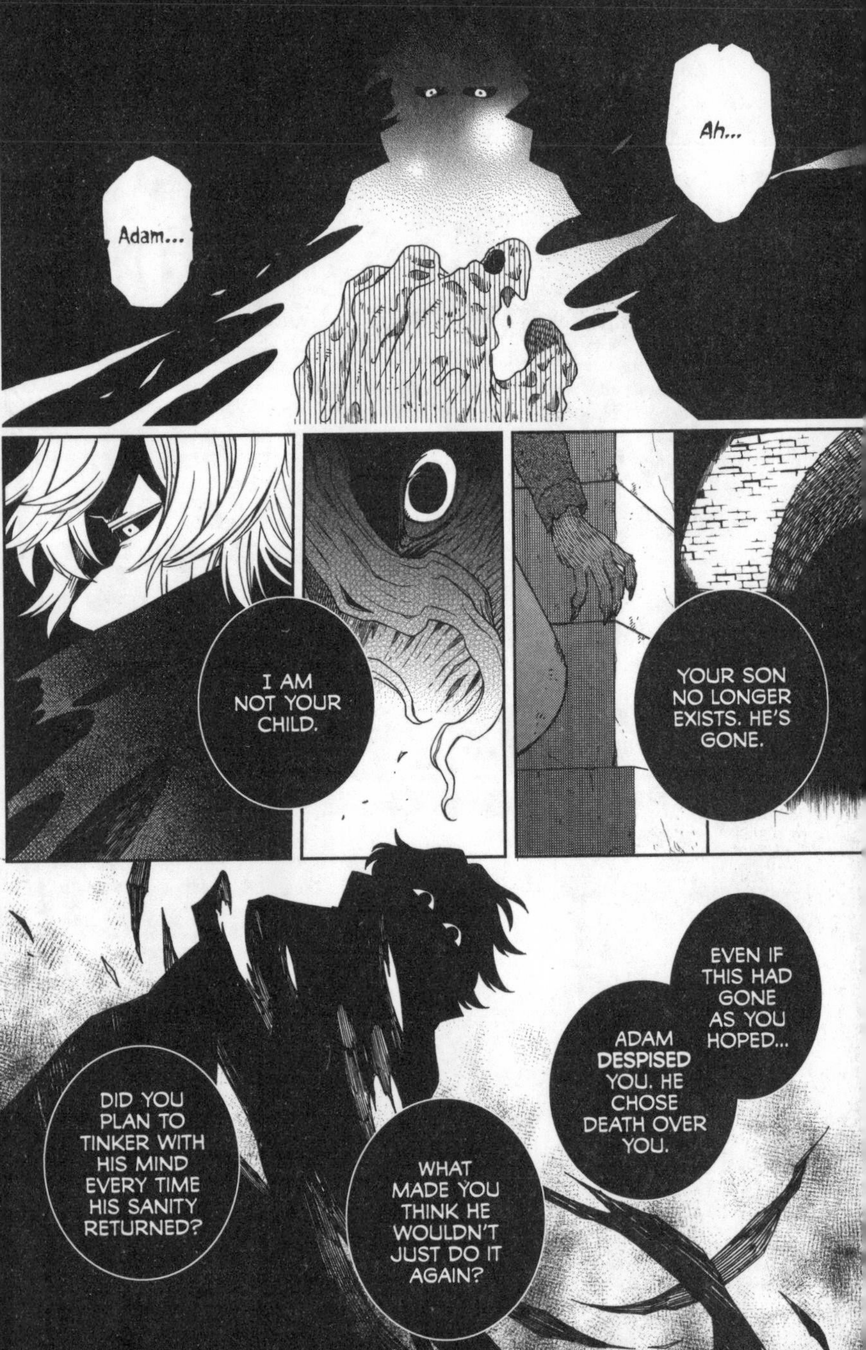
Ah...
Adam...
YOUR SON NO LONGER EXISTS. HE'S GONE.
I AM NOT YOUR CHILD.
EVEN IF THIS HAD GONE AS YOU HOPED...
ADAM DESPISED YOU. HE CHOSE DEATH OVER YOU.
WHAT MADE YOU THINK HE WOULDN'T JUST DO IT AGAIN?
DID YOU PLAN TO TINKER WITH HIS MIND EVERY TIME HIS SANITY RETURNED?

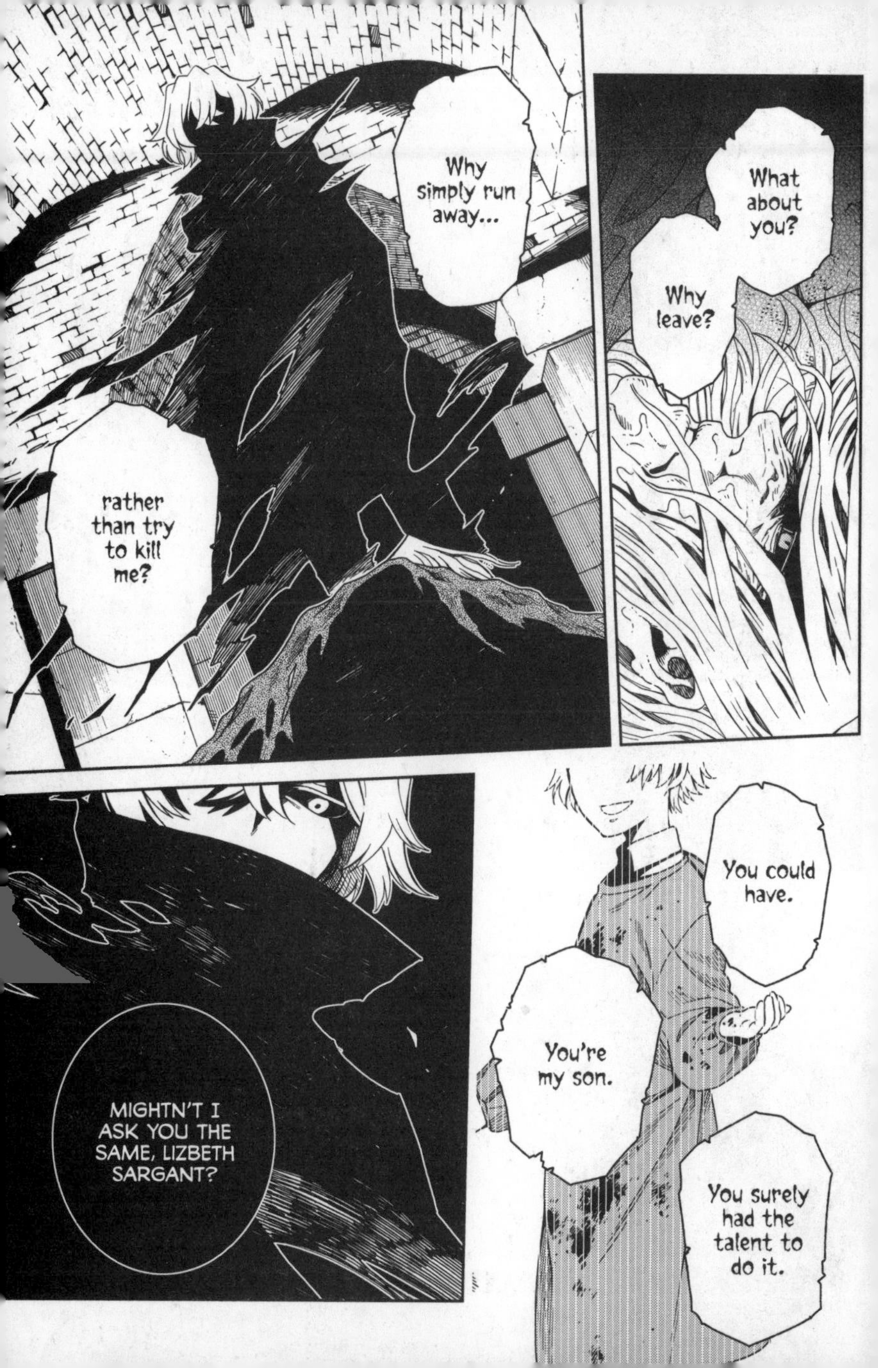
What about you?
Why leave?
Why simply run away...
rather than try to kill me?
You could have.
You're my son.
You surely had the talent to do it.
MIGHTN'T I ASK YOU THE SAME, LIZBETH SARGANT?

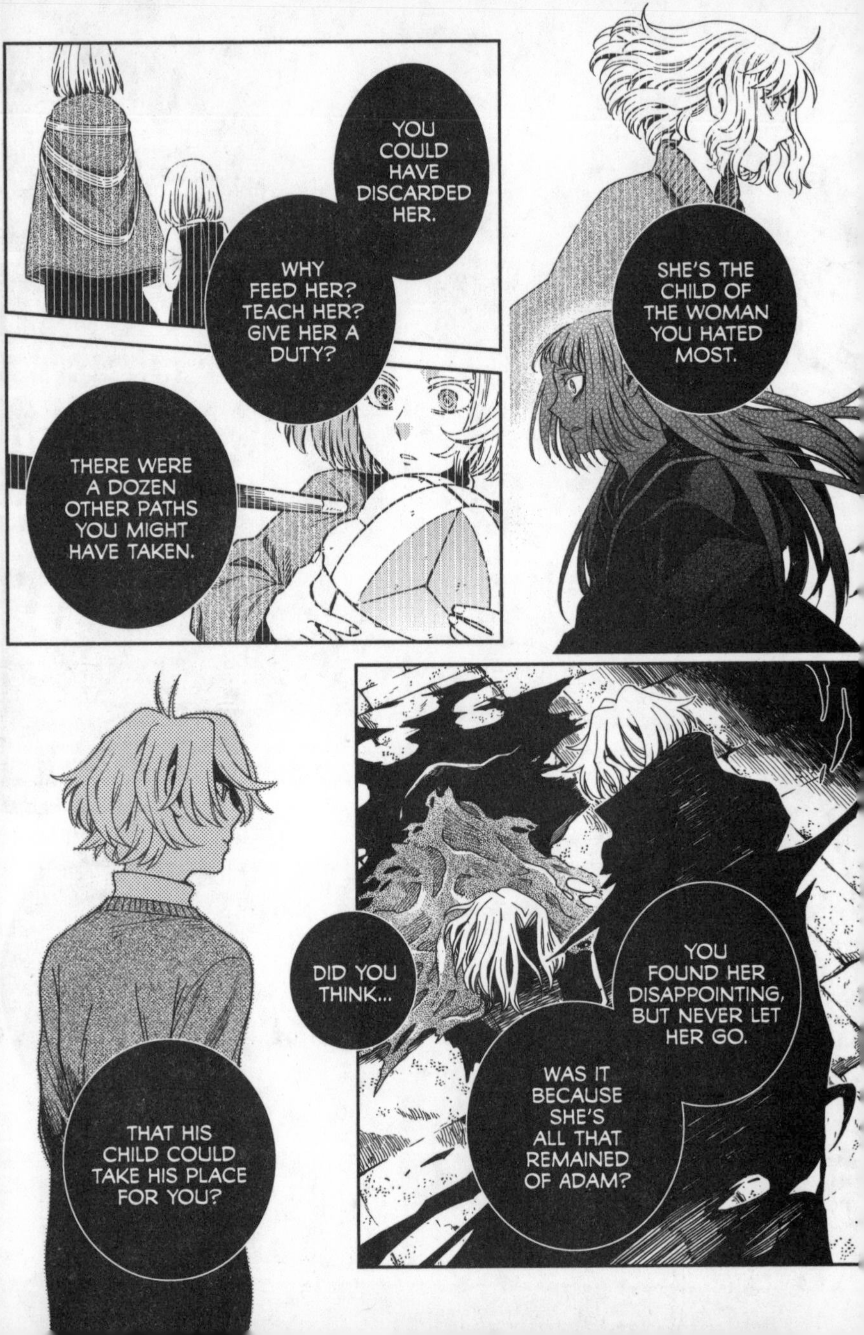
SHE'S THE CHILD OF THE WOMAN YOU HATED MOST.
YOU COULD HAVE DISCARDED HER.
WHY FEED HER? TEACH HER? GIVE HER A DUTY?
THERE WERE A DOZEN OTHER PATHS YOU MIGHT HAVE TAKEN.
YOU FOUND HER DISAPPOINTING, BUT NEVER LET HER GO.
WAS IT BECAUSE SHE'S ALL THAT REMAINED OF ADAM?
DID YOU THINK...
THAT HIS CHILD COULD TAKE HIS PLACE FOR YOU?

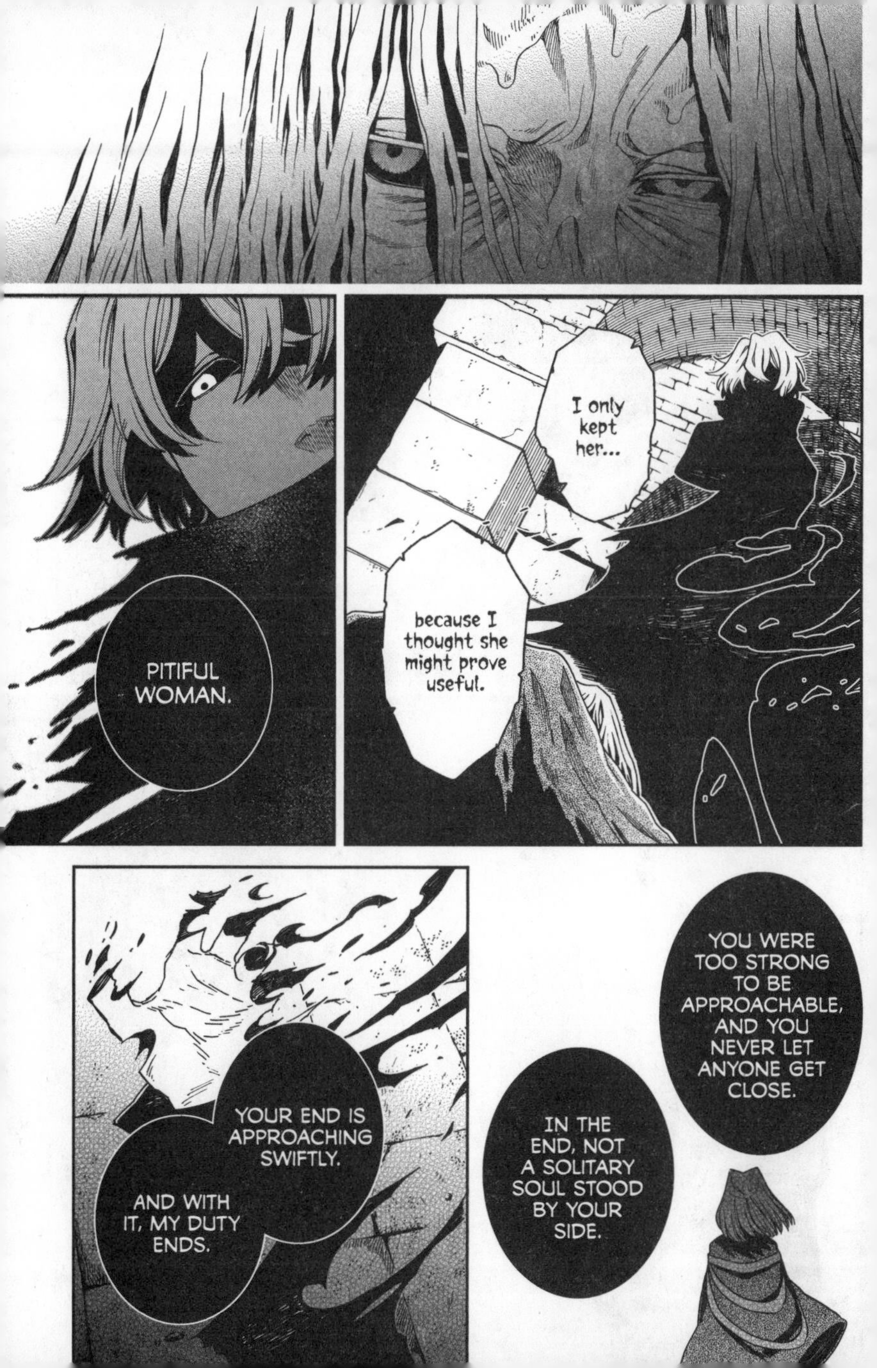
I only kept her...
because I thought she might prove useful.
PITIFUL WOMAN.
YOU WERE TOO STRONG TO BE APPROACHABLE, AND YOU NEVER LET ANYONE GET CLOSE.
IN THE END, NOT A SOLITARY SOUL STOOD BY YOUR SIDE.
YOUR END IS APPROACHING SWIFTLY.
AND WITH IT, MY DUTY ENDS.

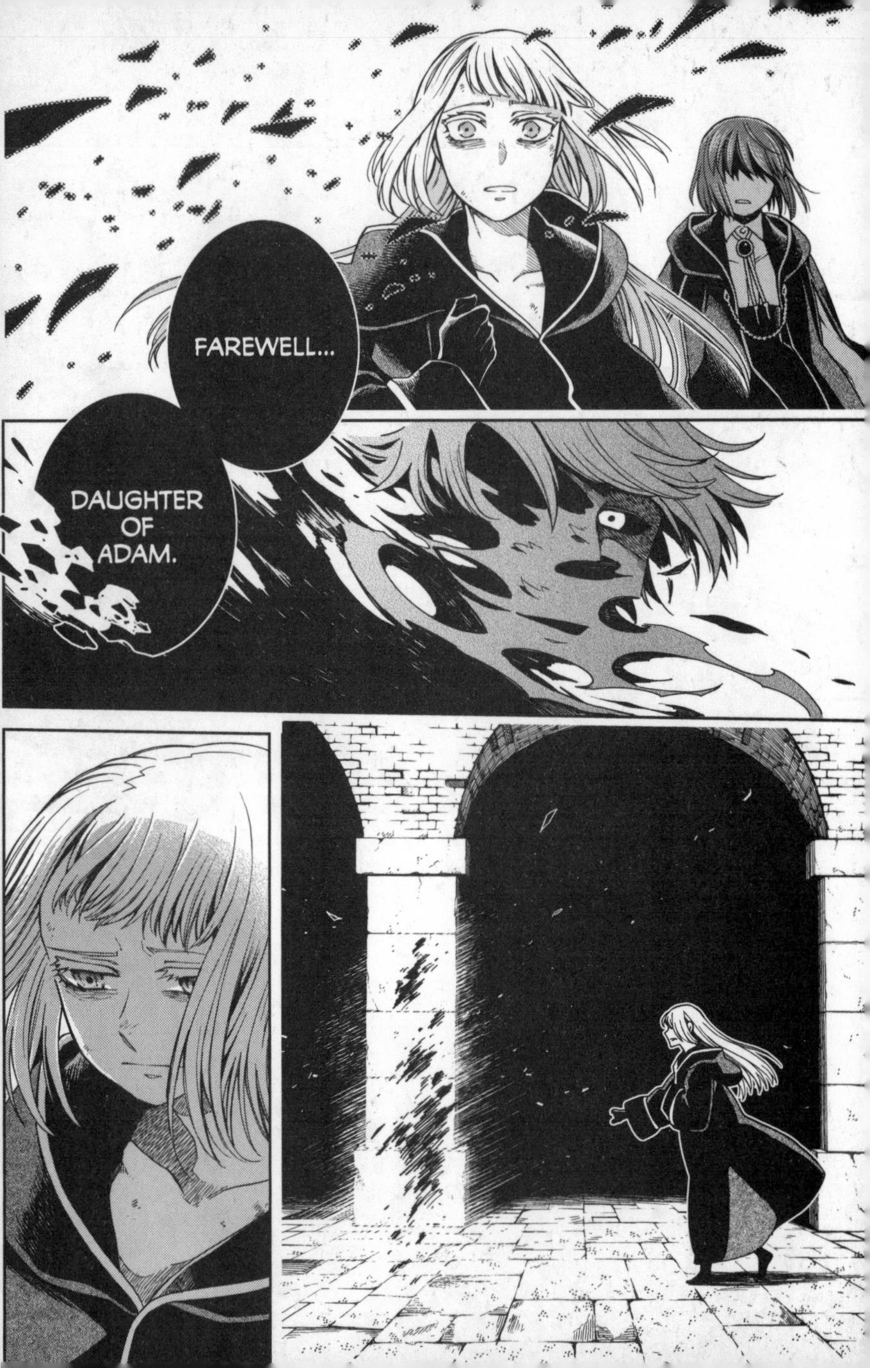
FAREWELL...
DAUGHTER OF ADAM.

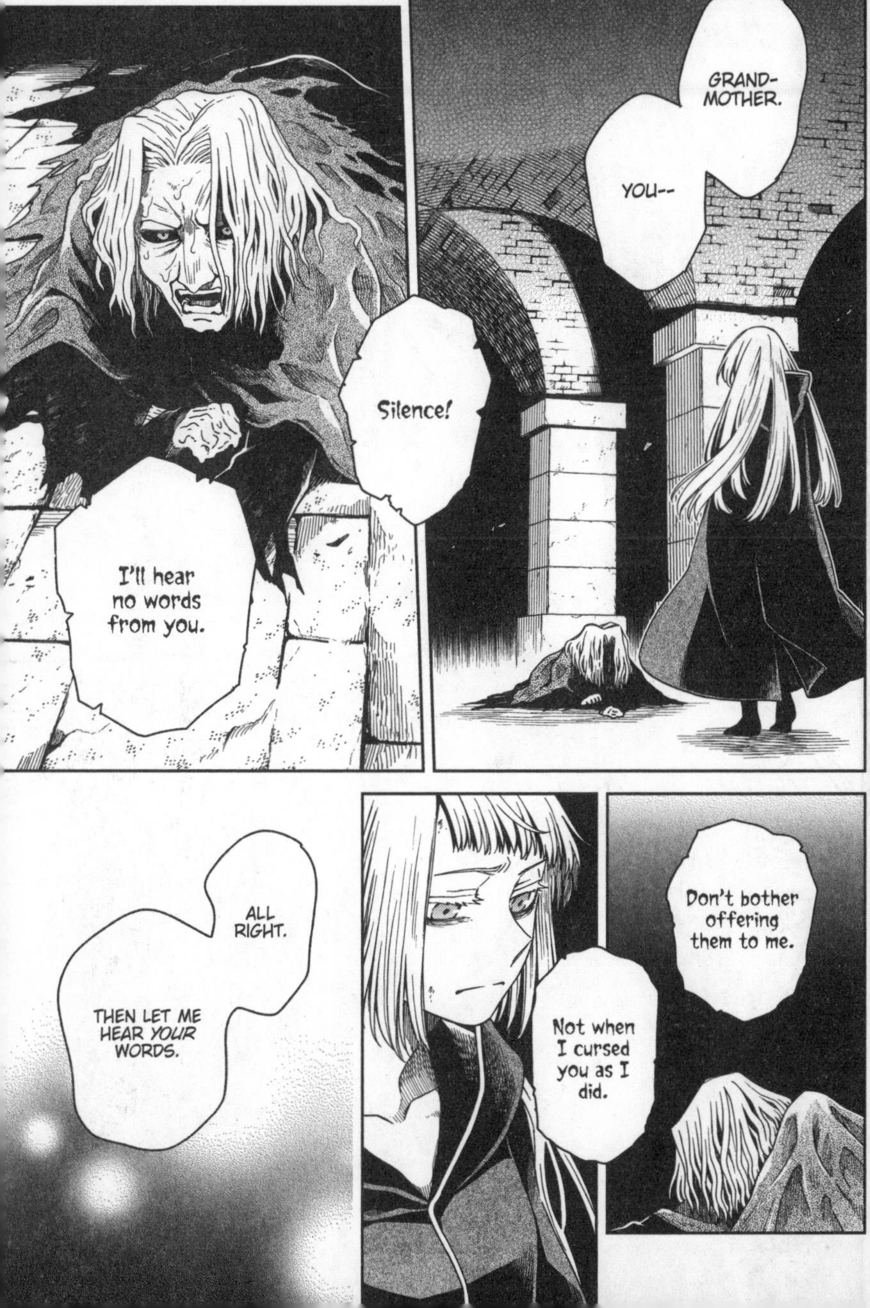
GRAND-MOTHER.
YOU--
Silence!
I'll hear no words from you.
Don't bother offering them to me.
Not when I cursed you as I did.
ALL RIGHT.
THEN LET ME HEAR *YOUR* WORDS.

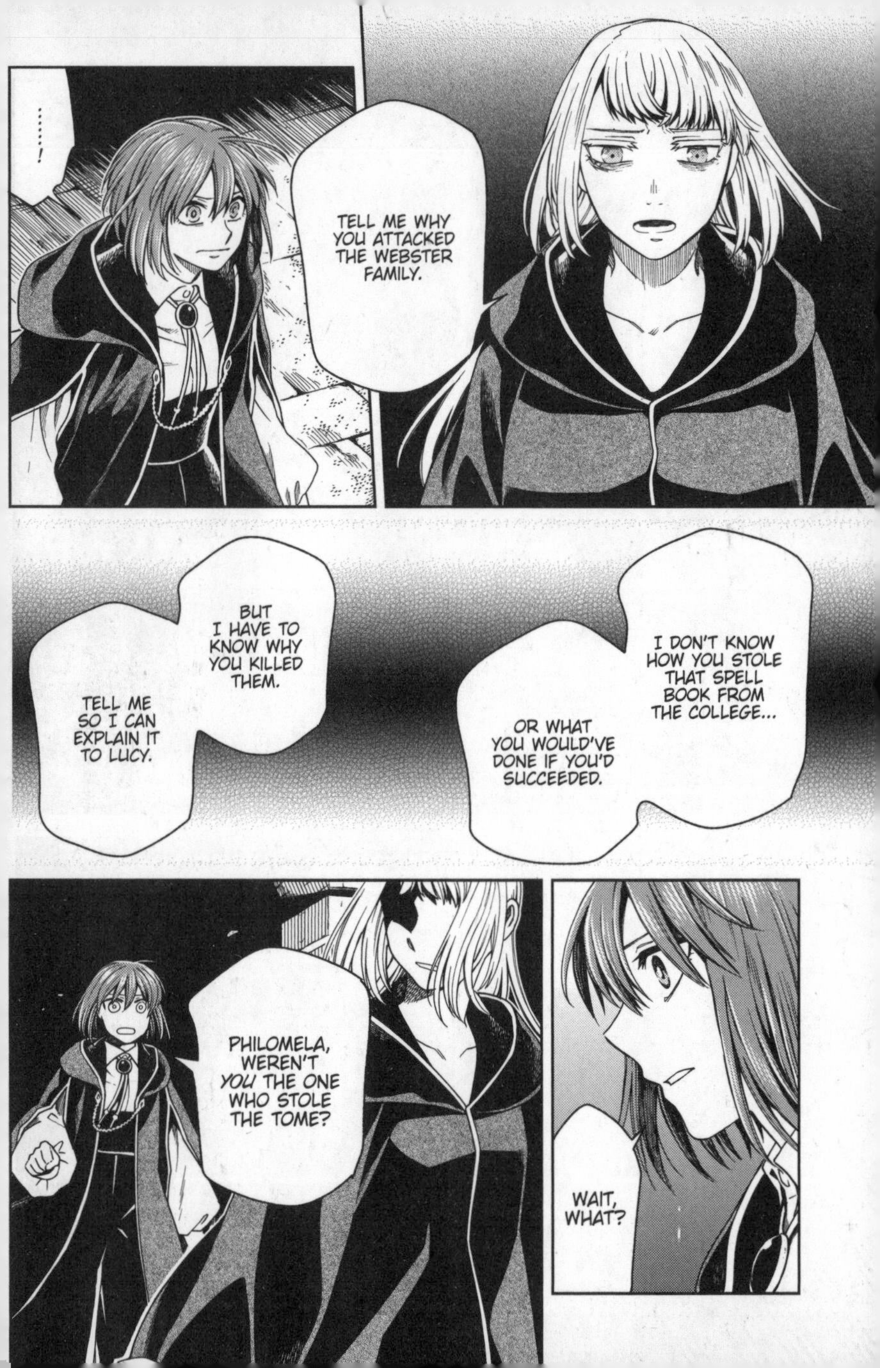
TELL ME WHY YOU ATTACKED THE WEBSTER FAMILY.
......!
I DON'T KNOW HOW YOU STOLE THAT SPELL BOOK FROM THE COLLEGE...
OR WHAT YOU WOULD'VE DONE IF YOU'D SUCCEEDED.
BUT I HAVE TO KNOW WHY YOU KILLED THEM.
TELL ME SO I CAN EXPLAIN IT TO LUCY.
PHILOMELA, WEREN'T *YOU* THE ONE WHO STOLE THE TOME?
WAIT, WHAT?

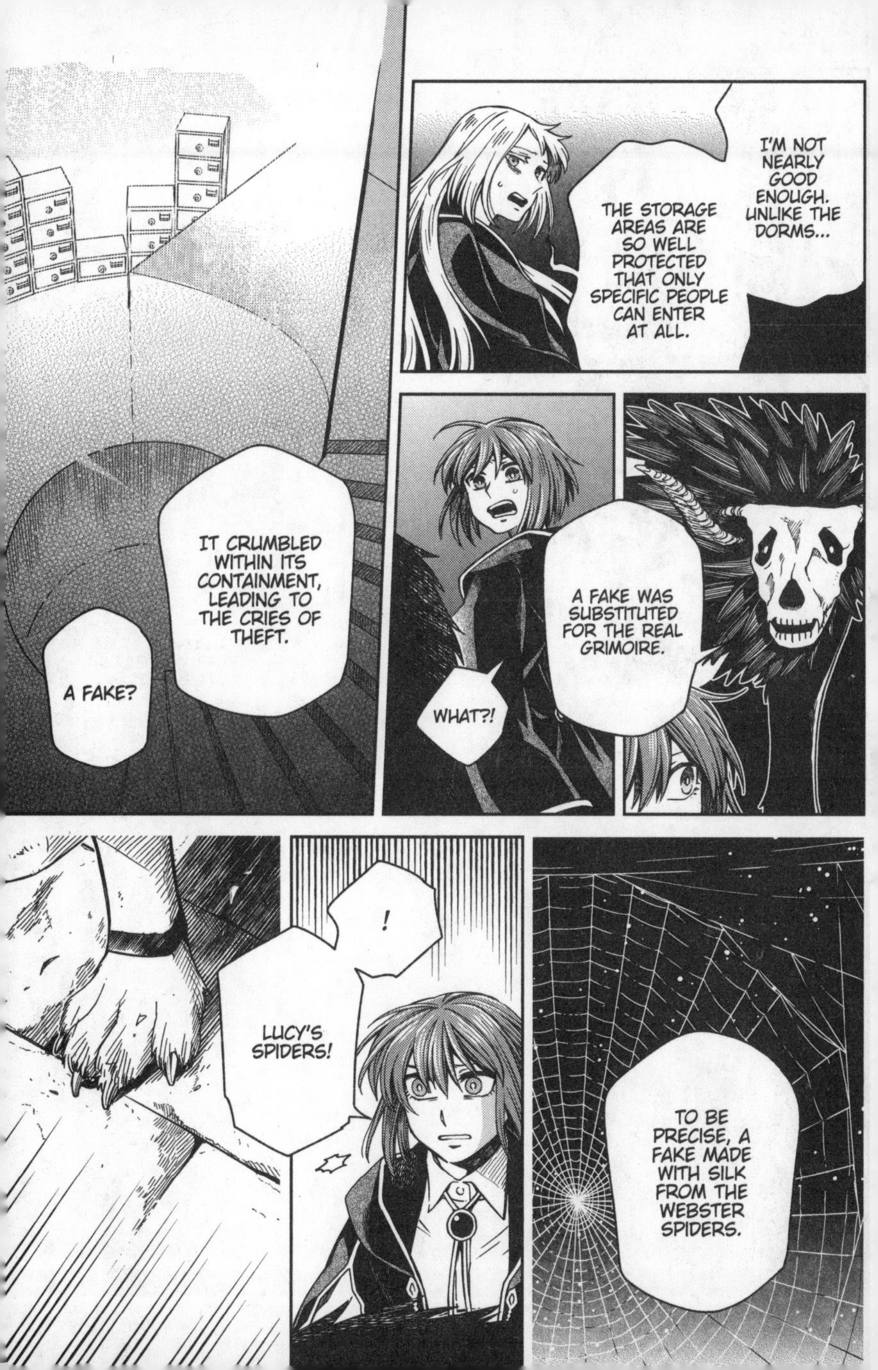
I'M NOT NEARLY GOOD ENOUGH. UNLIKE THE DORMS...
THE STORAGE AREAS ARE SO WELL PROTECTED THAT ONLY SPECIFIC PEOPLE CAN ENTER AT ALL.
A FAKE WAS SUBSTITUTED FOR THE REAL GRIMOIRE.
WHAT?!
IT CRUMBLED WITHIN ITS CONTAINMENT, LEADING TO THE CRIES OF THEFT.
A FAKE?
TO BE PRECISE, A FAKE MADE WITH SILK FROM THE WEBSTER SPIDERS.
!
LUCY'S SPIDERS!

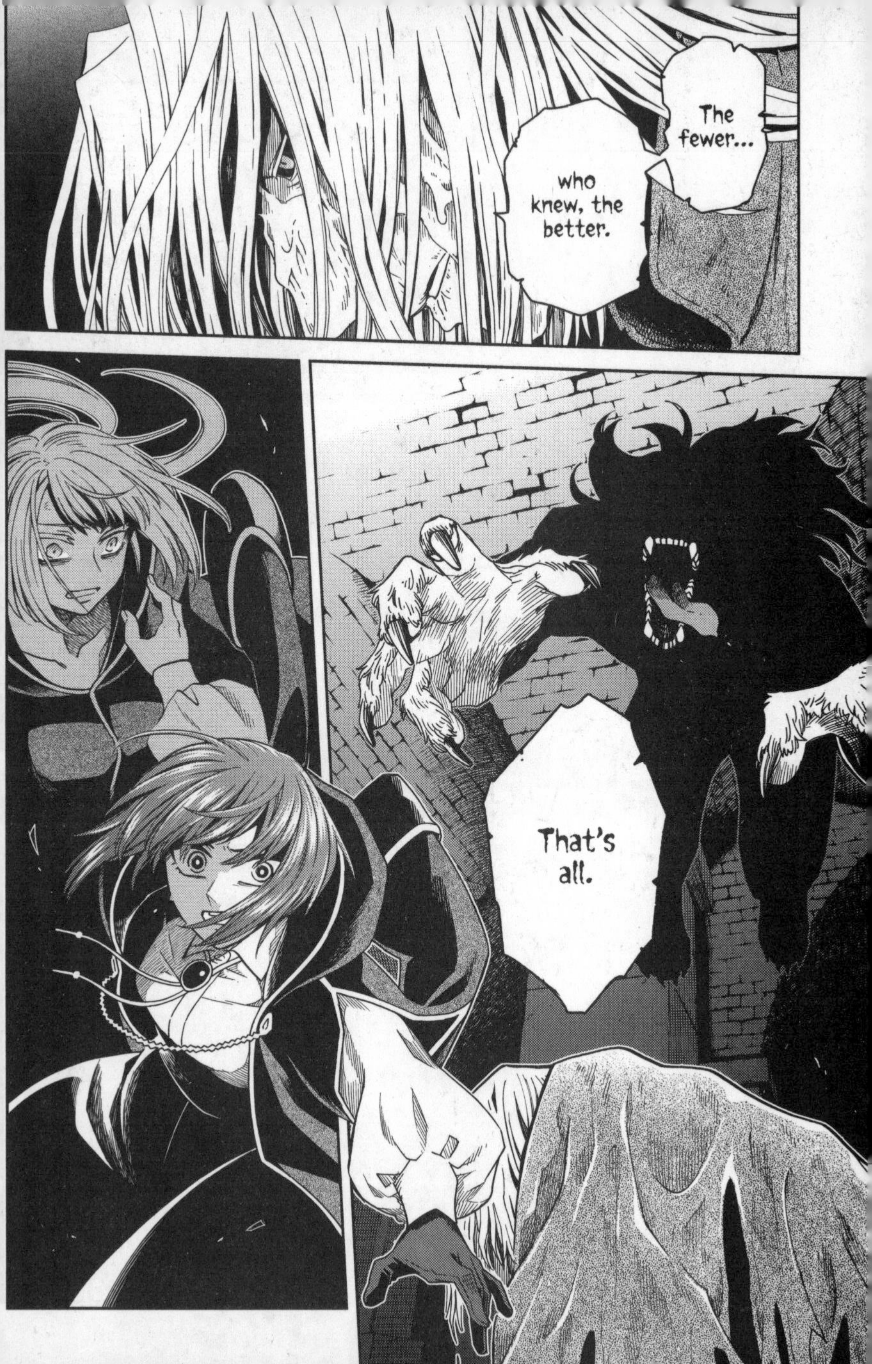
The fewer...
who knew, the better.
That's all.

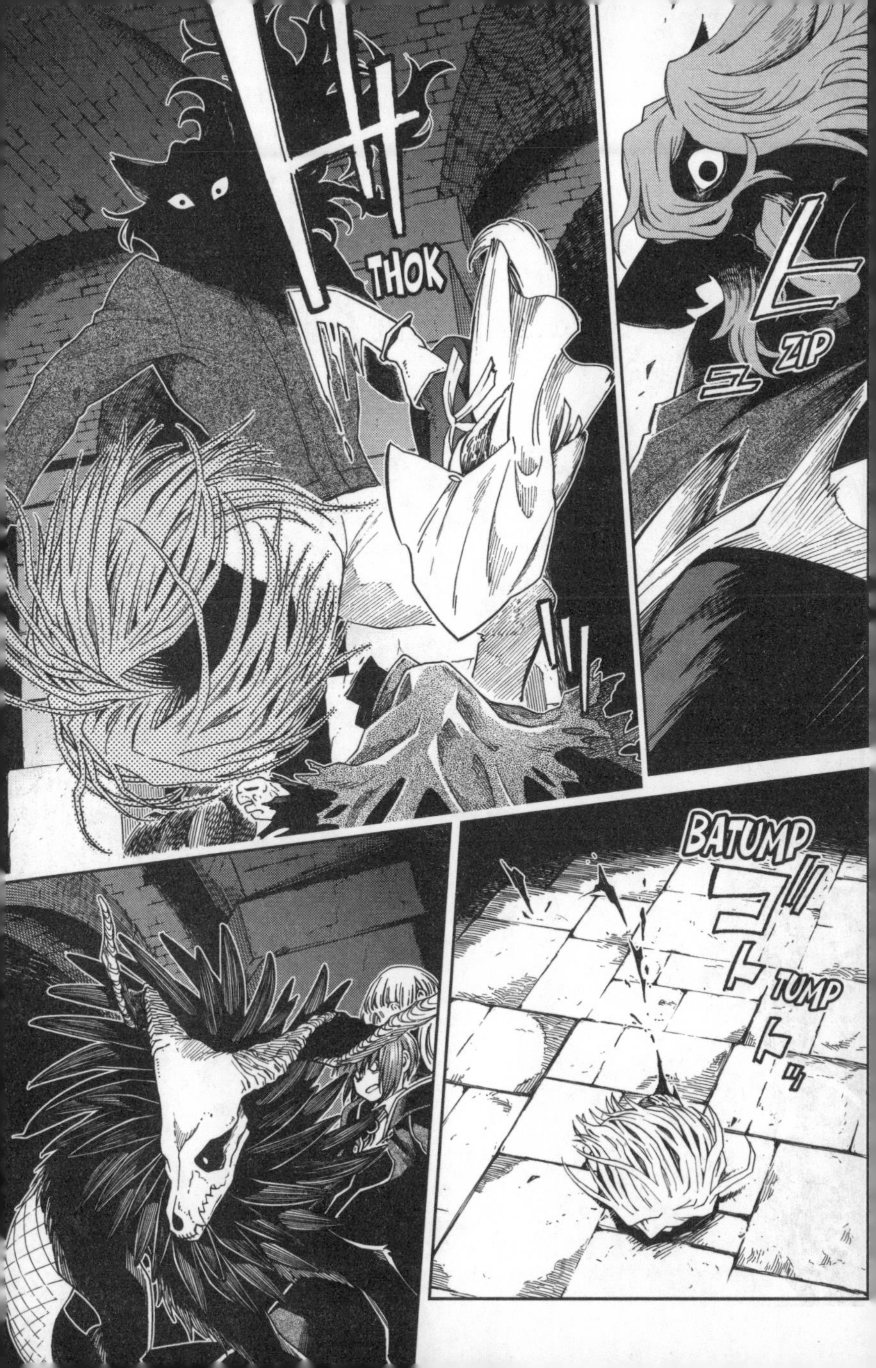
THOK
ZIP
BATUMP
TUMP

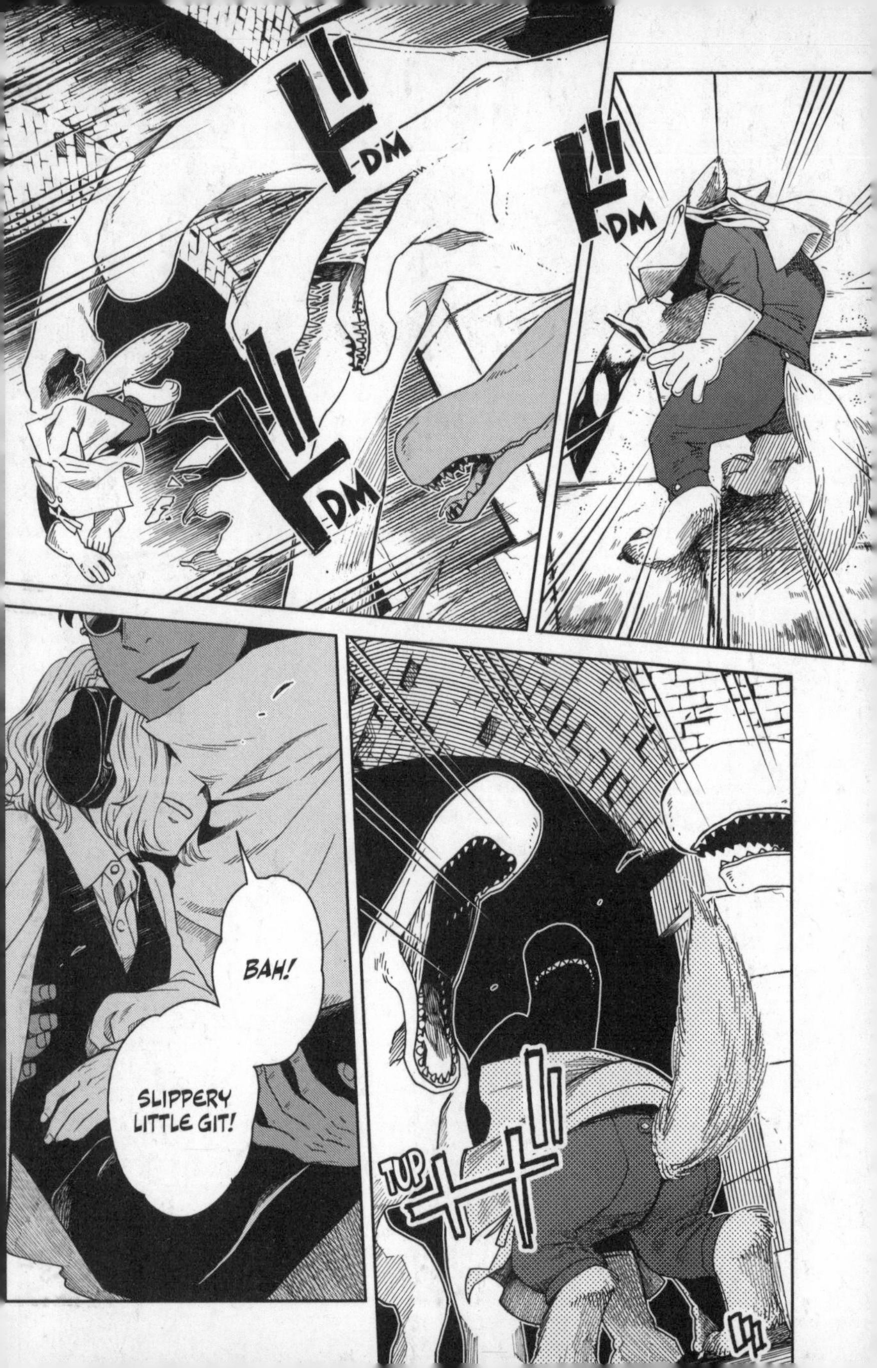
DM
DM
DM
TUP
BAH!
SLIPPERY LITTLE GIT!

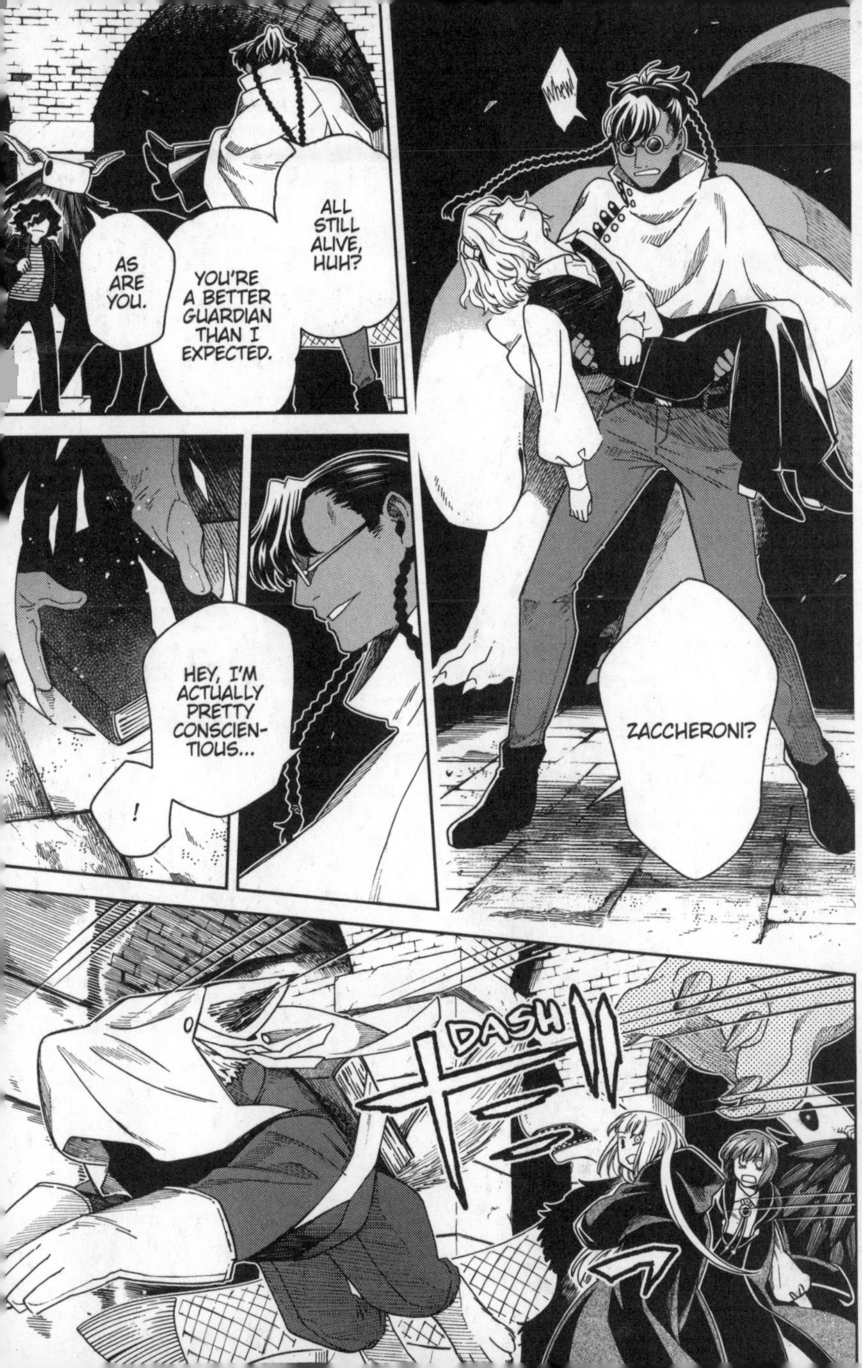
Whew!
ALL STILL ALIVE, HUH?
YOU'RE A BETTER GUARDIAN THAN I EXPECTED.
AS ARE YOU.
ZACCHERONI?
HEY, I'M ACTUALLY PRETTY CONSCIEN-TIOUS...
!
DASH

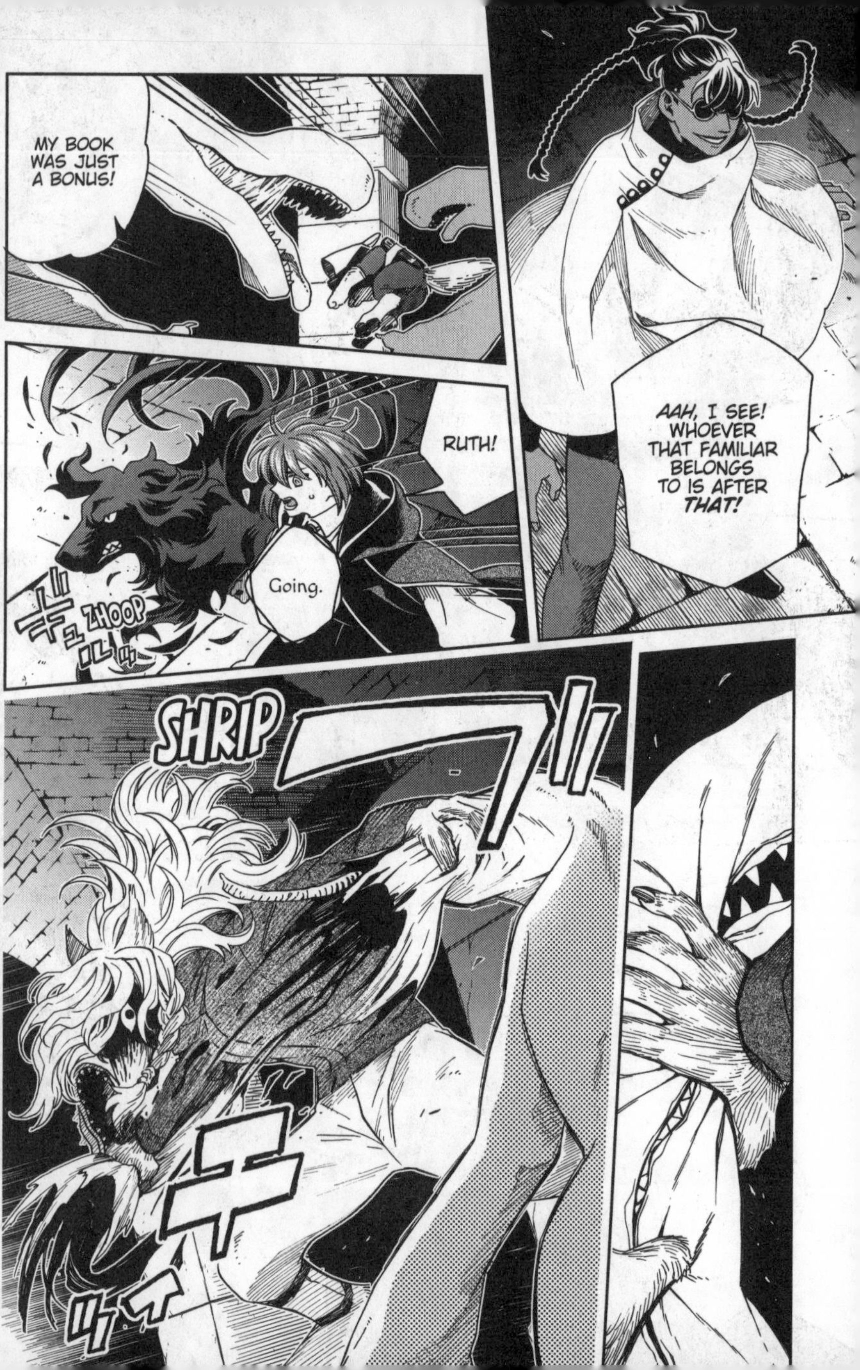

AAH, I SEE! WHOEVER THAT FAMILIAR BELONGS TO IS AFTER THAT!
MY BOOK WAS JUST A BONUS!
RUTH!
Going.
ZHOOP
SHRIP

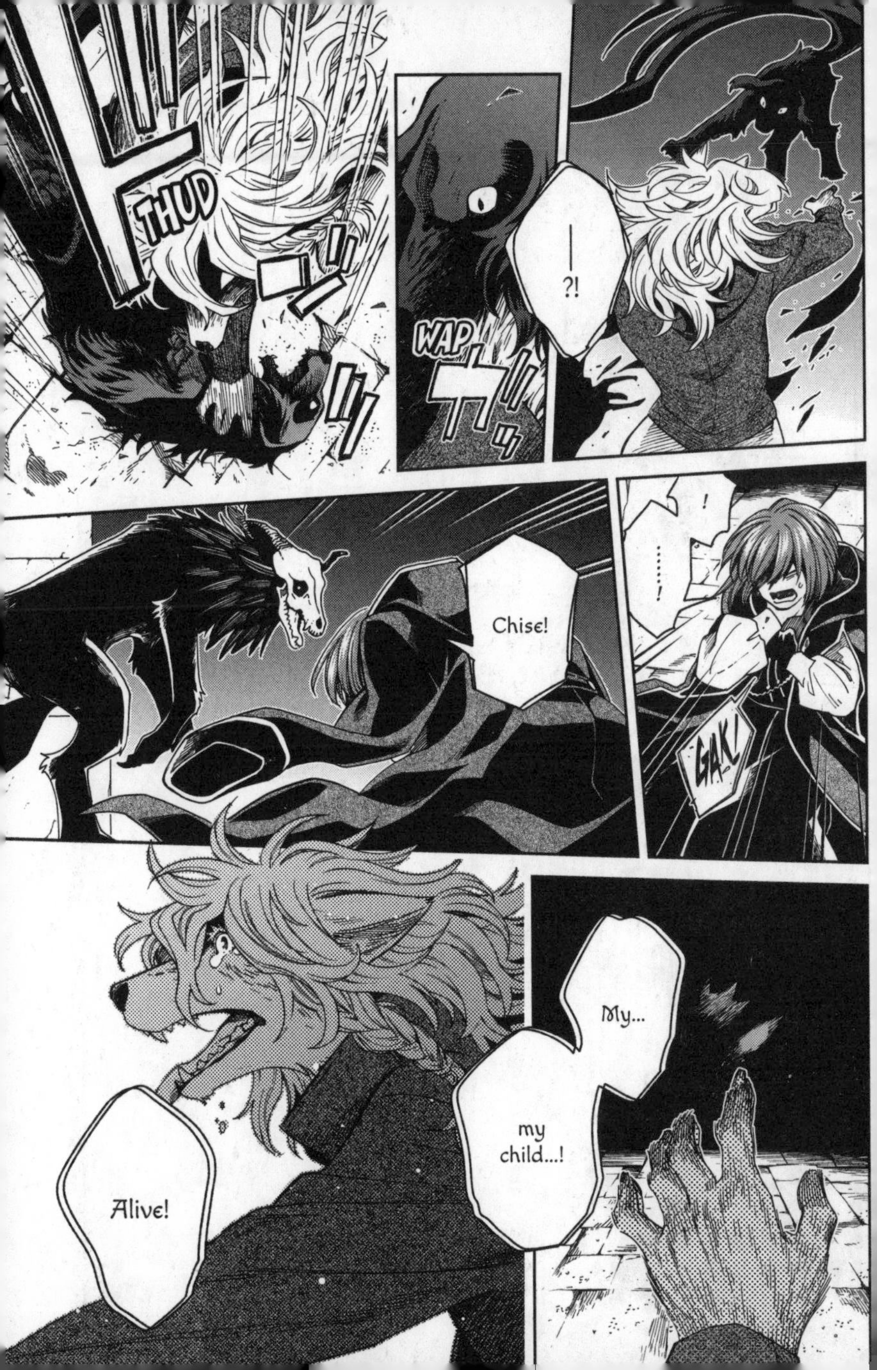
—?!
WAP
THUD
!
......!
GAK!
Chise!
My...
my child...!
Alive!

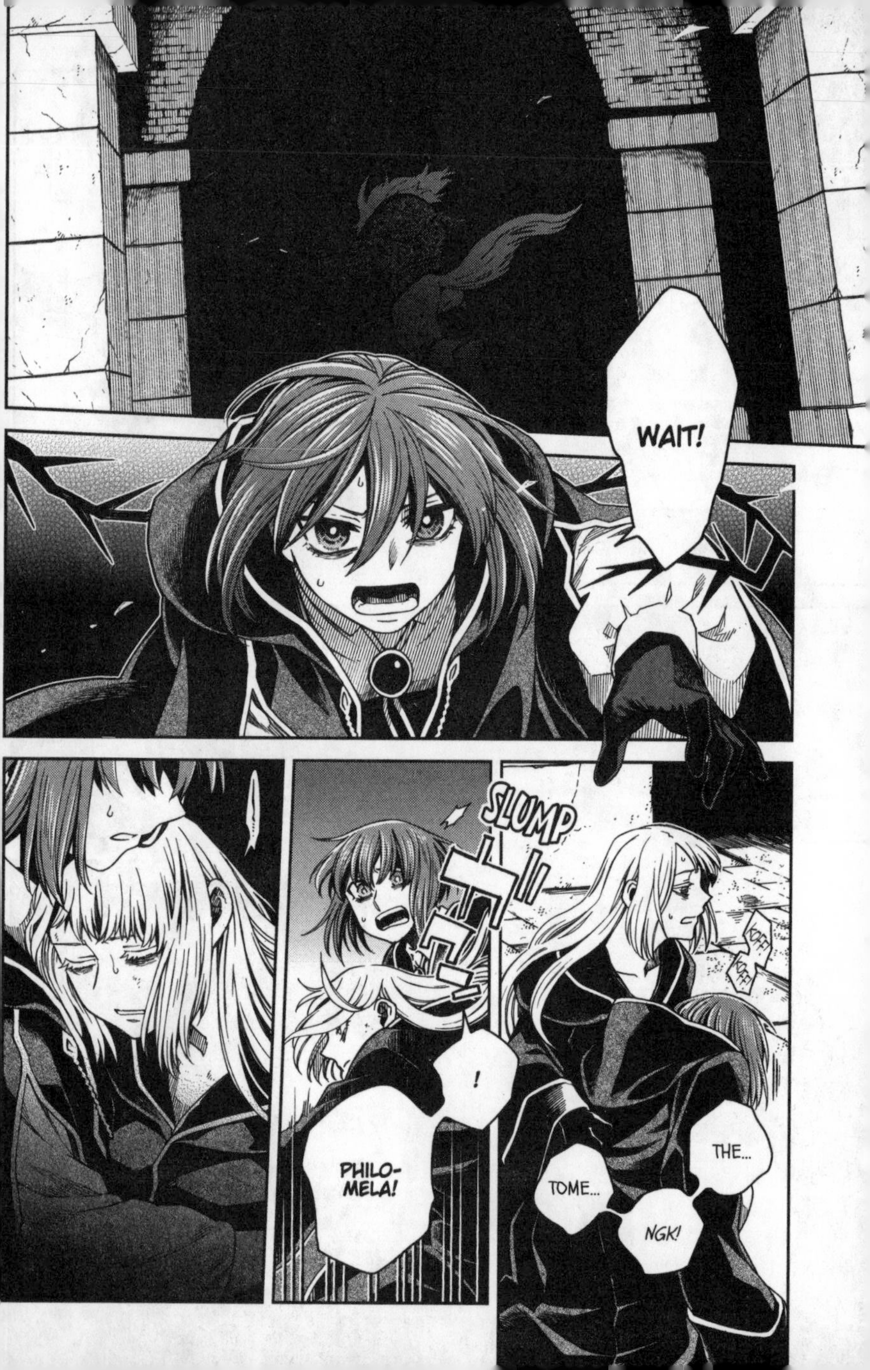
WAIT!
KOFF
KOFF
THE...
NGK!
TOME...
SLUMP
!
PHILO-
MELA!

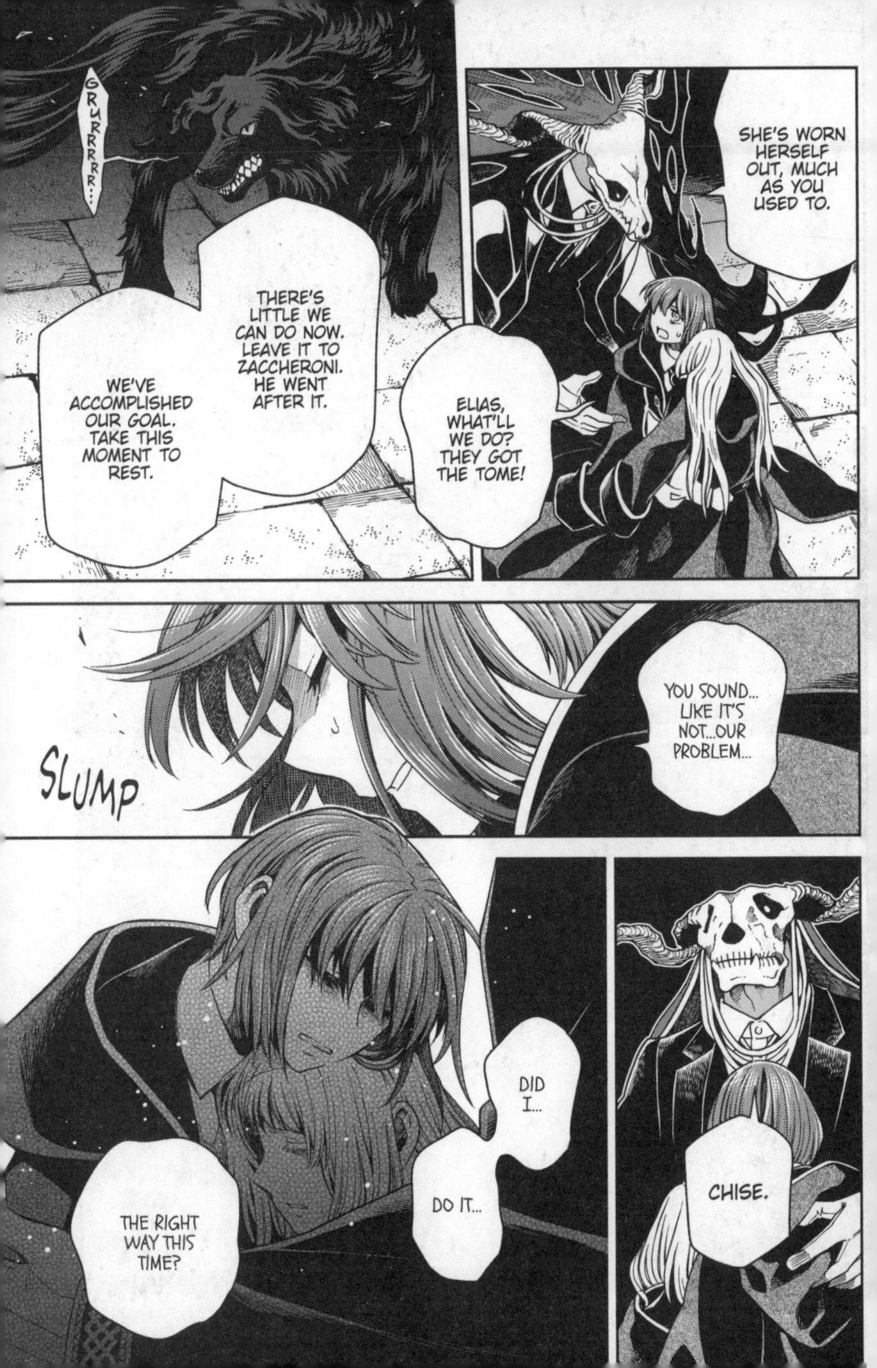
SHE'S WORN HERSELF OUT, MUCH AS YOU USED TO.
ELIAS, WHAT'LL WE DO? THEY GOT THE TOME!
THERE'S LITTLE WE CAN DO NOW. LEAVE IT TO ZACCHERONI. HE WENT AFTER IT.
WE'VE ACCOMPLISHED OUR GOAL. TAKE THIS MOMENT TO REST.
GRURRRRR...
YOU SOUND... LIKE IT'S NOT...OUR PROBLEM...
SLUMP
CHISE.
DID I...
DO IT...
THE RIGHT WAY THIS TIME?

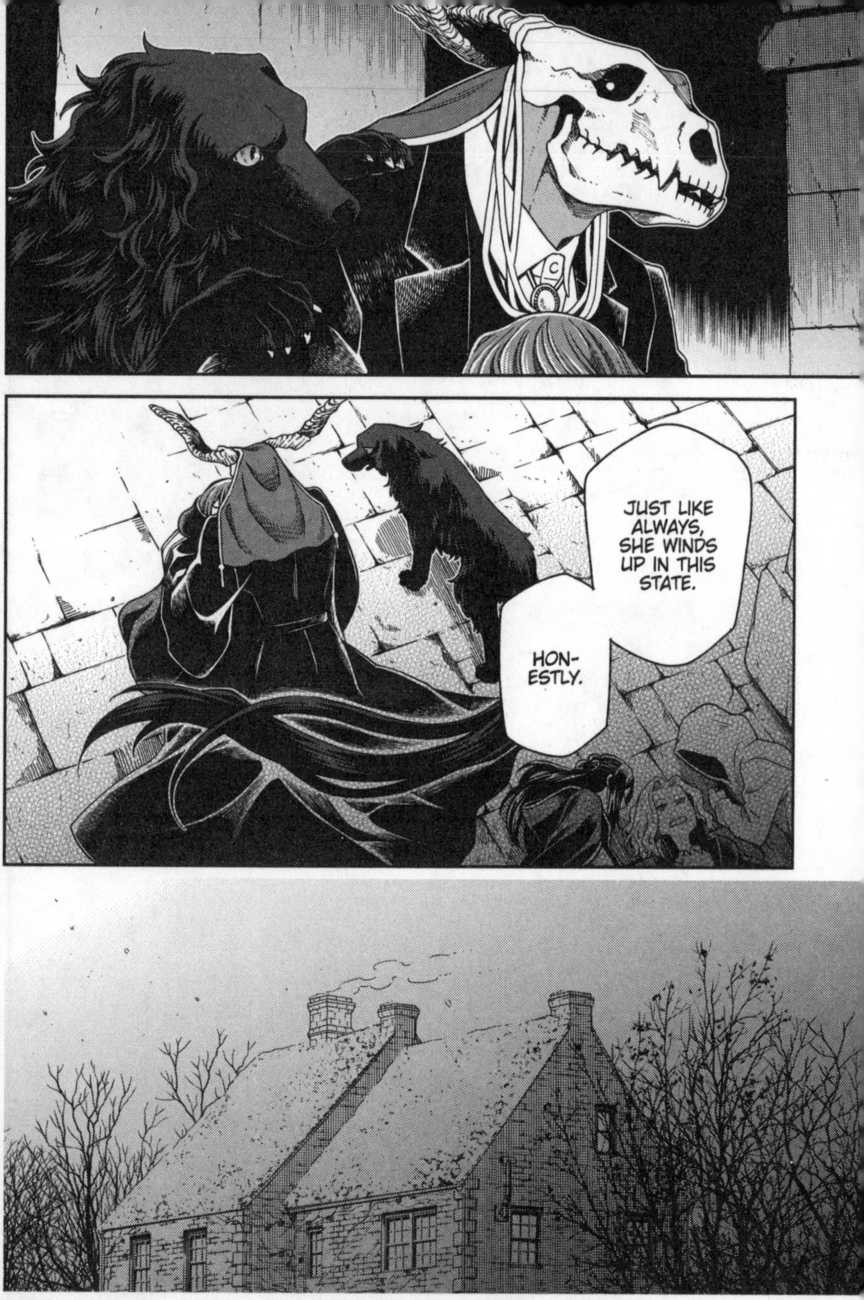
JUST LIKE ALWAYS, SHE WINDS UP IN THIS STATE.
HON-ESTLY.

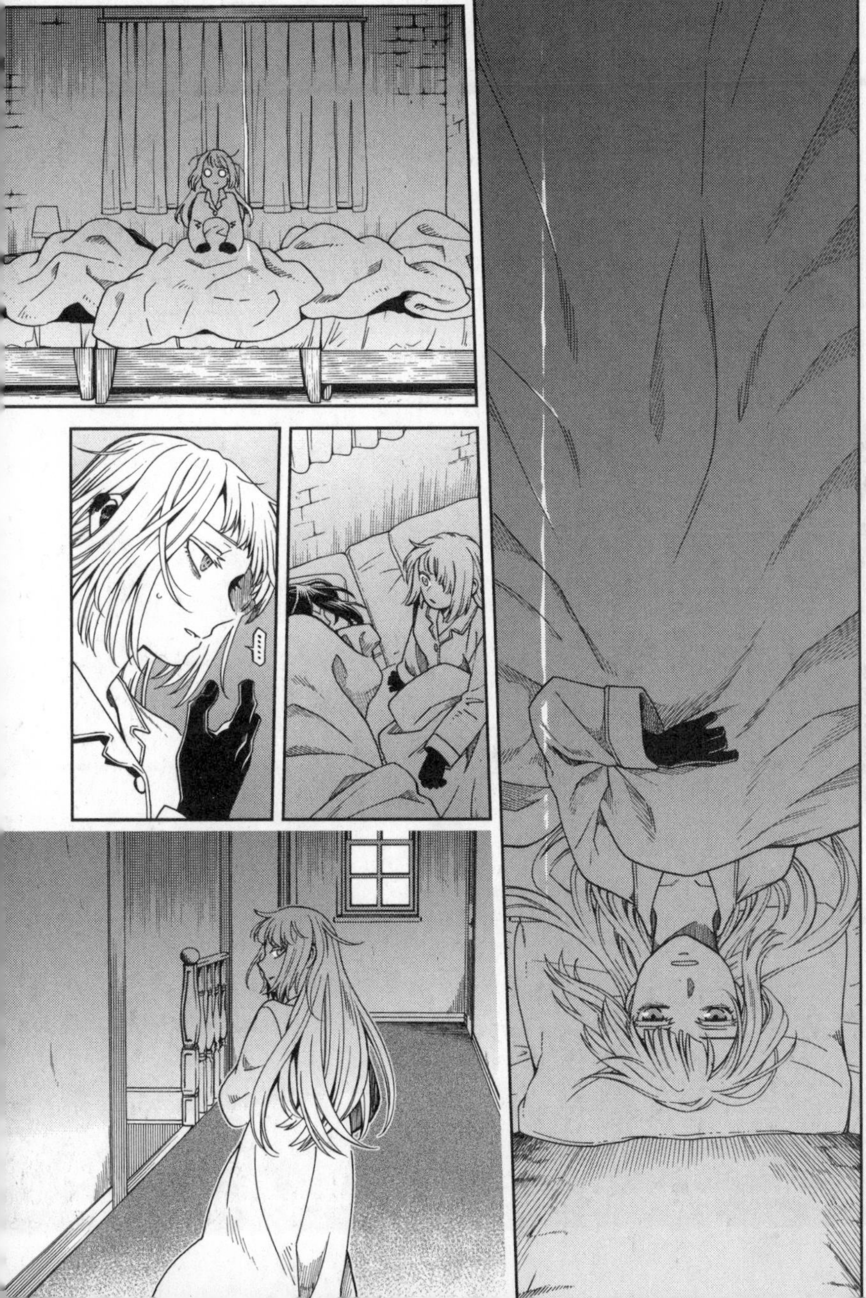
......

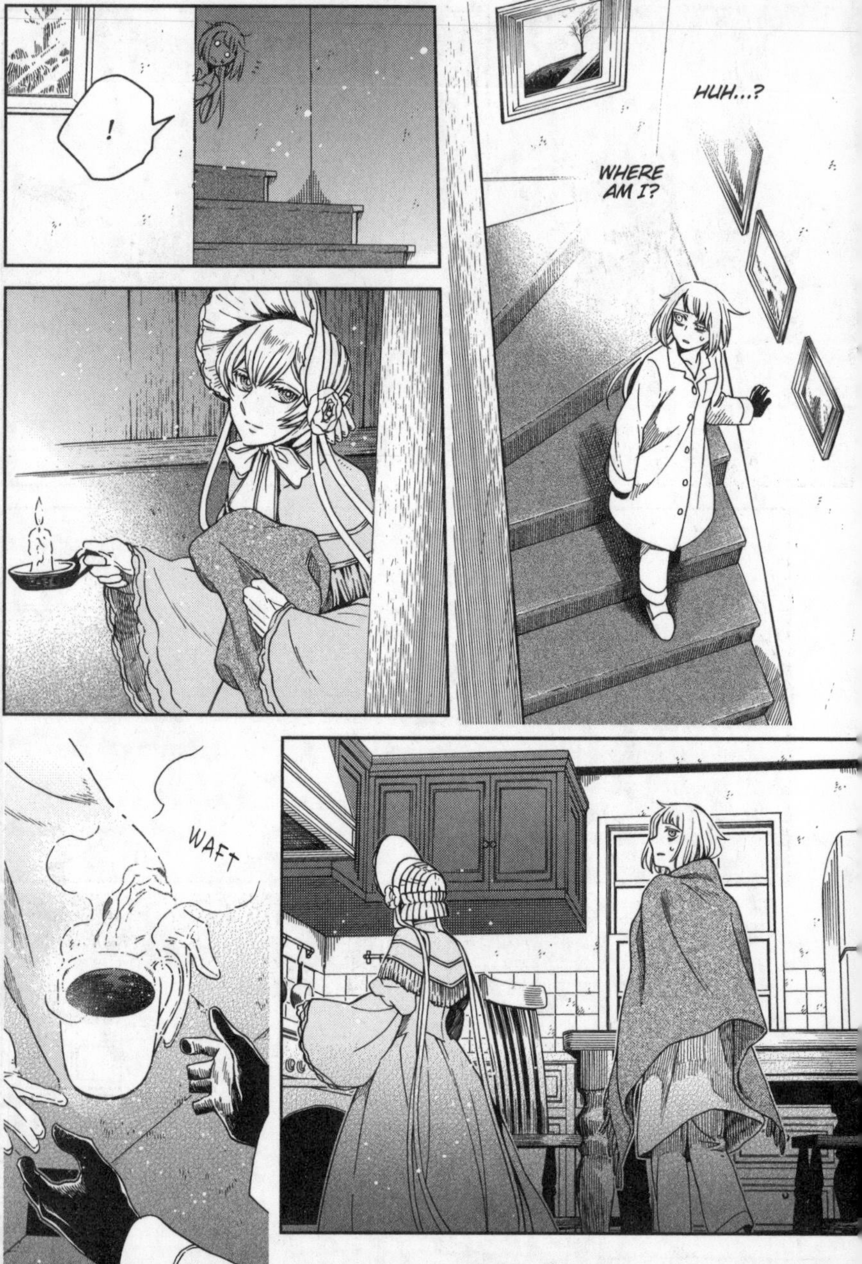
HUH...?
WHERE AM I?
!
WAFT

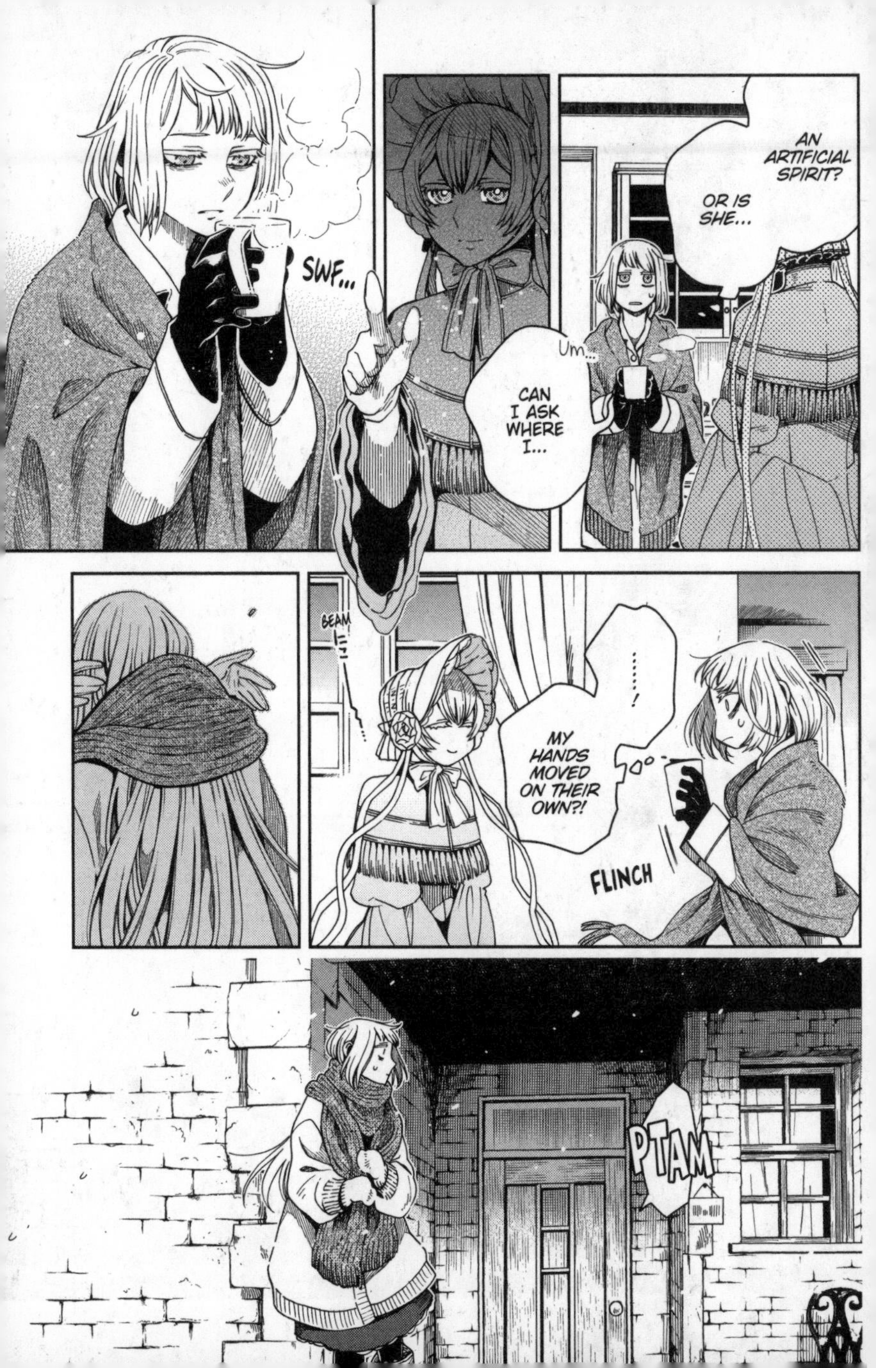
AN ARTIFICIAL SPIRIT?
OR IS SHE...
Um...
CAN I ASK WHERE I...
SWF...
......!
MY HANDS MOVED ON THEIR OWN?!
FLINCH
BEAM
PTAM

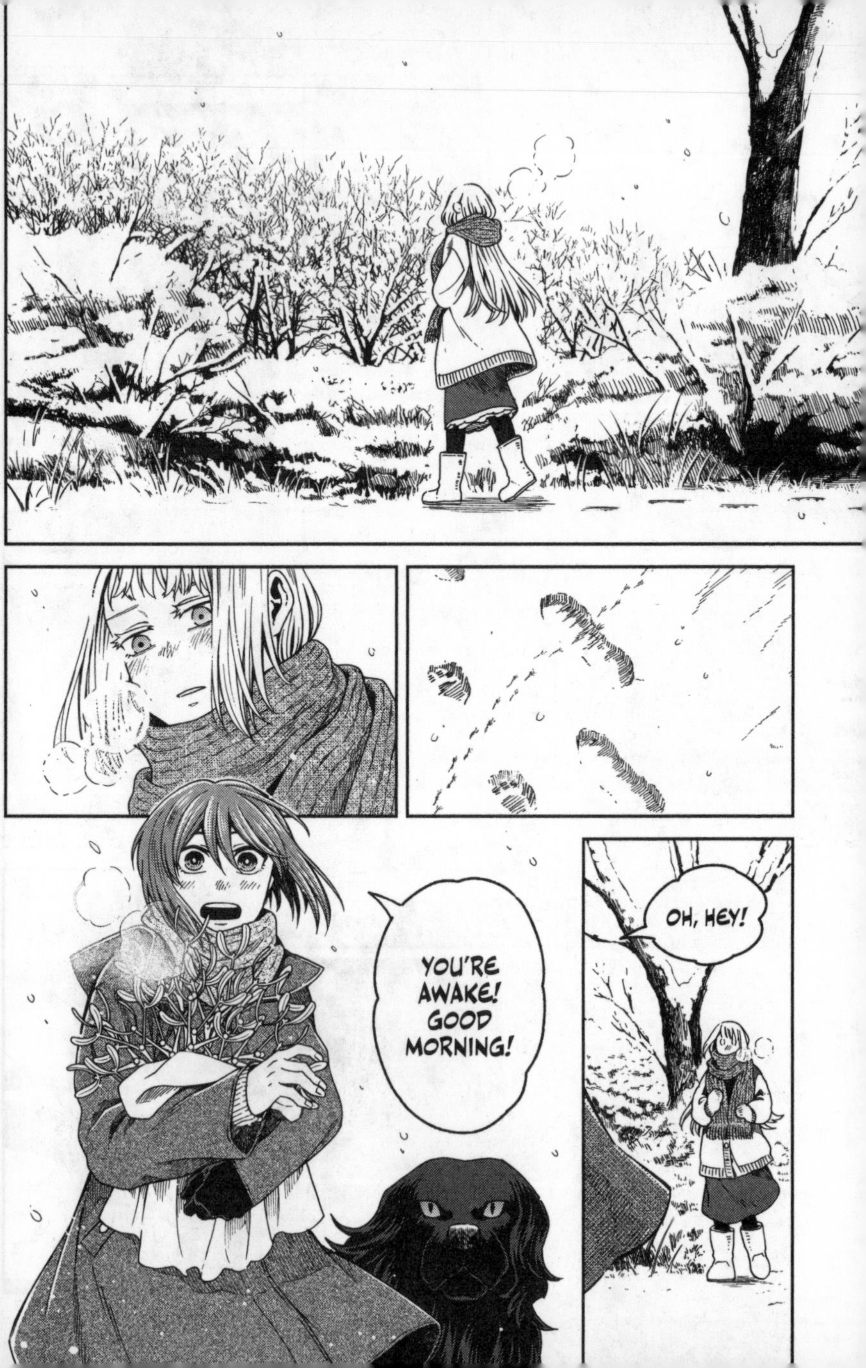
OH, HEY!
YOU'RE AWAKE! GOOD MORNING!

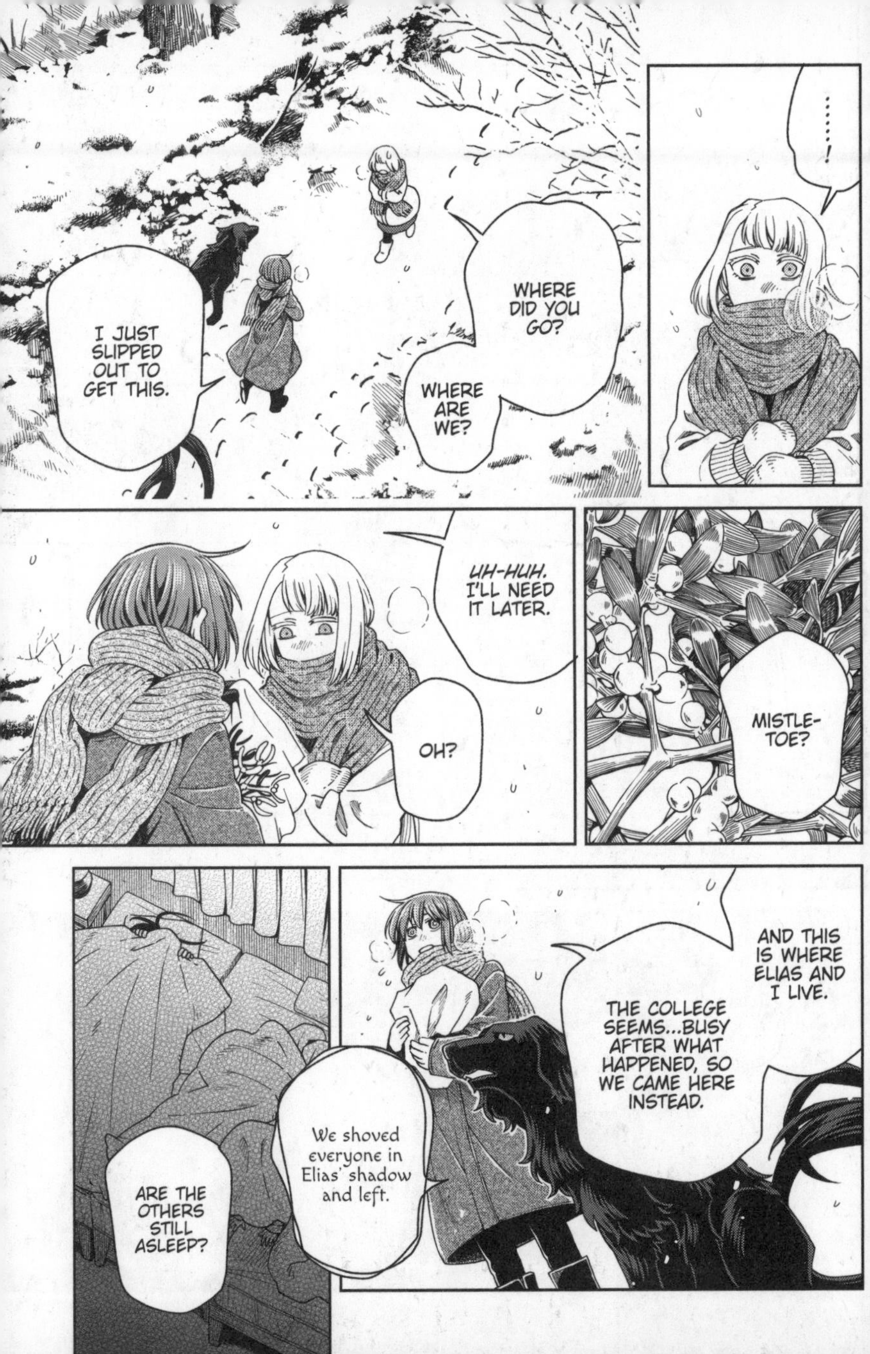
......!
WHERE DID YOU GO?
WHERE ARE WE?
I JUST SLIPPED OUT TO GET THIS.
MISTLE-TOE?
UH-HUH. I'LL NEED IT LATER.
OH?
AND THIS IS WHERE ELIAS AND I LIVE.
THE COLLEGE SEEMS...BUSY AFTER WHAT HAPPENED, SO WE CAME HERE INSTEAD.
We shoved everyone in Elias' shadow and left.
ARE THE OTHERS STILL ASLEEP?

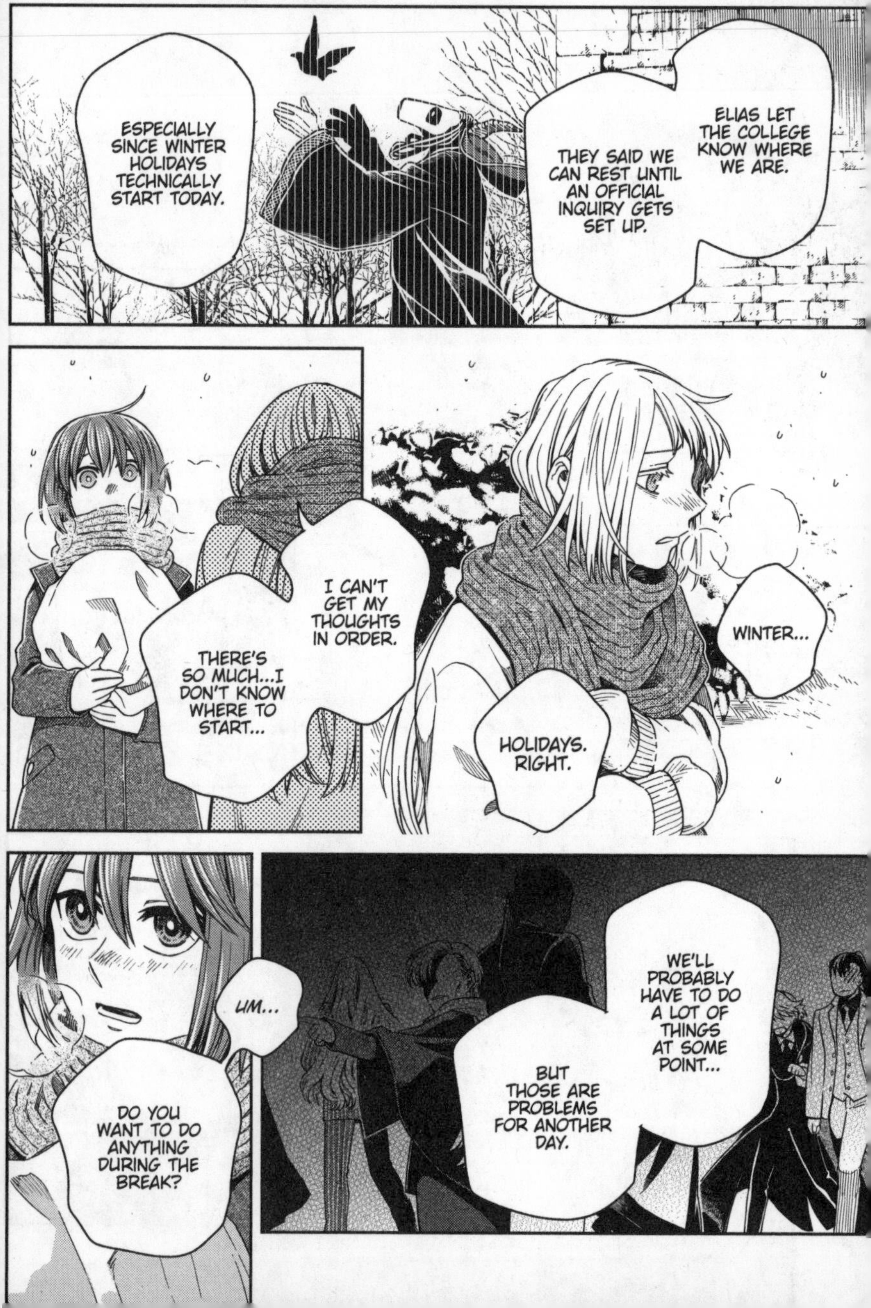
ELIAS LET THE COLLEGE KNOW WHERE WE ARE.
THEY SAID WE CAN REST UNTIL AN OFFICIAL INQUIRY GETS SET UP.
ESPECIALLY SINCE WINTER HOLIDAYS TECHNICALLY START TODAY.
WINTER...
HOLIDAYS. RIGHT.
I CAN'T GET MY THOUGHTS IN ORDER.
THERE'S SO MUCH...I DON'T KNOW WHERE TO START...
WE'LL PROBABLY HAVE TO DO A LOT OF THINGS AT SOME POINT...
BUT THOSE ARE PROBLEMS FOR ANOTHER DAY.
UM...
DO YOU WANT TO DO ANYTHING DURING THE BREAK?

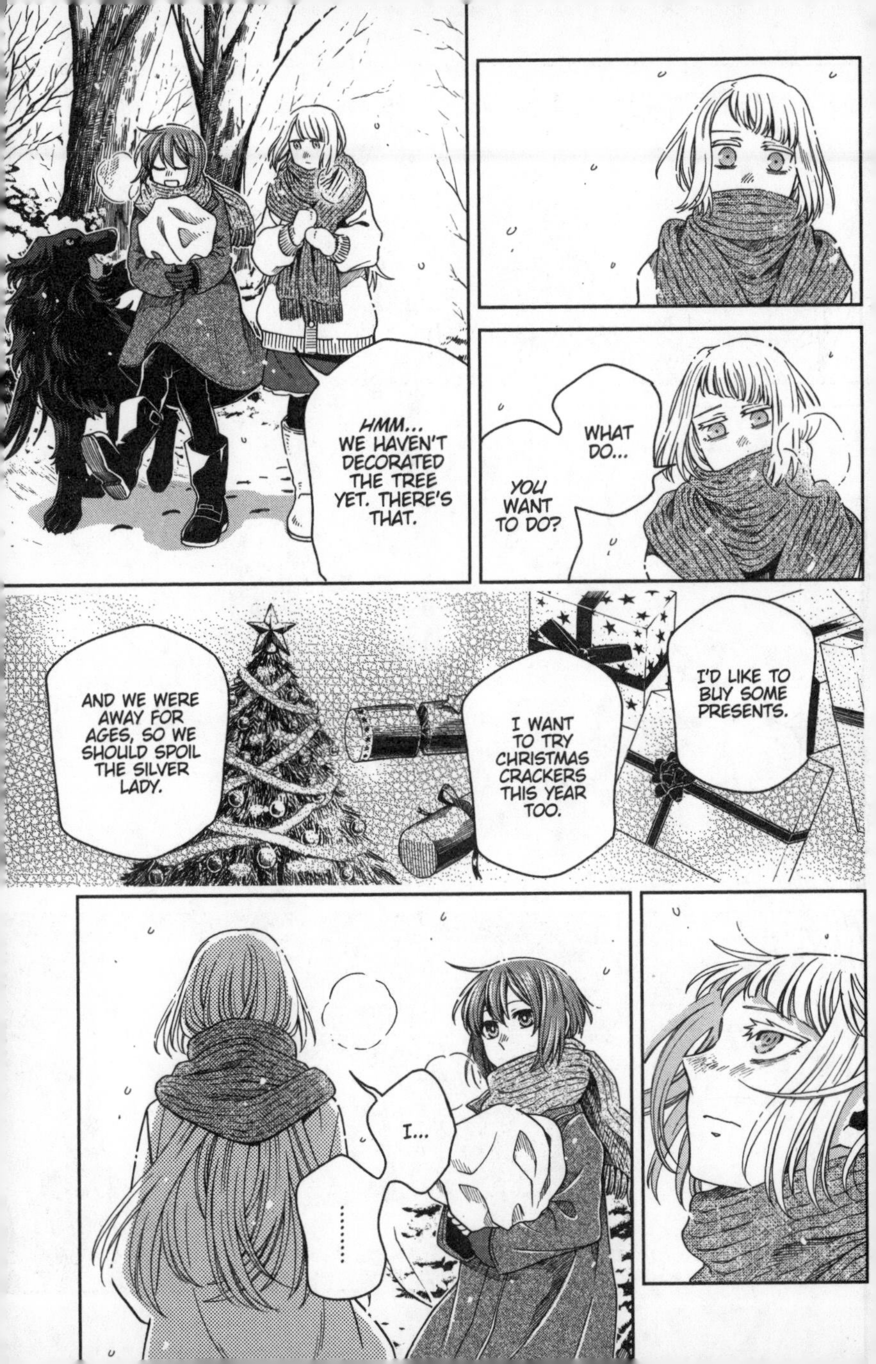
WHAT DO...
YOU WANT TO DO?
HMM... WE HAVEN'T DECORATED THE TREE YET. THERE'S THAT.
I'D LIKE TO BUY SOME PRESENTS.
I WANT TO TRY CHRISTMAS CRACKERS THIS YEAR TOO.
AND WE WERE AWAY FOR AGES, SO WE SHOULD SPOIL THE SILVER LADY.
I...
......

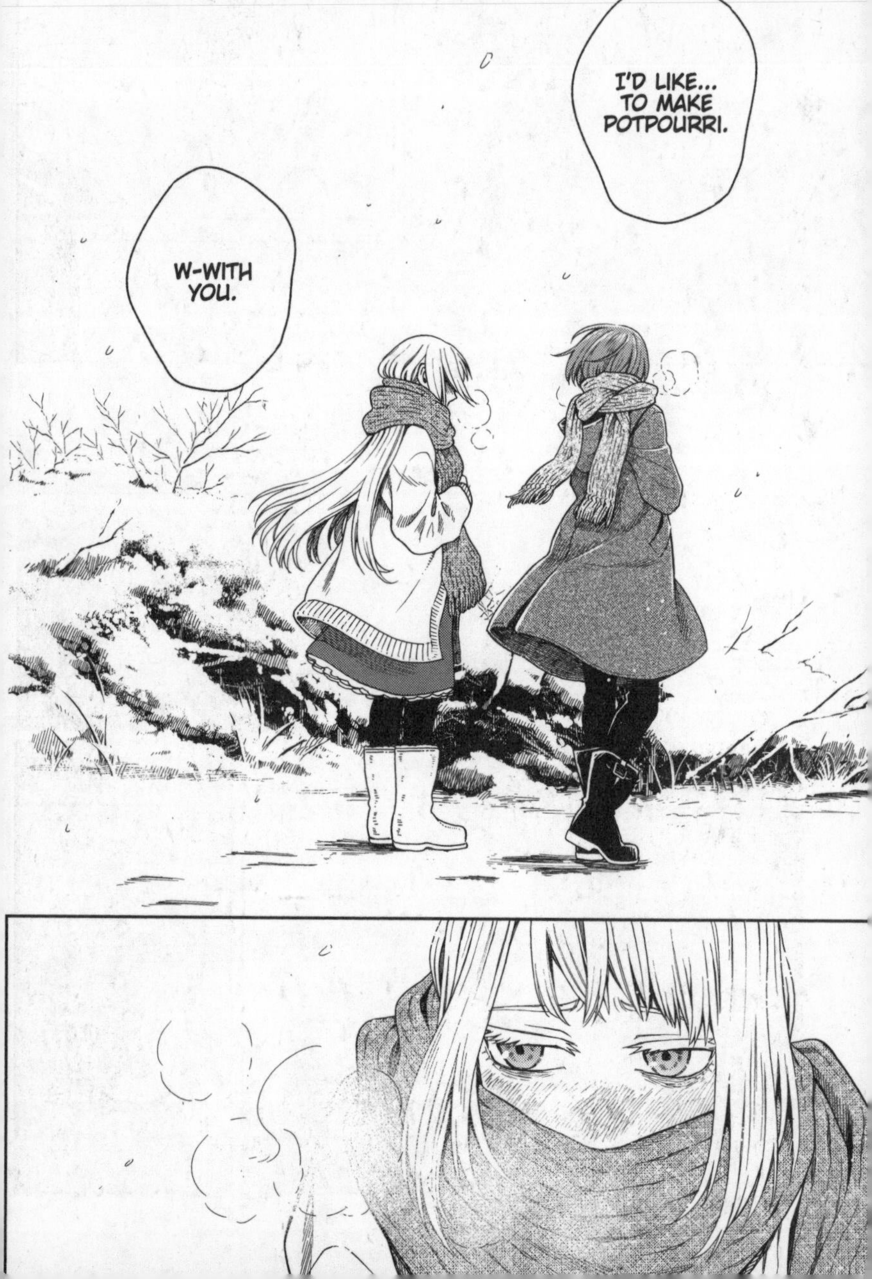
I'D LIKE... TO MAKE POTPOURRI.
W-WITH YOU.

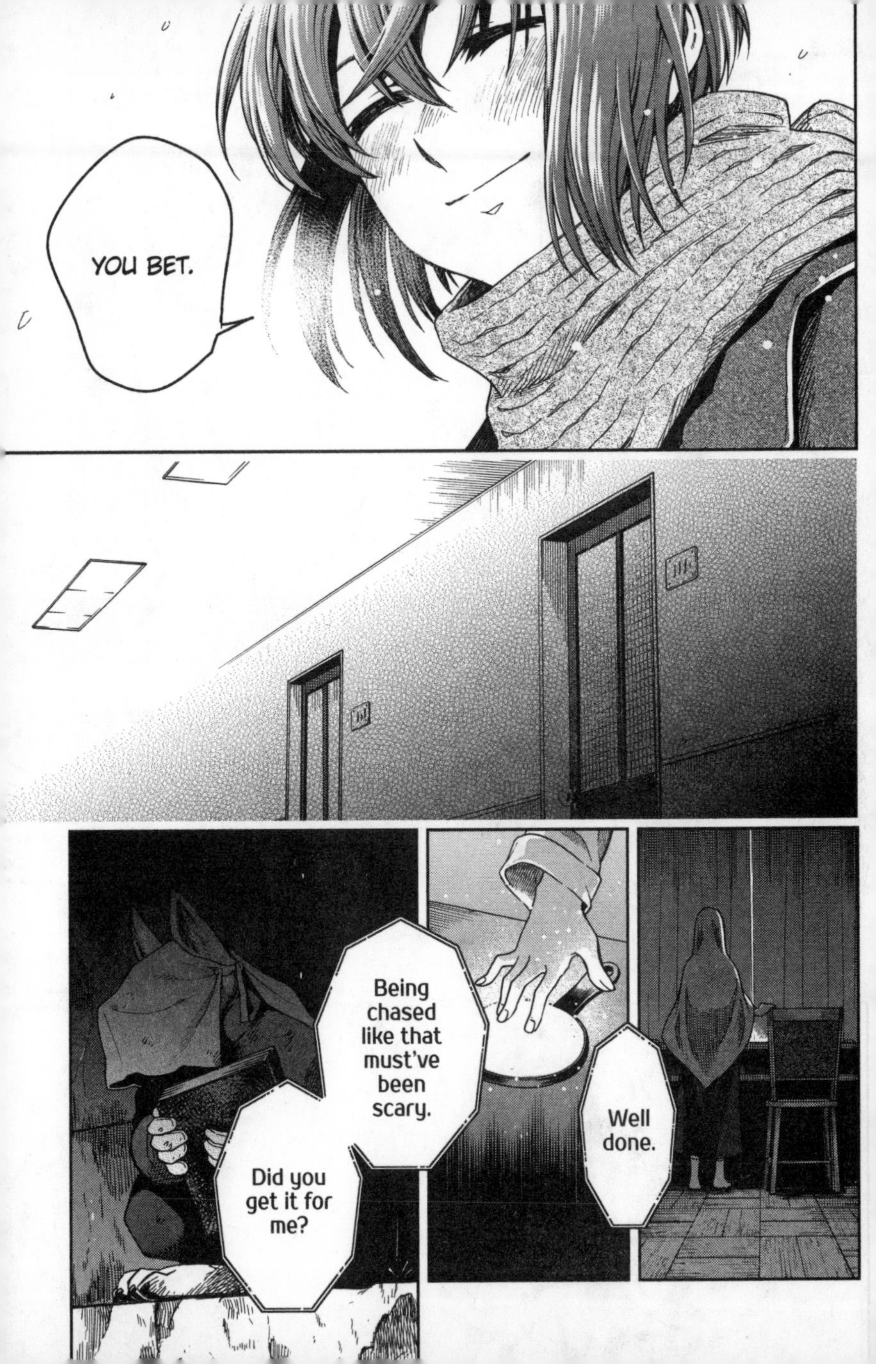
YOU BET.
Well done.
Being chased like that must've been scary.
Did you get it for me?

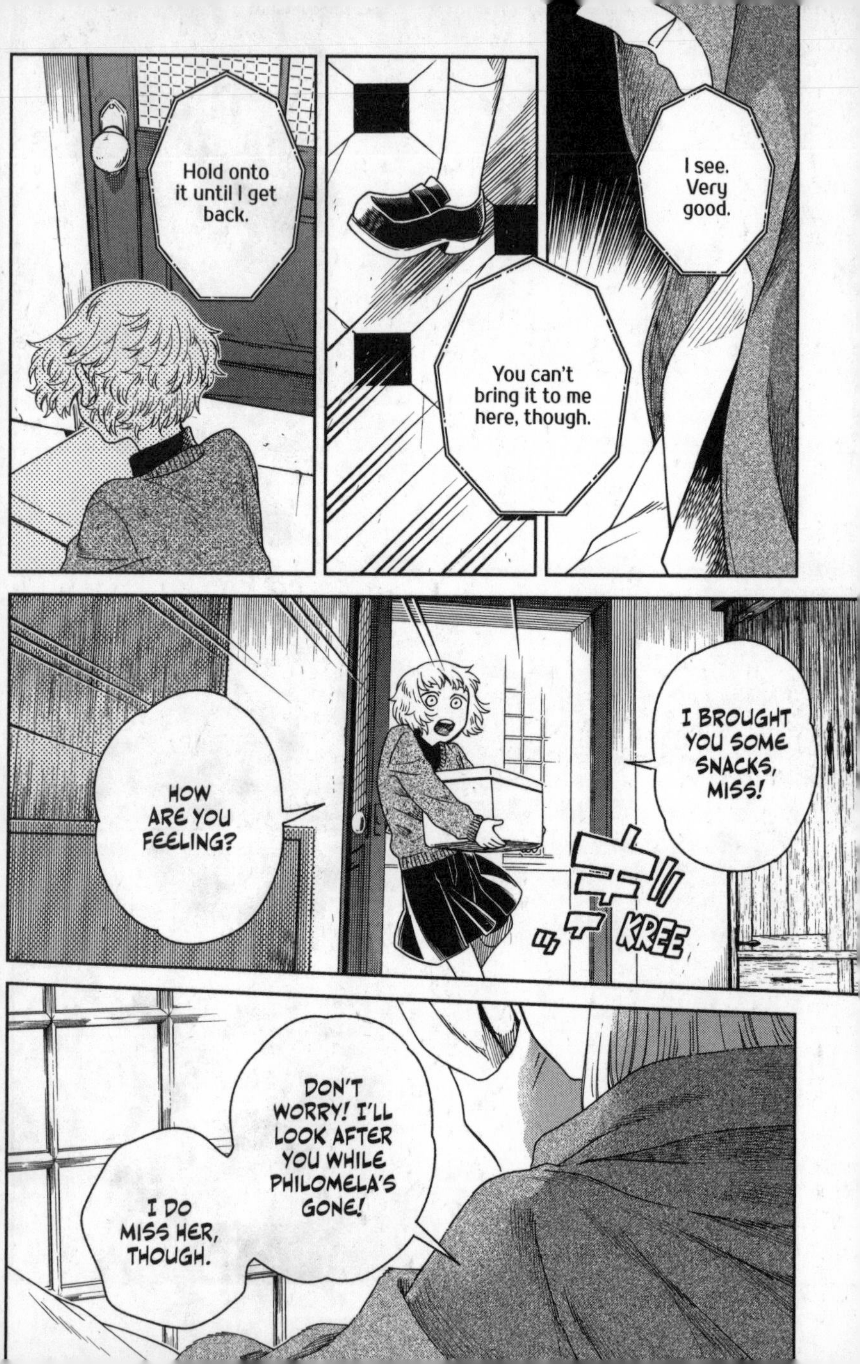
Hold onto it until I get back.
You can't bring it to me here, though.
I see. Very good.
I BROUGHT YOU SOME SNACKS, MISS!
KREE
HOW ARE YOU FEELING?
DON'T WORRY! I'LL LOOK AFTER YOU WHILE PHILOMELA'S GONE!
I DO MISS HER, THOUGH.

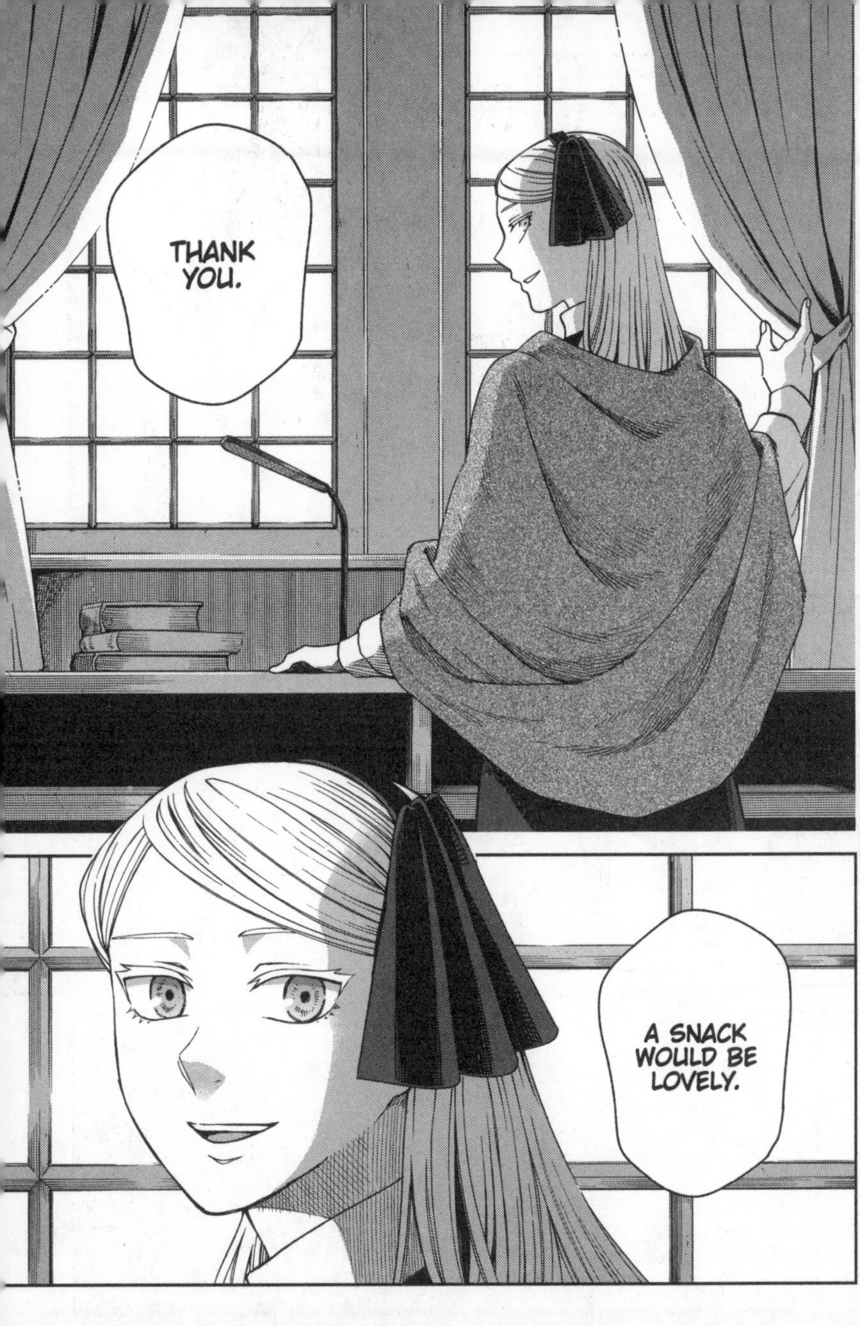
THANK YOU.
A SNACK WOULD BE LOVELY.

The Ancient Magus' Bride

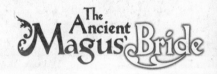

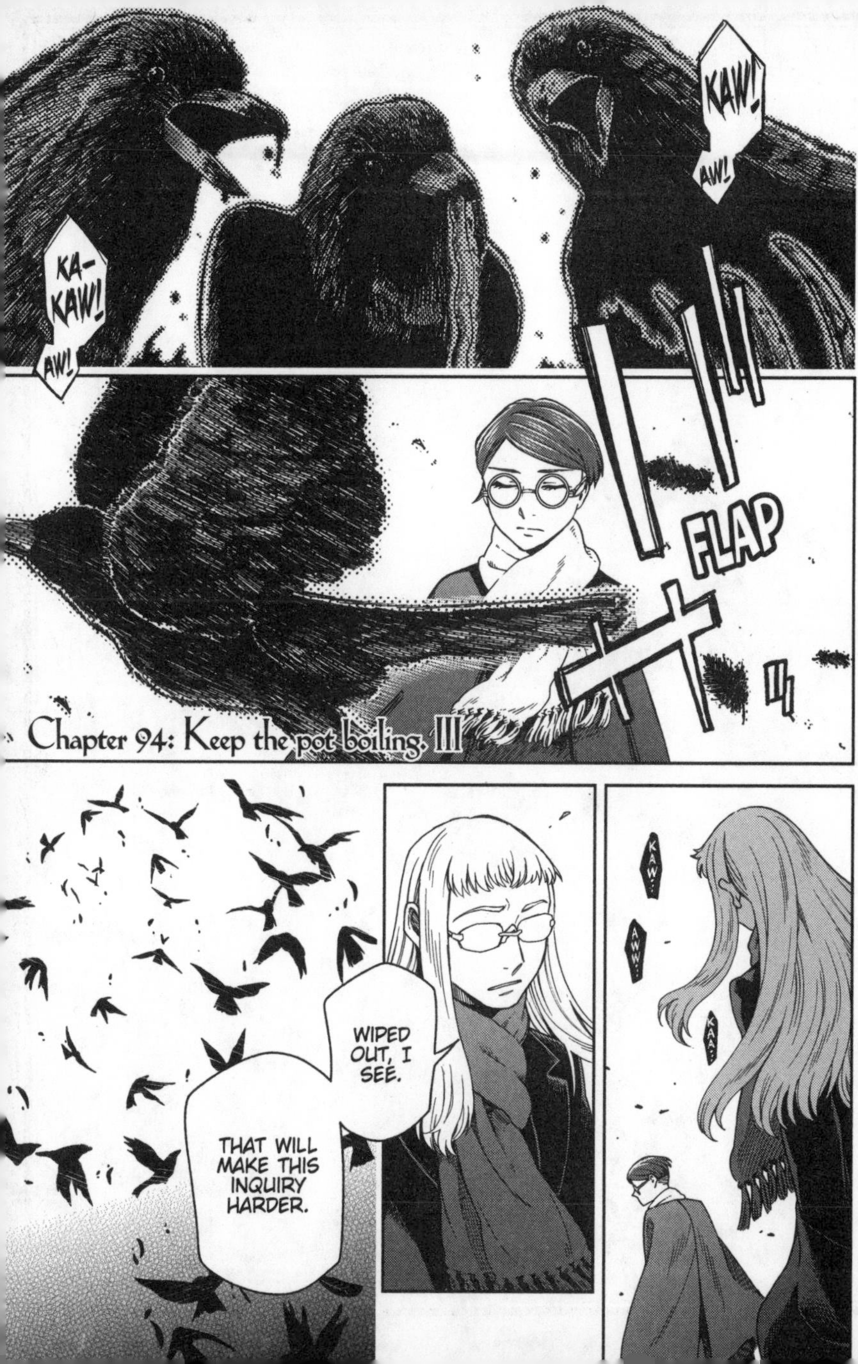
KAW!
AW!
KA-KAW!
AW!
FLAP
Chapter 94: Keep the pot boiling. III
KAW...
AWW...
KAA...
WIPED OUT, I SEE.
THAT WILL MAKE THIS INQUIRY HARDER.

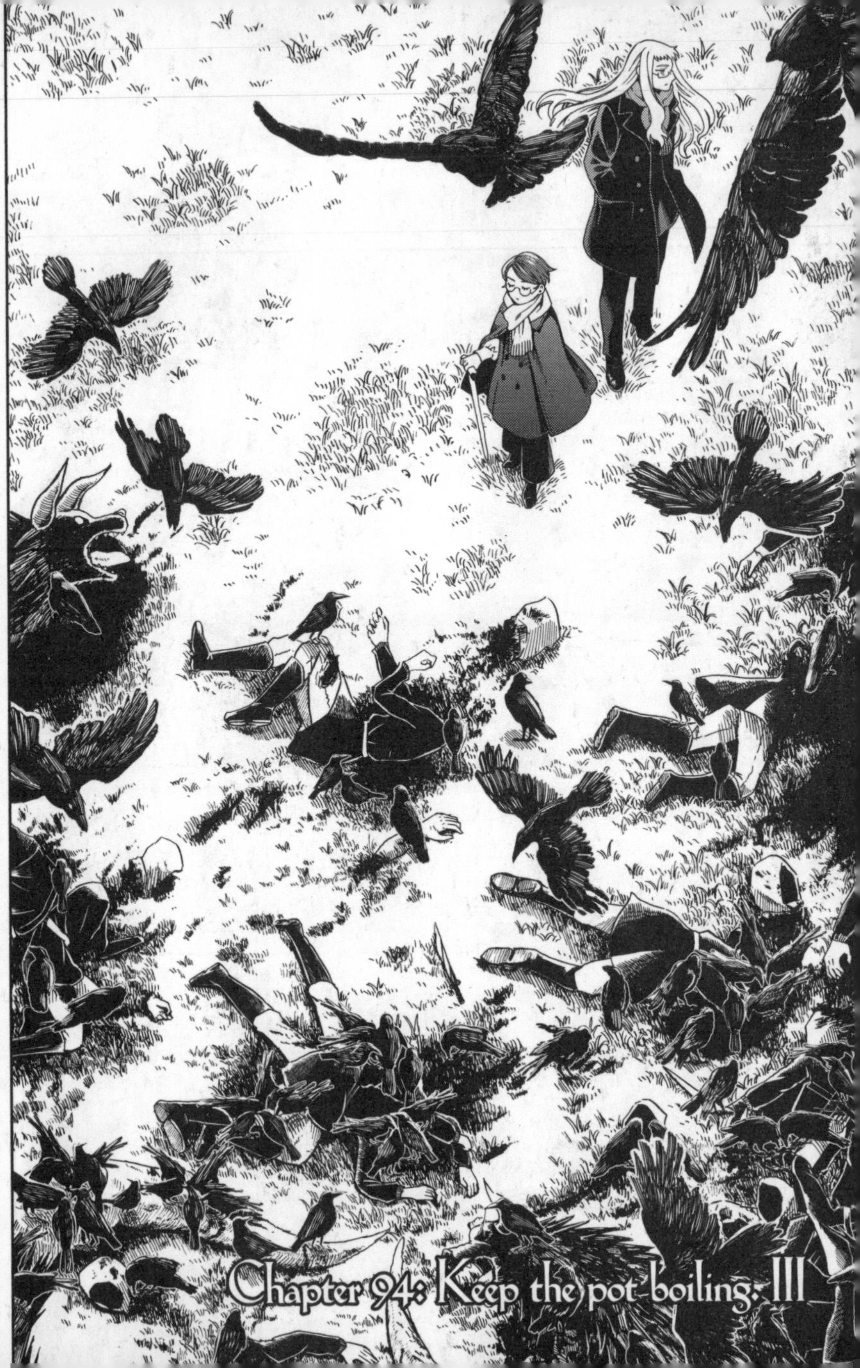
Chapter 94: Keep the pot boiling: III

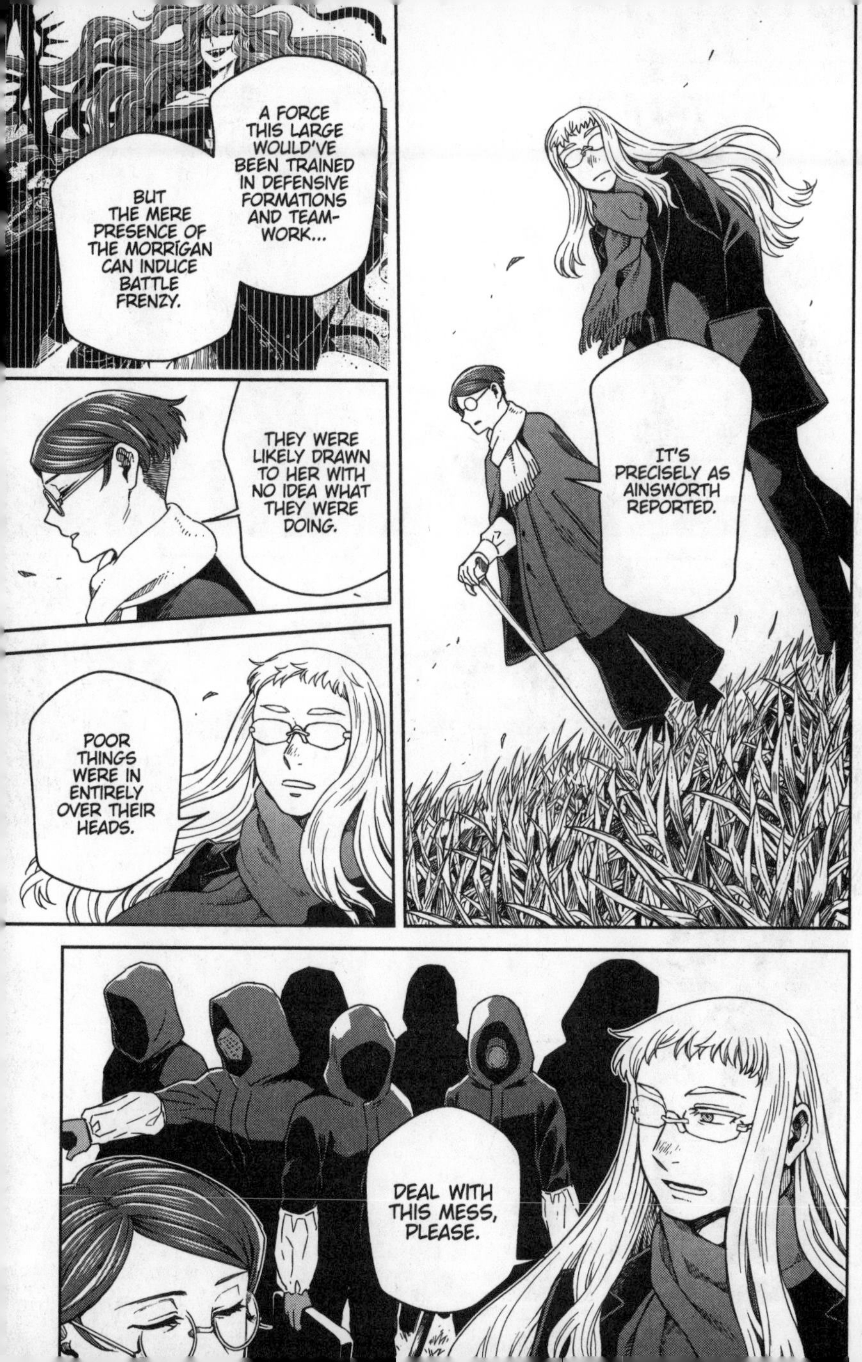
IT'S PRECISELY AS AINSWORTH REPORTED.
A FORCE THIS LARGE WOULD'VE BEEN TRAINED IN DEFENSIVE FORMATIONS AND TEAM-WORK...
BUT THE MERE PRESENCE OF THE MORRIGAN CAN INDUCE BATTLE FRENZY.
THEY WERE LIKELY DRAWN TO HER WITH NO IDEA WHAT THEY WERE DOING.
POOR THINGS WERE IN ENTIRELY OVER THEIR HEADS.
DEAL WITH THIS MESS, PLEASE.

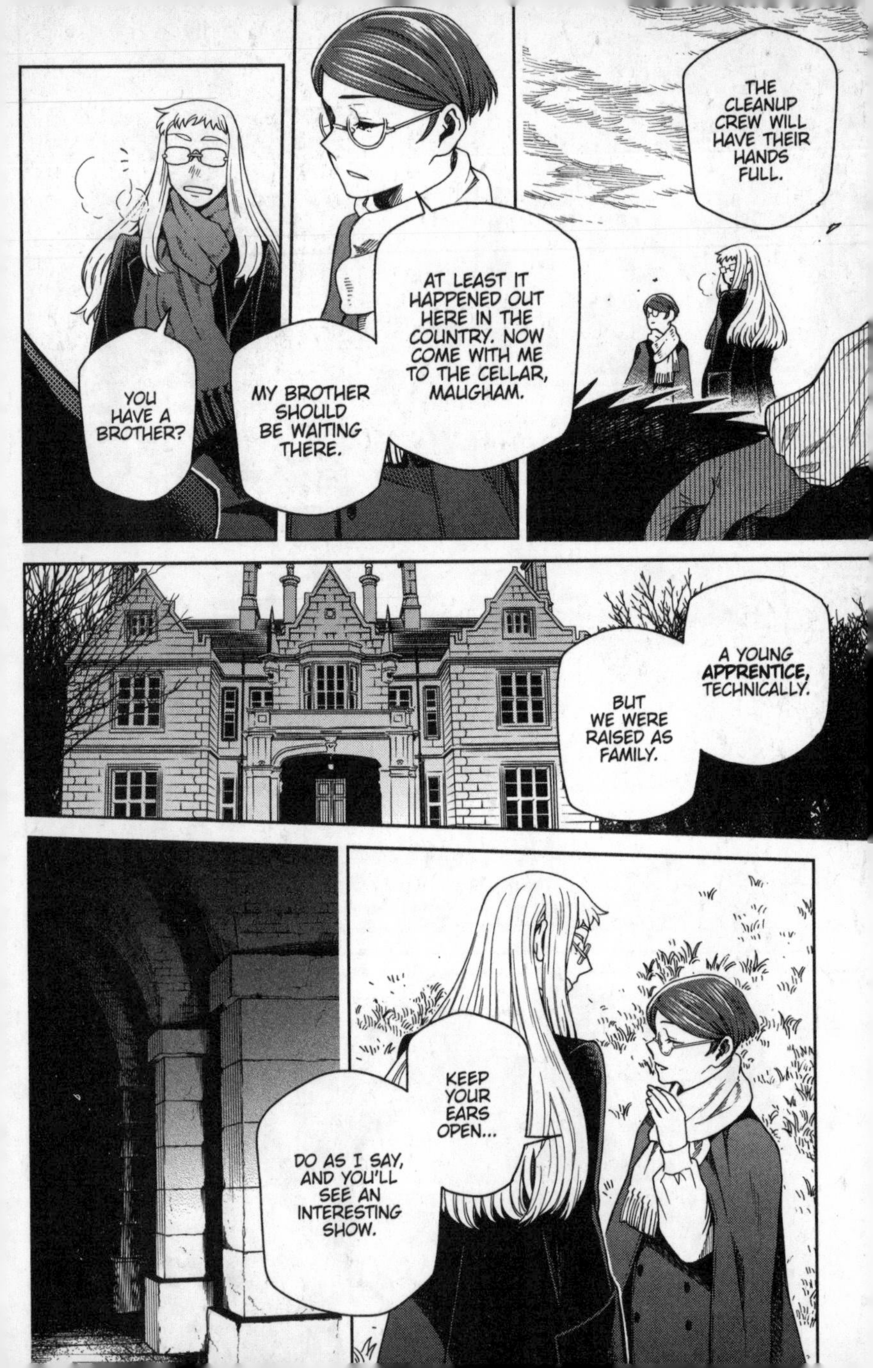
THE CLEANUP CREW WILL HAVE THEIR HANDS FULL.
AT LEAST IT HAPPENED OUT HERE IN THE COUNTRY. NOW COME WITH ME TO THE CELLAR, MAUGHAM.
MY BROTHER SHOULD BE WAITING THERE.
YOU HAVE A BROTHER?
A YOUNG **APPRENTICE**, TECHNICALLY.
BUT WE WERE RAISED AS FAMILY.
KEEP YOUR EARS OPEN...
DO AS I SAY, AND YOU'LL SEE AN INTERESTING SHOW.

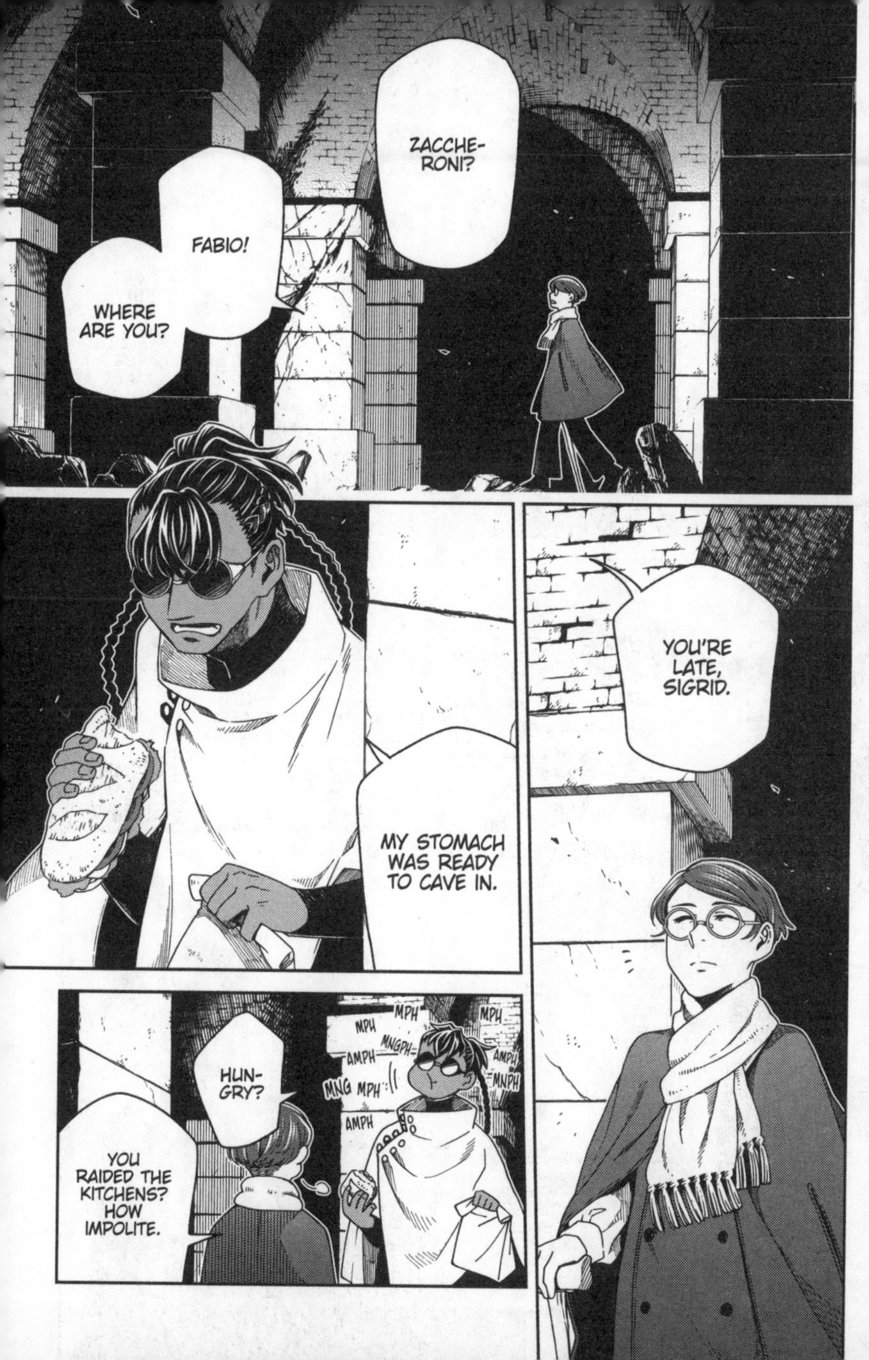
ZACCHE-
RONI?
FABIO!
WHERE
ARE YOU?
YOU'RE
LATE,
SIGRID.
MY STOMACH
WAS READY
TO CAVE IN.
MPH
MPH
MPH
MNGPH
AMPH
AMPH
MNPH
MNG MPH
AMPH
HUN-
GRY?
YOU
RAIDED THE
KITCHENS?
HOW
IMPOLITE.

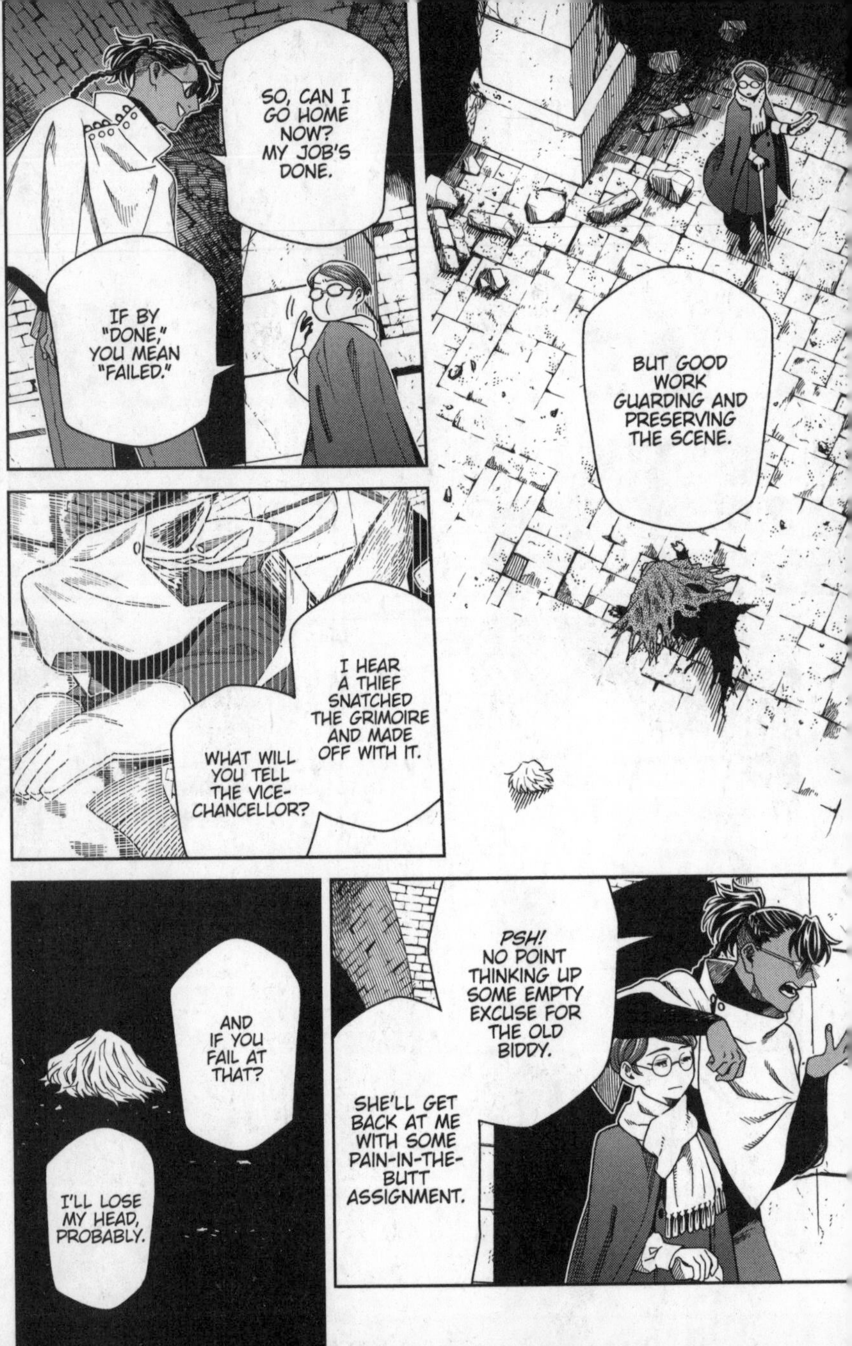
SO, CAN I GO HOME NOW? MY JOB'S DONE.
IF BY "DONE," YOU MEAN "FAILED."
BUT GOOD WORK GUARDING AND PRESERVING THE SCENE.
I HEAR A THIEF SNATCHED THE GRIMOIRE AND MADE OFF WITH IT.
WHAT WILL YOU TELL THE VICE-CHANCELLOR?
PSH! NO POINT THINKING UP SOME EMPTY EXCUSE FOR THE OLD BIDDY.
SHE'LL GET BACK AT ME WITH SOME PAIN-IN-THE-BUTT ASSIGNMENT.
AND IF YOU FAIL AT THAT?
I'LL LOSE MY HEAD, PROBABLY.

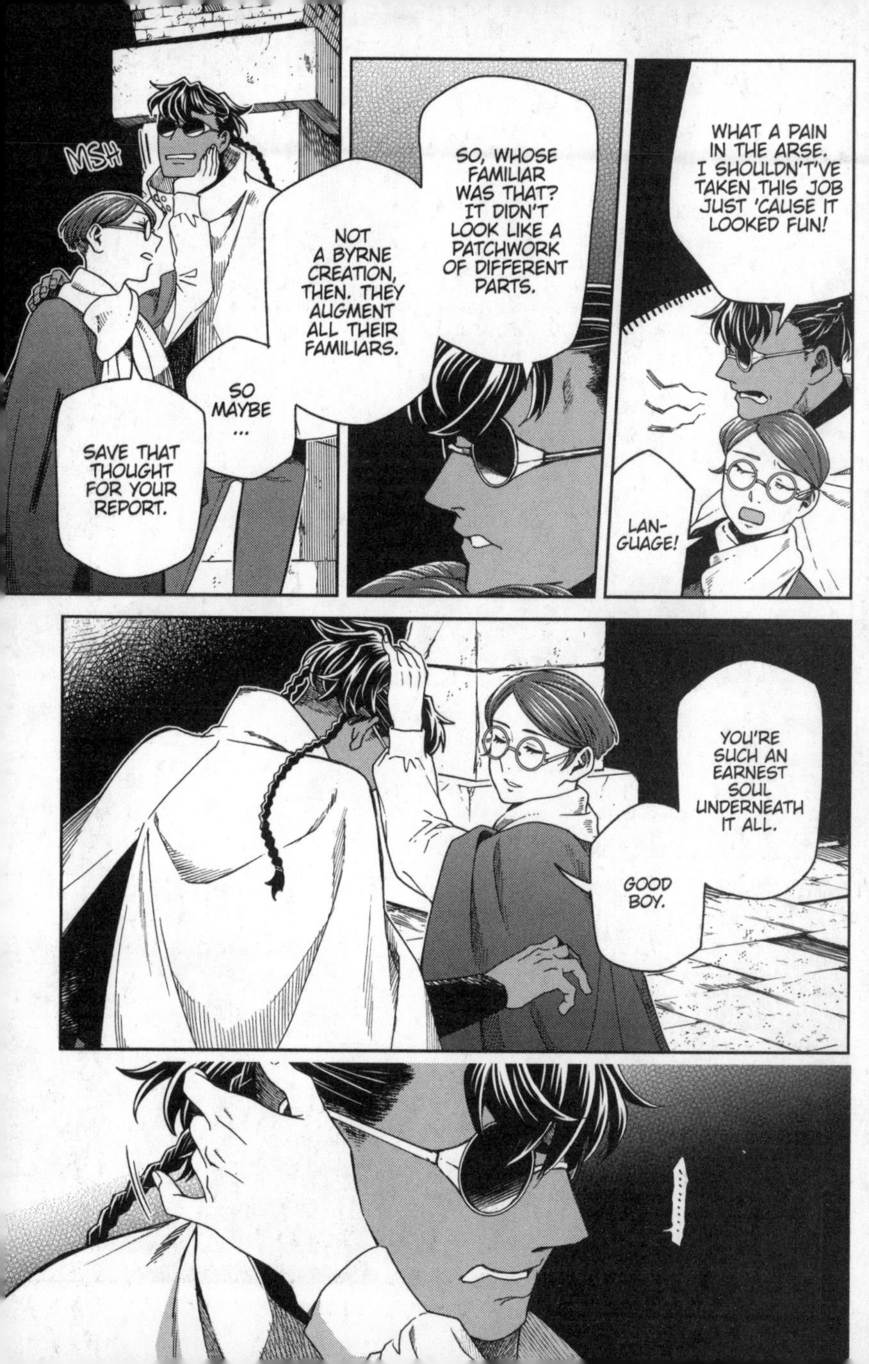
WHAT A PAIN IN THE ARSE. I SHOULDN'T'VE TAKEN THIS JOB JUST 'CAUSE IT LOOKED FUN!
LAN-GUAGE!
SO, WHOSE FAMILIAR WAS THAT? IT DIDN'T LOOK LIKE A PATCHWORK OF DIFFERENT PARTS.
NOT A BYRNE CREATION, THEN. THEY AUGMENT ALL THEIR FAMILIARS.
SO MAYBE ...
SAVE THAT THOUGHT FOR YOUR REPORT.
MSH
YOU'RE SUCH AN EARNEST SOUL UNDERNEATH IT ALL.
GOOD BOY.
......!

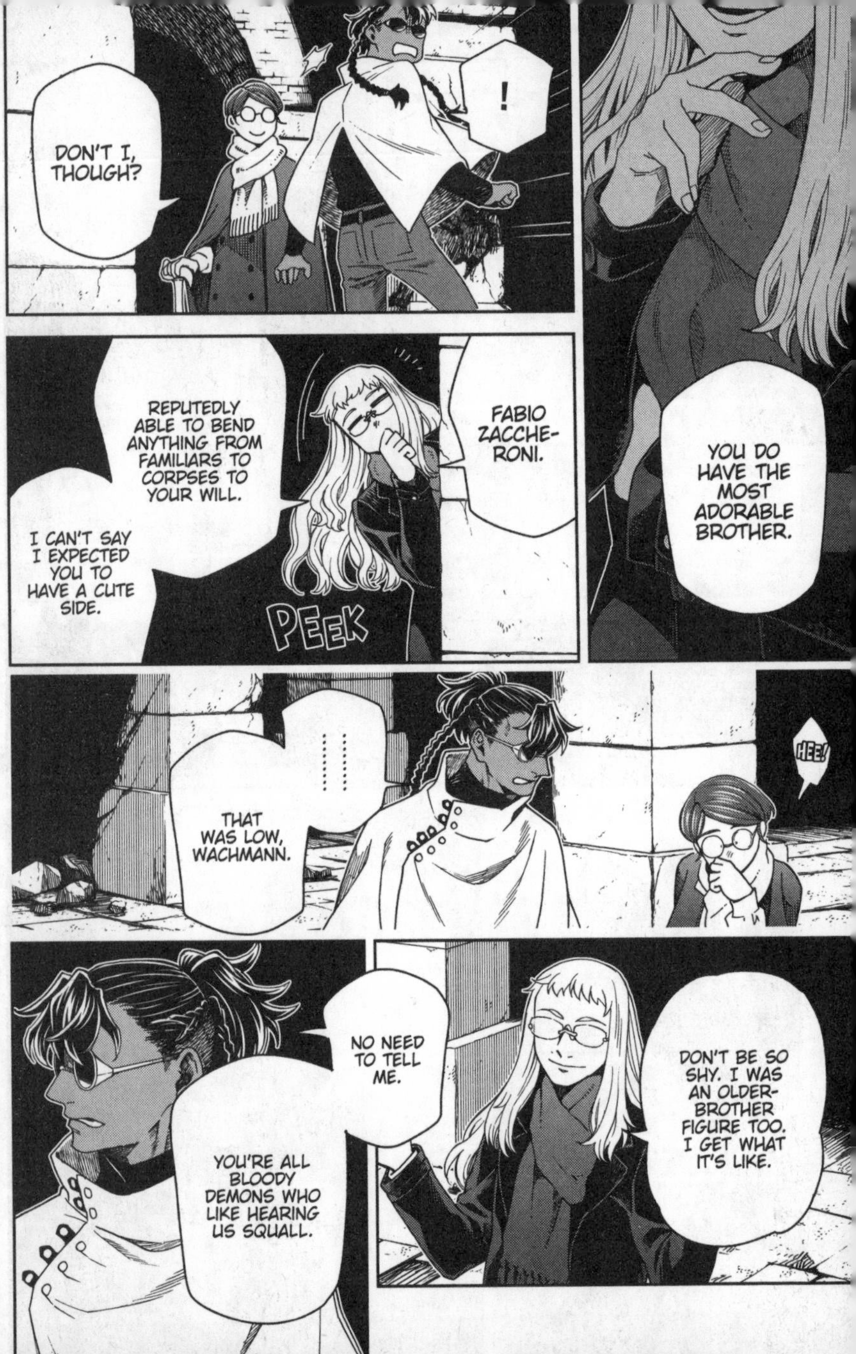
YOU DO HAVE THE MOST ADORABLE BROTHER.
!
DON'T I, THOUGH?
FABIO ZACCHE-RONI.
REPUTEDLY ABLE TO BEND ANYTHING FROM FAMILIARS TO CORPSES TO YOUR WILL.
I CAN'T SAY I EXPECTED YOU TO HAVE A CUTE SIDE.
PEEK
HEE!
......
THAT WAS LOW, WACHMANN.
DON'T BE SO SHY. I WAS AN OLDER-BROTHER FIGURE TOO. I GET WHAT IT'S LIKE.
NO NEED TO TELL ME.
YOU'RE ALL BLOODY DEMONS WHO LIKE HEARING US SQUALL.

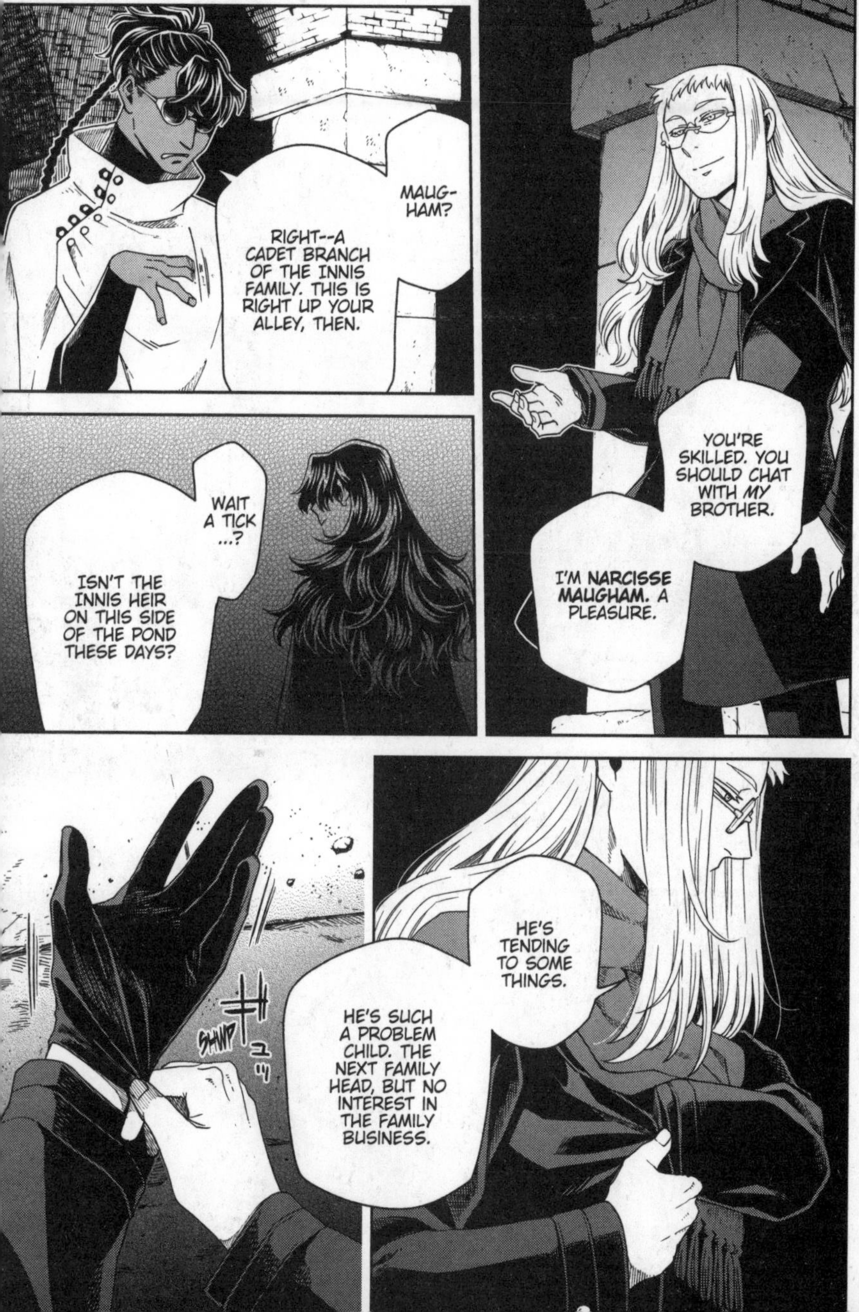
YOU'RE SKILLED. YOU SHOULD CHAT WITH *MY* BROTHER.
I'M **NARCISSE MAUGHAM**. A PLEASURE.
MAUG-HAM?
RIGHT--A CADET BRANCH OF THE INNIS FAMILY. THIS IS RIGHT UP YOUR ALLEY, THEN.
WAIT A TICK ...?
ISN'T THE INNIS HEIR ON THIS SIDE OF THE POND THESE DAYS?
HE'S TENDING TO SOME THINGS.
HE'S SUCH A PROBLEM CHILD. THE NEXT FAMILY HEAD, BUT NO INTEREST IN THE FAMILY BUSINESS.
SHWIP

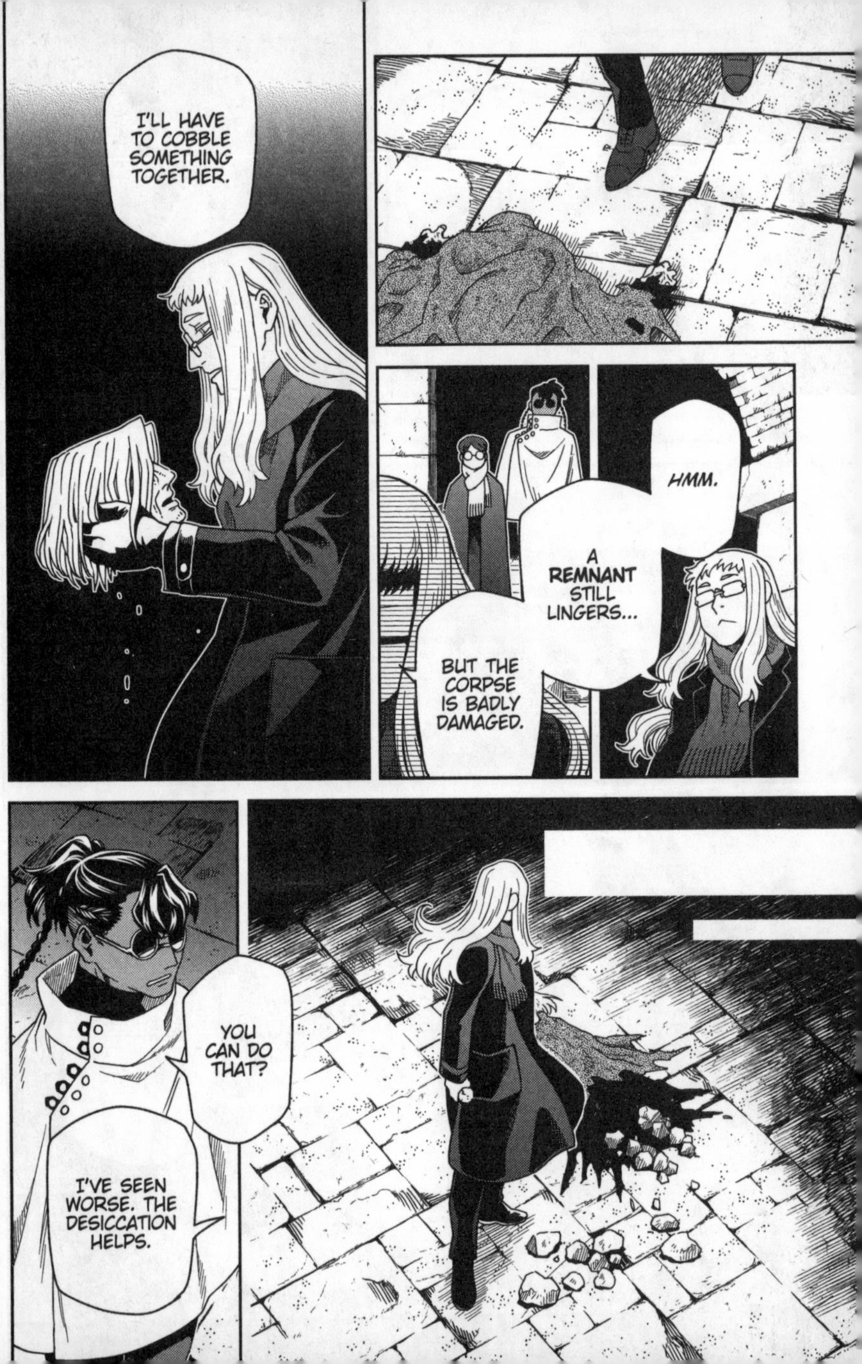
HMM.
A REMNANT STILL LINGERS...
BUT THE CORPSE IS BADLY DAMAGED.
I'LL HAVE TO COBBLE SOMETHING TOGETHER.
YOU CAN DO THAT?
I'VE SEEN WORSE. THE DESICCATION HELPS.

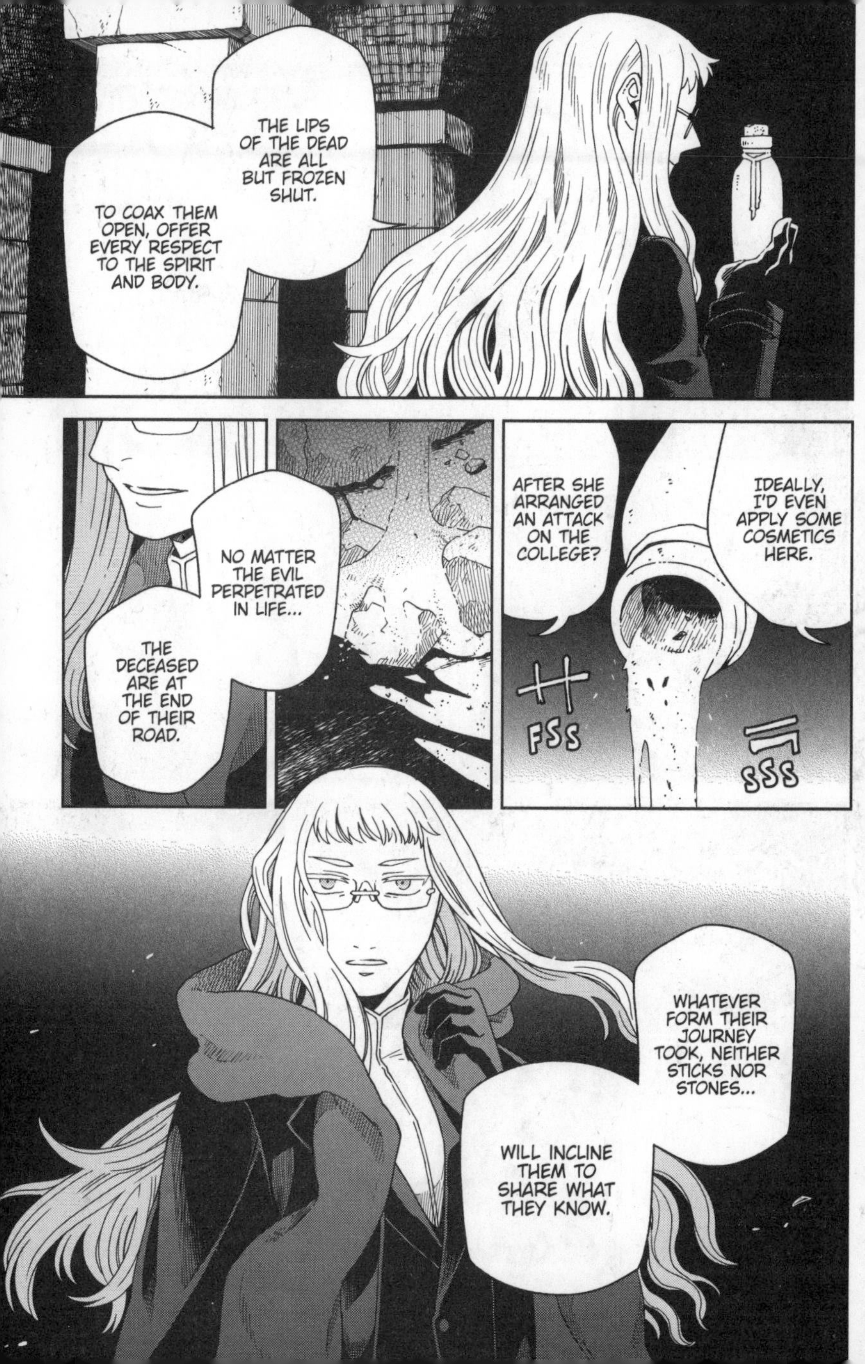
THE LIPS OF THE DEAD ARE ALL BUT FROZEN SHUT.
TO COAX THEM OPEN, OFFER EVERY RESPECT TO THE SPIRIT AND BODY.
IDEALLY, I'D EVEN APPLY SOME COSMETICS HERE.
AFTER SHE ARRANGED AN ATTACK ON THE COLLEGE?
SSS
FSS
NO MATTER THE EVIL PERPETRATED IN LIFE...
THE DECEASED ARE AT THE END OF THEIR ROAD.
WHATEVER FORM THEIR JOURNEY TOOK, NEITHER STICKS NOR STONES...
WILL INCLINE THEM TO SHARE WHAT THEY KNOW.

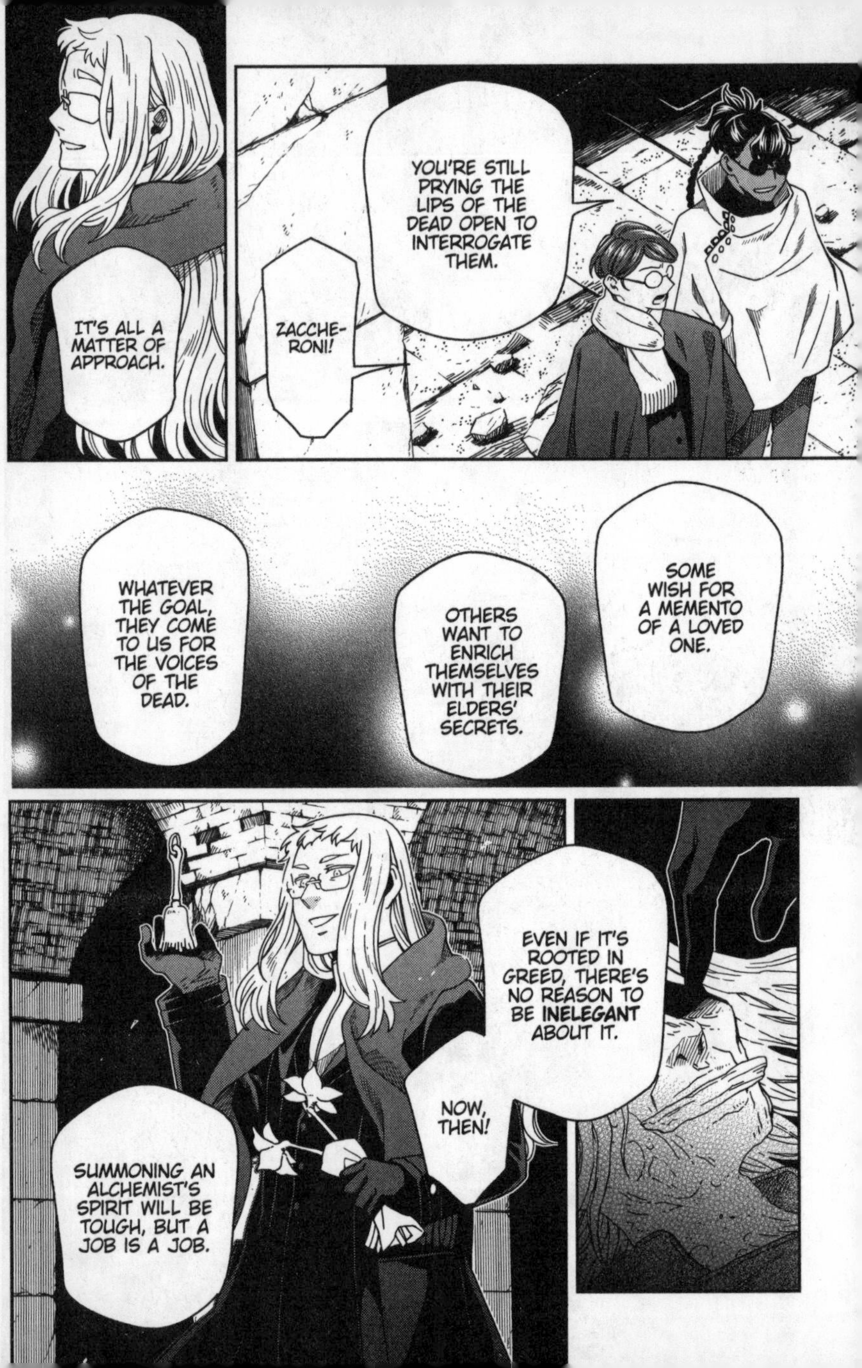
YOU'RE STILL PRYING THE LIPS OF THE DEAD OPEN TO INTERROGATE THEM.
ZACCHE-RONI!
IT'S ALL A MATTER OF APPROACH.
SOME WISH FOR A MEMENTO OF A LOVED ONE.
OTHERS WANT TO ENRICH THEMSELVES WITH THEIR ELDERS' SECRETS.
WHATEVER THE GOAL, THEY COME TO US FOR THE VOICES OF THE DEAD.
EVEN IF IT'S ROOTED IN GREED, THERE'S NO REASON TO BE INELEGANT ABOUT IT.
NOW, THEN!
SUMMONING AN ALCHEMIST'S SPIRIT WILL BE TOUGH, BUT A JOB IS A JOB.

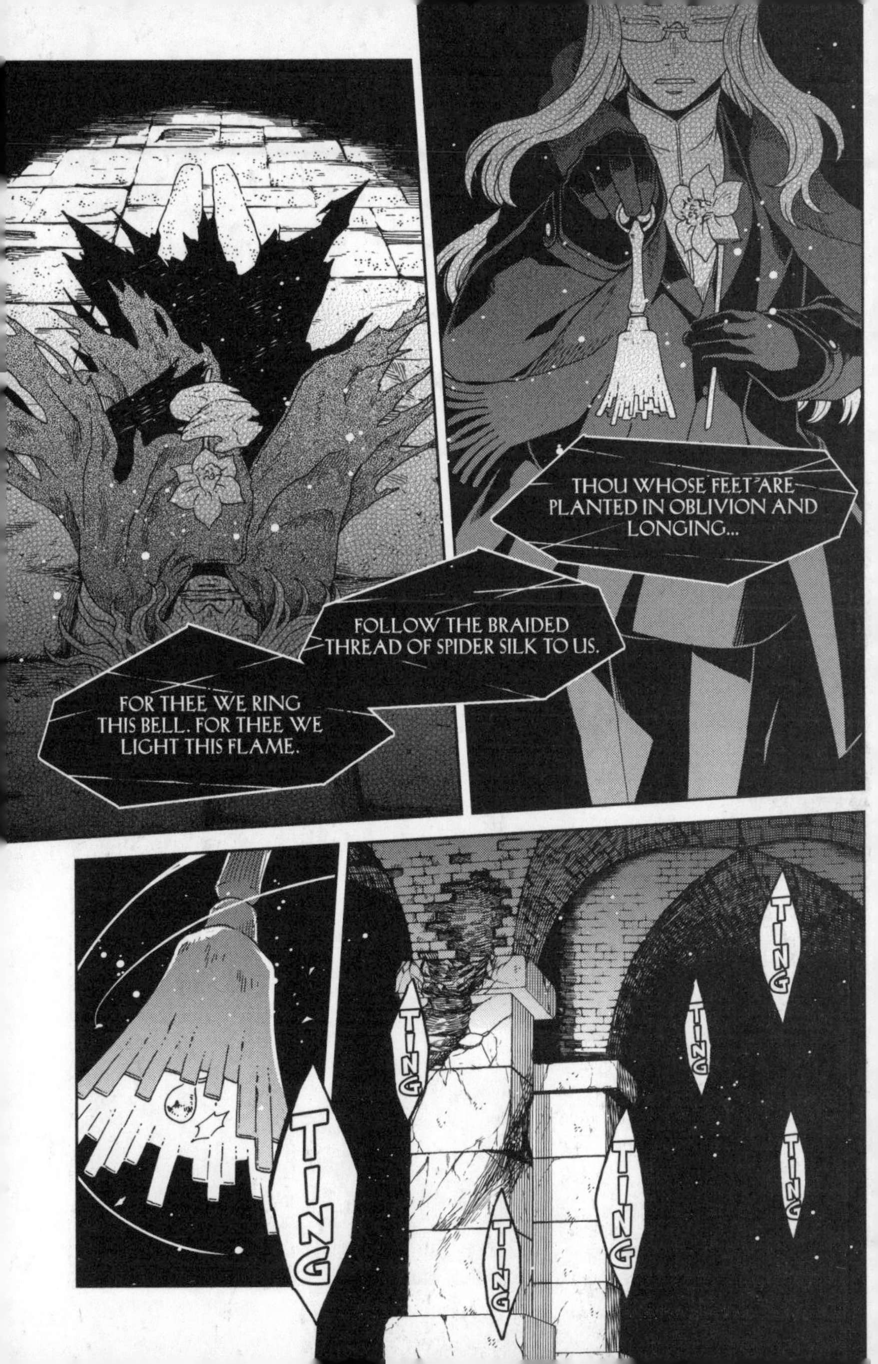
THOU WHOSE FEET ARE PLANTED IN OBLIVION AND LONGING...
FOLLOW THE BRAIDED THREAD OF SPIDER SILK TO US.
FOR THEE WE RING THIS BELL. FOR THEE WE LIGHT THIS FLAME.
TING
TING
TING
TING
TING
TING
TING

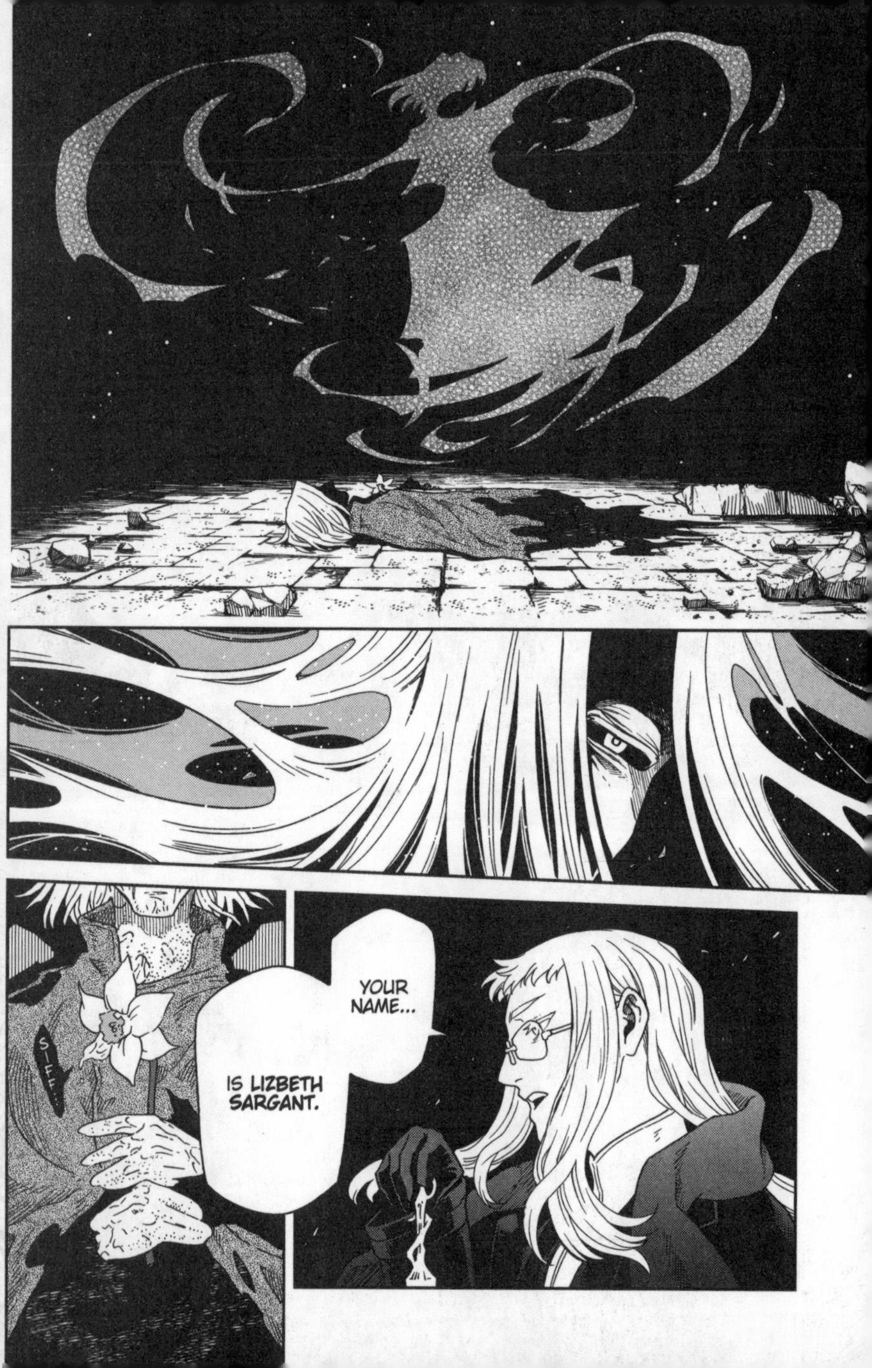
SIFF.
YOUR NAME...
IS LIZBETH SARGANT.

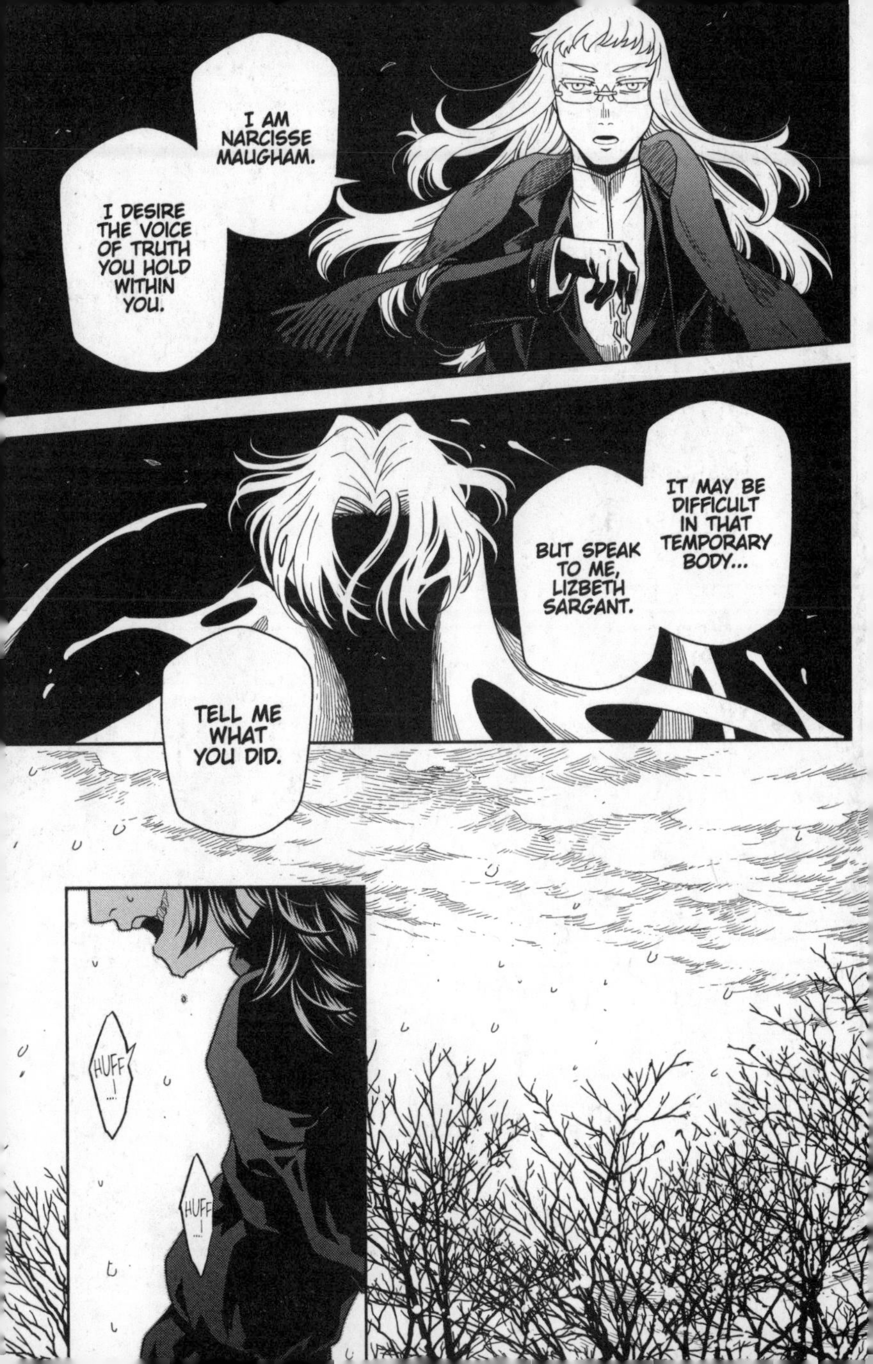
I AM NARCISSE MAUGHAM.
I DESIRE THE VOICE OF TRUTH YOU HOLD WITHIN YOU.
IT MAY BE DIFFICULT IN THAT TEMPORARY BODY...
BUT SPEAK TO ME, LIZBETH SARGANT.
TELL ME WHAT YOU DID.
HUFF!...
HUFF!...

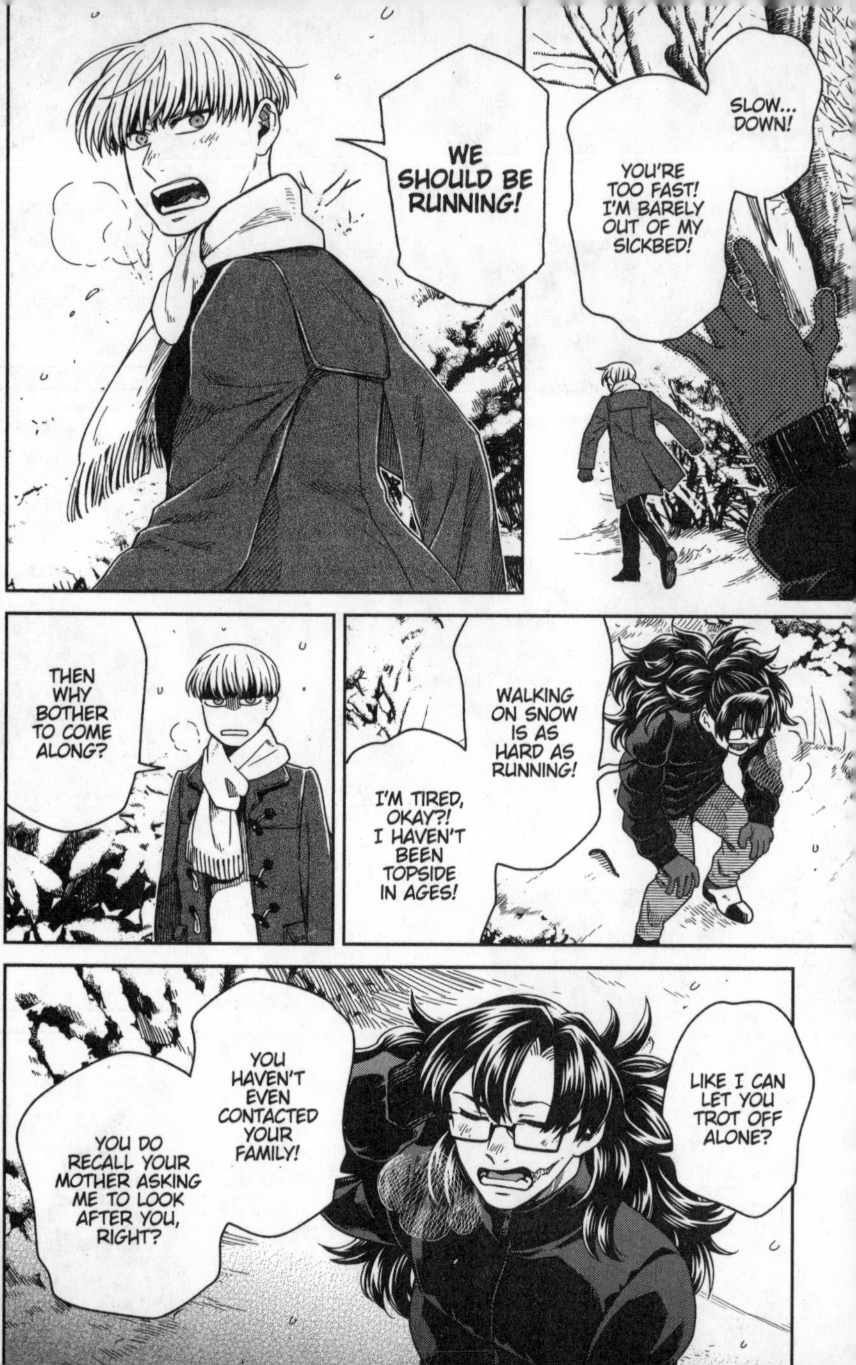
SLOW... DOWN!
YOU'RE TOO FAST! I'M BARELY OUT OF MY SICKBED!
WE SHOULD BE RUNNING!
WALKING ON SNOW IS AS HARD AS RUNNING!
I'M TIRED, OKAY?! I HAVEN'T BEEN TOPSIDE IN AGES!
THEN WHY BOTHER TO COME ALONG?
LIKE I CAN LET YOU TROT OFF ALONE?
YOU HAVEN'T EVEN CONTACTED YOUR FAMILY!
YOU DO RECALL YOUR MOTHER ASKING ME TO LOOK AFTER YOU, RIGHT?

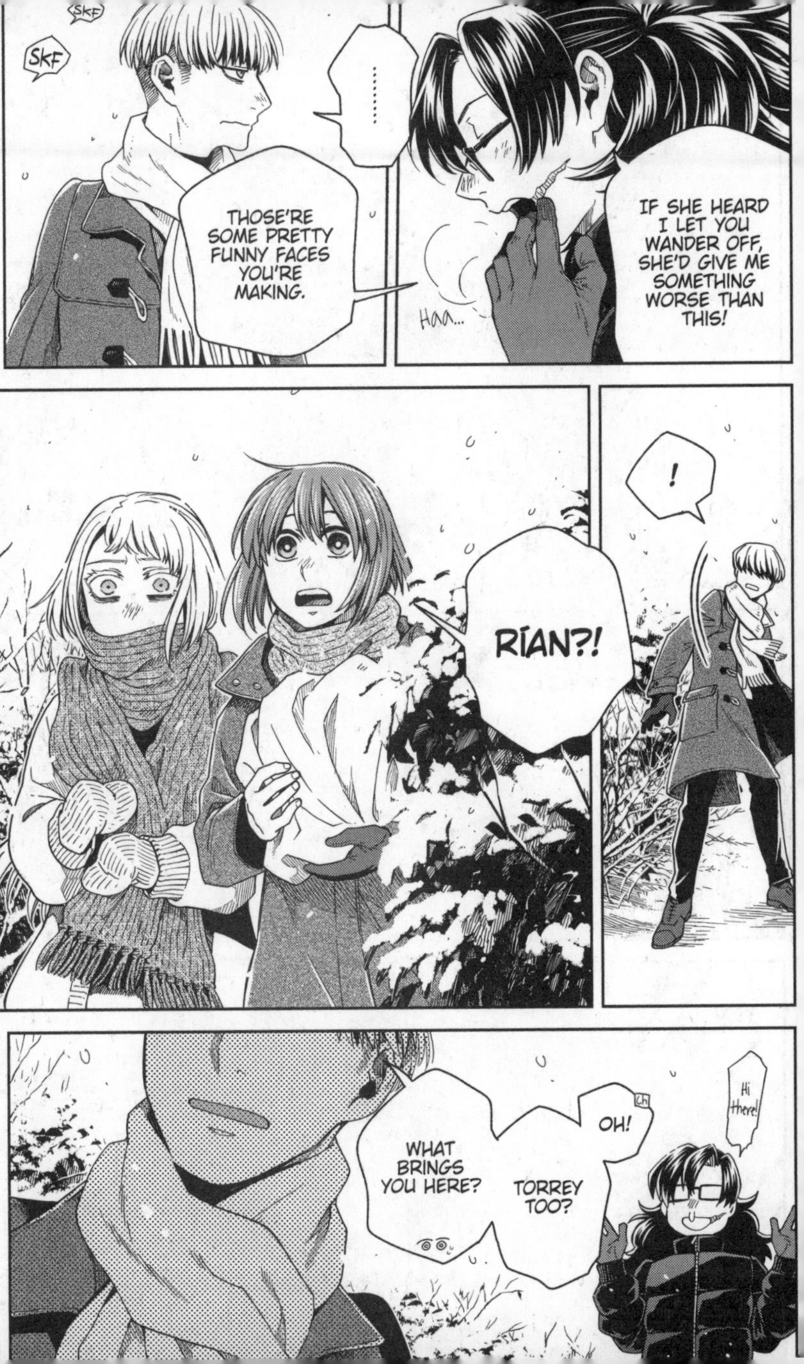
SKF
SKF
......
THOSE'RE SOME PRETTY FUNNY FACES YOU'RE MAKING.
Haa...
IF SHE HEARD I LET YOU WANDER OFF, SHE'D GIVE ME SOMETHING WORSE THAN THIS!
!
RIAN?!
Hi there!
OH!
TORREY TOO?
WHAT BRINGS YOU HERE?

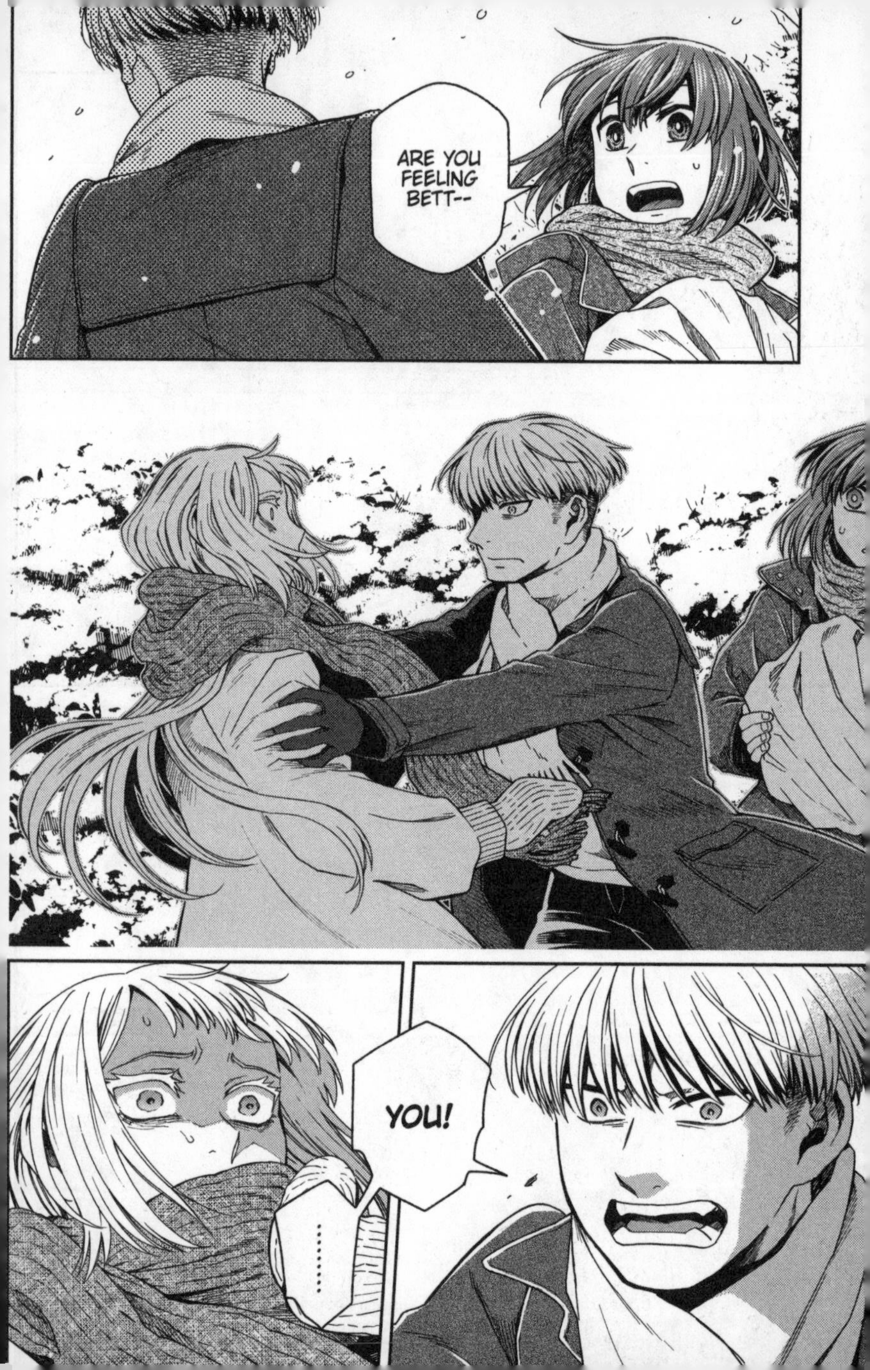
ARE YOU FEELING BETT--
YOU!
......

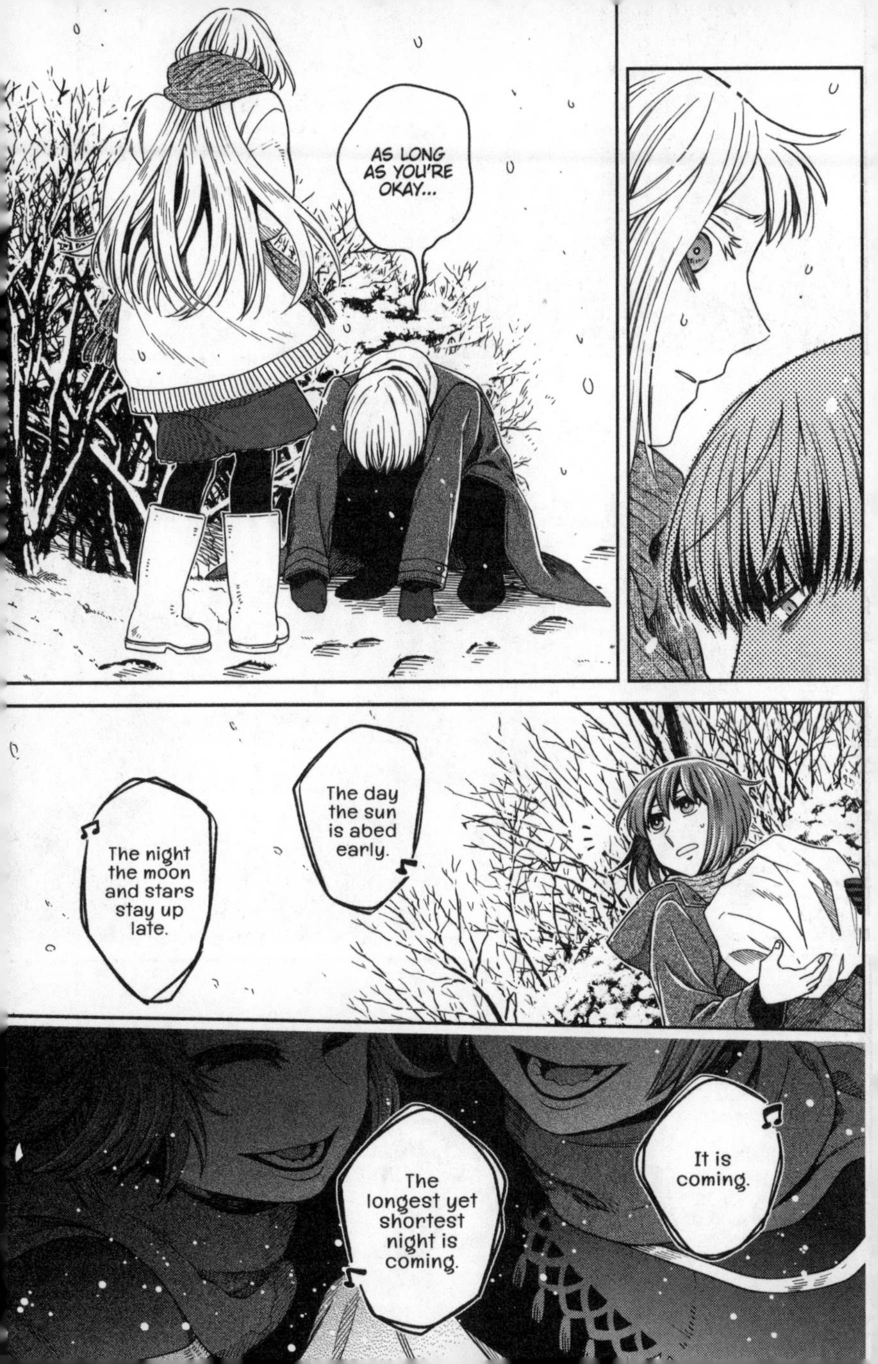
AS LONG AS YOU'RE OKAY...
The day the sun is abed early.
The night the moon and stars stay up late.
It is coming.
The longest yet shortest night is coming.

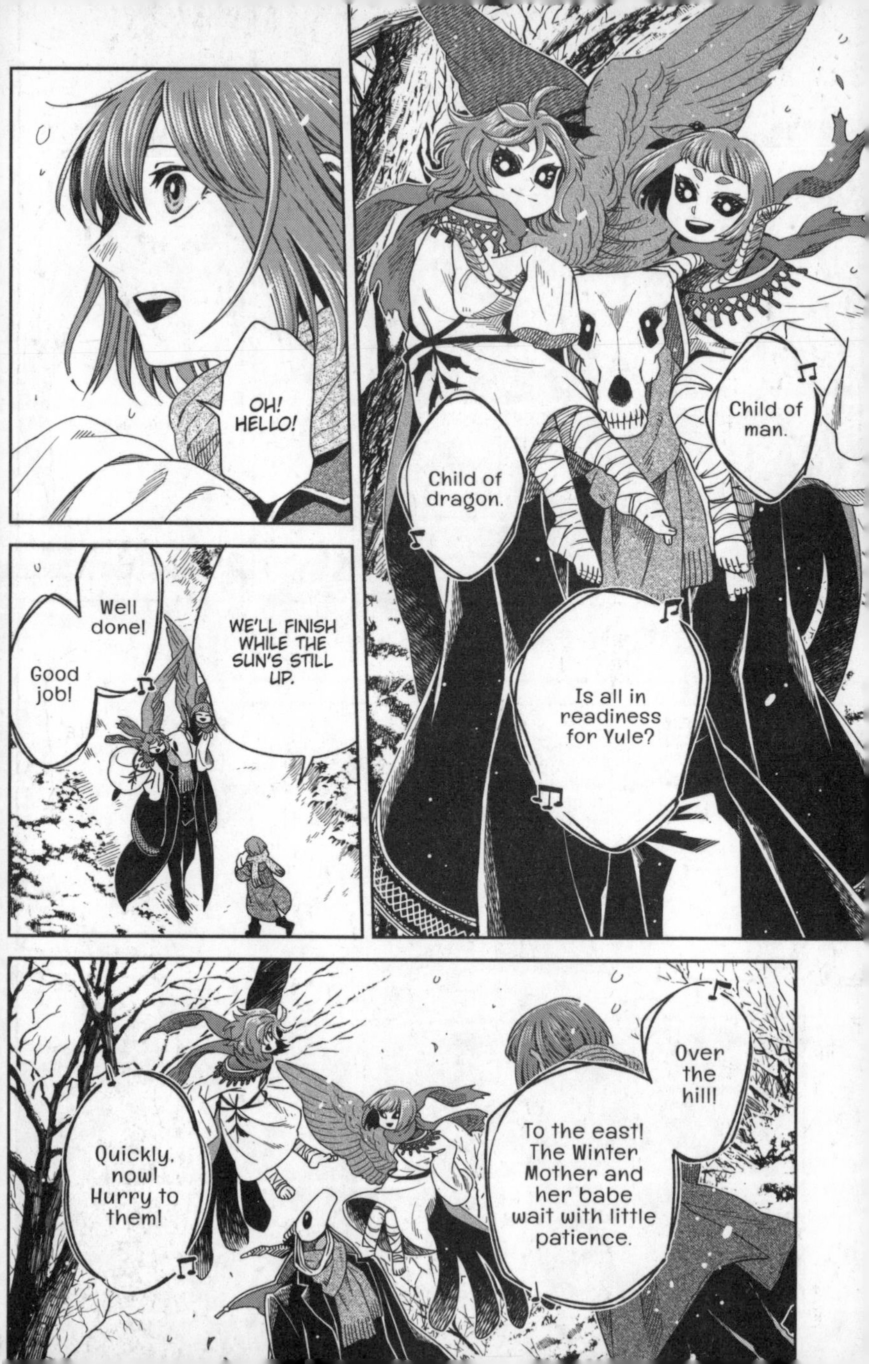
Child of man.
Child of dragon.
Is all in readiness for Yule?
OH! HELLO!
WE'LL FINISH WHILE THE SUN'S STILL UP.
Well done!
Good job!
Over the hill!
To the east! The Winter Mother and her babe wait with little patience.
Quickly, now! Hurry to them!

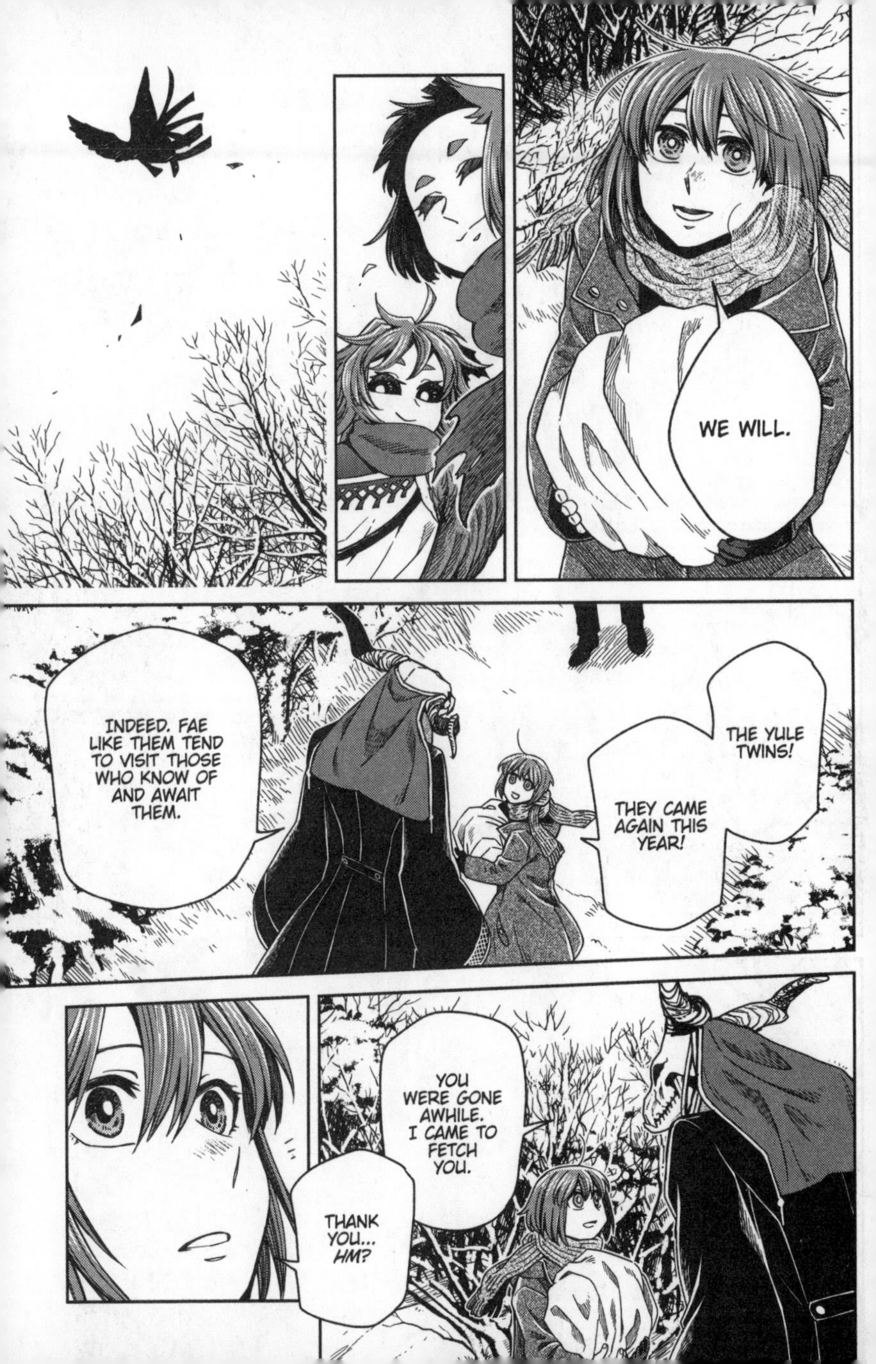
WE WILL.
THE YULE TWINS!
THEY CAME AGAIN THIS YEAR!
INDEED. FAE LIKE THEM TEND TO VISIT THOSE WHO KNOW OF AND AWAIT THEM.
YOU WERE GONE AWHILE. I CAME TO FETCH YOU.
THANK YOU... HM?

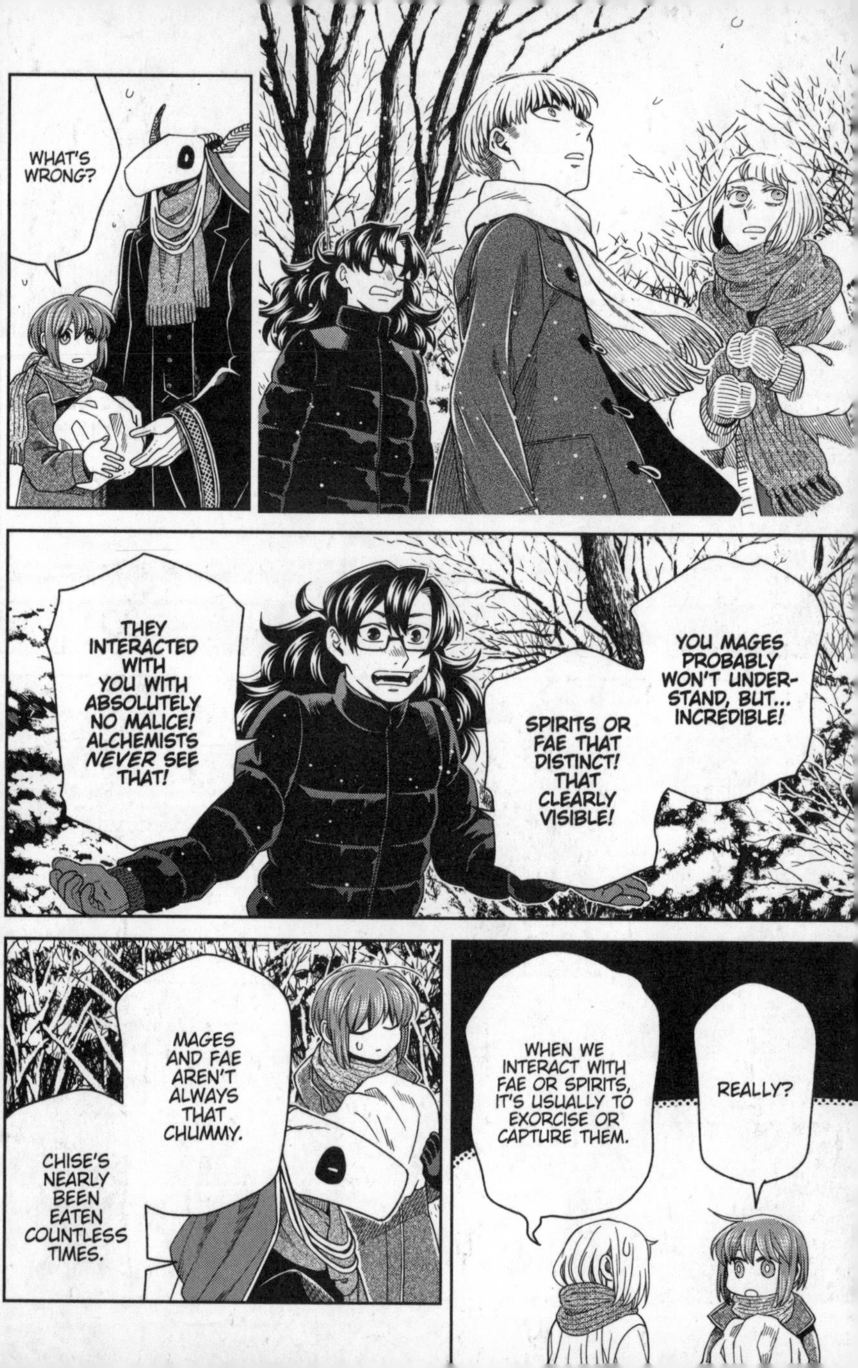
WHAT'S WRONG?
YOU MAGES PROBABLY WON'T UNDER-STAND, BUT... INCREDIBLE!
SPIRITS OR FAE THAT DISTINCT! THAT CLEARLY VISIBLE!
THEY INTERACTED WITH YOU WITH ABSOLUTELY NO MALICE! ALCHEMISTS *NEVER* SEE THAT!
REALLY?
WHEN WE INTERACT WITH FAE OR SPIRITS, IT'S USUALLY TO EXORCISE OR CAPTURE THEM.
MAGES AND FAE AREN'T ALWAYS THAT CHUMMY.
CHISE'S NEARLY BEEN EATEN COUNTLESS TIMES.

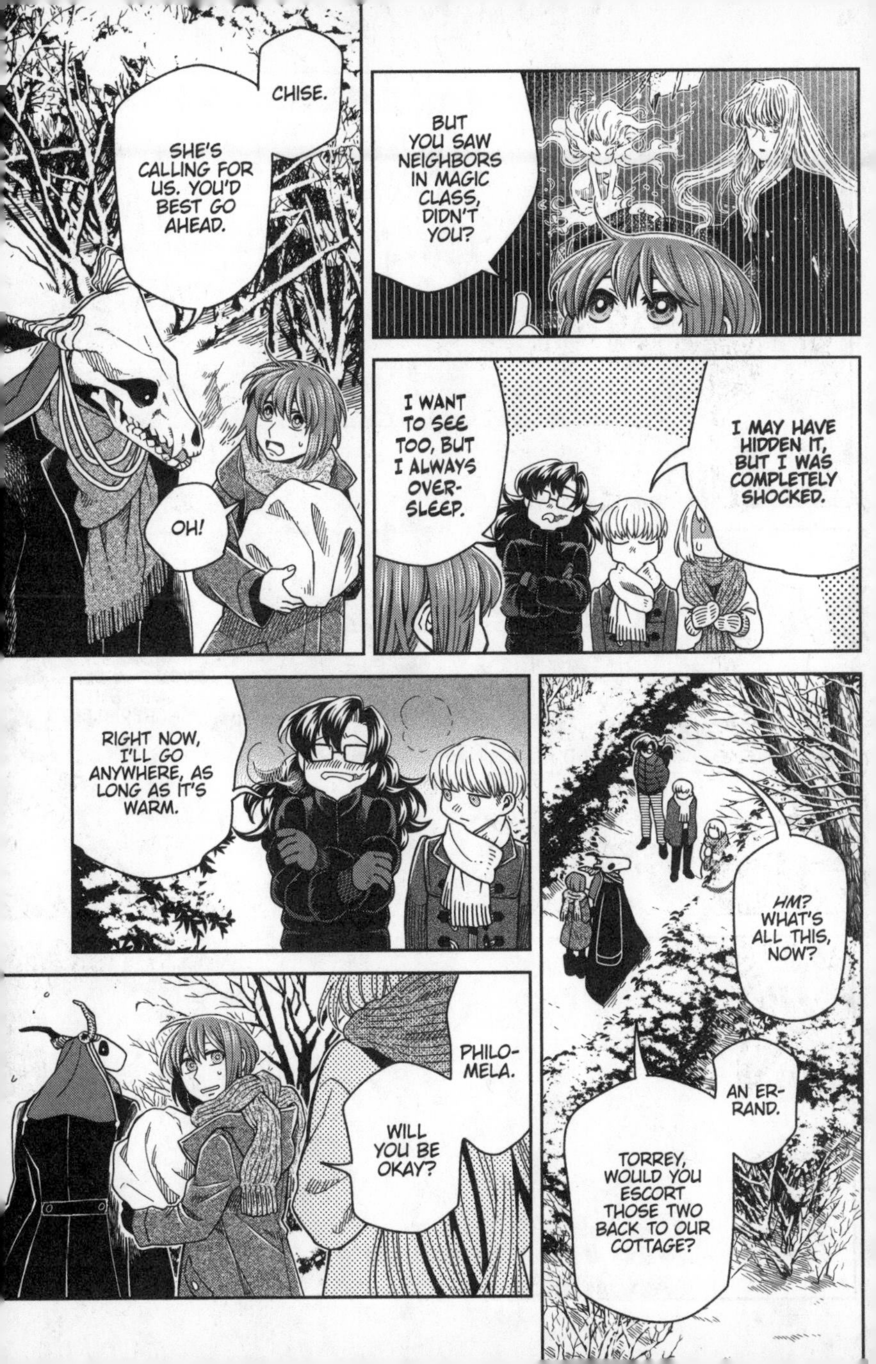
BUT YOU SAW NEIGHBORS IN MAGIC CLASS, DIDN'T YOU?
I MAY HAVE HIDDEN IT, BUT I WAS COMPLETELY SHOCKED.
I WANT TO SEE TOO, BUT I ALWAYS OVER-SLEEP.
CHISE.
SHE'S CALLING FOR US. YOU'D BEST GO AHEAD.
OH!
HM? WHAT'S ALL THIS, NOW?
AN ER-RAND.
TORREY, WOULD YOU ESCORT THOSE TWO BACK TO OUR COTTAGE?
RIGHT NOW, I'LL GO ANYWHERE, AS LONG AS IT'S WARM.
PHILO-MELA.
WILL YOU BE OKAY?

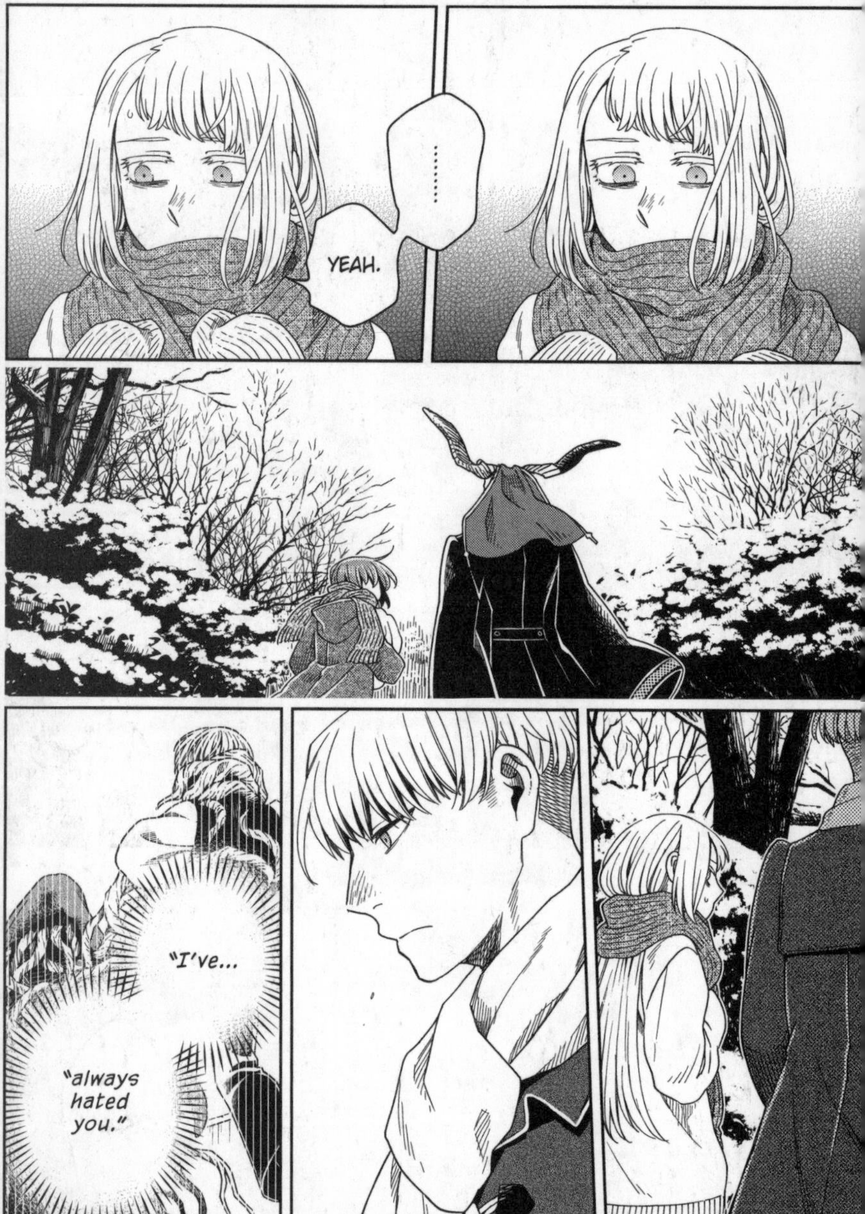
......
YEAH.
"I've...
"always hated you."

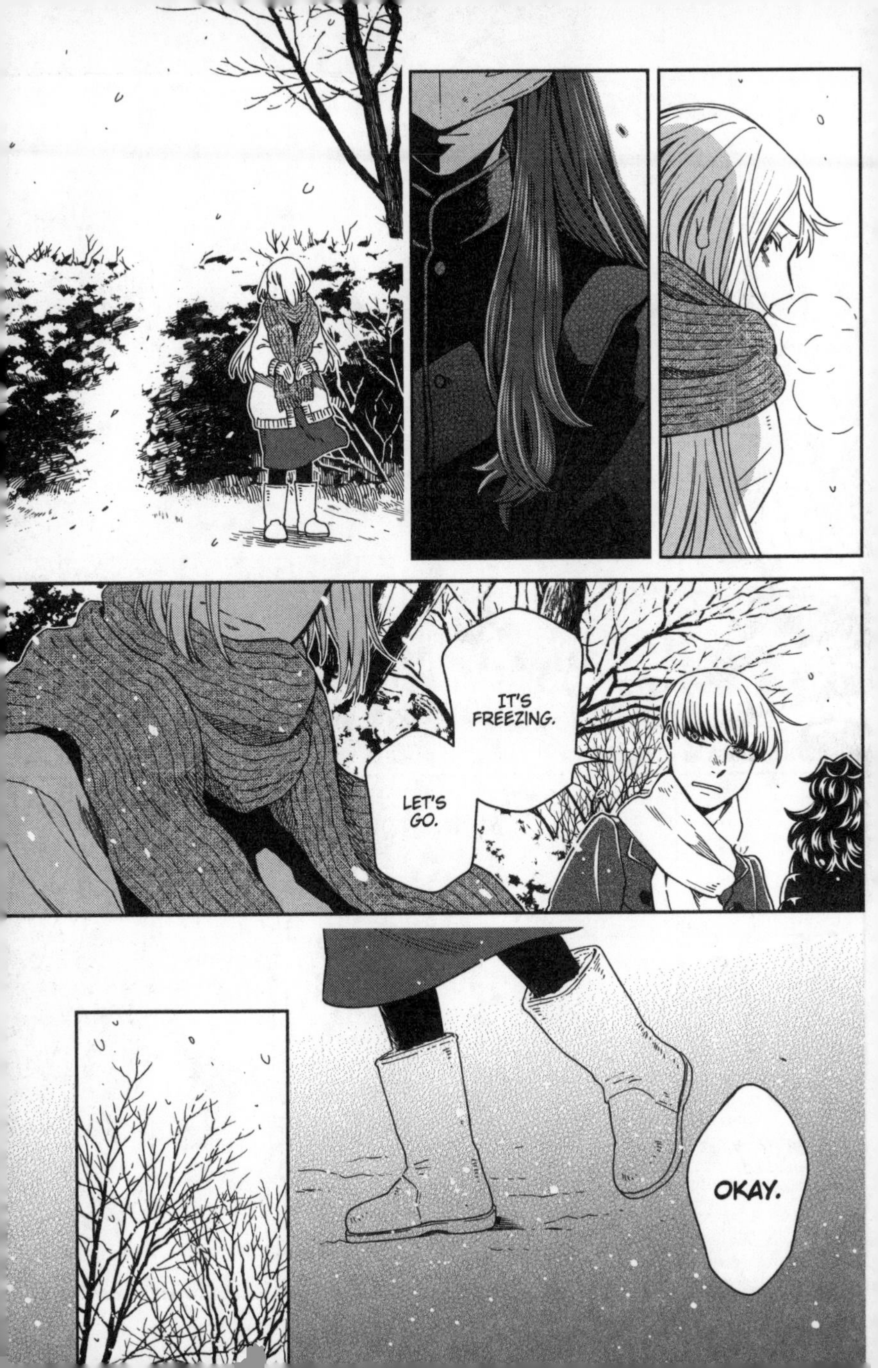
IT'S FREEZING.
LET'S GO.
OKAY.

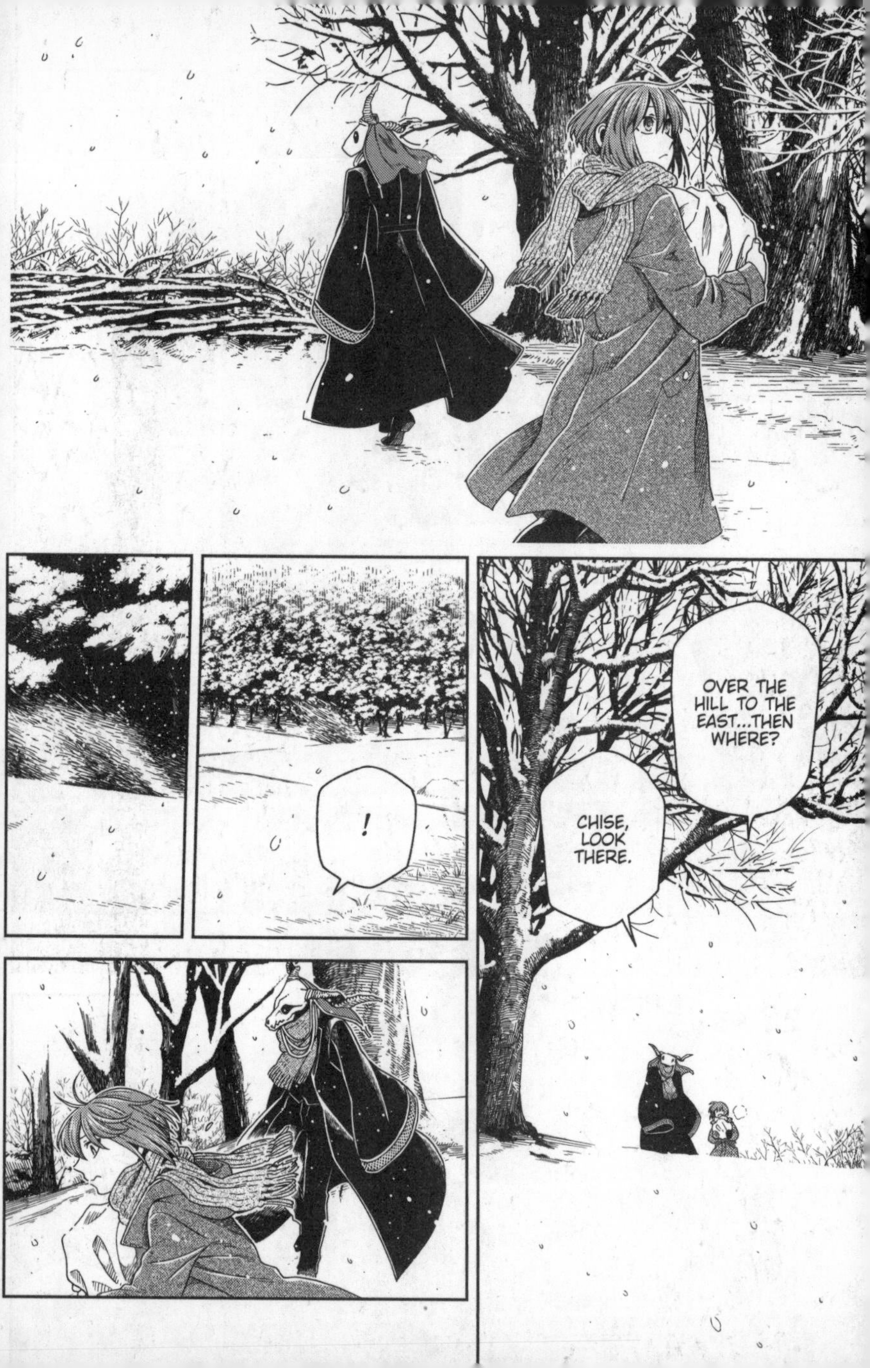
OVER THE HILL TO THE EAST...THEN WHERE?
CHISE, LOOK THERE.
!

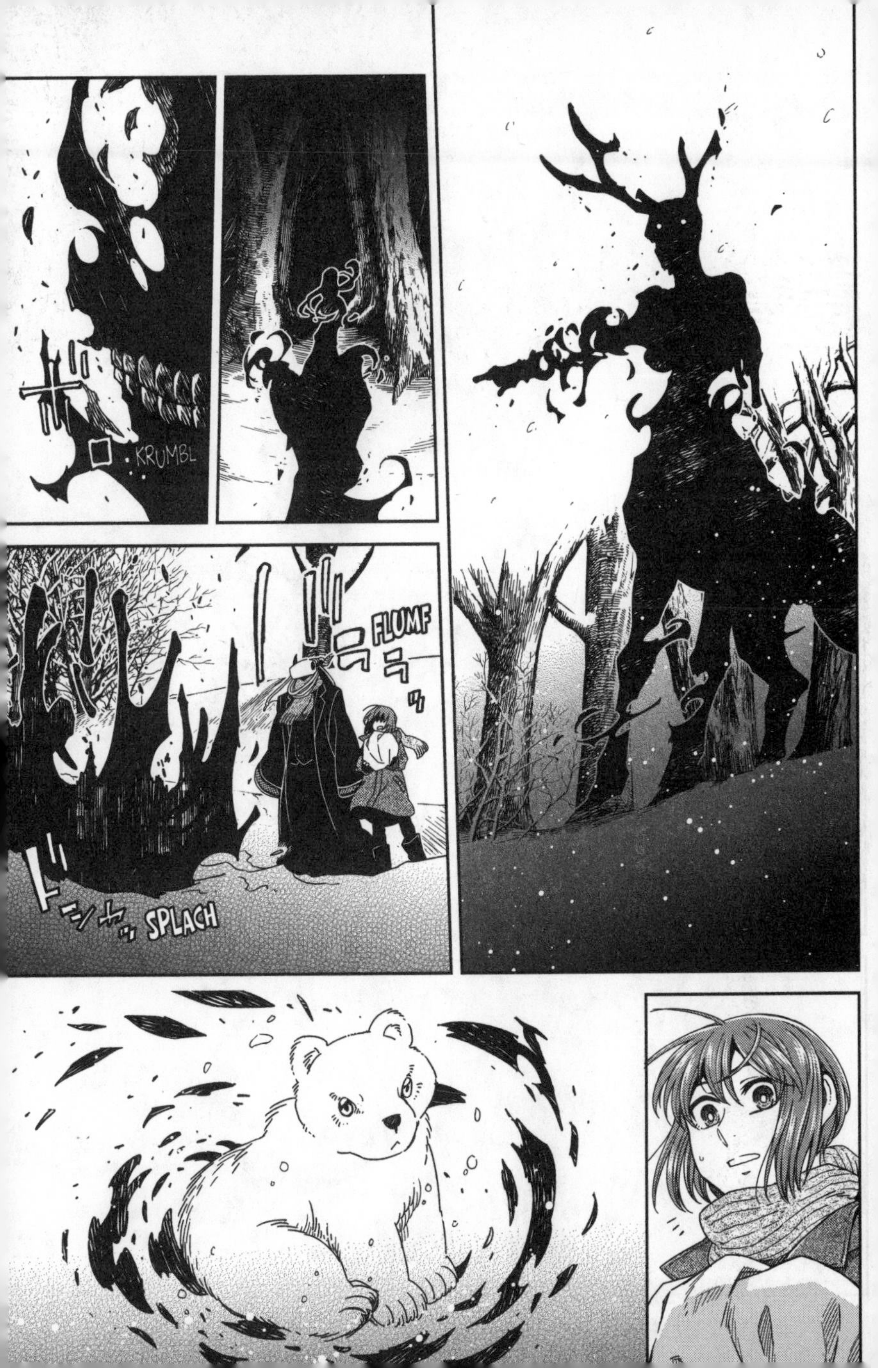
KRUMBL
FLUMF
SPLACH

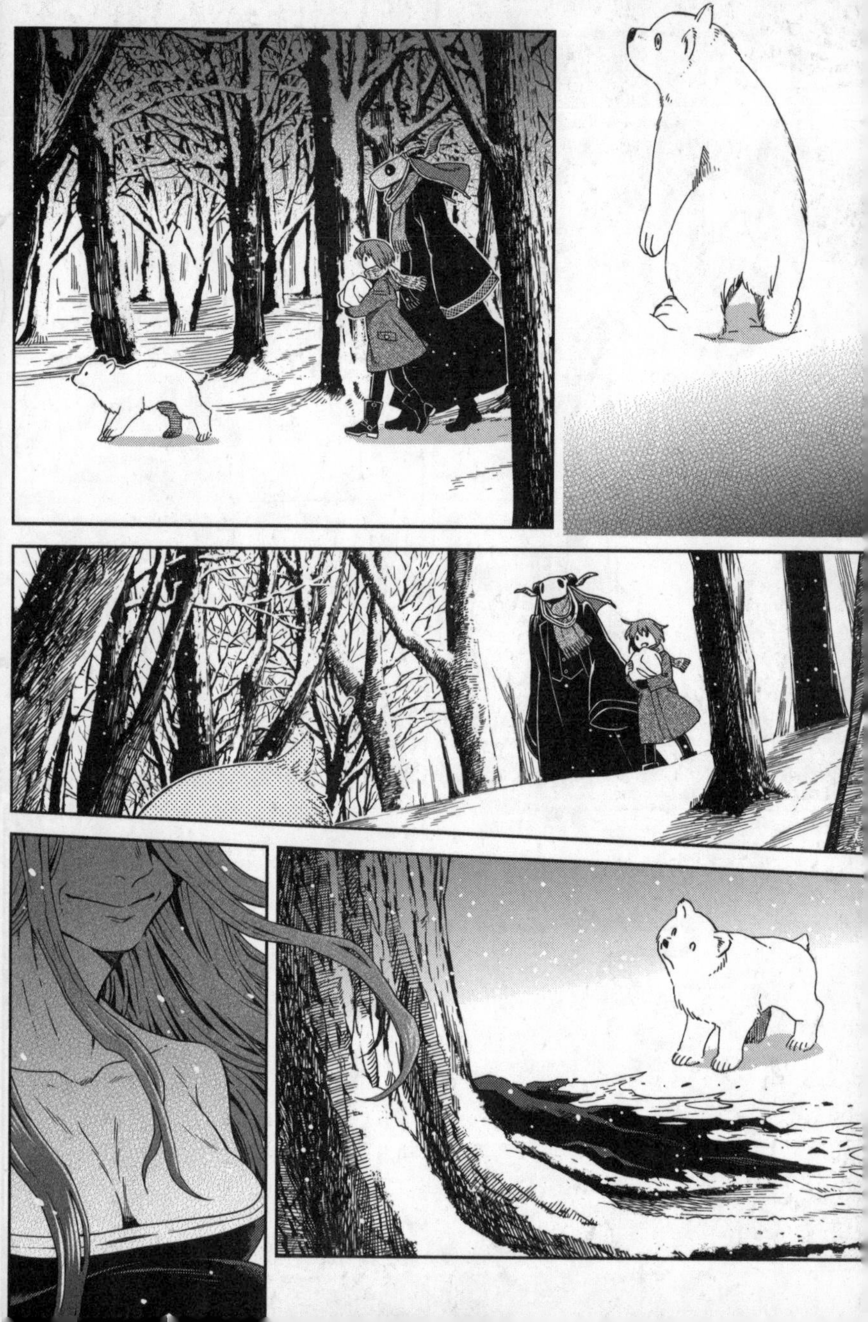

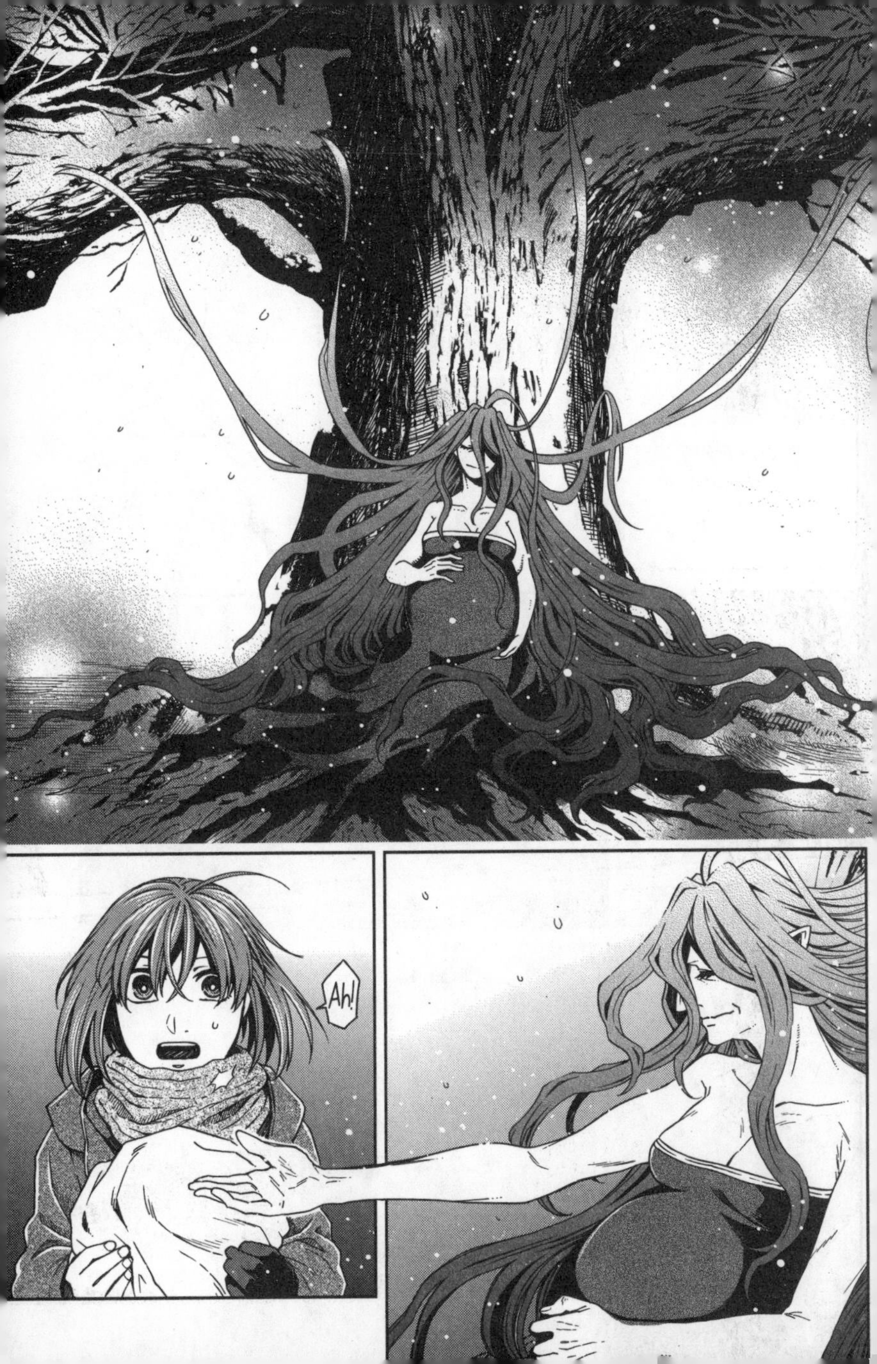
Ah!

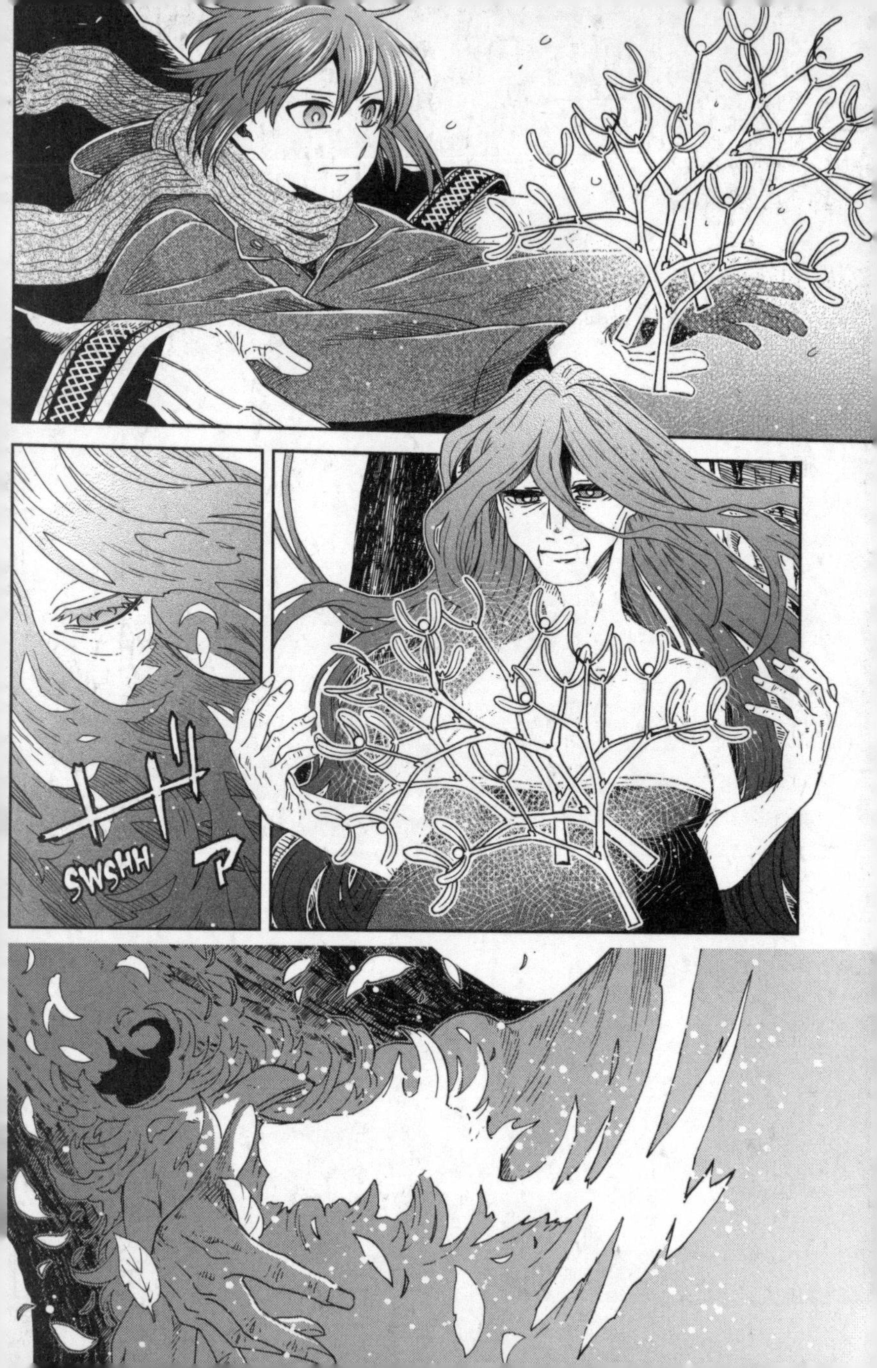

ザァ
SWSHH

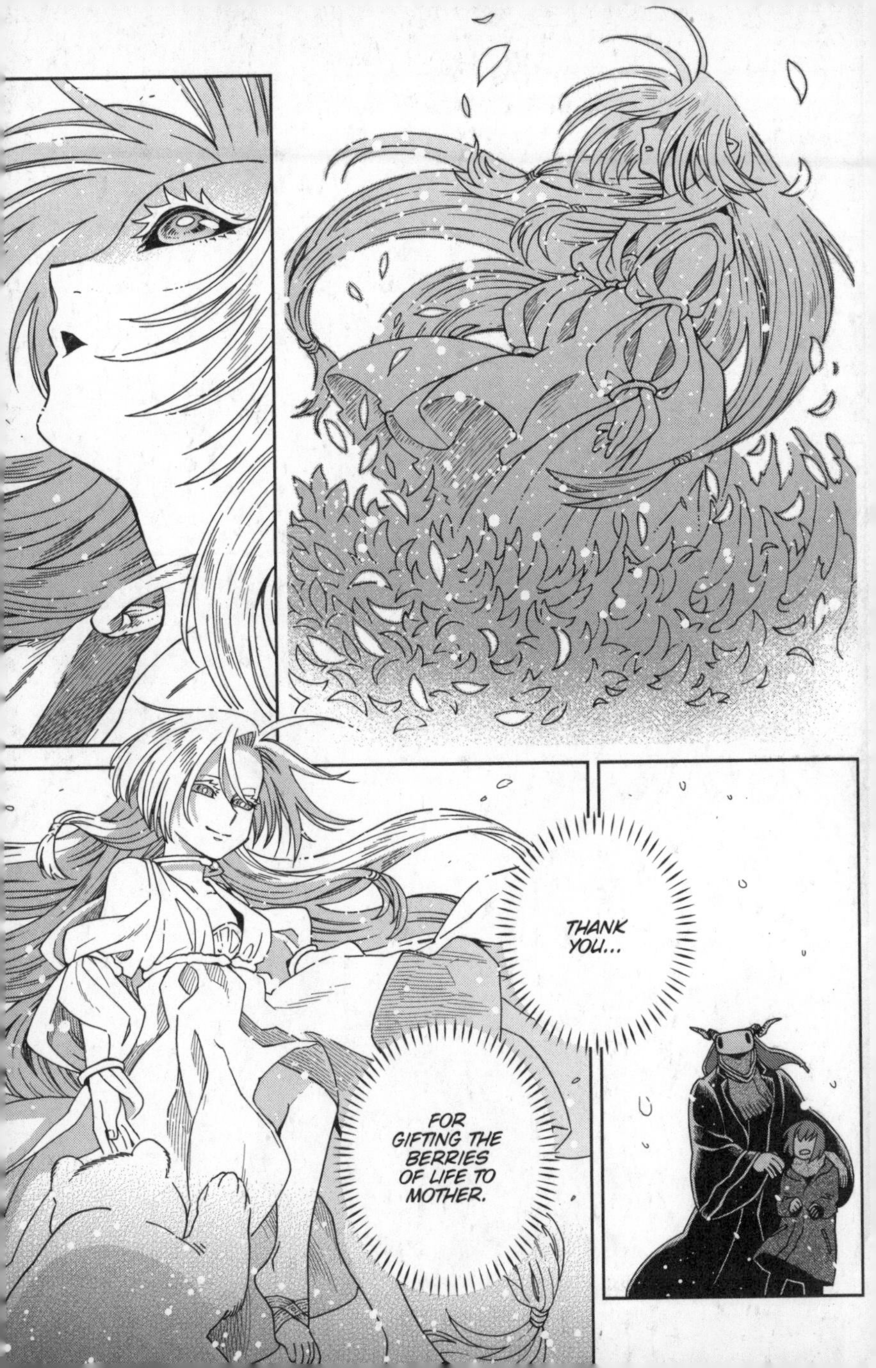
THANK YOU...
FOR GIFTING THE BERRIES OF LIFE TO MOTHER.

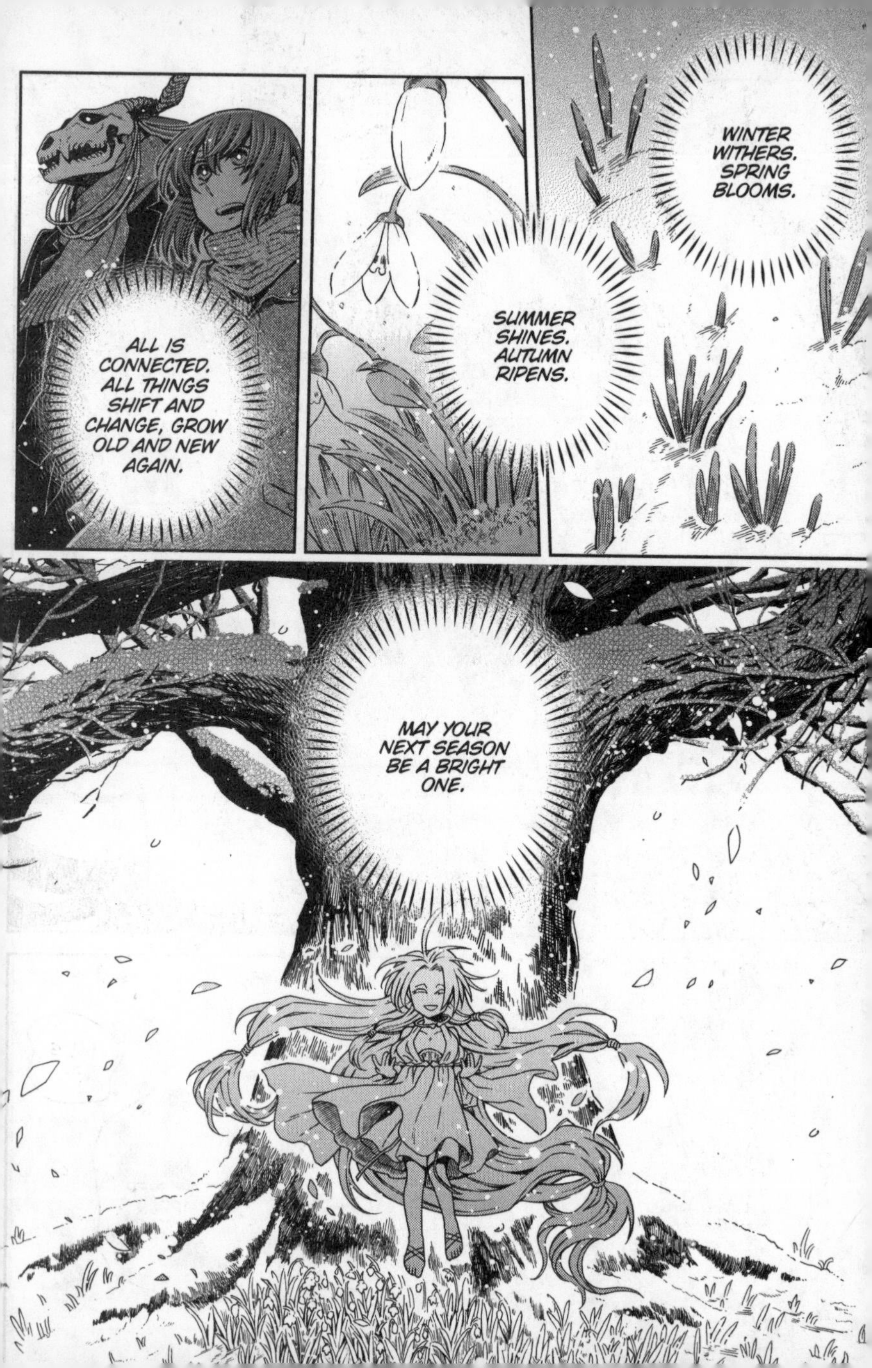
WINTER WITHERS. SPRING BLOOMS.
SUMMER SHINES. AUTUMN RIPENS.
ALL IS CONNECTED. ALL THINGS SHIFT AND CHANGE, GROW OLD AND NEW AGAIN.
MAY YOUR NEXT SEASON BE A BRIGHT ONE.

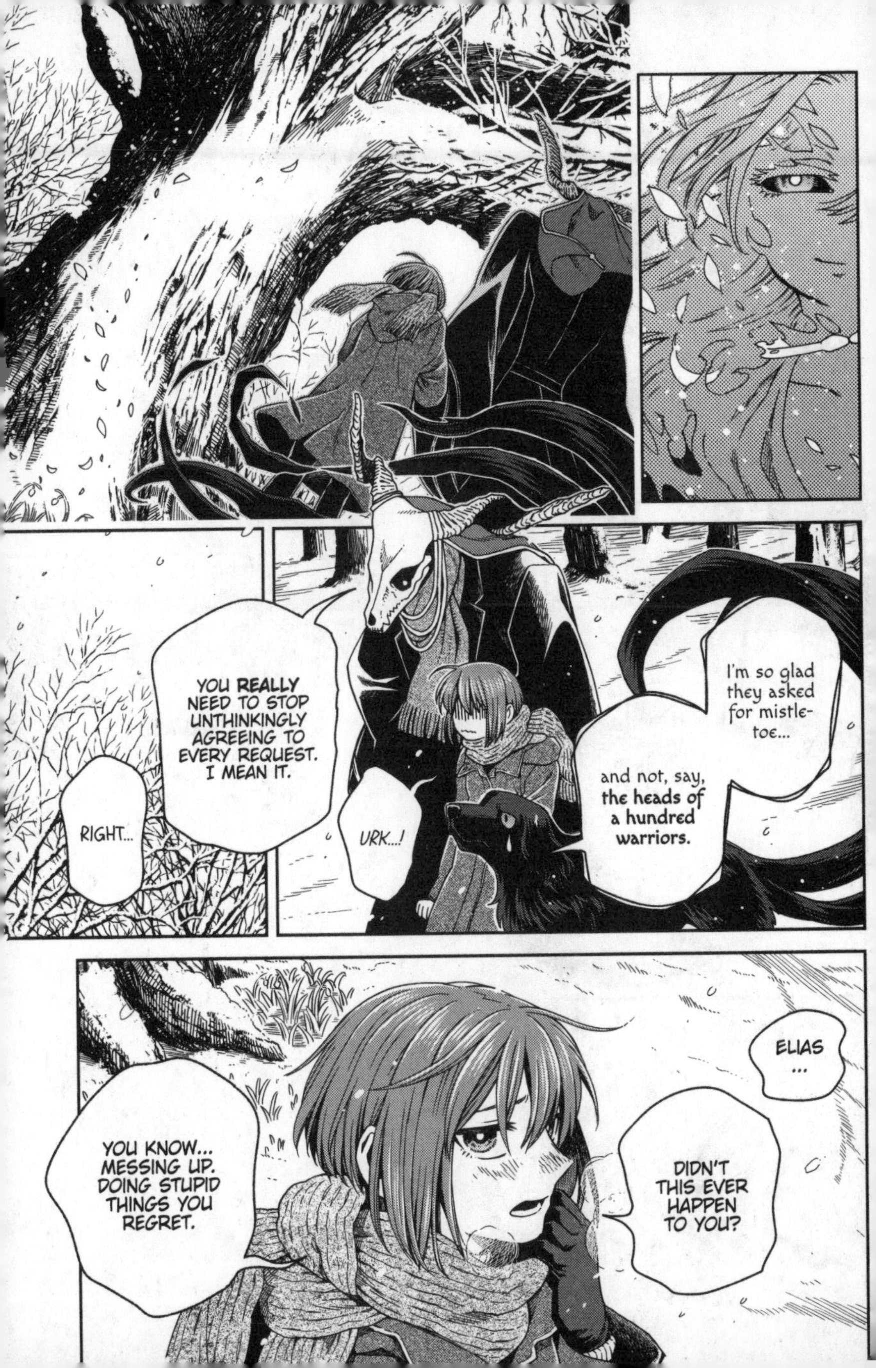
I'm so glad they asked for mistle-toe...
and not, say, the heads of a hundred warriors.
URK...!
YOU REALLY NEED TO STOP UNTHINKINGLY AGREEING TO EVERY REQUEST. I MEAN IT.
RIGHT...
ELIAS ...
DIDN'T THIS EVER HAPPEN TO YOU?
YOU KNOW... MESSING UP. DOING STUPID THINGS YOU REGRET.

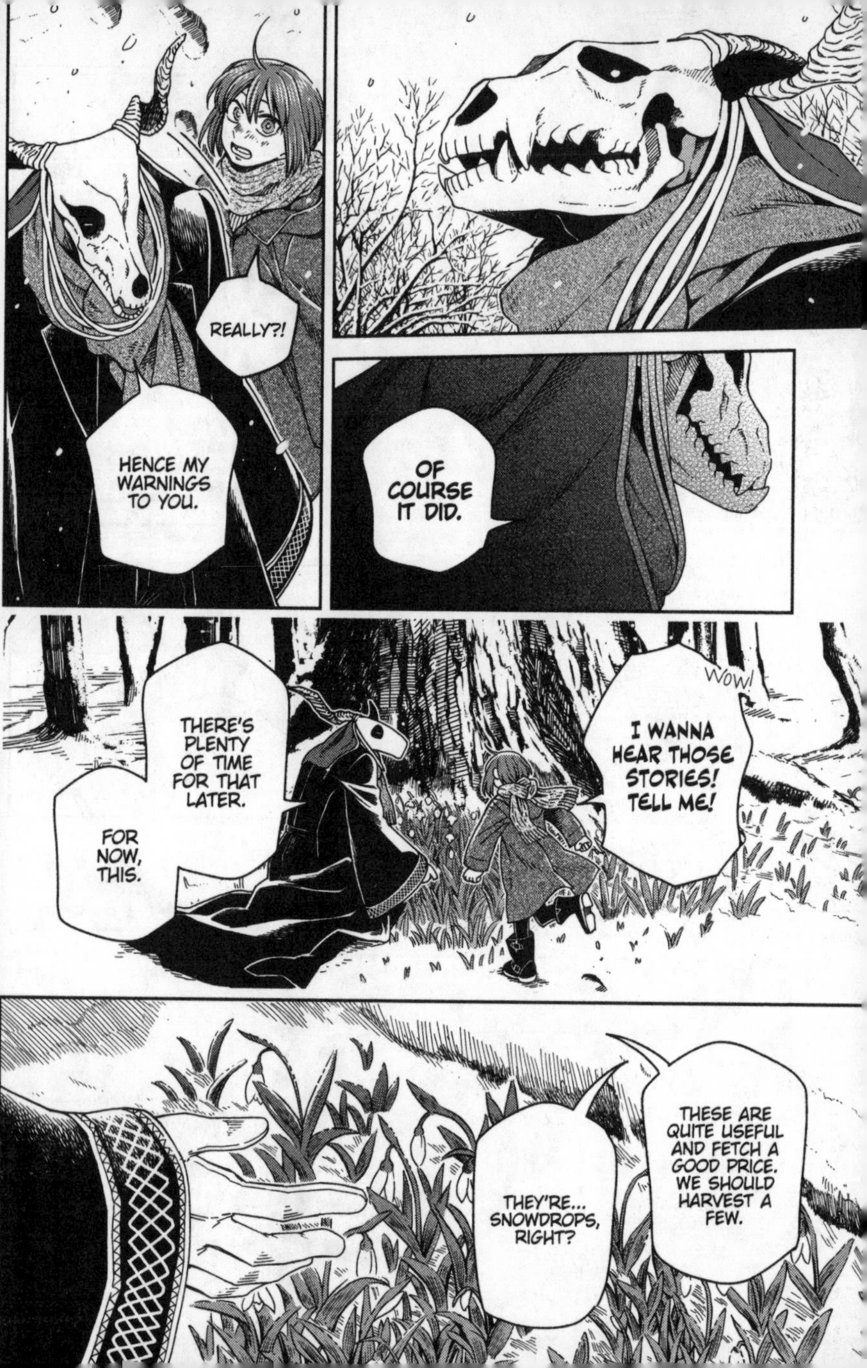
OF COURSE IT DID.
REALLY?!
HENCE MY WARNINGS TO YOU.
WOW!
I WANNA HEAR THOSE STORIES! TELL ME!
THERE'S PLENTY OF TIME FOR THAT LATER.
FOR NOW, THIS.
THESE ARE QUITE USEFUL AND FETCH A GOOD PRICE. WE SHOULD HARVEST A FEW.
THEY'RE... SNOWDROPS, RIGHT?

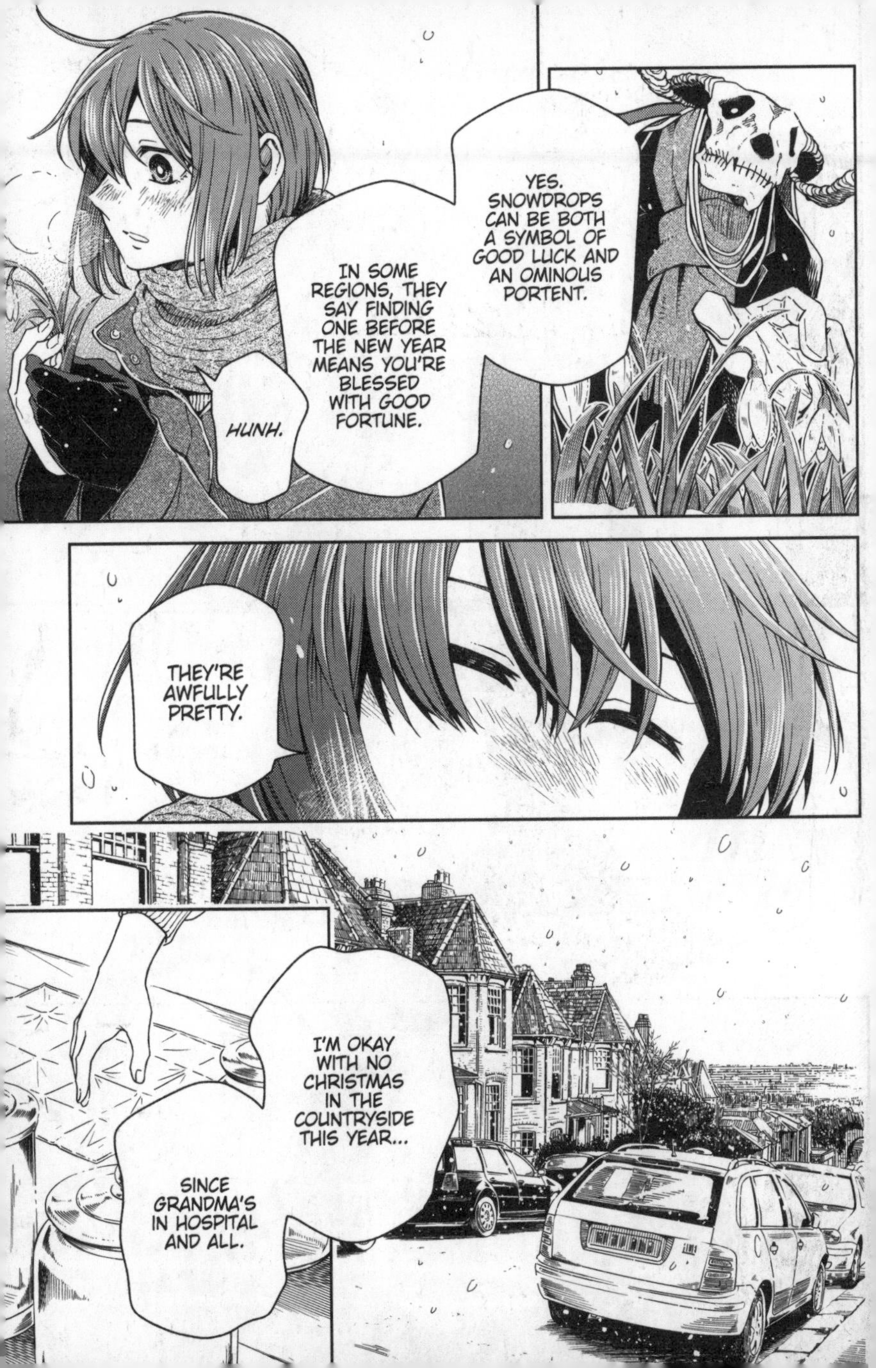
YES. SNOWDROPS CAN BE BOTH A SYMBOL OF GOOD LUCK AND AN OMINOUS PORTENT.
IN SOME REGIONS, THEY SAY FINDING ONE BEFORE THE NEW YEAR MEANS YOU'RE BLESSED WITH GOOD FORTUNE.
HUNH.
THEY'RE AWFULLY PRETTY.
I'M OKAY WITH NO CHRISTMAS IN THE COUNTRYSIDE THIS YEAR...
SINCE GRANDMA'S IN HOSPITAL AND ALL.

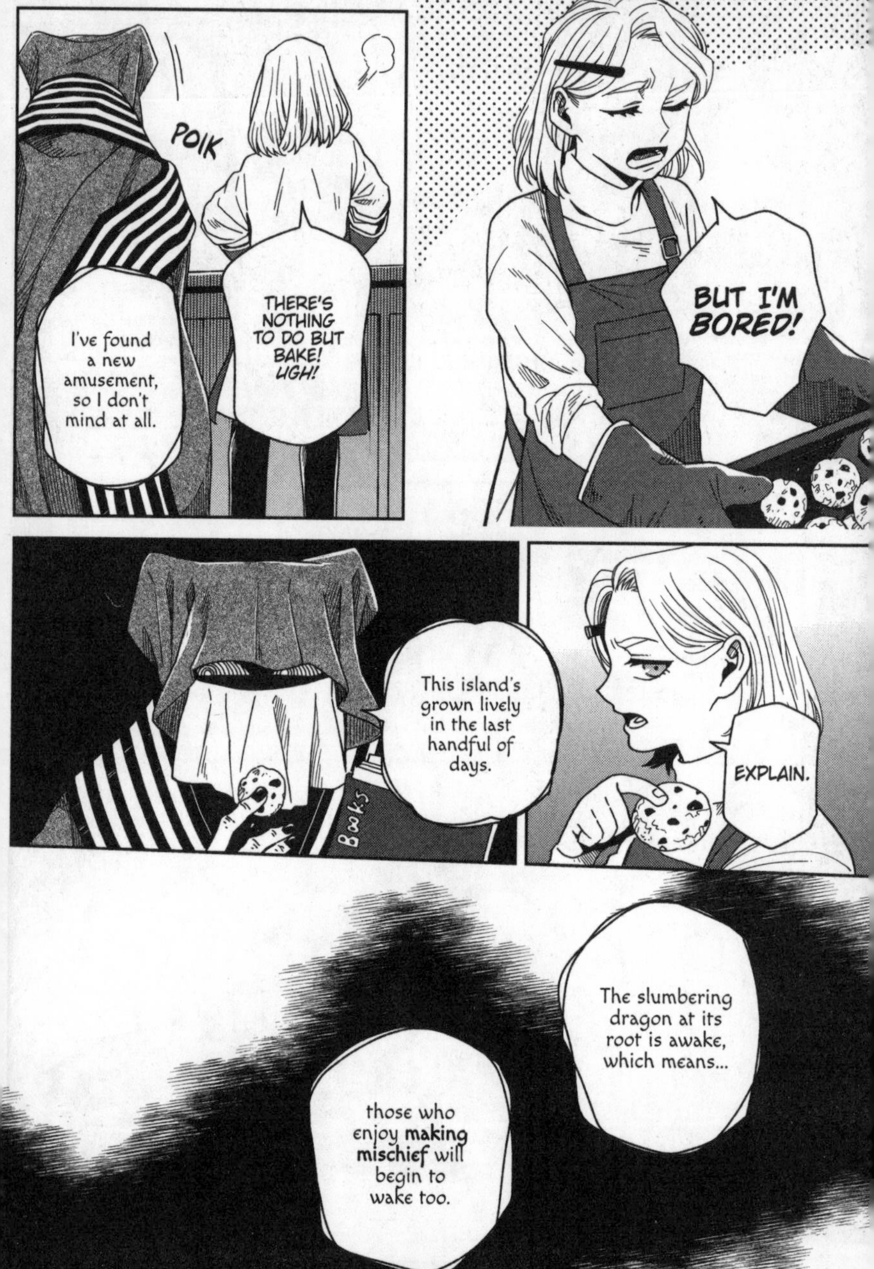
BUT I'M BORED!
POIK
THERE'S NOTHING TO DO BUT BAKE! UGH!
I've found a new amusement, so I don't mind at all.
EXPLAIN.
This island's grown lively in the last handful of days.
Books
The slumbering dragon at its root is awake, which means...
those who enjoy **making mischief** will begin to wake too.

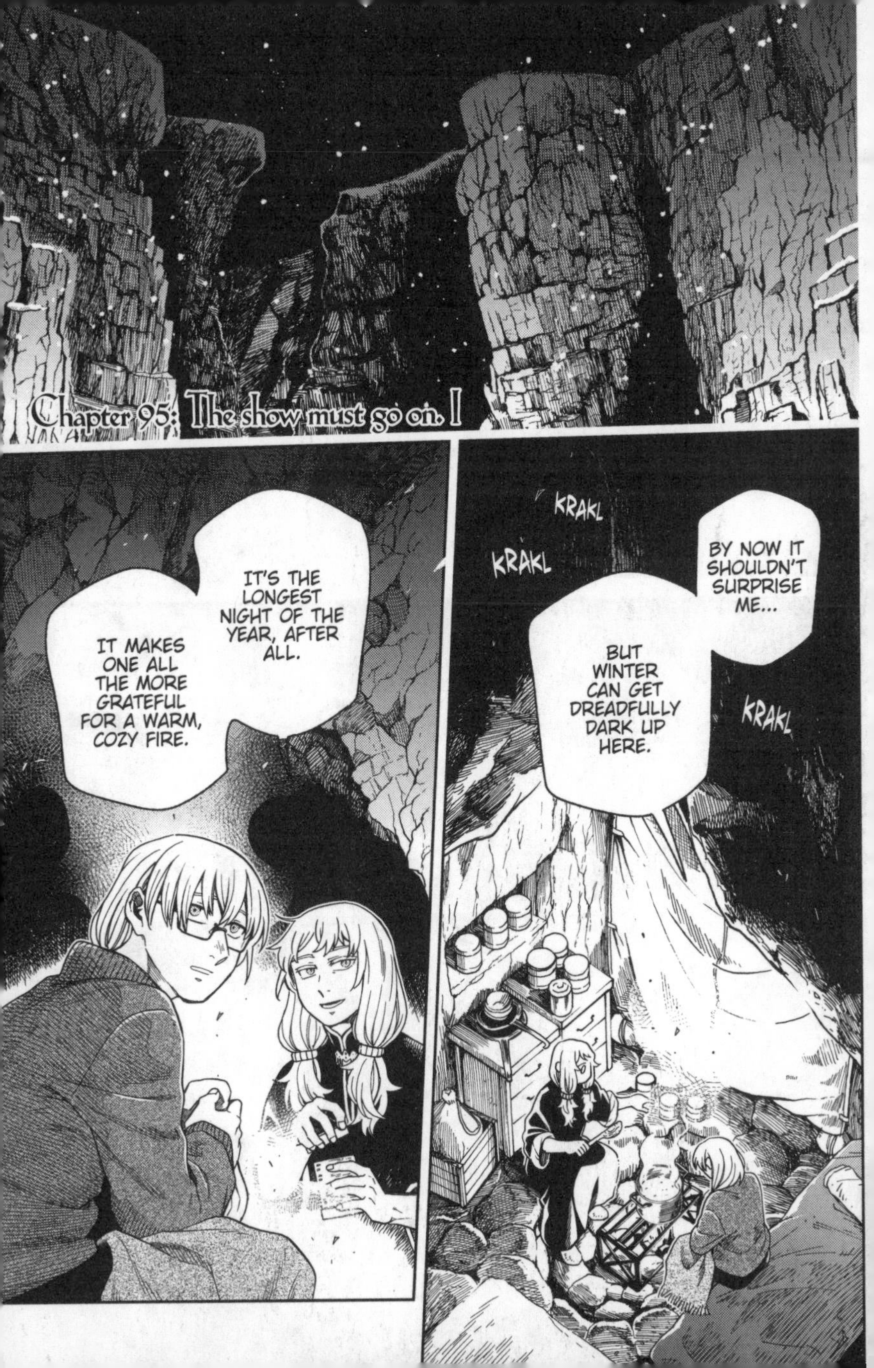
Chapter 95: The show must go on. I
KRAKL
KRAKL
KRAKL
BY NOW IT SHOULDN'T SURPRISE ME...
BUT WINTER CAN GET DREADFULLY DARK UP HERE.
IT'S THE LONGEST NIGHT OF THE YEAR, AFTER ALL.
IT MAKES ONE ALL THE MORE GRATEFUL FOR A WARM, COZY FIRE.

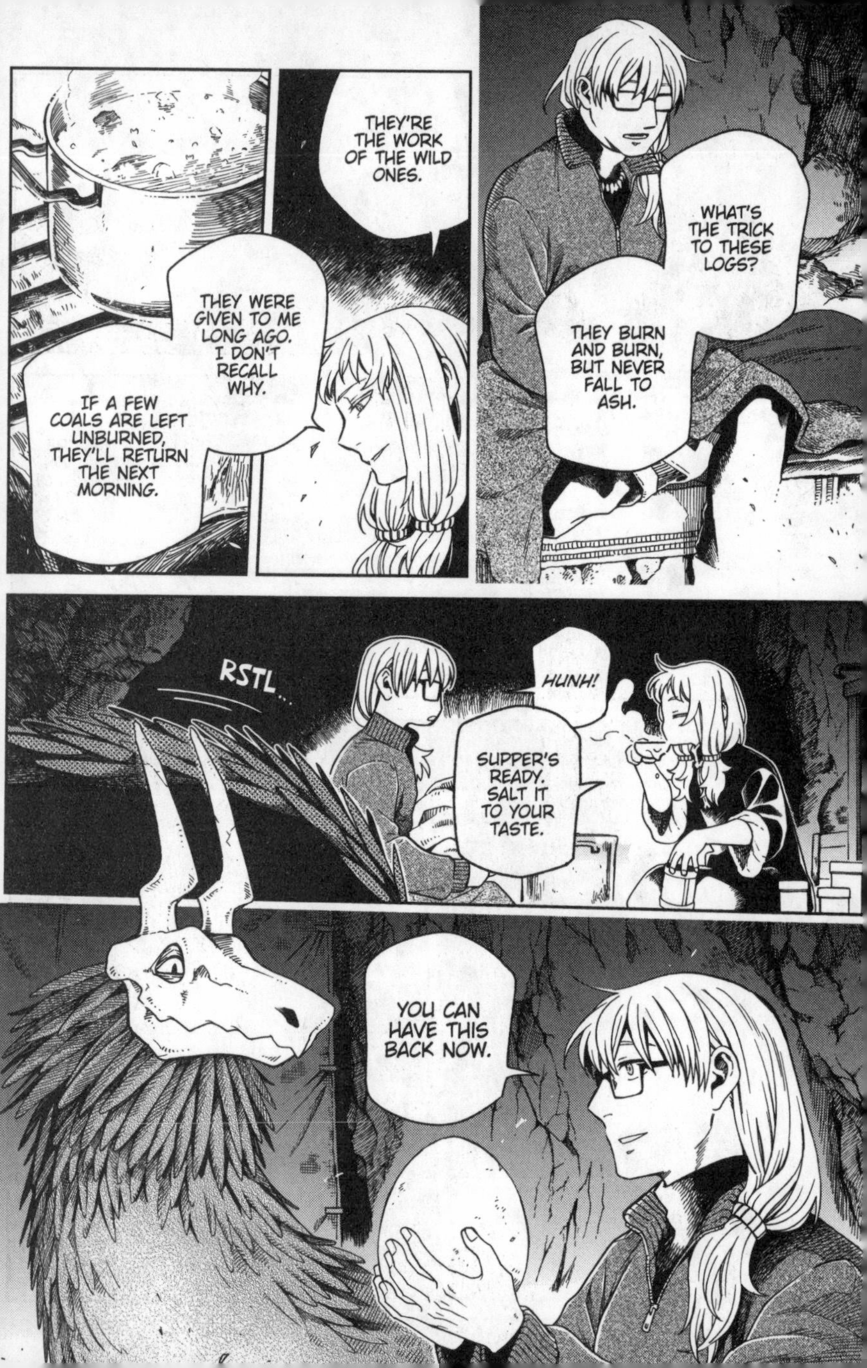
WHAT'S THE TRICK TO THESE LOGS?
THEY BURN AND BURN, BUT NEVER FALL TO ASH.
THEY'RE THE WORK OF THE WILD ONES.
THEY WERE GIVEN TO ME LONG AGO. I DON'T RECALL WHY.
IF A FEW COALS ARE LEFT UNBURNED, THEY'LL RETURN THE NEXT MORNING.
HUNH!
SUPPER'S READY. SALT IT TO YOUR TASTE.
RSTL...
YOU CAN HAVE THIS BACK NOW.

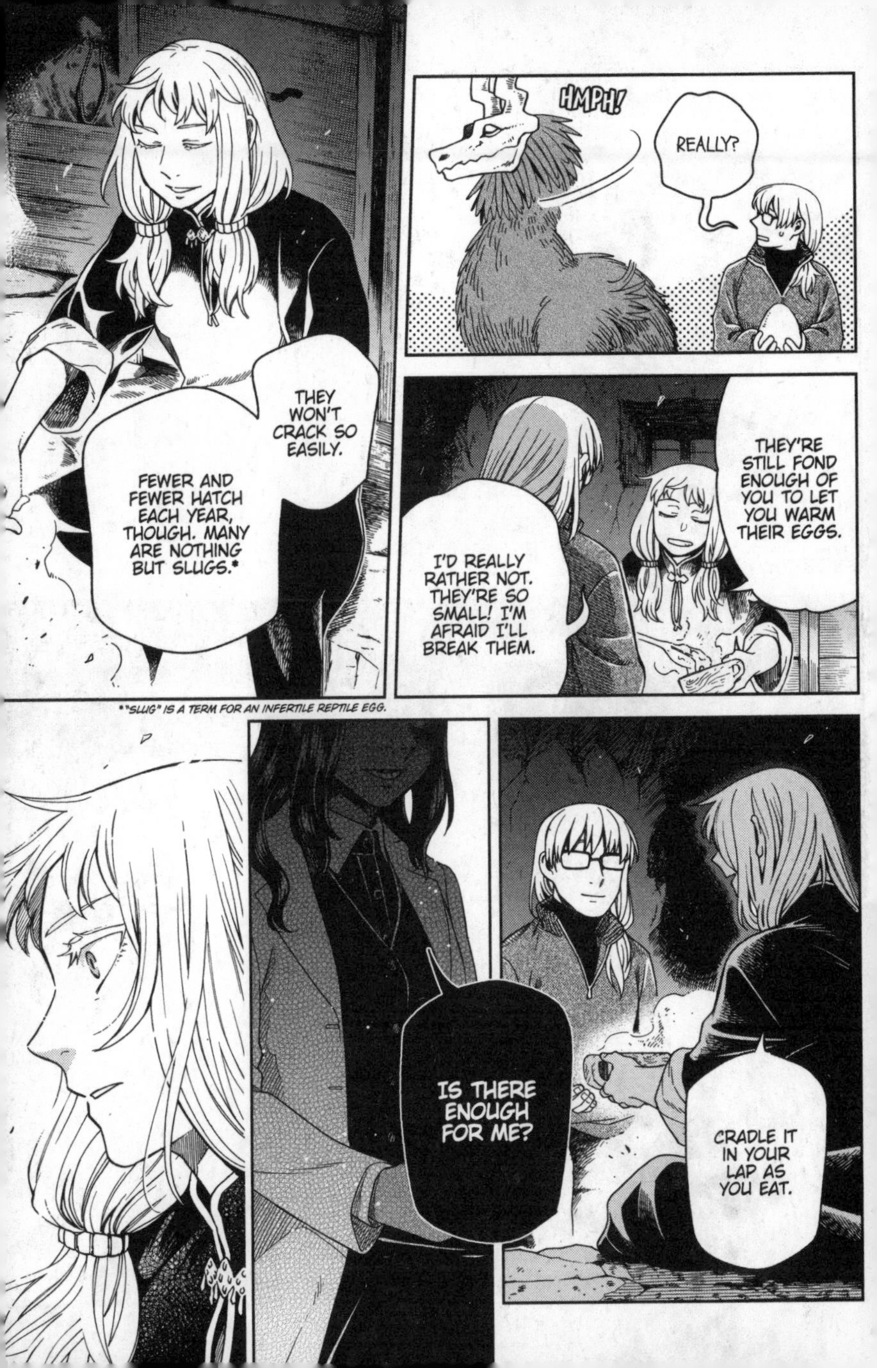
HMPH!
REALLY?
THEY'RE STILL FOND ENOUGH OF YOU TO LET YOU WARM THEIR EGGS.
I'D REALLY RATHER NOT. THEY'RE SO SMALL! I'M AFRAID I'LL BREAK THEM.
THEY WON'T CRACK SO EASILY.
FEWER AND FEWER HATCH EACH YEAR, THOUGH. MANY ARE NOTHING BUT SLUGS.*
CRADLE IT IN YOUR LAP AS YOU EAT.
IS THERE ENOUGH FOR ME?
*"SLUG" IS A TERM FOR AN INFERTILE REPTILE EGG.

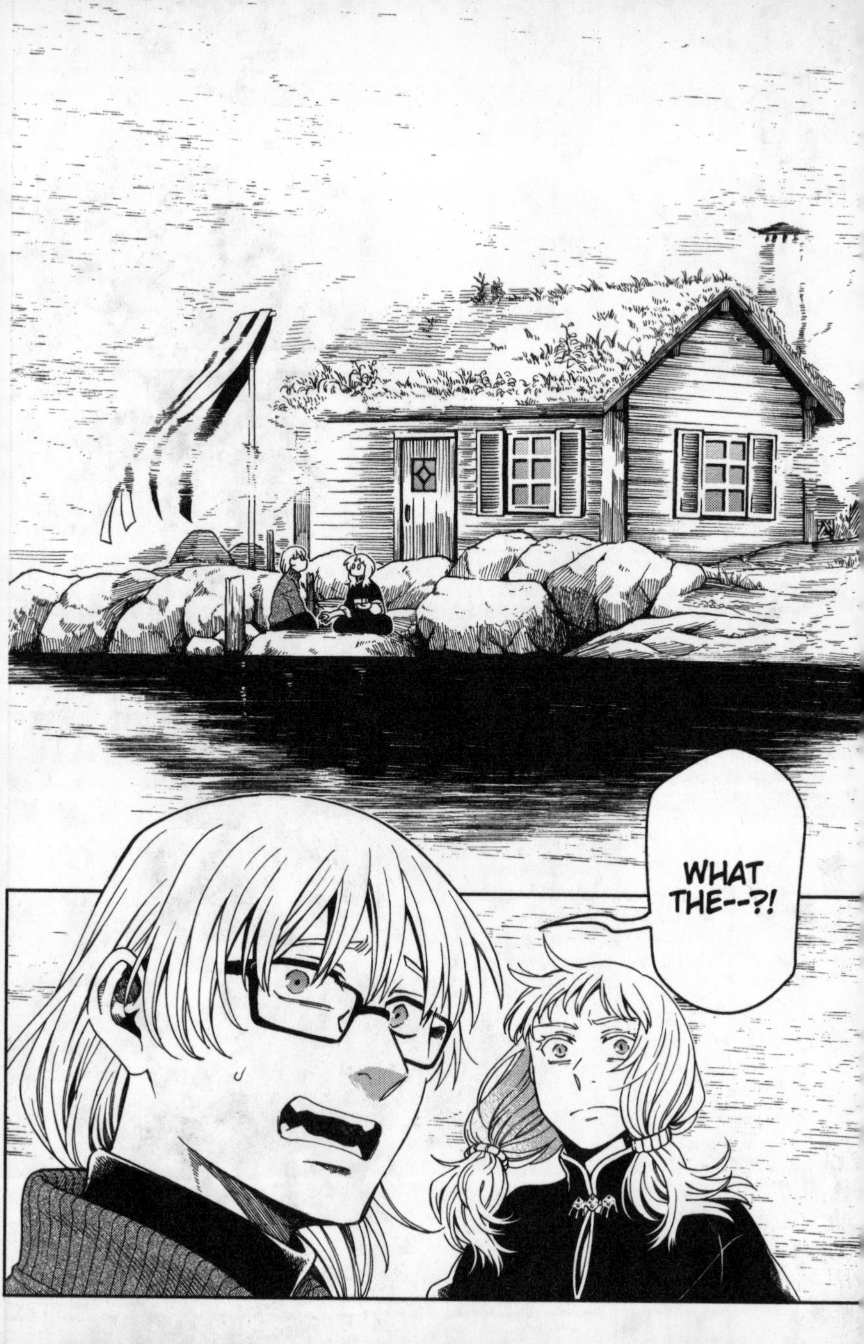
WHAT THE--?!

Chapter 95: The show must go on. I

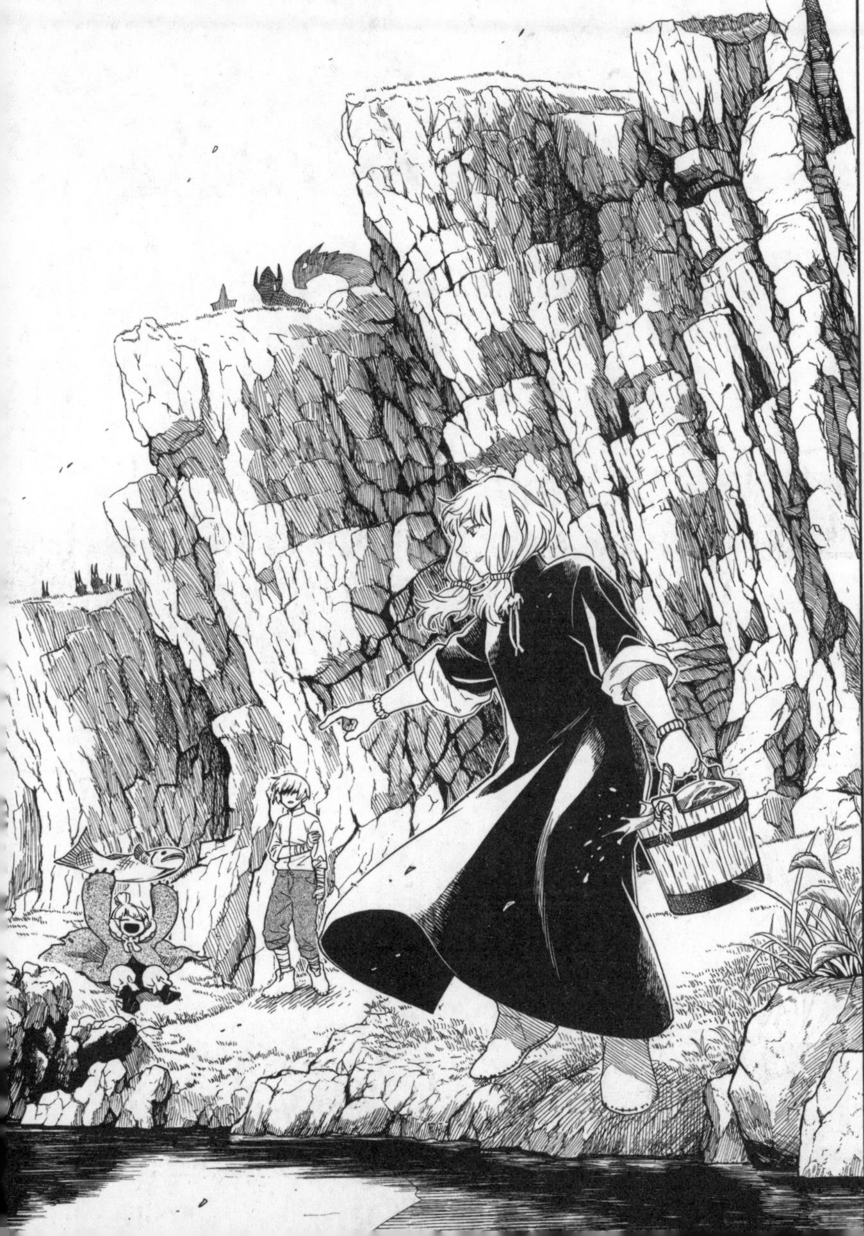

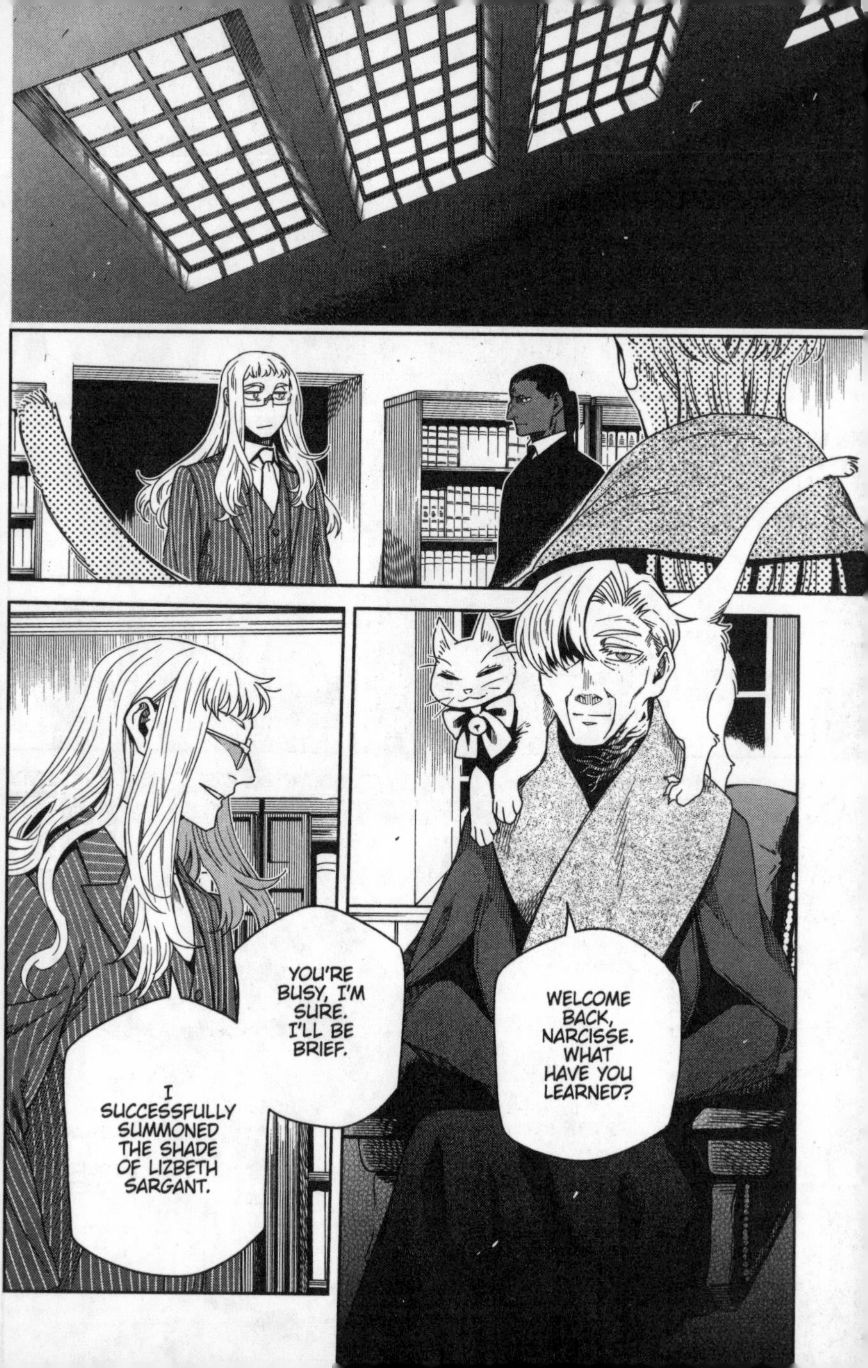
WELCOME BACK, NARCISSE. WHAT HAVE YOU LEARNED?
YOU'RE BUSY, I'M SURE. I'LL BE BRIEF.
I SUCCESSFULLY SUMMONED THE SHADE OF LIZBETH SARGANT.

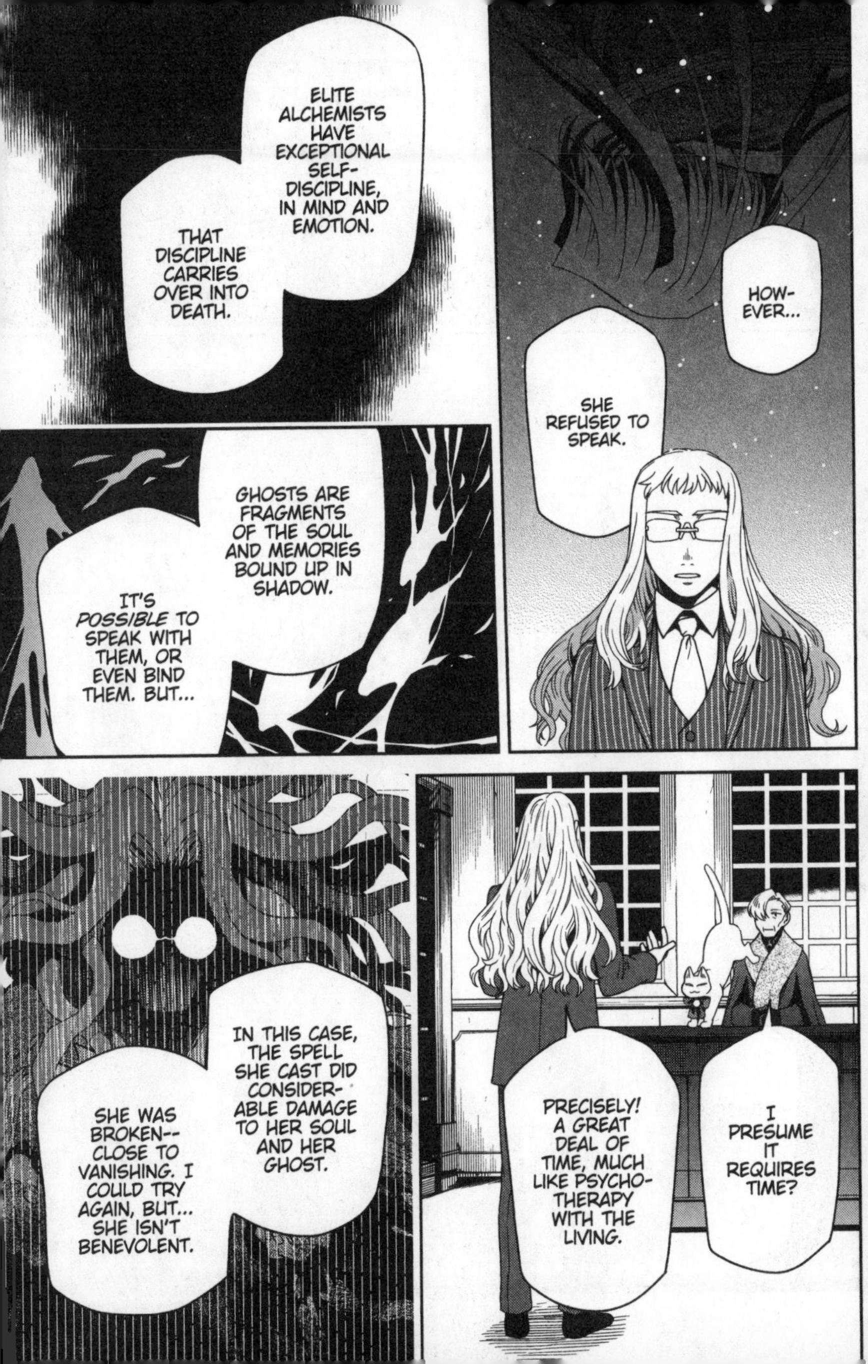
HOW-EVER...
SHE REFUSED TO SPEAK.
ELITE ALCHEMISTS HAVE EXCEPTIONAL SELF-DISCIPLINE, IN MIND AND EMOTION.
THAT DISCIPLINE CARRIES OVER INTO DEATH.
GHOSTS ARE FRAGMENTS OF THE SOUL AND MEMORIES BOUND UP IN SHADOW.
IT'S *POSSIBLE* TO SPEAK WITH THEM, OR EVEN BIND THEM. BUT...
I PRESUME IT REQUIRES TIME?
PRECISELY! A GREAT DEAL OF TIME, MUCH LIKE PSYCHO-THERAPY WITH THE LIVING.
IN THIS CASE, THE SPELL SHE CAST DID CONSIDER-ABLE DAMAGE TO HER SOUL AND HER GHOST.
SHE WAS BROKEN--CLOSE TO VANISHING. I COULD TRY AGAIN, BUT... SHE ISN'T BENEVOLENT.

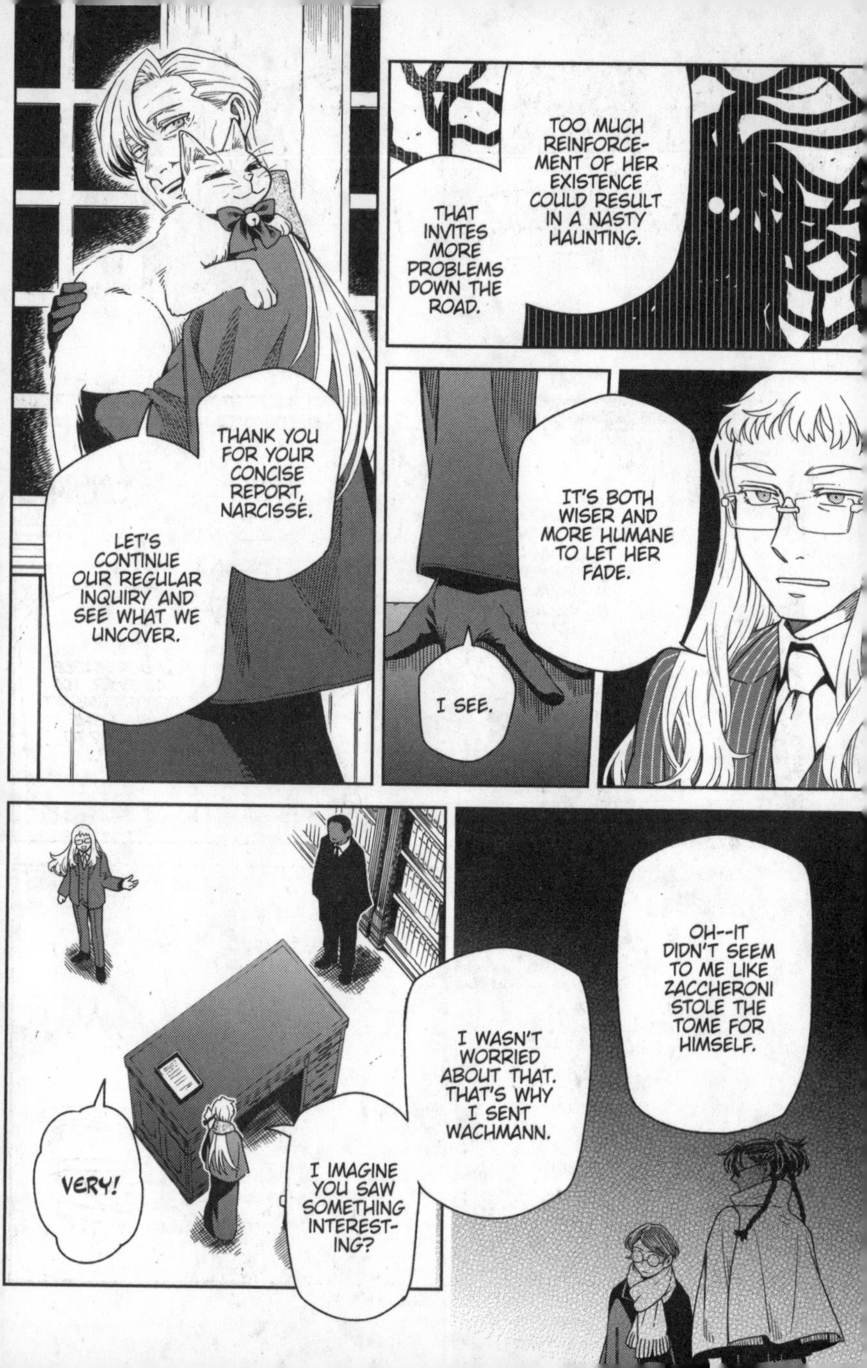
TOO MUCH REINFORCEMENT OF HER EXISTENCE COULD RESULT IN A NASTY HAUNTING.
THAT INVITES MORE PROBLEMS DOWN THE ROAD.
IT'S BOTH WISER AND MORE HUMANE TO LET HER FADE.
I SEE.
THANK YOU FOR YOUR CONCISE REPORT, NARCISSE.
LET'S CONTINUE OUR REGULAR INQUIRY AND SEE WHAT WE UNCOVER.
OH--IT DIDN'T SEEM TO ME LIKE ZACCHERONI STOLE THE TOME FOR HIMSELF.
I WASN'T WORRIED ABOUT THAT. THAT'S WHY I SENT WACHMANN.
I IMAGINE YOU SAW SOMETHING INTERESTING?
VERY!

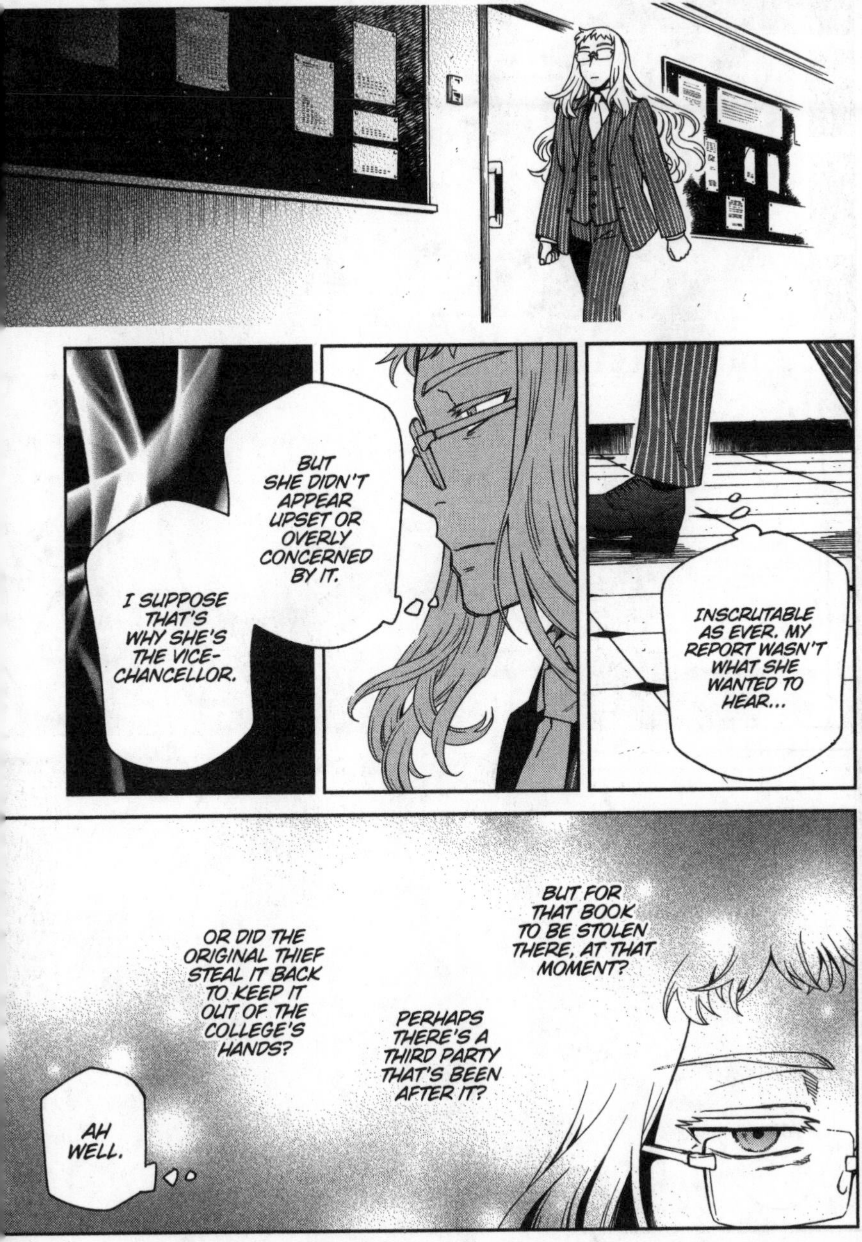
INSCRUTABLE AS EVER. MY REPORT WASN'T WHAT SHE WANTED TO HEAR...
BUT SHE DIDN'T APPEAR UPSET OR OVERLY CONCERNED BY IT.
I SUPPOSE THAT'S WHY SHE'S THE VICE-CHANCELLOR.
BUT FOR THAT BOOK TO BE STOLEN THERE, AT THAT MOMENT?
PERHAPS THERE'S A THIRD PARTY THAT'S BEEN AFTER IT?
OR DID THE ORIGINAL THIEF STEAL IT BACK TO KEEP IT OUT OF THE COLLEGE'S HANDS?
AH WELL.

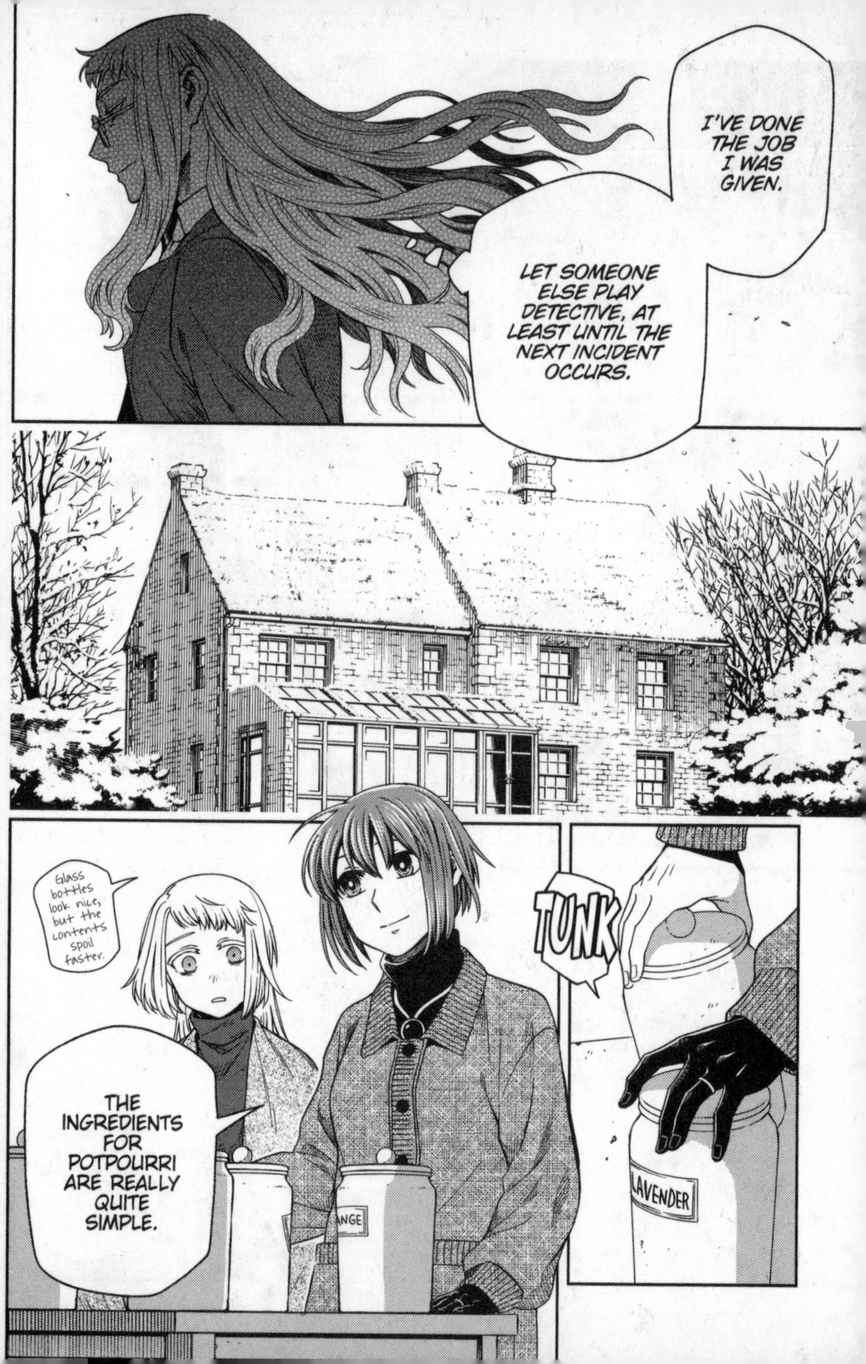
I'VE DONE THE JOB I WAS GIVEN.
LET SOMEONE ELSE PLAY DETECTIVE, AT LEAST UNTIL THE NEXT INCIDENT OCCURS.
TUNK
LAVENDER
Glass bottles look nice, but the contents spoil faster.
THE INGREDIENTS FOR POTPOURRI ARE REALLY QUITE SIMPLE.

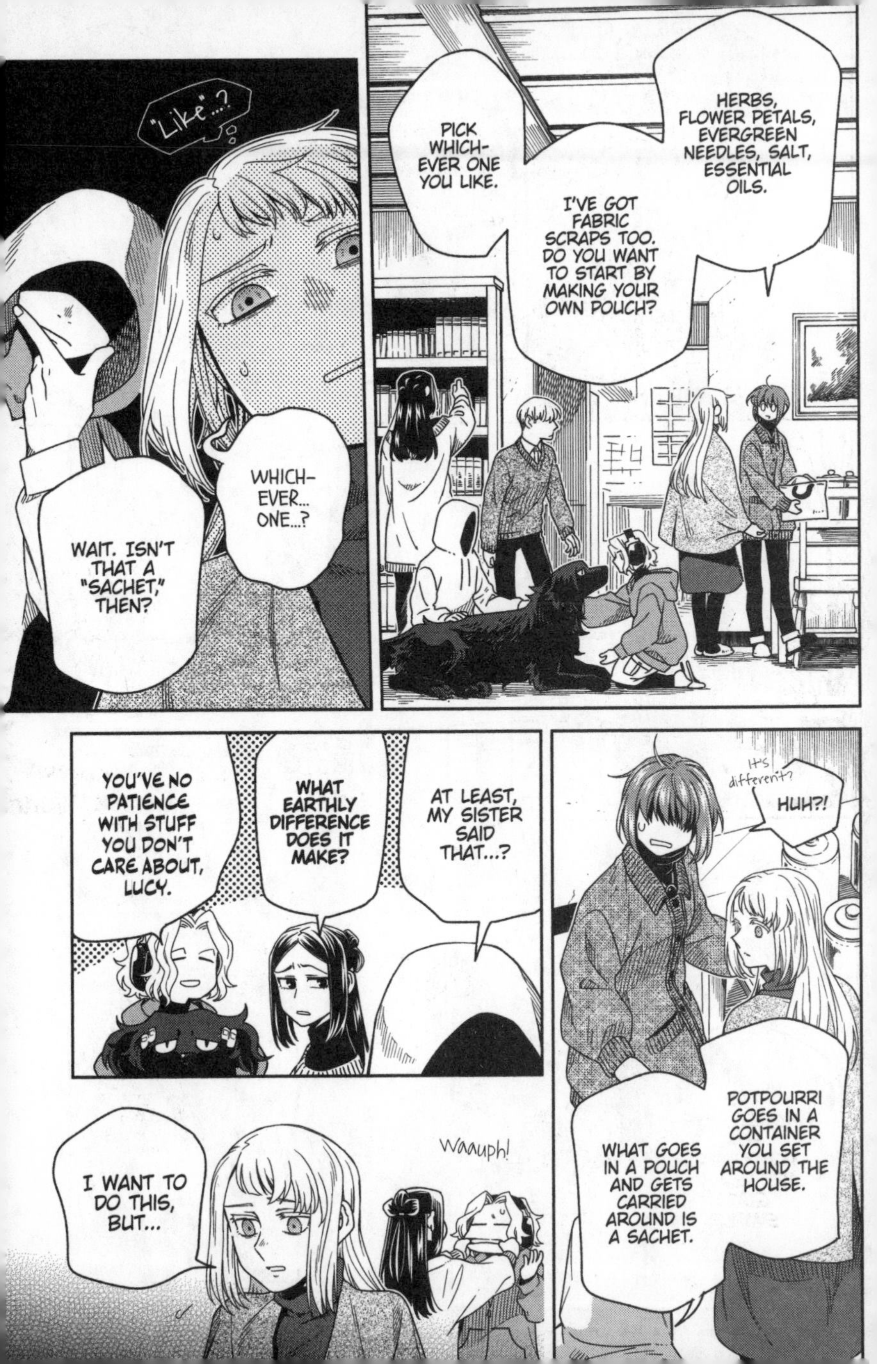
HERBS, FLOWER PETALS, EVERGREEN NEEDLES, SALT, ESSENTIAL OILS.
PICK WHICHEVER ONE YOU LIKE.
I'VE GOT FABRIC SCRAPS TOO. DO YOU WANT TO START BY MAKING YOUR OWN POUCH?
"Like"...?
WHICHEVER... ONE...?
WAIT. ISN'T THAT A "SACHET," THEN?
HUH?!
It's different?
AT LEAST, MY SISTER SAID THAT...?
WHAT EARTHLY DIFFERENCE DOES IT MAKE?
YOU'VE NO PATIENCE WITH STUFF YOU DON'T CARE ABOUT, LUCY.
POTPOURRI GOES IN A CONTAINER YOU SET AROUND THE HOUSE.
WHAT GOES IN A POUCH AND GETS CARRIED AROUND IS A SACHET.
Waauph!
I WANT TO DO THIS, BUT...

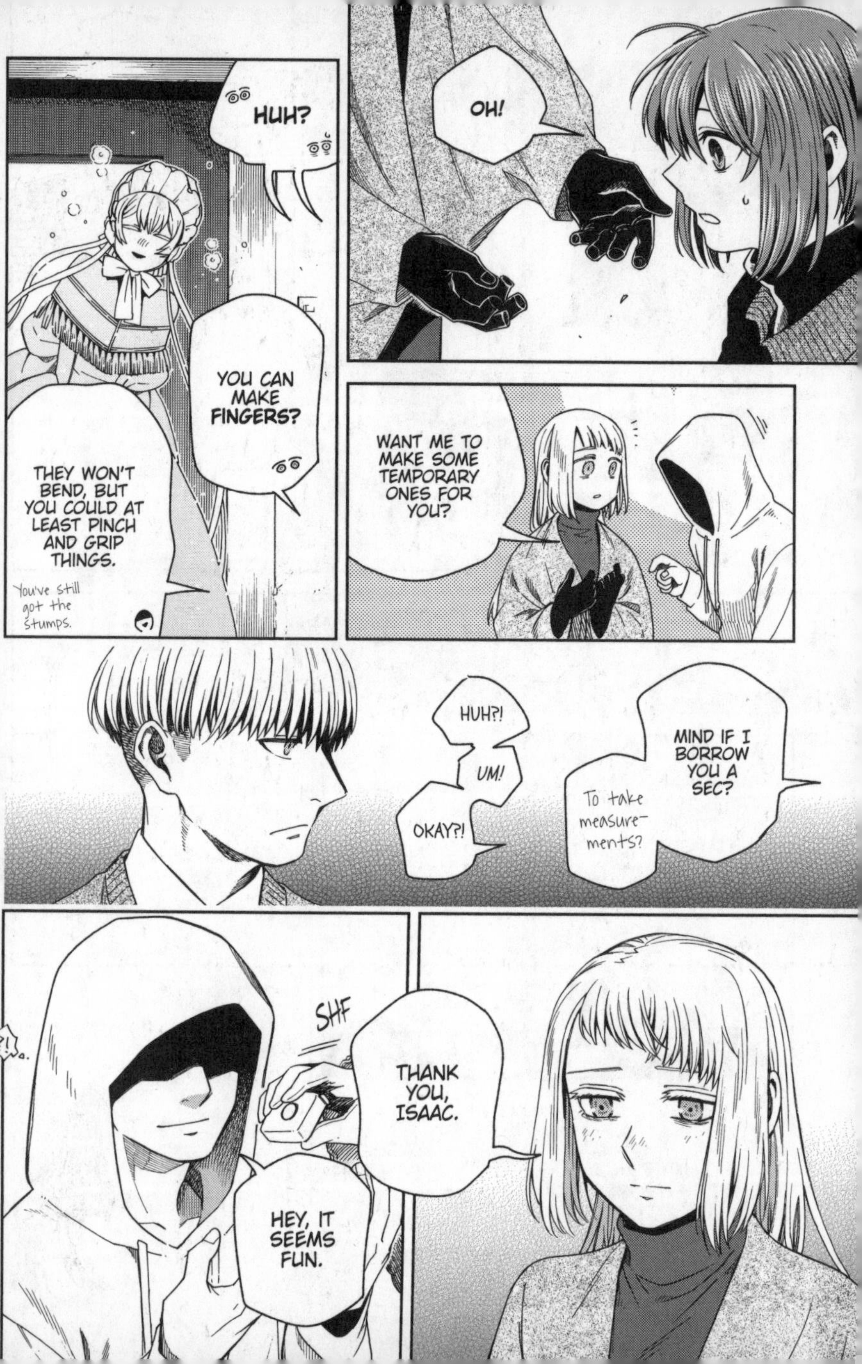
OH!
WANT ME TO MAKE SOME TEMPORARY ONES FOR YOU?
HUH?
YOU CAN MAKE FINGERS?
THEY WON'T BEND, BUT YOU COULD AT LEAST PINCH AND GRIP THINGS.
You've still got the stumps.
MIND IF I BORROW YOU A SEC?
To take measure-ments?
HUH?!
UM!
OKAY?!
THANK YOU, ISAAC.
SHF
?!
HEY, IT SEEMS FUN.

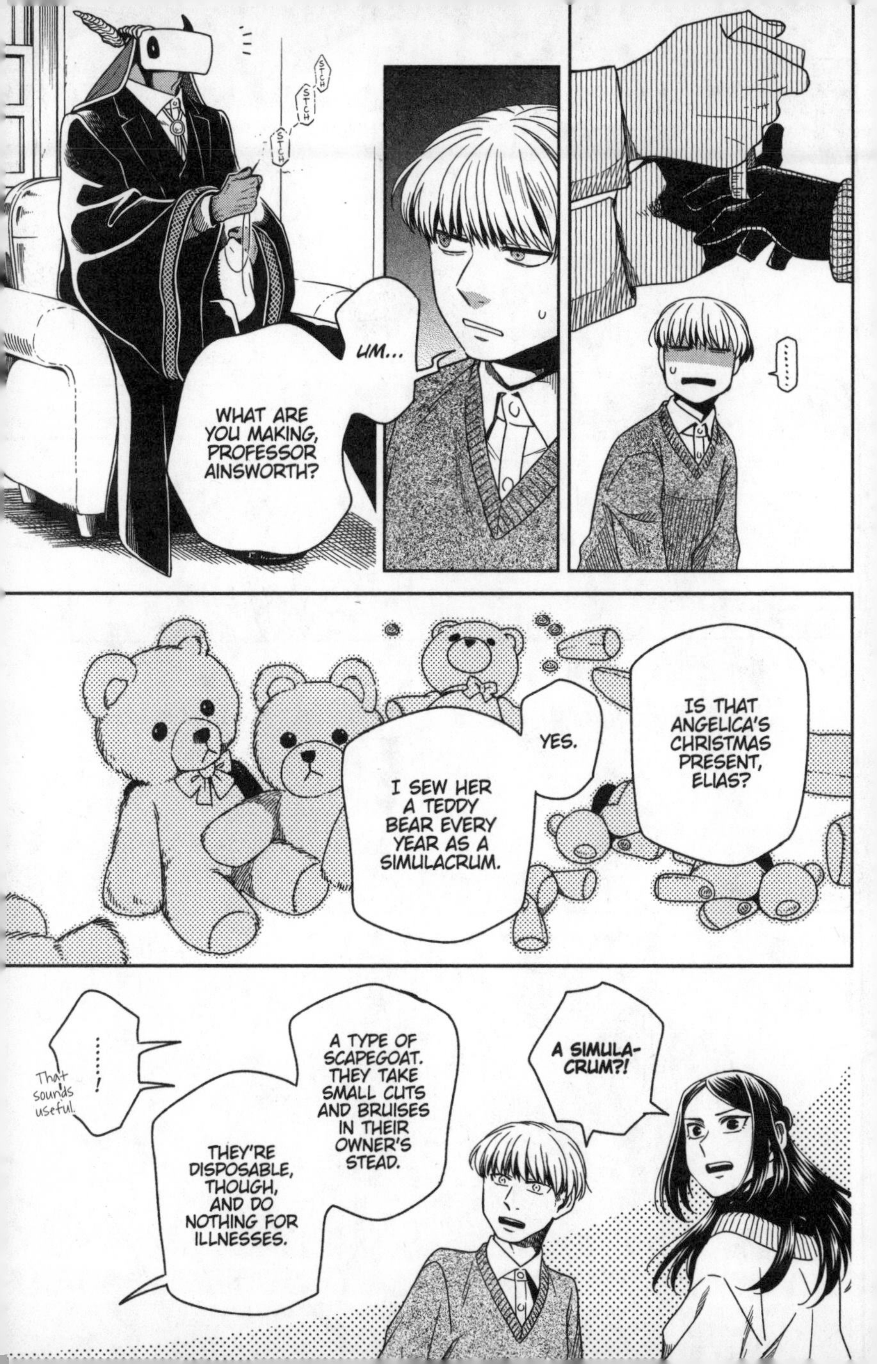
STCH
STCH
STCH
UM...
WHAT ARE YOU MAKING, PROFESSOR AINSWORTH?
......
IS THAT ANGELICA'S CHRISTMAS PRESENT, ELIAS?
YES.
I SEW HER A TEDDY BEAR EVERY YEAR AS A SIMULACRUM.
A SIMULA-CRUM?!
A TYPE OF SCAPEGOAT. THEY TAKE SMALL CUTS AND BRUISES IN THEIR OWNER'S STEAD.
THEY'RE DISPOSABLE, THOUGH, AND DO NOTHING FOR ILLNESSES.
......!
That sounds useful.

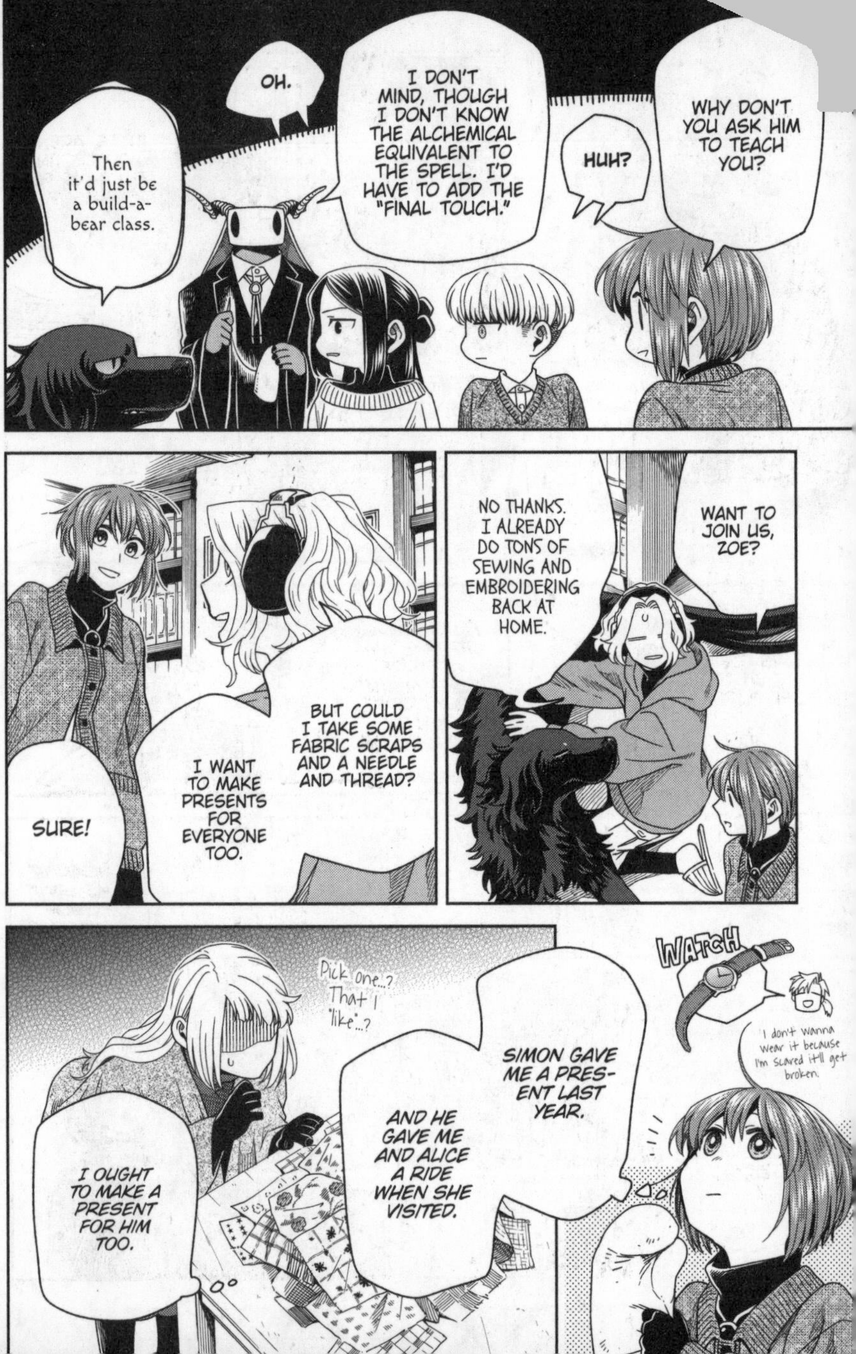
WHY DON'T YOU ASK HIM TO TEACH YOU?
HUH?
I DON'T MIND, THOUGH I DON'T KNOW THE ALCHEMICAL EQUIVALENT TO THE SPELL. I'D HAVE TO ADD THE "FINAL TOUCH."
OH.
Then it'd just be a build-a-bear class.
WANT TO JOIN US, ZOE?
NO THANKS. I ALREADY DO TONS OF SEWING AND EMBROIDERING BACK AT HOME.
BUT COULD I TAKE SOME FABRIC SCRAPS AND A NEEDLE AND THREAD?
I WANT TO MAKE PRESENTS FOR EVERYONE TOO.
SURE!
WATCH
I don't wanna wear it because I'm scared it'll get broken.
SIMON GAVE ME A PRESENT LAST YEAR.
AND HE GAVE ME AND ALICE A RIDE WHEN SHE VISITED.
Pick one...? That I "like"...?
I OUGHT TO MAKE A PRESENT FOR HIM TOO.

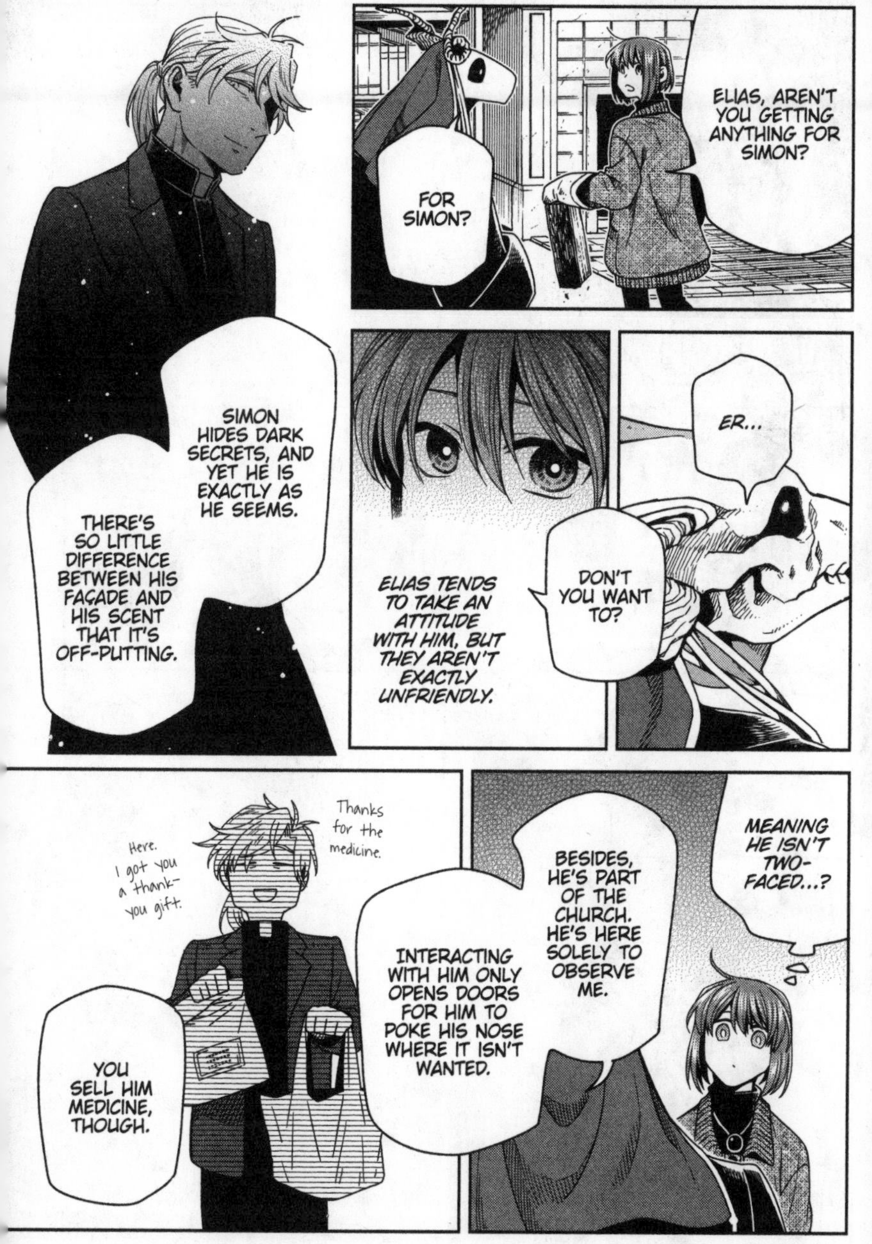
ELIAS, AREN'T YOU GETTING ANYTHING FOR SIMON?
FOR SIMON?
ER...
DON'T YOU WANT TO?
ELIAS TENDS TO TAKE AN ATTITUDE WITH HIM, BUT THEY AREN'T EXACTLY UNFRIENDLY.
SIMON HIDES DARK SECRETS, AND YET HE IS EXACTLY AS HE SEEMS.
THERE'S SO LITTLE DIFFERENCE BETWEEN HIS FAÇADE AND HIS SCENT THAT IT'S OFF-PUTTING.
MEANING HE ISN'T TWO-FACED...?
BESIDES, HE'S PART OF THE CHURCH. HE'S HERE SOLELY TO OBSERVE ME.
INTERACTING WITH HIM ONLY OPENS DOORS FOR HIM TO POKE HIS NOSE WHERE IT ISN'T WANTED.
YOU SELL HIM MEDICINE, THOUGH.
Thanks for the medicine.
Here. I got you a thank-you gift.

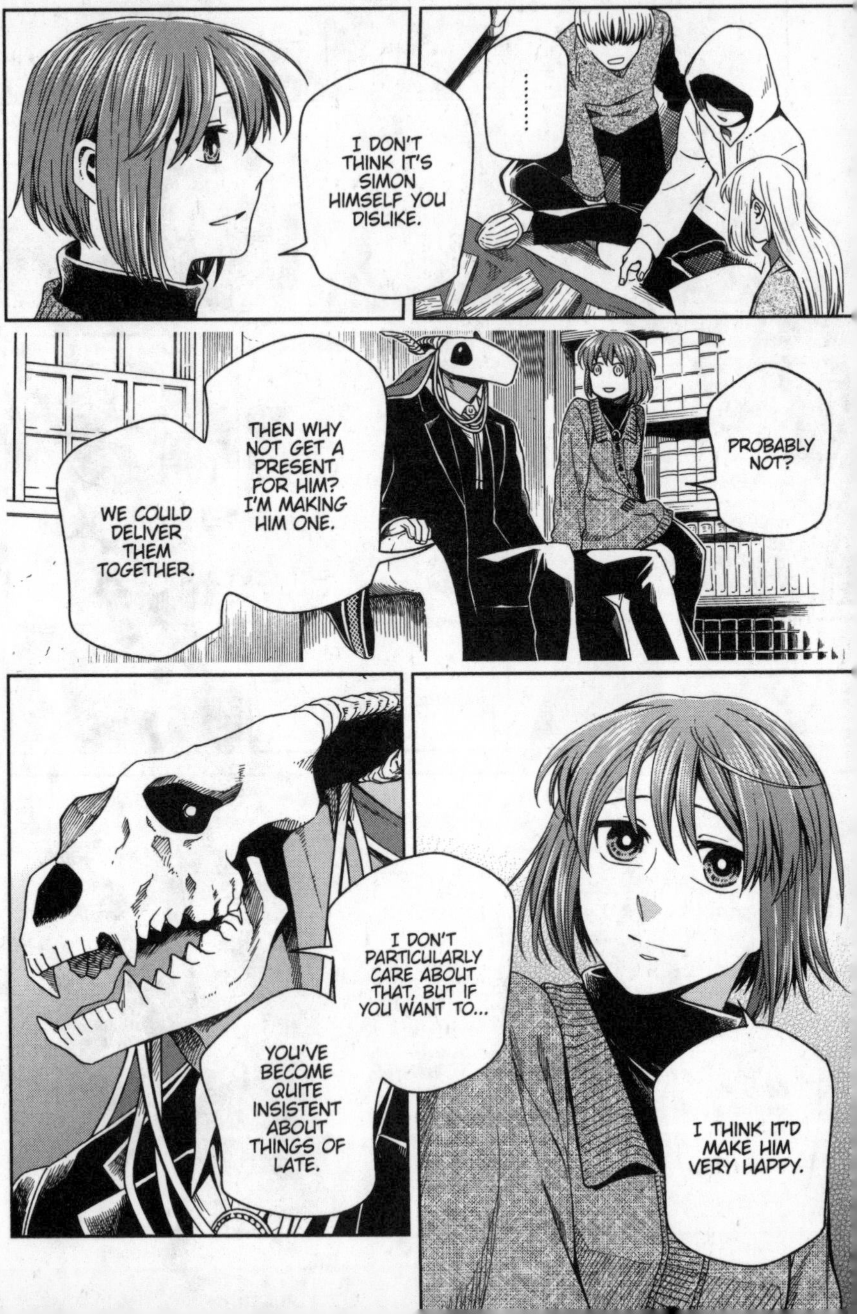
......
I DON'T THINK IT'S SIMON HIMSELF YOU DISLIKE.
PROBABLY NOT?
THEN WHY NOT GET A PRESENT FOR HIM? I'M MAKING HIM ONE.
WE COULD DELIVER THEM TOGETHER.
I THINK IT'D MAKE HIM VERY HAPPY.
I DON'T PARTICULARLY CARE ABOUT THAT, BUT IF YOU WANT TO...
YOU'VE BECOME QUITE INSISTENT ABOUT THINGS OF LATE.

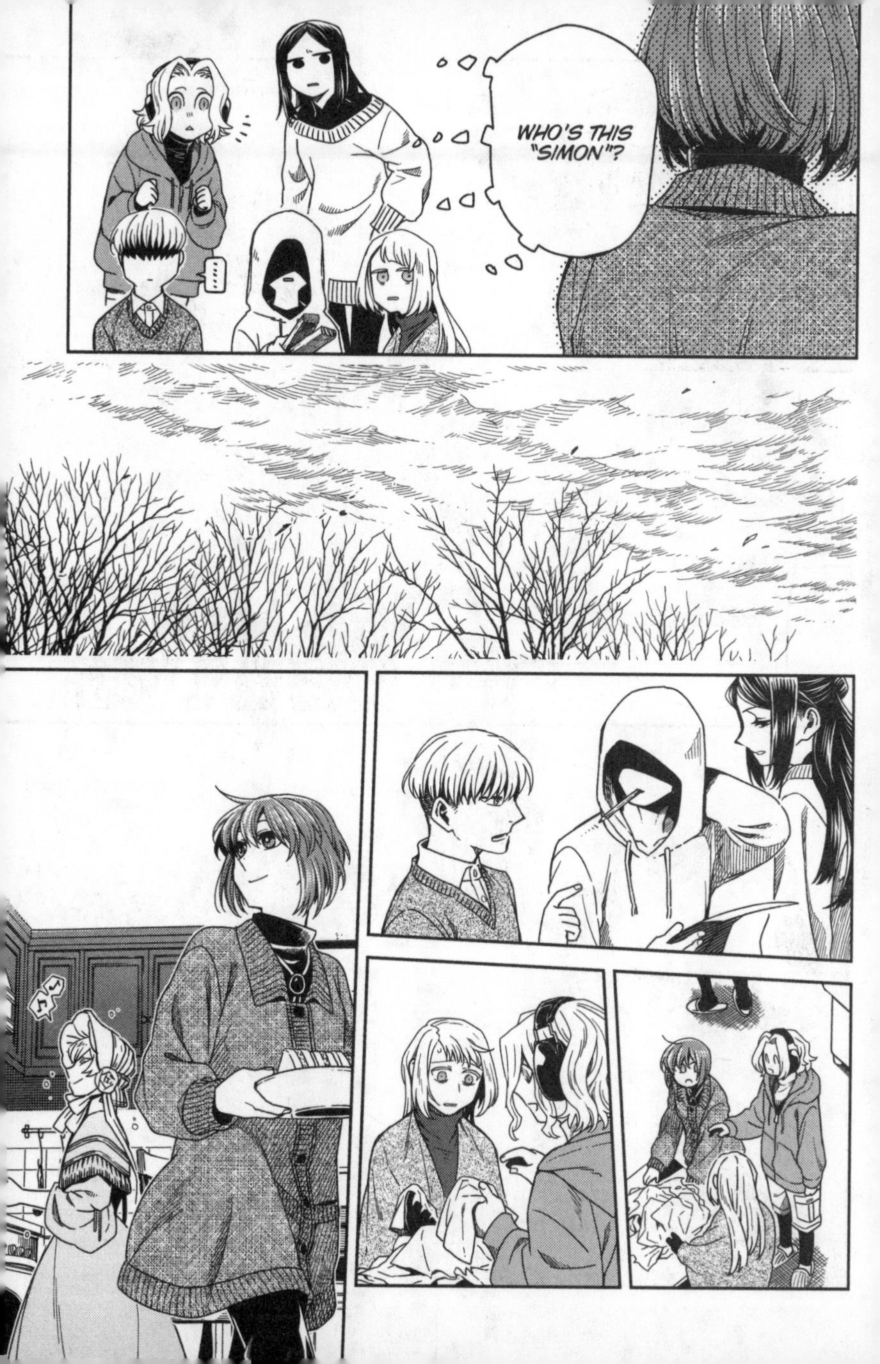
WHO'S THIS "SIMON"?

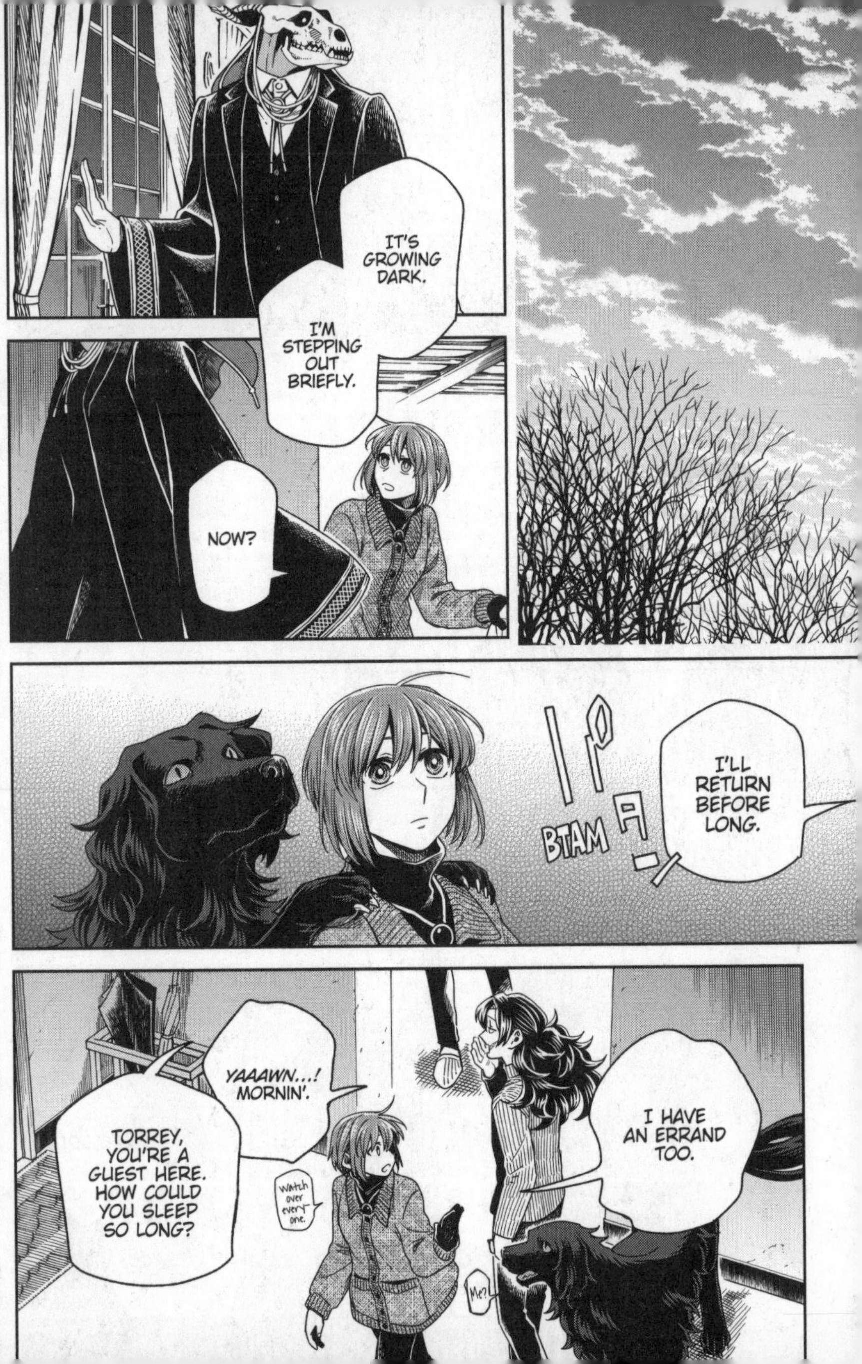
IT'S GROWING DARK.
I'M STEPPING OUT BRIEFLY.
NOW?
I'LL RETURN BEFORE LONG.
BTAM
I HAVE AN ERRAND TOO.
Watch over everyone.
Me?
YAAAWN...! MORNIN'.
TORREY, YOU'RE A GUEST HERE. HOW COULD YOU SLEEP SO LONG?

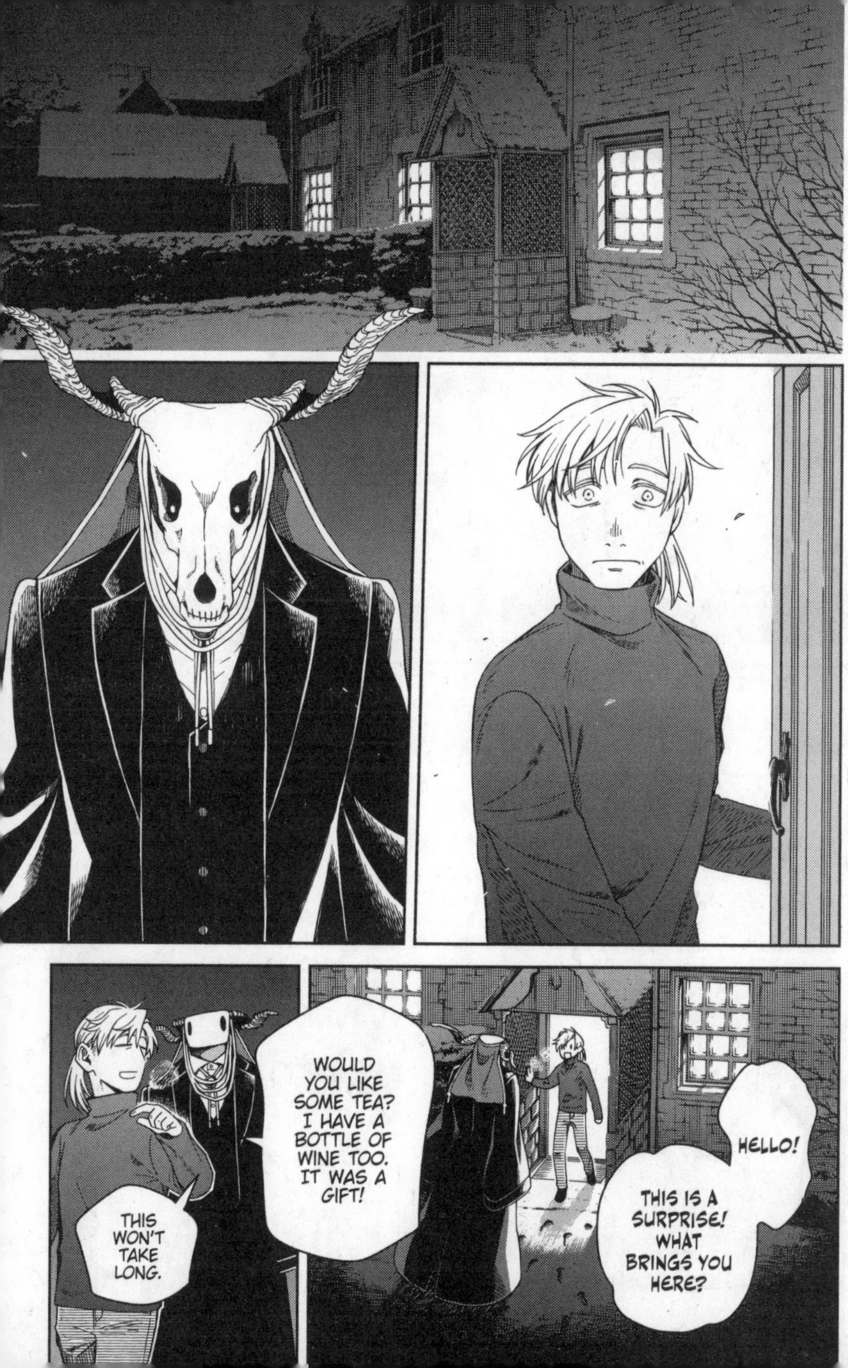
HELLO!
THIS IS A SURPRISE! WHAT BRINGS YOU HERE?
WOULD YOU LIKE SOME TEA? I HAVE A BOTTLE OF WINE TOO. IT WAS A GIFT!
THIS WON'T TAKE LONG.

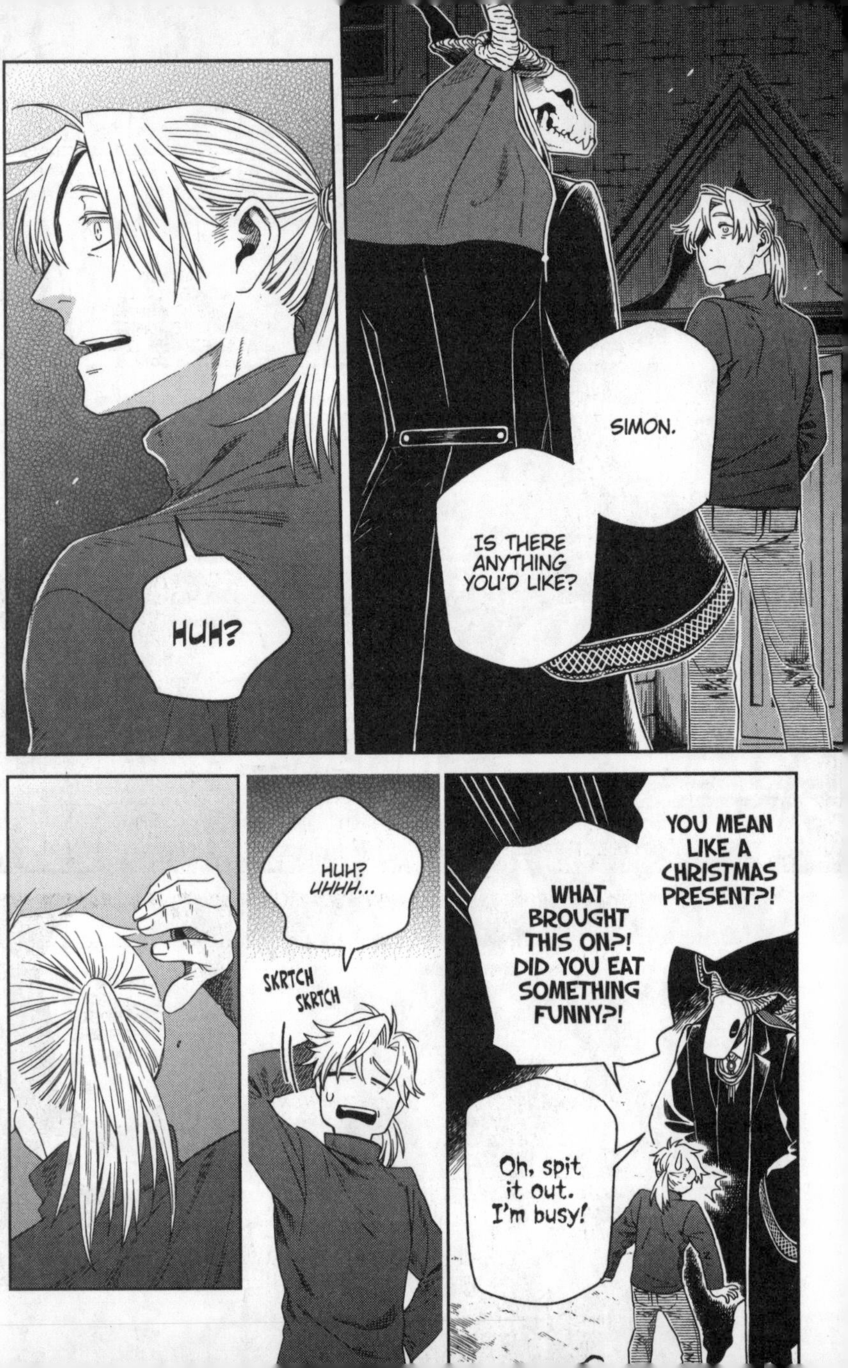
SIMON.
IS THERE ANYTHING YOU'D LIKE?
HUH?
YOU MEAN LIKE A CHRISTMAS PRESENT?!
WHAT BROUGHT THIS ON?! DID YOU EAT SOMETHING FUNNY?!
Oh, spit it out. I'm busy!
HUH? UHHH...
SKRTCH SKRTCH

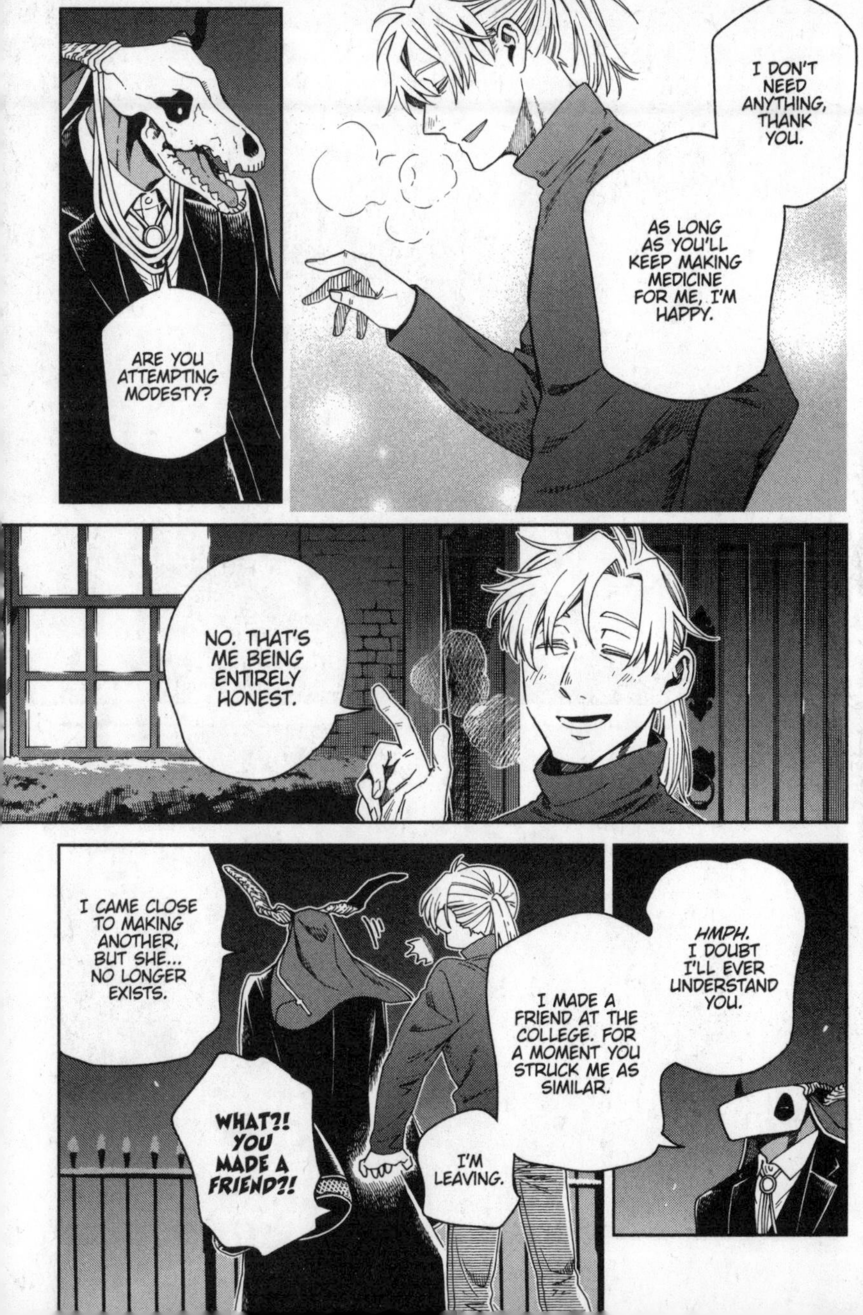
I DON'T NEED ANYTHING, THANK YOU.
AS LONG AS YOU'LL KEEP MAKING MEDICINE FOR ME, I'M HAPPY.
ARE YOU ATTEMPTING MODESTY?
NO. THAT'S ME BEING ENTIRELY HONEST.
HMPH. I DOUBT I'LL EVER UNDERSTAND YOU.
I MADE A FRIEND AT THE COLLEGE. FOR A MOMENT YOU STRUCK ME AS SIMILAR.
I CAME CLOSE TO MAKING ANOTHER, BUT SHE... NO LONGER EXISTS.
I'M LEAVING.
WHAT?! YOU MADE A FRIEND?!

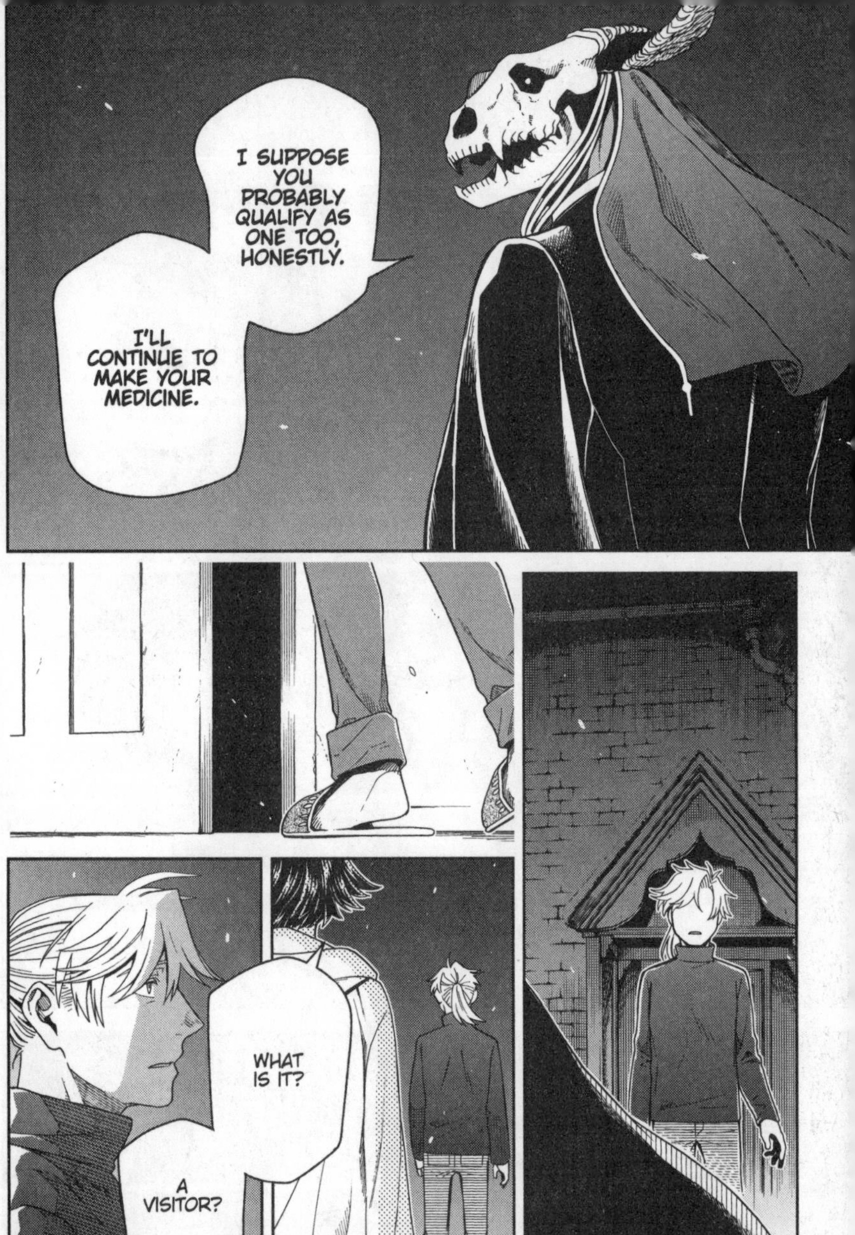
I SUPPOSE YOU PROBABLY QUALIFY AS ONE TOO, HONESTLY.
I'LL CONTINUE TO MAKE YOUR MEDICINE.
WHAT IS IT?
A VISITOR?

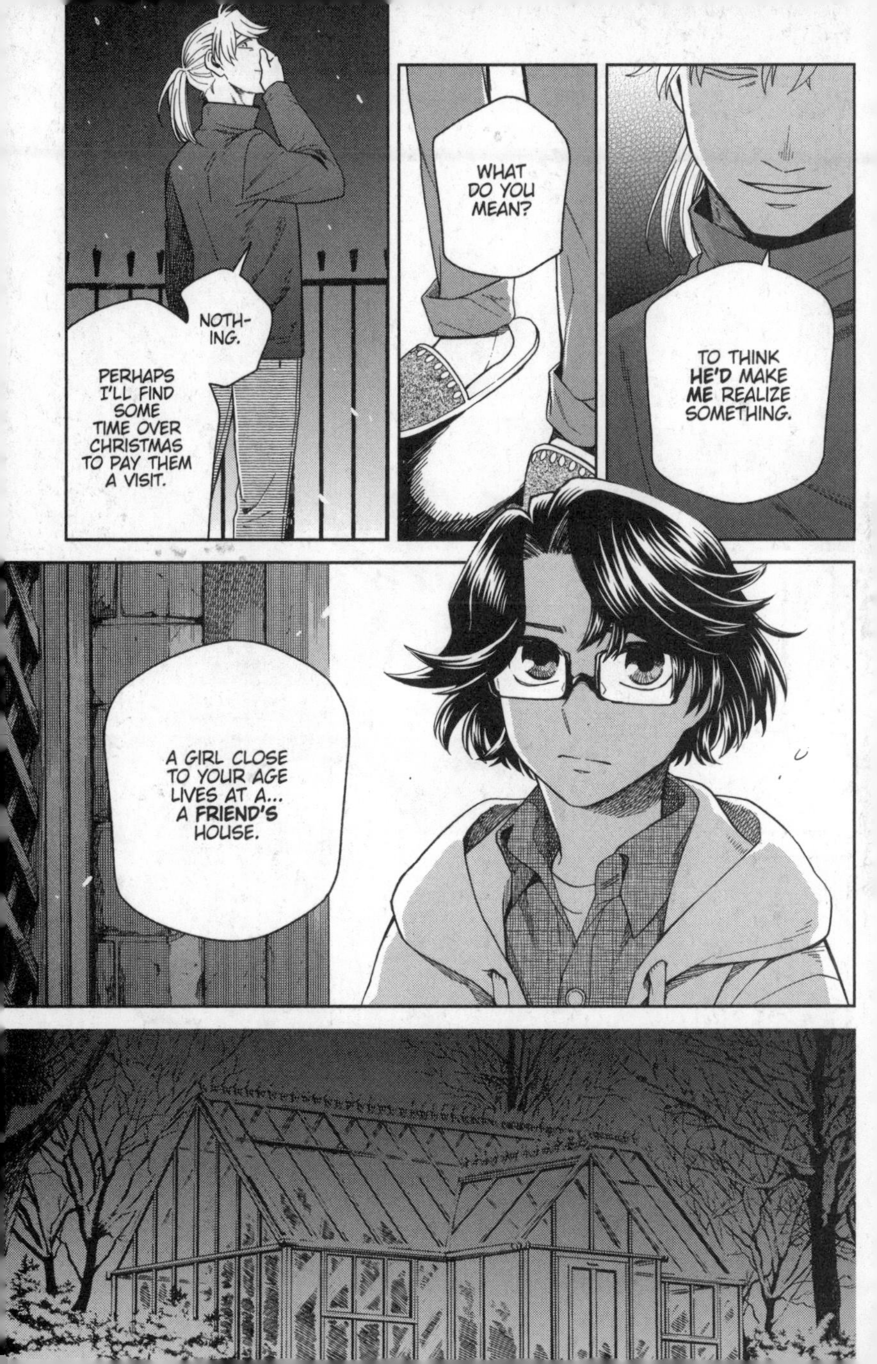
WHAT DO YOU MEAN?
TO THINK HE'D MAKE ME REALIZE SOMETHING.
NOTHING.
PERHAPS I'LL FIND SOME TIME OVER CHRISTMAS TO PAY THEM A VISIT.
A GIRL CLOSE TO YOUR AGE LIVES AT A... A FRIEND'S HOUSE.

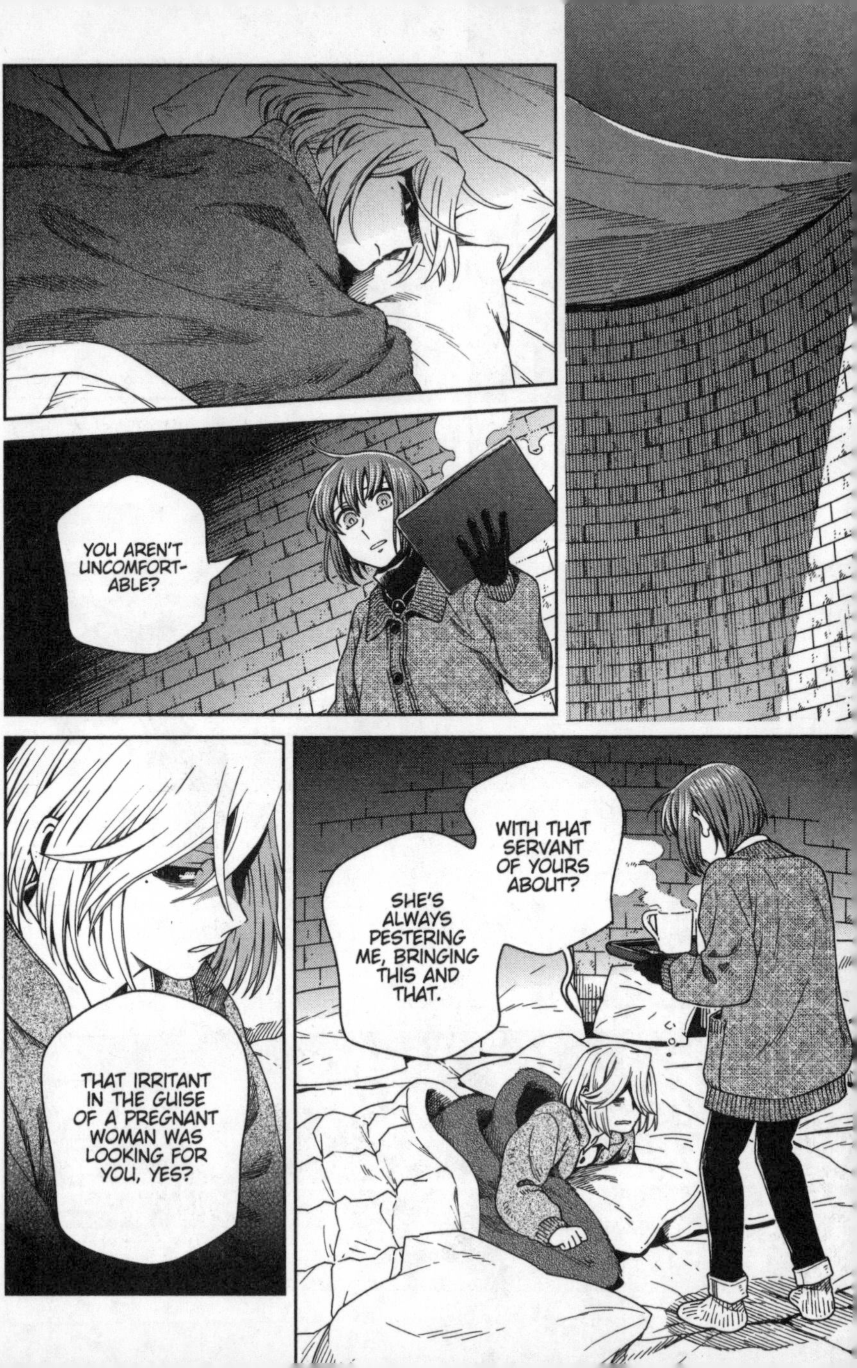
YOU AREN'T UNCOMFORTABLE?
WITH THAT SERVANT OF YOURS ABOUT?
SHE'S ALWAYS PESTERING ME, BRINGING THIS AND THAT.
THAT IRRITANT IN THE GUISE OF A PREGNANT WOMAN WAS LOOKING FOR YOU, YES?

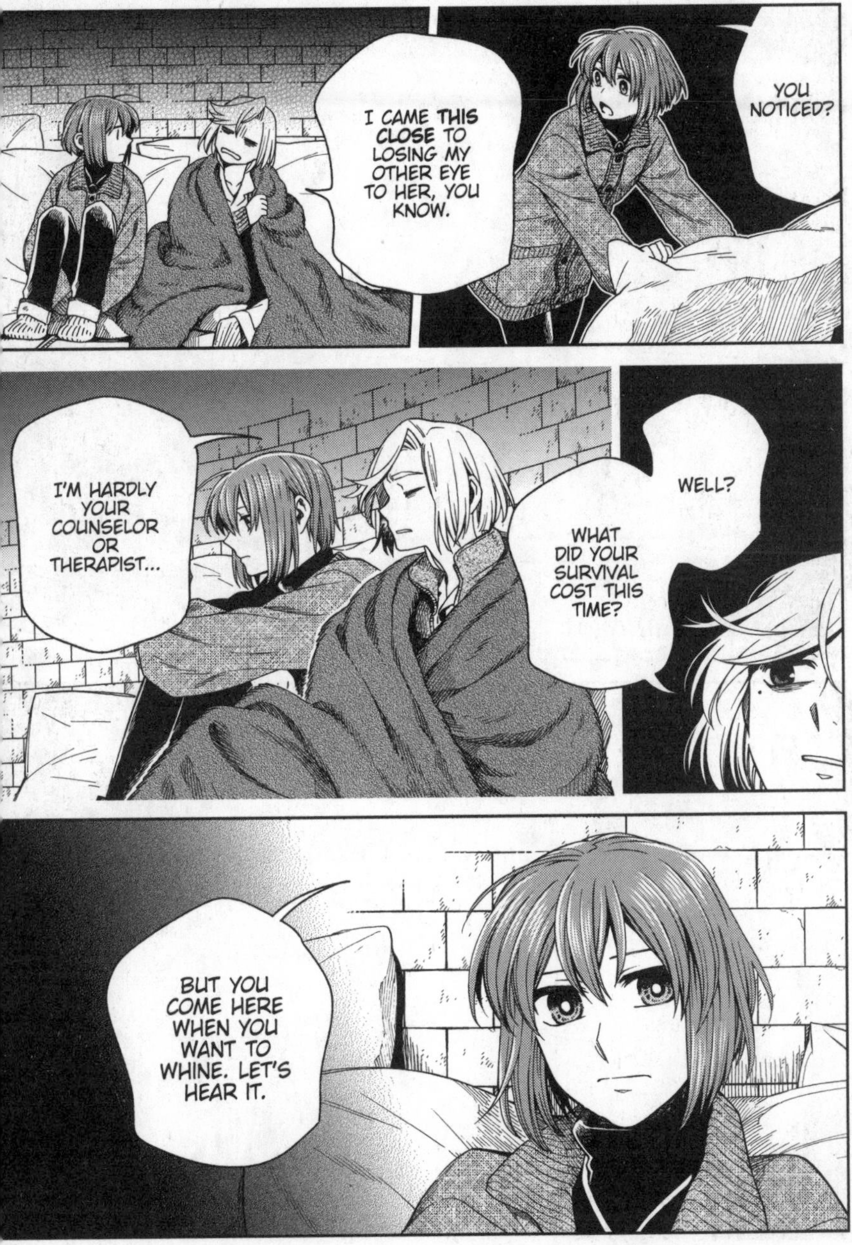
YOU NOTICED?
I CAME THIS CLOSE TO LOSING MY OTHER EYE TO HER, YOU KNOW.
WELL?
WHAT DID YOUR SURVIVAL COST THIS TIME?
I'M HARDLY YOUR COUNSELOR OR THERAPIST...
BUT YOU COME HERE WHEN YOU WANT TO WHINE. LET'S HEAR IT.

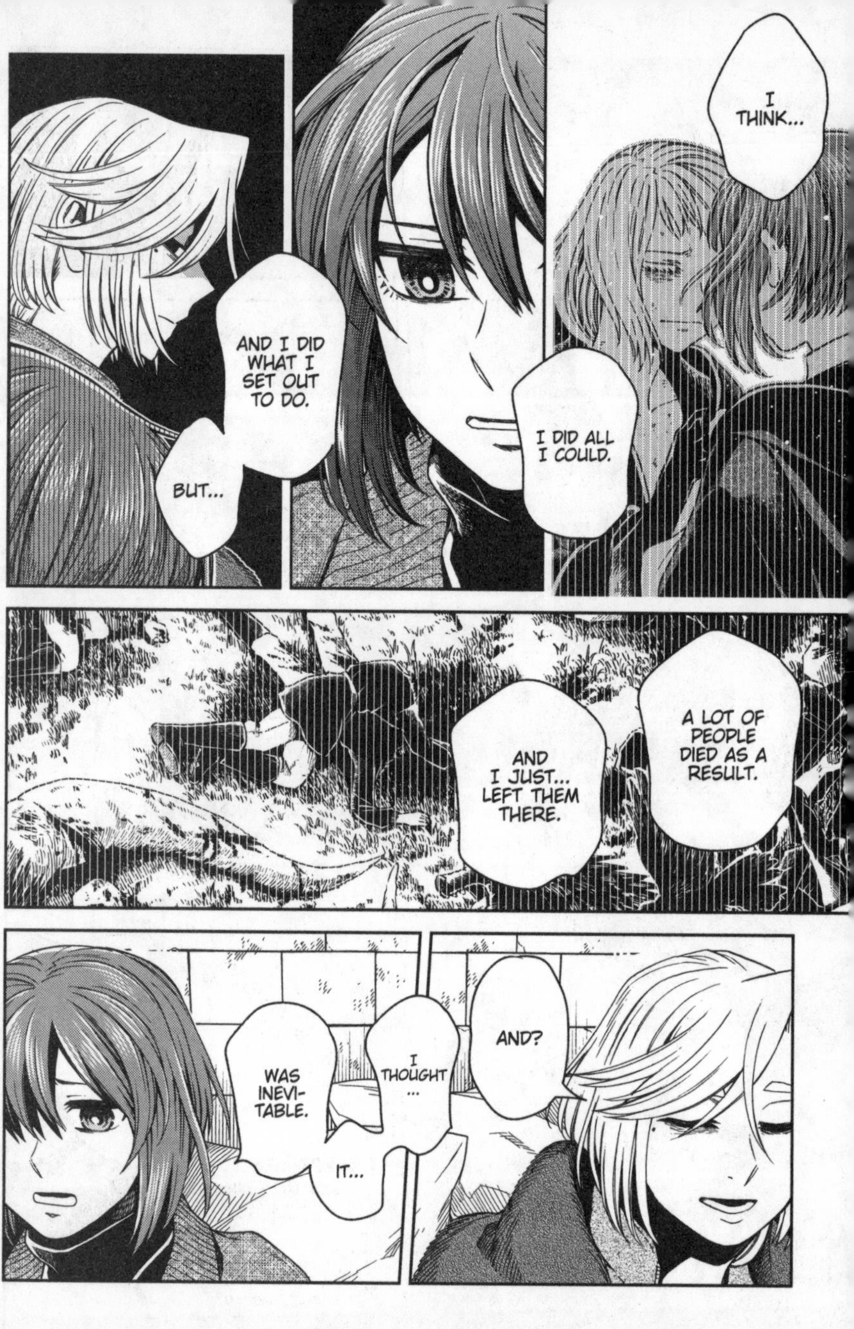
I THINK...
I DID ALL I COULD.
AND I DID WHAT I SET OUT TO DO.
BUT...
A LOT OF PEOPLE DIED AS A RESULT.
AND I JUST... LEFT THEM THERE.
AND?
I THOUGHT...
IT...
WAS INEVI-TABLE.

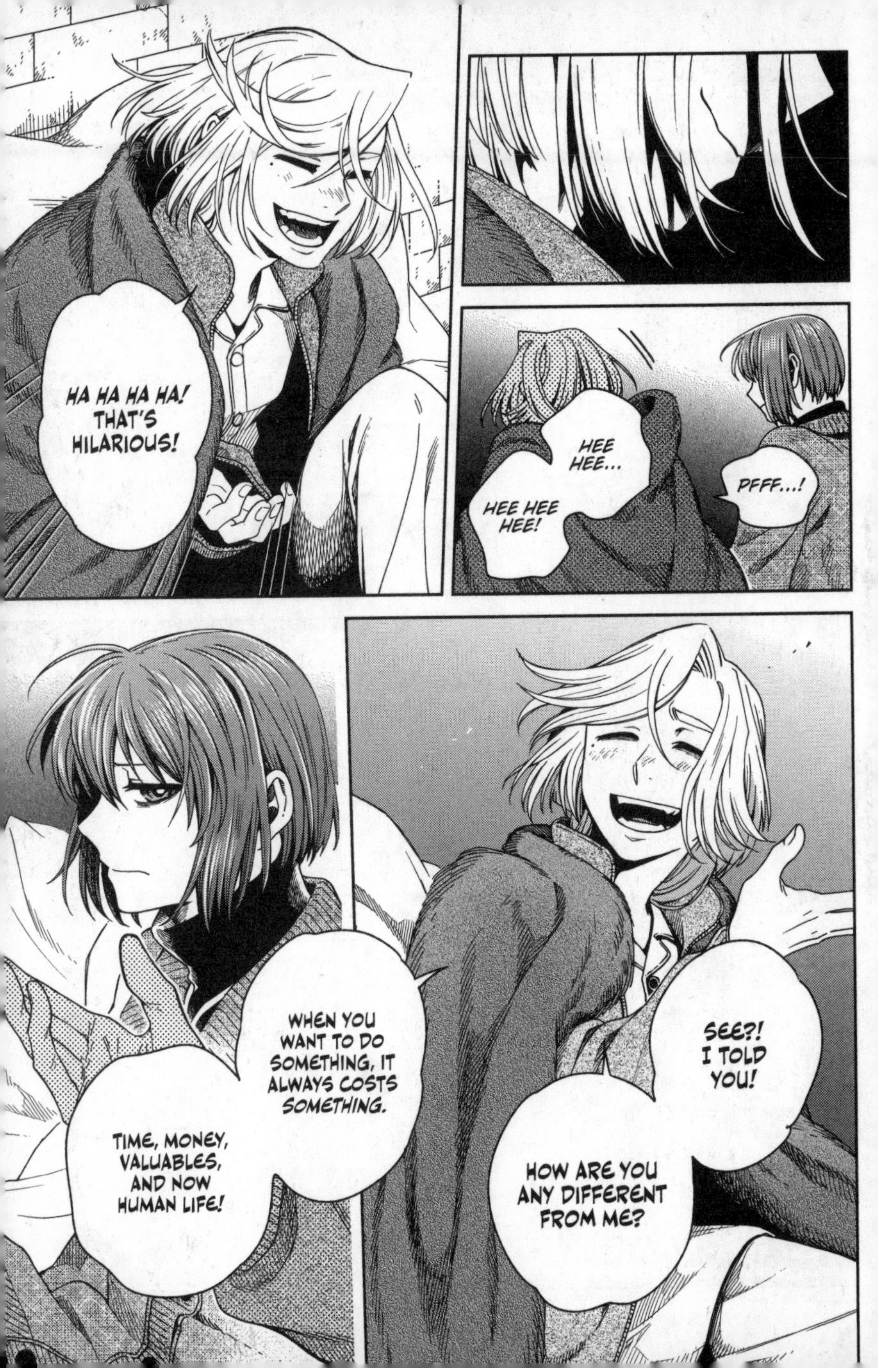
PFFF...!
HEE HEE...
HEE HEE HEE!
HA HA HA HA! THAT'S HILARIOUS!
SEE?! I TOLD YOU!
HOW ARE YOU ANY DIFFERENT FROM ME?
WHEN YOU WANT TO DO SOMETHING, IT ALWAYS COSTS SOMETHING.
TIME, MONEY, VALUABLES, AND NOW HUMAN LIFE!

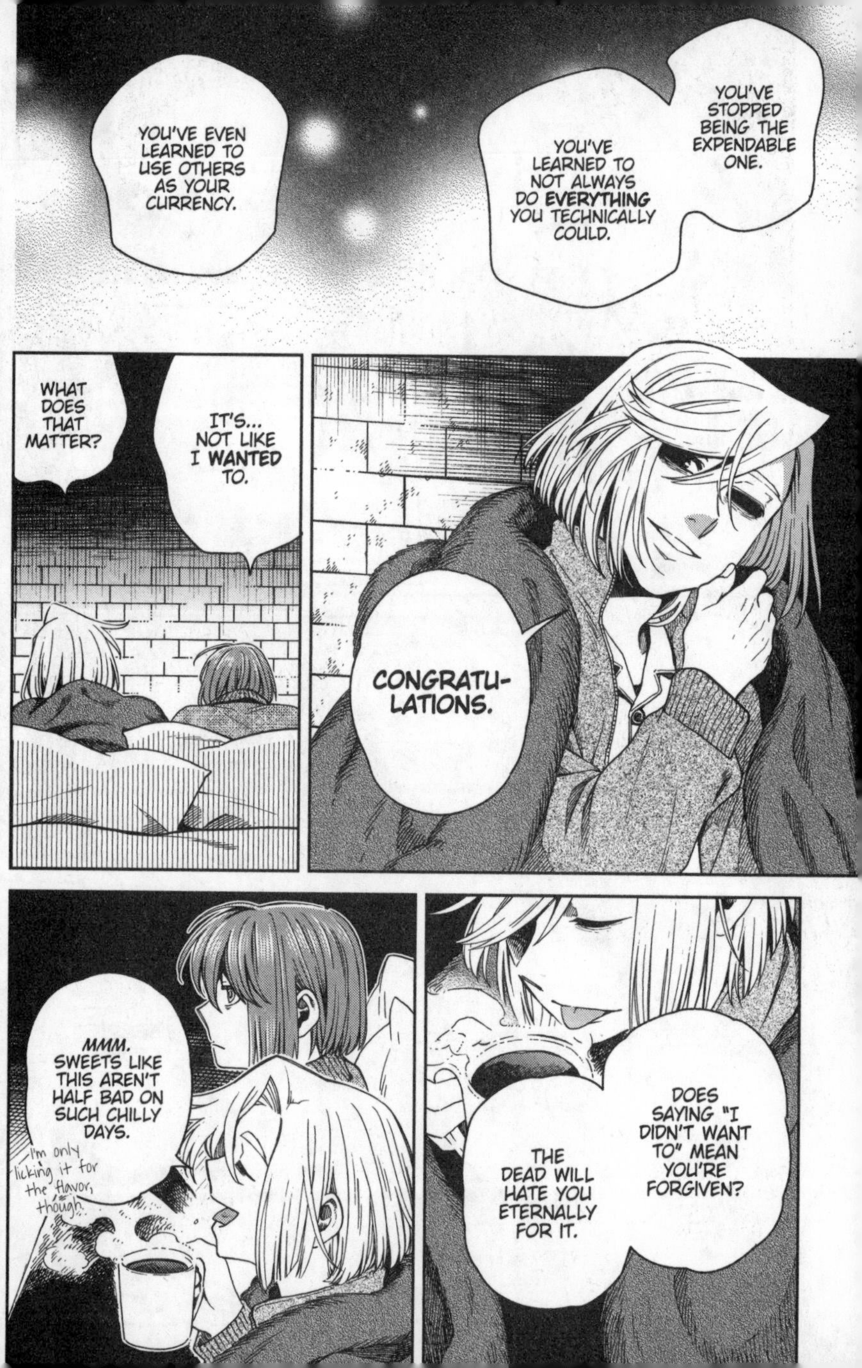
YOU'VE STOPPED BEING THE EXPENDABLE ONE.
YOU'VE LEARNED TO NOT ALWAYS DO **EVERYTHING** YOU TECHNICALLY COULD.
YOU'VE EVEN LEARNED TO USE OTHERS AS YOUR CURRENCY.
CONGRATULATIONS.
IT'S... NOT LIKE I **WANTED** TO.
WHAT DOES THAT MATTER?
DOES SAYING "I DIDN'T WANT TO" MEAN YOU'RE FORGIVEN?
THE DEAD WILL HATE YOU ETERNALLY FOR IT.
MMM. SWEETS LIKE THIS AREN'T HALF BAD ON SUCH CHILLY DAYS.
I'm only licking it for the flavor, though.

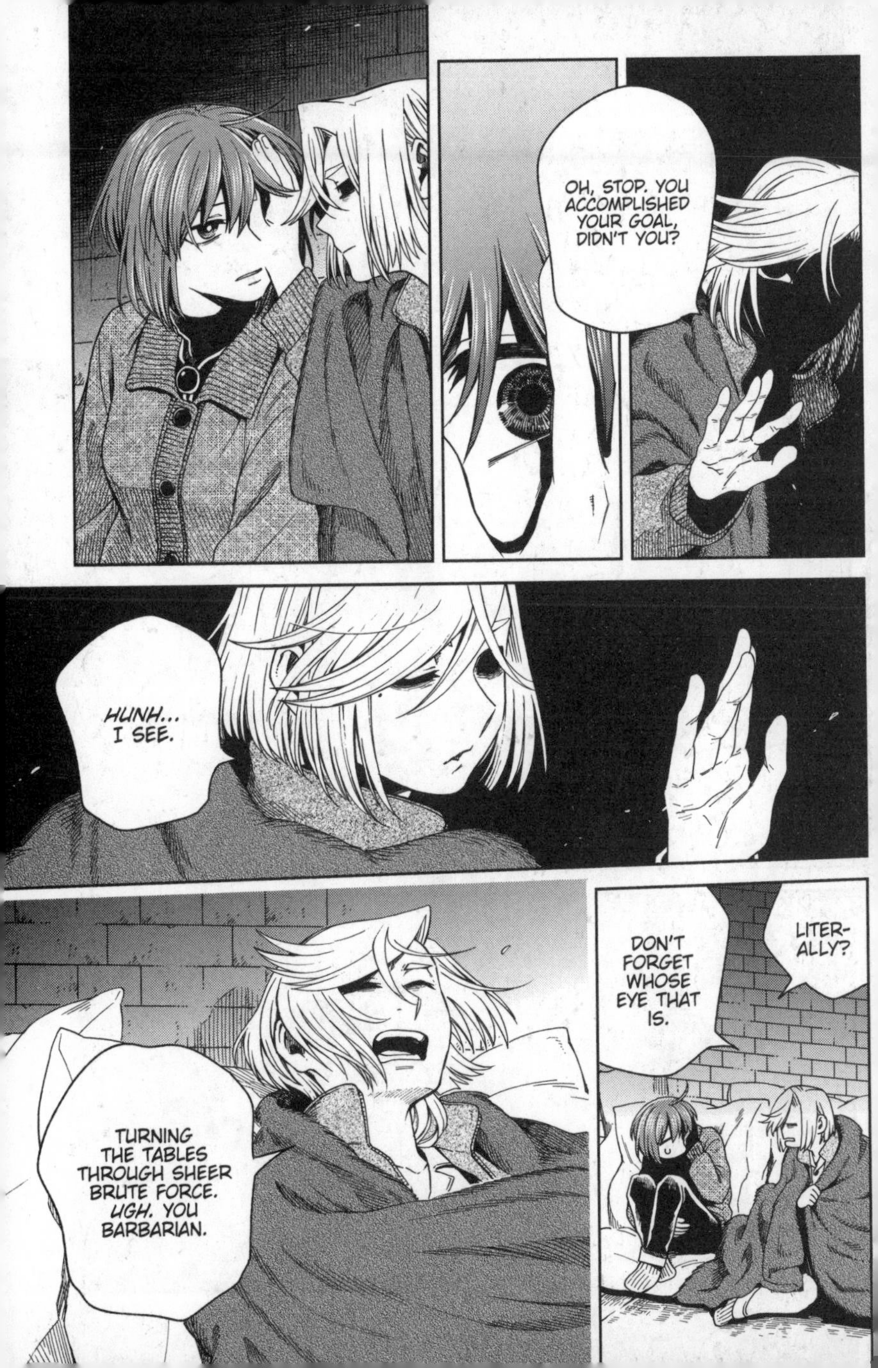

OH, STOP. YOU ACCOMPLISHED YOUR GOAL, DIDN'T YOU?
HUNH... I SEE.
LITER-ALLY?
DON'T FORGET WHOSE EYE THAT IS.
TURNING THE TABLES THROUGH SHEER BRUTE FORCE. *UGH.* YOU BARBARIAN.

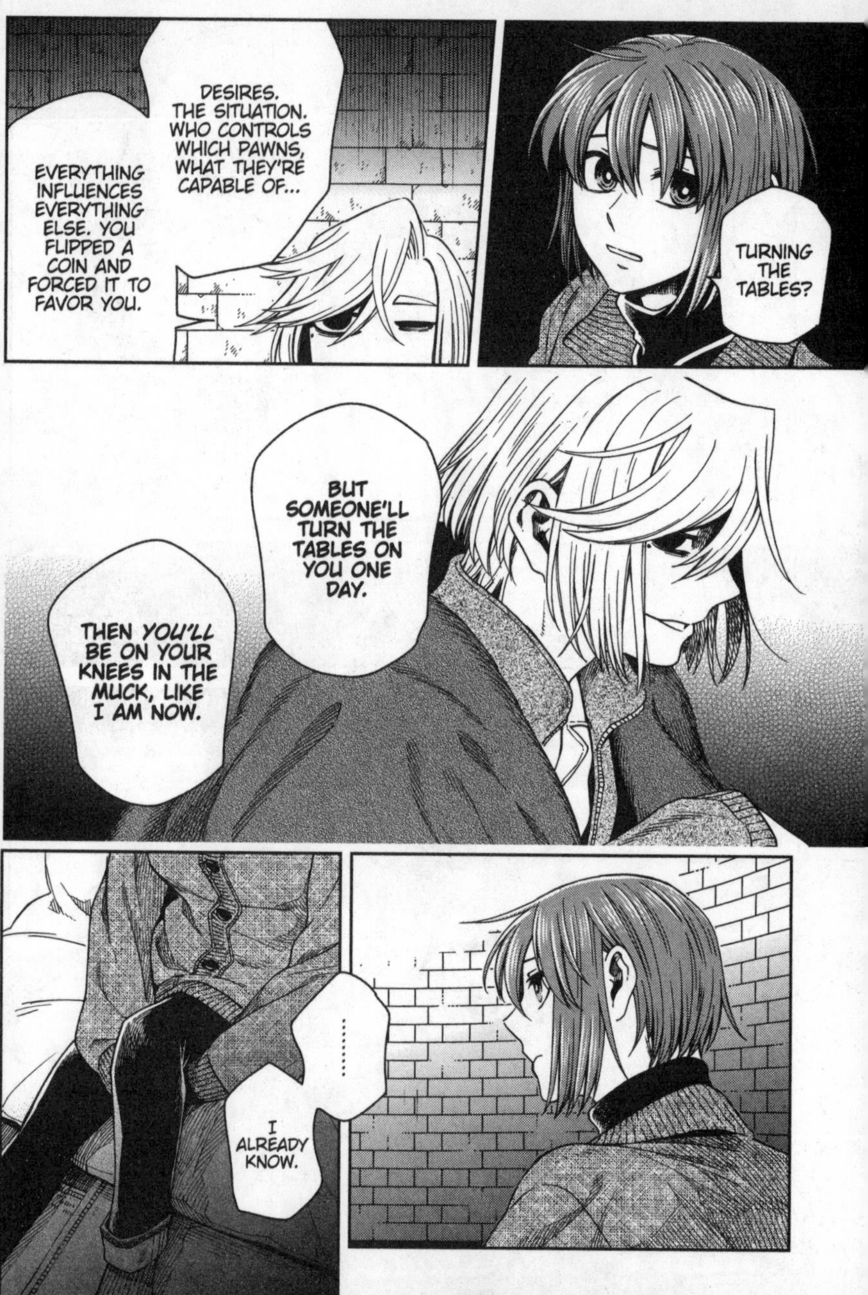
TURNING THE TABLES?
DESIRES. THE SITUATION. WHO CONTROLS WHICH PAWNS, WHAT THEY'RE CAPABLE OF...
EVERYTHING INFLUENCES EVERYTHING ELSE. YOU FLIPPED A COIN AND FORCED IT TO FAVOR YOU.
BUT SOMEONE'LL TURN THE TABLES ON YOU ONE DAY.
THEN *YOU'LL* BE ON YOUR KNEES IN THE MUCK, LIKE I AM NOW.
......
I ALREADY KNOW.

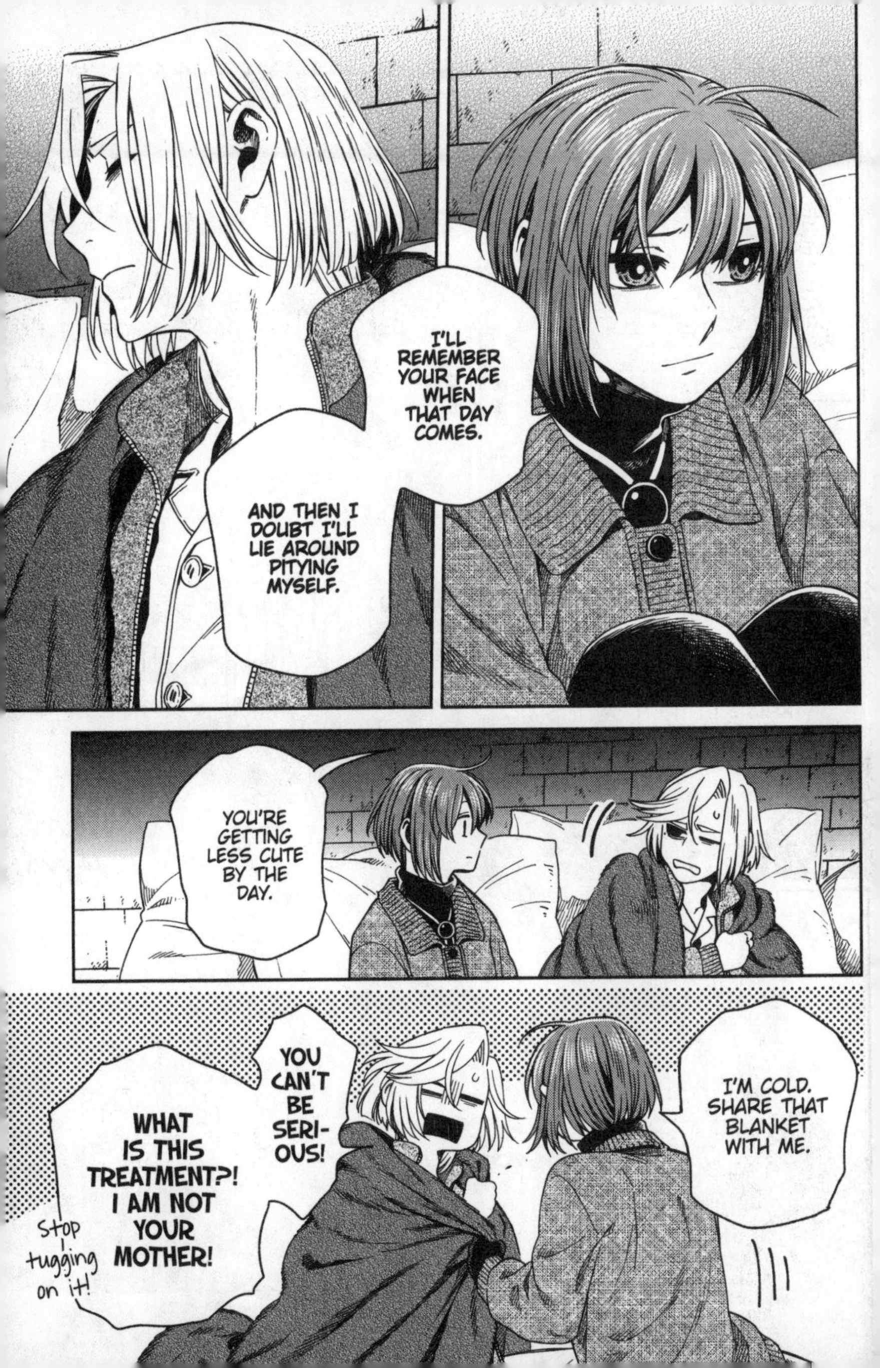
I'LL REMEMBER YOUR FACE WHEN THAT DAY COMES.
AND THEN I DOUBT I'LL LIE AROUND PITYING MYSELF.
YOU'RE GETTING LESS CUTE BY THE DAY.
I'M COLD. SHARE THAT BLANKET WITH ME.
YOU CAN'T BE SERI-OUS!
WHAT IS THIS TREATMENT?! I AM NOT YOUR MOTHER!
Stop tugging on it!

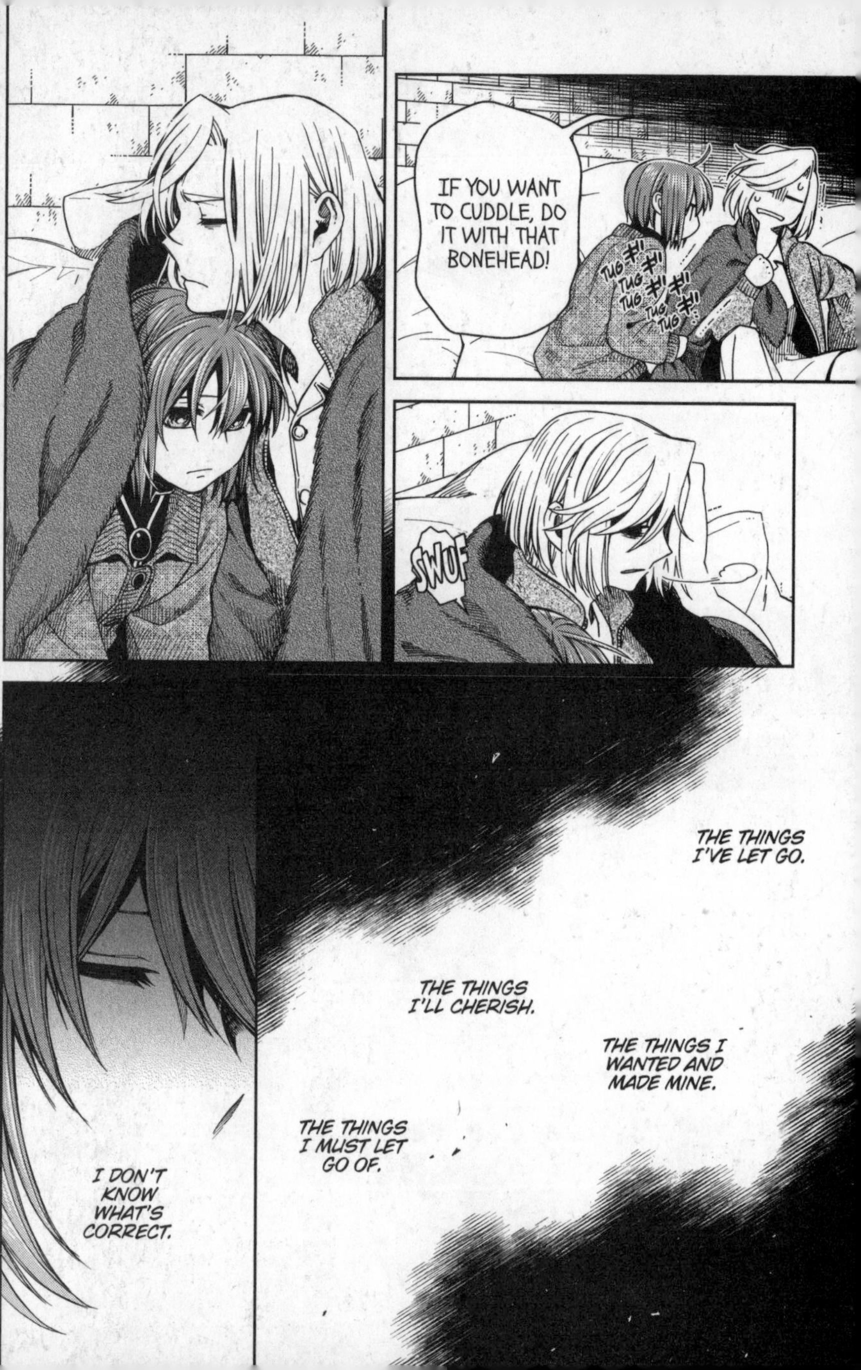
IF YOU WANT TO CUDDLE, DO IT WITH THAT BONEHEAD!
TUG TUG TUG TUG TUG
SWUF
THE THINGS I'VE LET GO.
THE THINGS I'LL CHERISH.
THE THINGS I WANTED AND MADE MINE.
THE THINGS I MUST LET GO OF.
I DON'T KNOW WHAT'S CORRECT.

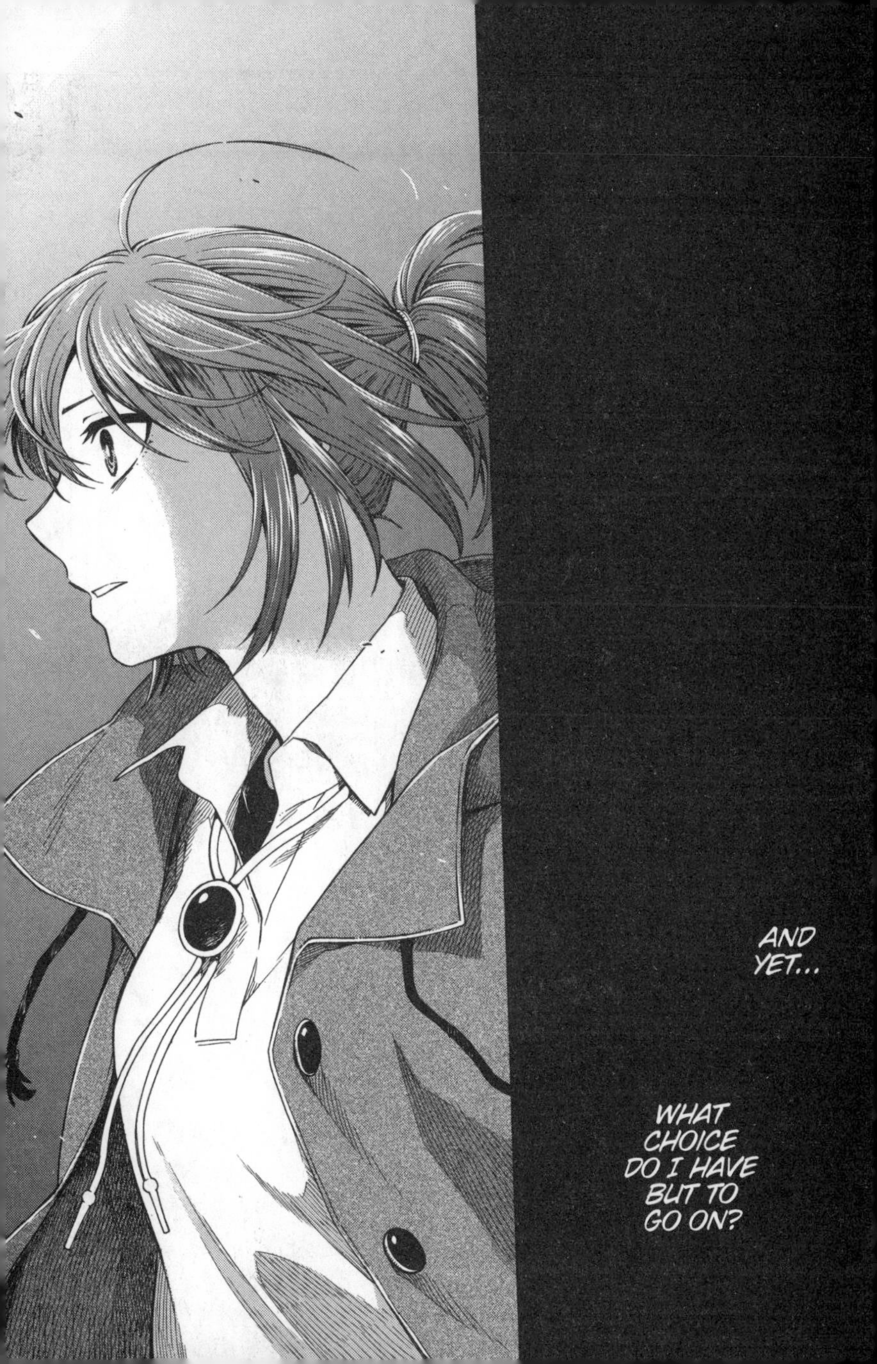
AND YET...
WHAT CHOICE DO I HAVE BUT TO GO ON?

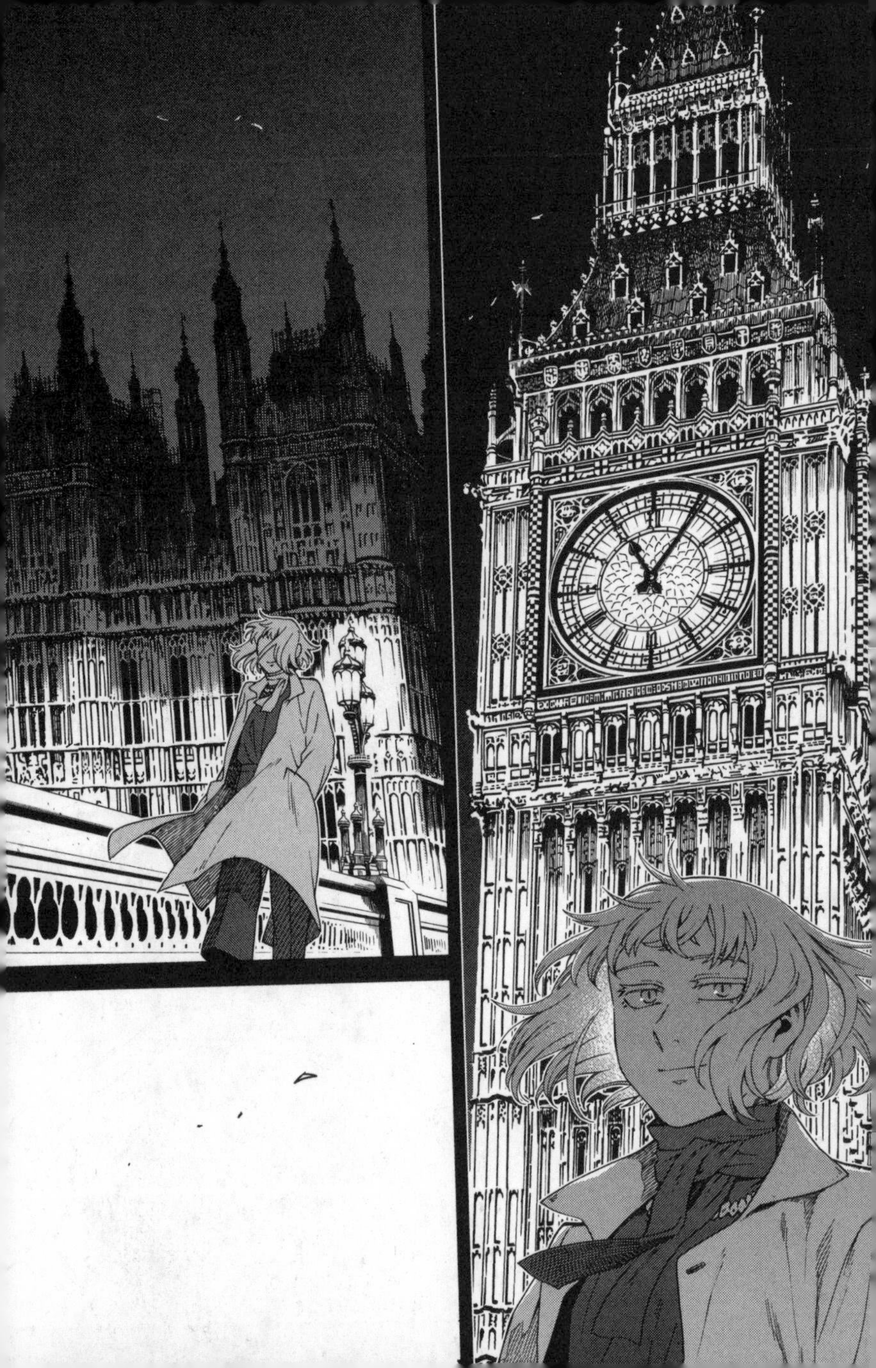

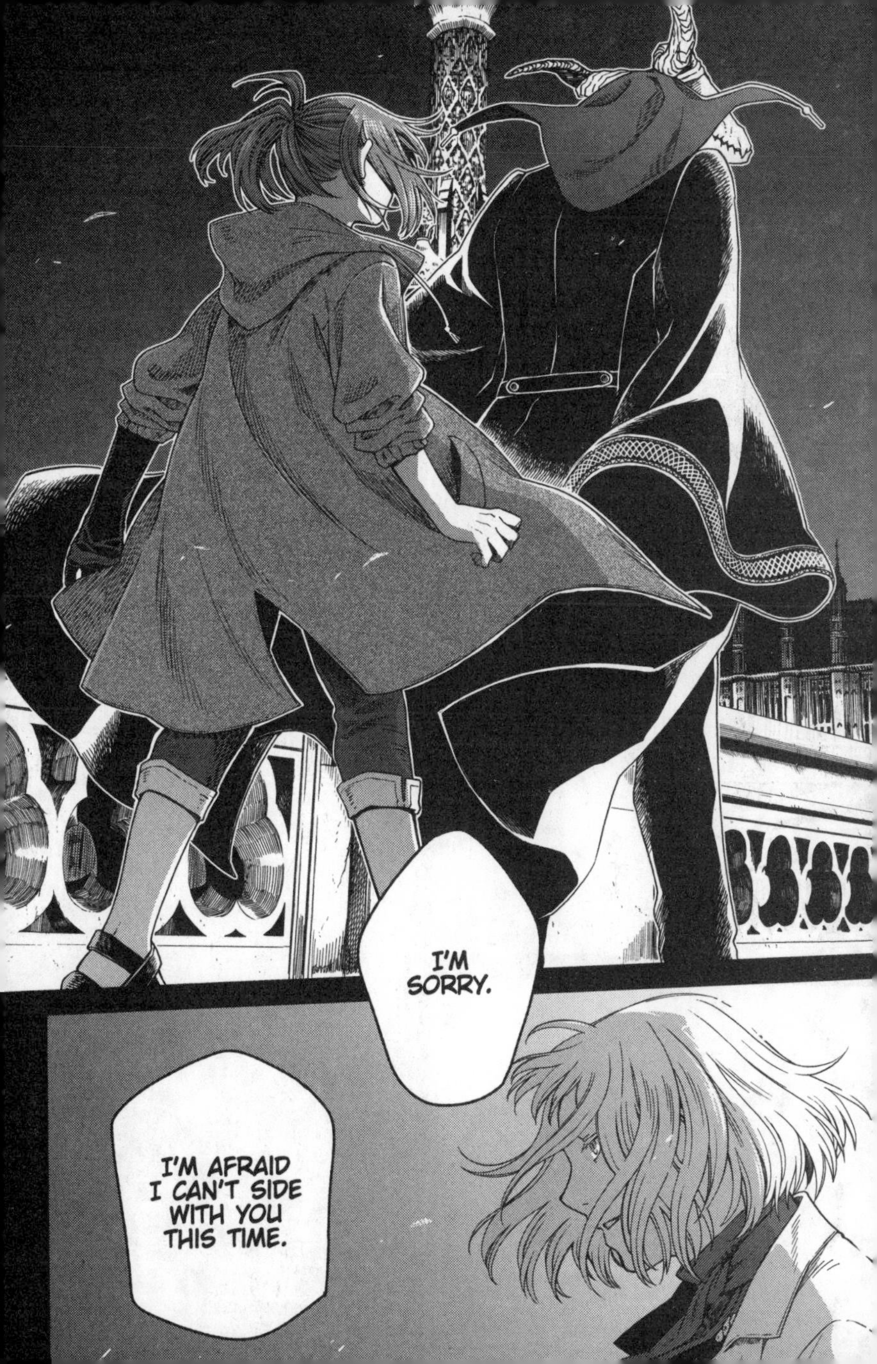
I'M SORRY.
I'M AFRAID I CAN'T SIDE WITH YOU THIS TIME.

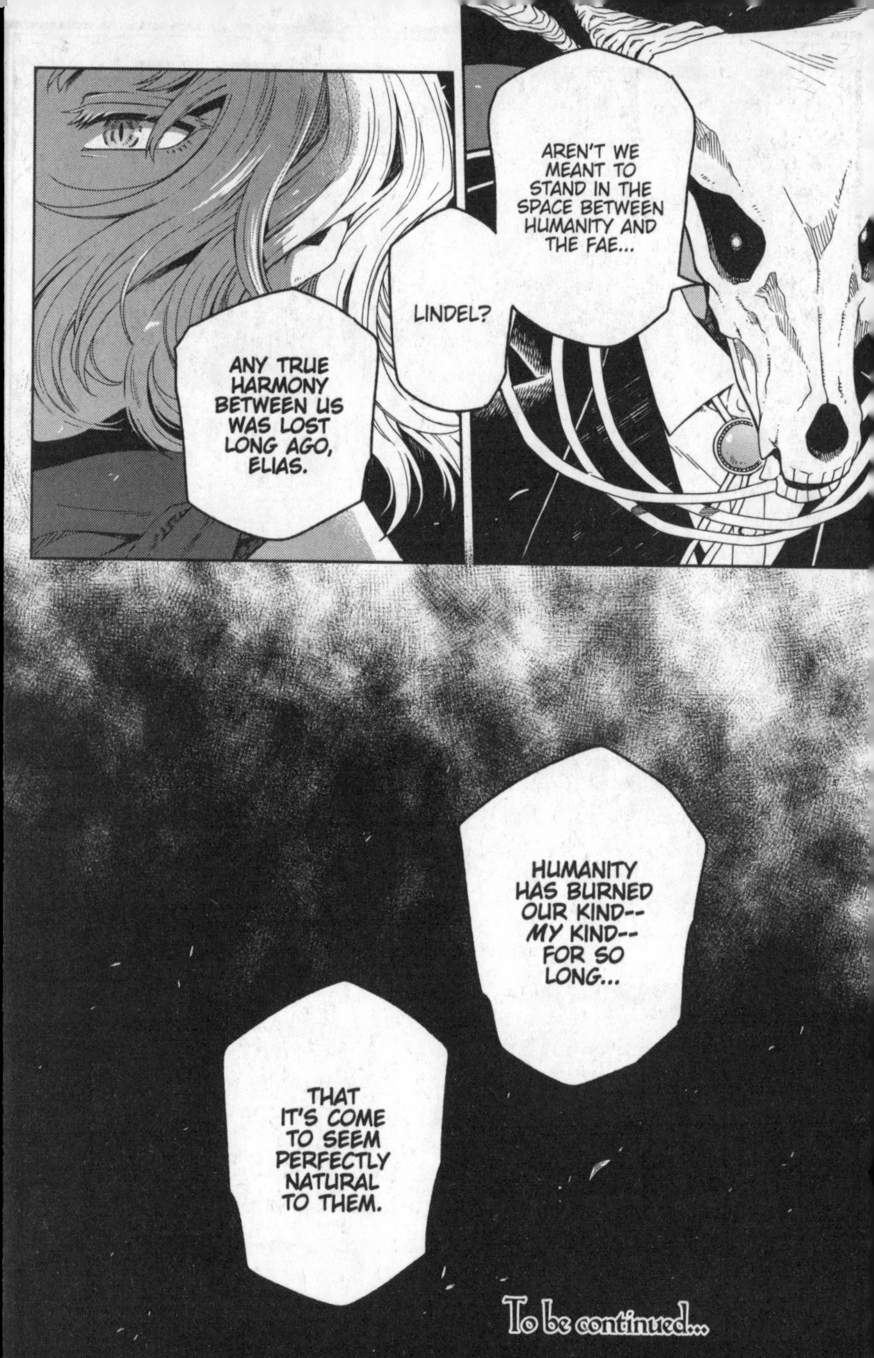
AREN'T WE MEANT TO STAND IN THE SPACE BETWEEN HUMANITY AND THE FAE...
LINDEL?
ANY TRUE HARMONY BETWEEN US WAS LOST LONG AGO, ELIAS.
HUMANITY HAS BURNED OUR KIND-- MY KIND-- FOR SO LONG...
THAT IT'S COME TO SEEM PERFECTLY NATURAL TO THEM.
To be continued...

A
New
Arc
Begins

The Ancient Magus' Bride

As one year at the College comes to a close, the howl of long-lost beasts echoes across England.

Interacting and bonding with other people
has helped both Chise and Elias grow. But
when they return to the little cottage in the
countryside, they're visited by Elias' "benefactor,"
and the story begins to move once again.

Meanwhile, the arrival of the red dragon sends
out tiny ripples across a world that has been
primarily human for a long, long time. The
resulting cracks will grow into chasms that may
eventually split England in two.

Human and inhuman, those of different status,
those with different mindsets...
are they fated to oppose each other in
the coming conflict?

For now, we'll rest, dreaming of the day
when we'll meet once again...

The Ancient Magus' Bride

The Ancient Magus' Bride

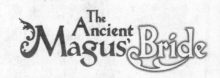

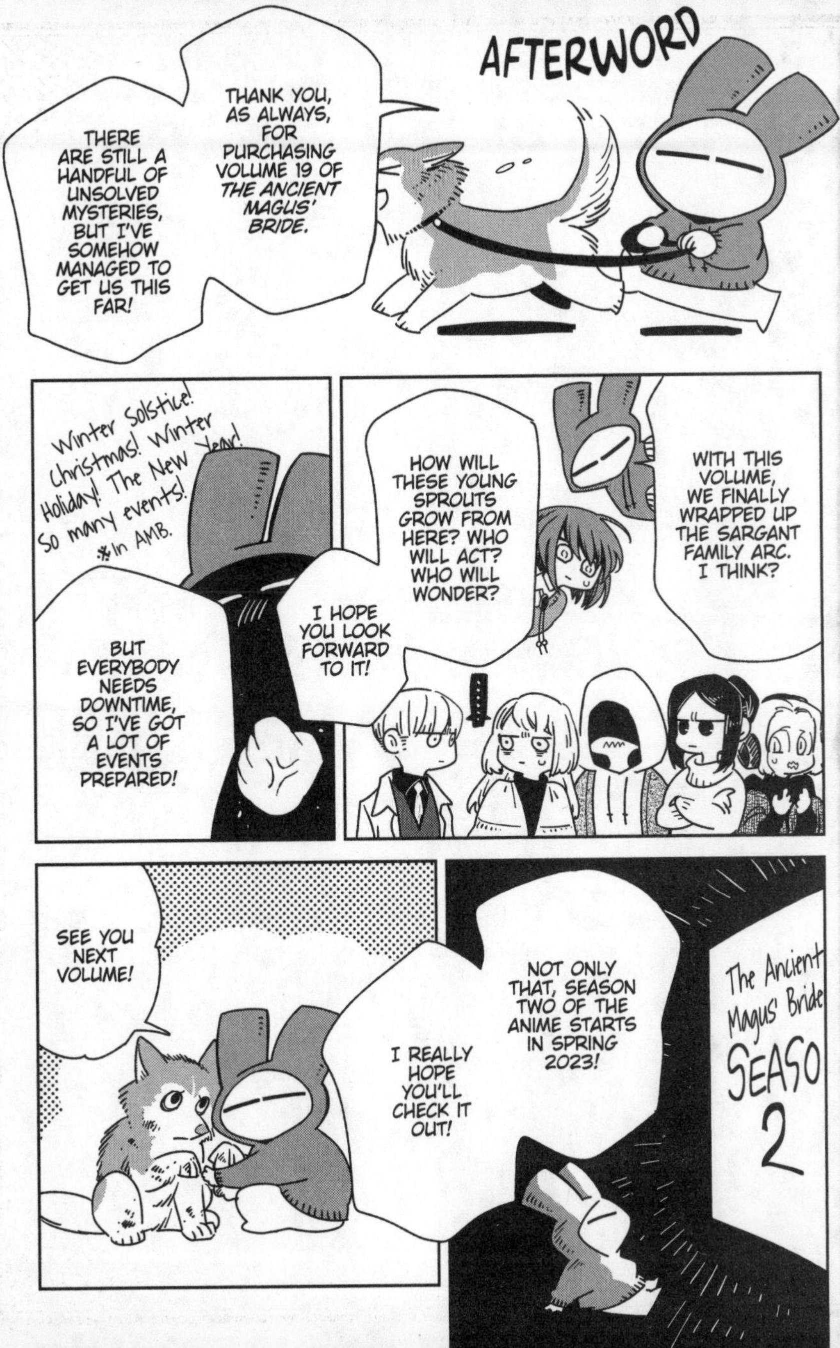
AFTERWORD
THANK YOU, AS ALWAYS, FOR PURCHASING VOLUME 19 OF *THE ANCIENT MAGUS' BRIDE.*
THERE ARE STILL A HANDFUL OF UNSOLVED MYSTERIES, BUT I'VE SOMEHOW MANAGED TO GET US THIS FAR!
WITH THIS VOLUME, WE FINALLY WRAPPED UP THE SARGANT FAMILY ARC. I THINK?
HOW WILL THESE YOUNG SPROUTS GROW FROM HERE? WHO WILL ACT? WHO WILL WONDER?
I HOPE YOU LOOK FORWARD TO IT!
Winter Solstice! Christmas! Winter Holiday! The New Year! So many events!
※In AMB.
BUT EVERYBODY NEEDS DOWNTIME, SO I'VE GOT A LOT OF EVENTS PREPARED!
NOT ONLY THAT, SEASON TWO OF THE ANIME STARTS IN SPRING 2023!
I REALLY HOPE YOU'LL CHECK IT OUT!
The Ancient Magus' Bride SEASO 2
SEE YOU NEXT VOLUME!

The Ancient Magus' Bride

THE ANCIENT MAGUS' BRIDE VOL. 19
STORY AND ART BY KORE YAMAZAKI

© Kore Yamazaki 2023
Originally published in Japan in 2023 by MAG Garden Corporation, TOKYO.
English translation rights arranged through TOHAN CORPORATION, Tokyo.

Translation: **Adrienne Beck**
Adaptation: **Ysabet Reinhardt MacFarlane**
Lettering: **Lys Blakeslee**
Cover Design: **Nicky Lim**
Proofreader: **Brett Hallahan**
Production Designer: **Christina McKenzie**
Senior Editor: **Shanti Whitesides**

Seven Seas Entertainment, Inc. | Publisher: **Jason DeAngelis** | Associate Publisher: **Adam Arnold**
Licensing Manager: **Yayoi Ihne** | Licensing Associate: **Lena LeRay** | Editor-In-Chief: **Julie Davis**
Managing Editors: **J.P. Sullivan & Shanti Whitesides** | Production Manager: **John Ramirez**
Prepress Technicians: **Melanie Ujimori & Jules Valera** | Sales & Marketing Director: **Lianne Sentar**
Marketing Associate: **Leanna Cruz** | Inventory & Logistics Manager: **Marsha Reid** | Administrative
Associate: **Danya Adair** | Digital Manager: **CK Russell**

ISBN: 979-8-88843-052-1
Printed in Canada
First Printing: December 2023
10 9 8 7 6 5 4 3 2 1